Legacy of a Governor
THE LIFE OF INDIANA'S
FRANK O'BANNON

ANDREW E. STONER

FOREWORD BY JUDY O'BANNON

ROOFTOP
publishing

Rooftop Publishing™
1663 Liberty Drive, Suite 200
Bloomington, IN 47403
Phone: 1-800-839-8640

This book is a work of non-fiction. Unless otherwise noted, the author and the publisher make no explicit guarantees as to the accuracy of the information contained in this book and in some cases, names of people and places have been altered to protect their privacy.

First published by Rooftop 09/15/2006

ISBN: 1-60008-017-0 (sc)
ISBN: 1-60008-012-X (dj)

Cover Photo: Gov. O'Bannon dedicates the new Prophetstown State Park in Tippecanoe County. **Photo credit: Steven Sellers**

Printed in the United States of America
Bloomington, Indiana

This book is printed on acid-free paper.

Foreword

For forty-seven incredible years, I shared a marriage with this man named Frank O'Bannon. While in the living of that time, the days often raced by without seeming so unusual. Many of the happenings were made up of the everyday goings and comings of life. One fails to give them their proper due because of their commonness, I'm afraid. But it was the steady, consistent, and always true nature of Frank that, seen in retrospect, was one of his most remarkable features.

Other events get lost in the absolute rush of the rapid changes and volume of activities of public service. Such lives are void of two great gifts in life: a time to anticipate and a time to reflect. It was, for years, a rush from one thing to another without a moment in between. So much is lost in the course of events that either fold in with life too easily or get pushed aside by the next demand.

If we are to gain hope from what we've seen in lives lived or guidance from them, we must have a time to take those experiences out, set them aside, and see them as a whole.

When Andrew Stoner suggested his wish to write a book about Frank O'Bannon, I felt a great relief in my responsibility to glean the jewels from a moment in history of which I had been a part. Personally, our family and those whose lives were in and out of Frank's years had been too involved in the actual activities of his life to automatically lay them all out to analyze. And for those who will only read his name on a plaque, this book will add human flesh and soul to their understanding.

Frank, in many ways, was a common man. This nature of his was a gift to us all. It was so easy to identify with him and to see our own calling within his. However, Frank put these common human traits into uncommon and awesome forms of wisdom and leadership. To understand this is the value of biographical writing. Andrew Stoner, in his many interviews with coworkers, family, and friends, has captured the essence of the man and for this, we are all grateful. There is an opportunity here to also study ourselves and find our route from looking at the life and times of one so open and involved.

My hope is that the reading of this book will cause you to see yourself in the timeline of Indiana life. May you recognize your interests and gifts to be put to service in our gathered community. Not all heroes become governors of a state, but most assuredly, they make a mark in our future. For this, Frank O'Bannon lived, and from his life, may we glean our individual and unique calling.

Judy O'Bannon
Indianapolis, Indiana
June 2006

Introduction & Acknowledgments

Shortly after I joined Governor Frank O'Bannon's staff in July 2001, a reporter asked me the question I had been dreading: "How does a guy like you, who worked for a Republican state treasurer, end up working for a Democratic governor?"

Quick on my feet, I replied, "I only work for state office holders with Irish surnames, O'Bannon and O'Laughlin."

My response drew a laugh and deflected further examination of my lack of a Democratic Party pedigree; I had been a convert to the party for only ten years at the time. In truth, I had come to the statehouse in 1987 as a Republican to work for another great Hoosier politician, State Treasurer Marjorie H. O'Laughlin, or "Marge O.," as we called her. With a little bit of life and learning, I eventually became a Democrat, a decision influenced in no small way by meeting the graceful and kind Frank O'Bannon of Corydon.

I did not plan to become involved with O'Bannon's 1996 campaign for governor. I just wanted to do all I could to keep his opponent from winning, so I plunked down $35 for an O'Bannon fundraiser in May 1996. My small contribution got me a handshake and a warm conversation with O'Bannon and his wife, Judy, and a whole lot more. I came away from that meeting convinced O'Bannon would be a great governor.

Some may suggest I'm not the best choice to write the story of Frank O'Bannon's life, because I only knew him during the last years of his life. But I like to think I am a good choice to journey back in discovery of the wonderful life of Frank O'Bannon. Like so many others who signed on with the O'Bannon team, once in, I was devoted and committed to the success of this generous and decent man. I signed up knowing little about him, but, as it turned out, I received a great gift in knowing Frank O'Bannon personally—a gift I didn't even know I needed.

My first interview for this book was with Dr. Ray Scheele from Ball State University, who wrote the Democratic bible, *Larry Conrad of Indiana*, which is shoved into the hands of interns, governor's fellows, and young, naïve politicos who jump into the crazy game of Indiana politics. His loving look at the life of Larry Conrad, one of Frank O'Bannon's friends, served as a guide to me. Dr. Scheele's advice rang in my ears the entire time: "Remember to stay devoted to your subject, Frank O'Bannon, and you can't go wrong."

I have made every attempt to honestly and fully report on the life of Frank O'Bannon, but this is less an analysis and more of a tribute. I am not objective when it comes to the subject of Governor O'Bannon. I am convinced he was one of the finest men to earn our state's highest office, so I will leave it to others to more fully evaluate his place in our state's history.

I found this journey to be thoroughly compelling, interesting, and fun and took great pleasure in hearing the stories of his life and imparting them here.

Many people have made this work possible—most important, Frank O'Bannon's life partner and love, Judy Asmus O'Bannon. Mrs. O'Bannon gave generously and graciously of her time and memories, telling some of her stories through tears and others through laughter. She also invited the O'Bannon children, Polly Zoeller, Jennifer

O'Bannon, and Jonathan O'Bannon, to share their stories. Two of Governor O'Bannon's sisters, Jane Parker and Rosamond Sample, also spent considerable time with me. Sadly, Mrs. Sample did not live to see the final version of this book, though she was excited to know it was being written.

The list of others who have helped is long. My friends Jonathan Swain and Mary Dieter helped fill in many details along the way, while my friends Randolph Scott and Kathy Stolz lent their ear to hear the voice that was becoming a book. Cindy Athey, Tim Joyce, Nancy Cira, Robin Winston, Pat Terrell, John Goss, David Johnson, and David Allen were extremely helpful. Alan January, at the Indiana State Archives, and Pam Bennett, at the Indiana State Historic Bureau, deserve special praise, as does Jerry Handfield for his oral history project that preserved forever the voice and views of Robert P. O'Bannon, the governor's father.

About one hundred Hoosiers sat down and talked of their time with Frank O'Bannon. I'm grateful to the legislators, journalists, state employees, residents of Harrison County, Phi Gamma Delta alumni, and others who gave of their time for this work. Moreover, I'm extremely grateful to each and every state employee who worked with me as a colleague, supervisor, or direct report. I enjoyed a wonderful career in Indiana state government, and I am especially grateful to some particularly important mentors to me: Marge O'Laughlin, Katie Humphreys, Phil Bremen, Mary Dieter, Sharon Bracey, Jon Laramore, William Bridges, Ann Barton, William Bryan Martin, and of course, Frank O'Bannon.

Special recognition belongs to Governor Joe Kernan, an incredible man worthy of his own book. Those of us who came to know "Joe," our state's forty-eighth governor, quickly saw the energy and ability of this man and understood even more fully why Frank O'Bannon trusted him always. I owe a debt of gratitude to Senator Evan Bayh, our state's forty-sixth governor, who shared freely of his memories and times with Frank O'Bannon. Each man answered every question put to him and remembered his friend with kindness and happiness.

My mother, Sandra J. Stoner, and my extended Stoner family, too numerous to mention, have been a great encouragement to me as I worked to tell the story I wanted to tell. The wonderful folks at Rooftop Publishing have been a joy to work with and shared my vision of a book that paid proper tribute to this fine man. I especially thank Kevin King, Nick Obradovich, Lora Bolton, and Lesley Bolton. To all, thank you.

Ultimately, I hope I have written a book that Frank O'Bannon would enjoy reading. I've tried, as advised by one of his Fiji fraternity brothers, to avoid "canonizing" him. He wasn't perfect, but he was a Hoosier we should never forget.

Andrew E. Stoner
Indianapolis, Indiana
June 2006

Dedication

In memory of and with thanksgiving for my loving father,
Duane E. Stoner

Contents

1

A Governor Passes

On September 19, 2003, four F-16 fighter jets roared north to south above the Indiana Statehouse at 300 miles per hour; one jet pulled out and flew upward in the "missing-man formation" and was lost to the low clouds covering Indianapolis. Below, the roar of the jets lingered several moments longer and temporarily drowned out the sobs but not the grief shared by all of us gathered there of one accord to honor our fallen governor, our fallen friend—Frank O'Bannon.

We had soldiered on during the eloquent eulogies, the moving tributes, even the original musical score written for the overcast day that brought a hint of autumn coolness. But the nineteen-cannon salute from the Indiana National Guard that boomed through the state government complex and the playing of "Taps" by a U.S. Air Force Honor Guard had been our undoing. The goose bumps rose on our arms and necks as this grand, final tribute confirmed what we—those of us who had known, worked with, or cared for Frank O'Bannon and his administration—had always thought and had come to know: that we had been a part of something very, very special.

Even the more festive sounds of the children from the Key School of Indianapolis singing their rousing version of "Back Home Again in Indiana" struggled to replace our tears and our sorrow.

But then, there she was, the new widow of the man who had drawn us all here, more than 5,000 strong, about to duck into the statehouse through the massive carved wood doors. As Judy O'Bannon ascended the west steps of the statehouse, she paused for a brief moment at the top. She wanted to capture the very last moment of the event, so as applause rang out for her and her family, she pulled from her coat pocket a small, card-sized digital camera that had belonged to her loving husband. She held the camera in front of her and clicked one final picture. With that, she signaled a smiling and confident thumbs-up to the crowd of friends and disappeared into the statehouse.

Chief Justice Randall Shepard described the event as "vintage O'Bannon"[1] and so was Judy's signal to all of us gathered there that day and all the others watching on local television and across the country on C-SPAN. Thumbs-up was Judy's signal of hope amidst our shared grief, a moment of cheer nestled at the end of our sometimes tearful remembrance of this simple, decent man from tiny Corydon, Indiana, who had, as Congresswoman Julia Carson said, "…brought together (so many) in the same place, and in the same spirit."[2]

As the massive memorial service drew to a close, the stubborn September clouds gave way to let in a few warming rays of sunshine—signifying the hope we had experienced together.

Frank O'Bannon could never have known that his life would lead to such a day and would impact so many people along the way. For me, like so many others, meeting him was all it took for me to understand that he was a very special person, a person worthy of my very best. Literally thousands of people who had given countless amounts of their time, talent, and treasure to ensure that one of the last pure Hoosiers, Frank O'Bannon, became the leader of Indiana gathered on that September day. Mixed in were people who had come to power on the wave of the Evan Bayh phenomenon in 1988 and just could not bring themselves to walk away when Bayh's eight years were complete. They chose to stay on to help a guy they just as often called "Frank" as "Governor." Others who came had known "Frank" since he was young and had always felt he was someone very, very special. Some never knew him personally at all; they had voted for him and watched him on TV or read of his work in the newspaper and considered him "their governor" and came to share in the grief of his passing.

For those of us a generation removed from Frank O'Bannon, he represented much of what we had seen and known in our parents and grandparents. His patriotism, his commitment to hard work, his love and trust of God, and his desire to help his fellow man were all evident qualities, though never ones he wore on his sleeve. He embodied all these qualities because, as Rabbi Sandy Sasso said at the memorial service, "...throughout his life, Frank O'Bannon wore with dignity and with humility the crown of a good name."[3]

For many of us, he represented what we hoped or strived to be. He was the good guy, finishing first for once, the quietly confident man moved to the front of the room.

Leadership had sought him, not the other way around. He had answered the call of his family, companions, and neighbors and stepped up to serve. He was that rare combination of a politician with true humility. He was, as Joe Kernan said, "a gentleman from sole to crown."[4]

Judy's reminder to us that day, with her quick flash of the thumbs-up, was that our work together had meant something important, that we *had* connected and loved one another as much as we felt we had. We had pushed and pulled to move Indiana in a positive, progressive direction, making our state a better place to live and call home. We had done our very best—not always succeeding, but always earnestly trying to make a difference for the better.

Frank O'Bannon built his adult life and his political career around such values. He advocated patience, tolerance, and respect in politics for the good and the unity of the state and worried that inflexible devotion to individual issues was creating barriers between people and rendering consensus difficult.[5] As the Indiana Senate minority leader at the 1979

Indiana Democratic Editorial Association, he said, "Compromising is not selling your soul. Freedom is the right of many different souls to work together and the result is often compromise."[6] His remarks came on the threshold of the coming Reagan revolution in 1980 that would knock a Democrat out of the White House, remove Birch Bayh and a Democratic majority from the U.S. Senate, and retain the Indiana governor's chair for the first four of eight more years, and served as warning for Indiana Democrats who, many feared, were on the verge of being cast aside as a permanent minority party in Indiana and across the nation amidst the rise of special interest groups around a variety of domestic and international issues.

Despite the hard days that lay ahead for Democrats in Indiana, Frank O'Bannon stayed in the game fighting, encouraging others not to give up on the process, asking us all to think of the ways we could contribute, and leading by example. He was, to turn a phrase, a Democrat when being a Democrat wasn't cool though his position represented very little in terms of real power in Indiana.

Although his remarks went by mostly unnoticed at the time, they foreshadowed what would become of the senator from Corydon who would earn a solid reputation as a man willing to compromise and work with others toward common goals. He and Judy embarked on a decades-long journey that took them to the far corners of Indiana through big cities and small towns all along the way. Their journey would involve long nights spent away from family and home and long drives back to Corydon in the dark of the night from yet another important political event, followed by an early start the next day for the next important event. The path of patience, tolerance, and mutual respect, however, would offer Frank O'Bannon great rewards and would inspire the heartfelt affection of millions of his fellow Hoosiers before his journey was over.

2
Deep Roots

THE FIRST CAPITAL

Frank O'Bannon's journey started far from the center of power in tiny Corydon, Indiana—an archetypical Hoosier town that was an important influence and a source of pride to him. He embodied, in his simple demeanor, the qualities of all the kind, cautious, unassuming, and earnest people of his small Indiana town deep in the hills. Corydon figured prominently in the initial stages of Indiana statehood, and O'Bannon's roots ran deepest of any governor in Indiana, instilling an unsurpassed love for Indiana.

In order to understand Frank O'Bannon, it is necessary to know something about his hometown. Corydon is situated in Southern Indiana bordering the Ohio River. For those who are willing to venture off Interstate 64, the George Rogers Clark Trail, named for the great American explorers, George Rogers Clark and Meriwether Lewis, roughly follows Indiana State Route 62, stretching from tiny Lanesville west to Corydon. Hills and valleys of great beauty roll out before you as the now softened, sloping curves are negotiated until you reach the town of Corydon. Indiana began here, where Hoosier forefathers gathered in the summer of 1816 to form a new state and a new state constitution. Corydon sits at the heart of Harrison County, named for William Henry Harrison (1773-1841) who served as governor of the Indiana Territory for thirteen years prior to Indiana statehood.[1]

In 1809, after Illinois was cut off from the territory, the original territorial seat at Vincennes was no longer the geographic or political center of Indiana. In 1813, the U.S. House of Representatives approved an act to move the Hoosier capital to Corydon, effective May 1, 1813.[2]

In June 1816, forty-three delegates met in Corydon to draft the state's first constitution. Much of their work was done outside under the shade of an elm tree, known as the "Constitution Elm." On December 11, 1816, Indiana was admitted as the nineteenth state of the Union. Corydon remained the state capital until it was moved to Indianapolis in December 1825.[3]

THE O'BANNON FAMILY MAKES ITS MARK

Frank O'Bannon grew up in Corydon, amidst a people who have rightfully and frequently celebrated their place in Indiana history. Who could predict this patriotic and historic town could also boast that it was the home base for the O'Bannon family, who would become one of Indiana's most important political families?

Lew McClellan O'Bannon (1864-1943) was the patriarch of the O'Bannons' political aspirations. His life and accomplishments would tower high above the O'Bannon family for the better part of a century. As his brother, son, and grandson followed his lead and gave generously of their lives in public service to the people of Harrison County and Indiana, they would often recall his words and life.

Lew O'Bannon lived all but a decade of his life in Harrison County, having been born on the family farm near Elizabeth, Indiana in 1864. He completed only the eighth grade and surprised himself by how much he was able to accomplish as a man who never attended high school. Despite his lack of education, he was hired as a country school teacher at the age of seventeen. Lew was only twenty years old and single when he was tapped to serve as Harrison County surveyor, but he had to wait until his twenty-first birthday to assume his duties in 1885. That job, for which he had to "...walk over a considerable portion of the county,"[4] was only the start of many forays into local and state politics, including a separate, later term as Harrison County recorder, for which he failed to win his reelection bid.

By the end of 1895, Lew settled on a career split between being a "country lawyer" (without a law degree), a newspaper publisher, and a county official. Always in love with politics and never at a loss for words to argue his Democratic views, Lew O'Bannon kept his political options and aspirations always open. A 1909 classified ad in the *Corydon Democrat* lists: "Lew M. O'Bannon, Attorney At Law. Will practice in all the courts. All kinds of legal business attended to. Will write deeds and mortgages and other legal instruments. Notary public in office."[5] His law office was eventually affiliated with local judge R.S. Kirkham.

He lived away from Corydon only once, from 1897 to 1907, when he served in Washington, D.C. as a secretary to an Indiana congressman from Corydon, William Taylor Zenor (1846-1916).

In 1897, the same year he accepted the job in Washington, D.C., Lew O'Bannon married Lillian Keller (1867-1939), a daughter of one of the most prominent families in Corydon. Robert Presley O'Bannon, Senior, was born on September 10, 1898, in the young couple's first home in Corydon on the northeast corner of Elliott Street and Capitol Avenue, just north of downtown, while his father was away at Washington, D.C. His brother, Lewis Keller O'Bannon (1901-1920), and his sister, Lillian Elizabeth (O'Bannon) Alltop (1905-1978), were both born in Washington, D.C.

The O'Bannon children marveled at their father's stories and worked hard to please him. He was a strict but fair disciplinarian. When one of the children disobeyed, he never left them in fear, but instead, wishing they had not disappointed him. In his home life, Lew O'Bannon mixed intelligence, perseverance, and joy into everything. Many of the same personality traits that made him a fair and loving husband and father would later win him the praise and admiration of Hoosiers throughout his life—an affirmation similarly enjoyed by his son, Robert, Sr., and his grandson, Frank, as they entered public life.

THE CORYDON DEMOCRAT

Out of work following Zenor's reelection loss and back in Corydon, Lew learned one of the co-publishers of the *Corydon Democrat* was ill with tuberculosis and looking for a buyer. Local Democrats were worried that the town would be left with only a Republican weekly. O'Bannon took the $1,200 he had saved from his small salary working for Congressman Zenor and borrowed another $2,700 to purchase a half-interest in the paper in 1907. Before the year was out, he owned the paper outright, as the other owner sold him his portion of the ownership. The *Democrat* would outlive its Republican counterpart and remain for more than a century as the town's only newspaper—and prove beneficial to the O'Bannon family across multiple generations.

He promised that the paper would earn its Democratic title. "This is also a political paper—a democratic paper—and whatever it may contain that is political, we shall earnestly endeavor to make fully deserving of the label, 'Democratic'..."[6]

By 1909, 517 weekly and 172 daily newspapers were publishing in Indiana, with mergers and financial struggles trimming that number considerably in the years ahead. The *Corydon Democrat* was published every Wednesday and competed fiercely with its rival the *Corydon Republican*, which was published on Tuesdays.[7] In business matters, it was a friendly competition. The *Democrat* readily typeset advertisements from local merchants who planned to buy ads in both papers and shared those with their Republican counterparts at no cost.[8]

"He would write these editorials about Republicans that were just terrible. People talk about how people act in politics today, but what he wrote back then, they sure were what we'd call politically incorrect now," granddaughter Rosamond (O'Bannon) Sample said. She describes her grandfather as an overweight, "unplayful" man whom they called "Daddy O'B." and says his personality differed from that of her father, Robert, Sr., and Frank.[9]

Another granddaughter, Jane (O'Bannon) Parker, concurs saying that her grandfather was very serious and not prone to joking. "I can recall a time we went to eat lunch at my grandparents, the O'Bannons, about the time Franklin Roosevelt was running against Herbert Hoover for president, and I was in first grade. I told my grandparents that they had asked us in first grade who we would be voting for in this election, if we could vote, and my grandfather O'Bannon asked, 'Whom did you say you would vote for?' I said, 'Hoover!' And he asked me, 'Why?!' and I said, 'Because we have a Hoover sweeper.' I had no notion about these things and these people. He immediately said to my dad, 'You had better teach these kids on where they stand.' I can remember sitting there at that table and my grandfather was not happy with my answer."[10]

During his tenure at the *Democrat*, Lew O'Bannon moved the newspaper from a small, one-room operation in a frame building on the east side of the Harrison County Courthouse square to its current location in a three-story brick building on Capitol Avenue.

LEW O'BANNON AND THE INDIANA HISTORICAL COMMISSION

A statewide role emerged for Lew O'Bannon with his 1915 appointment by Governor Samuel M. Ralston (1857-1925) to the first Indiana Historical Commission, which was created to prepare Indiana statehood centennial celebrations in 1916. The commission survived for ten years, with Lew O'Bannon's name faithfully appearing in the commission minutes up until 1925. He was the only member serving who did not possess a college (or in his case, even a high school) education, and he was extremely proud of his appointment.[11]

Because of his position as publisher and editor of a newspaper, Lew O'Bannon was also called upon to address the state's centennial at a meeting of the Newspaper Editors' Conference at Bloomington. He would eventually speak before many organizations statewide, including one joint meeting involving Governor Ralston where Lew O'Bannon—not the governor—was the keynote speaker.

Lew O'Bannon held onto his Historical Commission appointment far beyond Governor Ralston's term, through a succession of four Republican governors. Voters kept the Democrats out of the governor's office from 1916 to 1932 despite tremendous scandals that rocked and degraded the Indiana Republican Party. The disgust of Democrats and many Hoosiers continued to rise, however, and it was during this period that Lew O'Bannon formally entered Indiana politics beyond Harrison County.

Lew had maintained active leadership in the Indiana Democratic Editorial Association (IDEA), frequently speaking at the organization's annual meetings. Between 1912 and 1917, he held an IDEA office each year, including president.

O'BANNON FOR LIEUTENANT GOVERNOR

Lew O'Bannon's political peak would come in the summer of 1924 when he accepted the Democratic nomination for lieutenant governor.

His friendships included the powerful and elite of Indiana politics of that time—including Democratic powerbroker Thomas Taggart (1856-1929), a former Indianapolis mayor and U.S. Senator. He built many of these relationships through work in the IDEA, as well as through state and national participation in the congregationally driven Christian Church (Disciples of Christ).

According to Robert O'Bannon, Sr., his father was "middle of the road with broad-minded principles" and enjoyed talking to people from all social strata. Lew O'Bannon could "find something of interest about any person he ever knew."[12]

He made his 1924 statewide campaign into a "travelogue" column for the *Democrat* during the final month of the campaign, sending back to Corydon each week letters detailing stops and visits he and his wife, Lillian, had made all through the state—emphasizing any former Corydon or Harrison County folks he met along the way. In total, he and Mrs. O'Bannon campaigned by automobile and train in eighty-four of the state's ninety-two counties. He focused his campaign where he enjoyed most of his support: in Southern Indiana. It was a "southern strategy" his grandson, Frank, would one day also employ.

Lew O'Bannon tried to encourage the vastly outnumbered Indiana Democrats, noting the confidence of many Democrats he encountered and that "Many Republicans are going to vote with us this year."[13]

During his final week of campaigning across northern Indiana, he met a former Corydon resident in Warsaw who would one day become his daughter-in-law, Faith Dropsey.

The 1924 election was a watershed year in Indiana politics. Although he ultimately lost the election, history has been favorable to Lew O'Bannon. In balloting separate from the governor's race, O'Bannon was soundly defeated by the Republican nominee for lieutenant governor, State Senator F. Harold Van Orman (1884-1958) of Evansville, owner of the historic McCurdy Hotel at Evansville. Van Orman was a colorful character in Indiana political history, attributed with first uttering the oft-repeated quote: "Indiana has the best legislature money can buy."

Lew's wife, Lillian O'Bannon, a devoted Prohibitionist, was quite angry in 1924 that Van Orman and Governor Edward Jackson (1873-1954) won the support of the state's Anti-Saloon League. Voters perceived Indiana Democrats, even conservative and southern "Butternut Democrats" like Lew O'Bannon, to be "wet" and not supportive of Prohibition.

Van Orman won the support of Prohibitionists (or the "Anti-Saloon League") despite rumors that he was "weak" on keeping Indiana "dry"— perhaps because he owned a large hotel in Evansville where drinking occurred. In the closing days of the campaign, Van Orman declared before a Republican rally in his hometown of Evansville, "I have been charged with being wet. I want to say to you who are my friends, and among whom I live, that I believe whole-heartedly in the constitution in Indiana and of the United States. I believe in the sacredness of those documents. By this I mean I believe in all the amendments to the constitution, including the 18th amendment."[14]

Van Orman and Jackson also received heavy, albeit somewhat more confidential support, from members of the state's powerful Ku Klux Klan. Despite that fact, Jackson and Van Orman still courted black voters in their campaign. The *Indianapolis Star* reported on Republican rallies in Rockport and Evansville in the closing days of the campaign: "Speaking before the meeting of colored persons, Mr. Jackson renewed his stand in favor of the protection of religious and civil liberty of all citizens regardless of race, creed or color. Every man, he said, has a right to worship God as he chooses, and he said that any man who aspires to the governorship of Indiana, and who cannot assume the duties of that office without malice, ill will or prejudice against any citizen 'is wholly unfit even to aspire to such a position and wholly unworthy of the consideration or support of a single citizen.'"[15]

Jackson's words rang hollow, however, as he went on to preside over the most scandalized administration in state history. Jackson remained a fervent, yet private, supporter of the Ku Klux Klan in Indiana. He was also the second consecutive Republican Indiana governor to face criminal indictment and only escaped a prison cell because the statute of limitations on his crimes had expired. Van Orman's fierce loyalty to Jackson and the Republican bosses in control meant his reputation became tainted by the same scandal that eventually brought down Jackson. With one of Jackson's predecessors, Governor Warren T. McCray (1865-1938), serving a federal prison term for mail fraud, the Republicans went from overwhelming power to complete disgrace.

However, in 1924, the Republicans were riding high, sweeping all of the state offices and the presidency that year. President Calvin Coolidge (1872-1933) won a wide margin of victory in Indiana that year, as did Jackson—though Jackson's totals were hurt by the first major retreat of black voters from the ranks of the Republican Party to the anti-Klan Democrats: O'Bannon and his running mate, Dr. Carleton B. McCulloch (1897-1949).

In the end, Jackson vanquished Dr. McCulloch by a wide margin of 654,784 to 572,303. O'Bannon fared no better in separate balloting for lieutenant governor, losing to Van Orman by a statewide mark of 639,224 to 568,327.

Following the Jackson-Van Orman win, one of the GOP's top supporters, one-time Grand Dragon of the Ku Klux Klan in Indiana, D.C. Stephenson (1891-1966), was widely quoted by news reporters celebrating the GOP's win and declaring the Republican victory as "the beginning of our work to drive all vicious radicalism out of the Republic and satisfy the honest and misguided workers of the nation" and proclaimed that "the struggle of the future will be between leadership and the mob. The Democratic Party has passed into oblivion...those forces in the country which would conserve best and construct for the future must henceforth work through the Republican Party against radicalism."[16]

Stephenson's commentary on the future of the republic came just one year ahead of his 1925 Hamilton County conviction for the rape, torture, and murder of a female statehouse clerk.

Lew O'Bannon did not editorialize about his loss in his own newspaper. He instead ran a poem about thankfulness and ended his final campaign letter as he did all his columns: "We trust we have recited some facts herein that will interest the readers of the *Democrat*. We are glad to get back home and at our regular job. Call to see us. Lew M. O'Bannon."[17]

Despite being unsuccessful in his only statewide run for office, Lew O'Bannon remained active in Indiana Democratic Party politics. He served as permanent chair of the Indiana Democratic State Convention in 1928 and was mentioned in 1914 and again in 1932 as a possible candidate for the U.S. Senate.

LILLIAN (KELLER) O'BANNON

Lew's wife, Lillian Keller O'Bannon, was more reserved and traditional than her husband. She and her twin sister, Rose, were the daughters of the established Keller family of Corydon. The Kellers were an ambitious and devoutly Christian family who started the successful Keller Manufacturing Company, employing generations of Harrison County residents. The Kellers also owned the general store in Corydon, which Lillian's father and her brothers ran. While kind-hearted and quiet, Lillian could grow irritated with Lew's "mountaineer" ideas and big stories. In the end, many believed Lew O'Bannon, born on a nineteenth-century farm in rural Harrison County, had married well and perhaps above himself, but most also agreed that Lew and Lillian were deeply in love with one another.

Lillian carried a heavy responsibility for the care of her second son, Lewis, who acquired Pott's disease during one of the family's stays in Washington, D.C. At the time, Pott's disease, an infection of the spinal cord resulting from tuberculosis, was generally untreatable. It meant Lewis was eventually unable to stand upright as he walked. He developed a "hunchback," and the hope of attending school and leading a normal life away from his parents' home slipped away from him. Lew and Lillian were determined to try anything they could to help their son. Despite his condition, Lewis bravely and painfully boarded trains with his father to visit doctors in Louisville, New York, and Chicago, each of whom promised new treatments and help for the ailing boy. The treatment finally decided upon, using straps to hold Lewis's body in place against a board, succeeded in straightening his spine but rendered his legs paralyzed.

The O'Bannons pitched in and helped make life as normal and happy for Lewis as they could. A tutor came from the school after a couple of years when it became apparent Lewis wouldn't be able to make it to school and back without great difficulty. Lewis remained intellectually busy, filling his long hours with reading almost anything he could get his hands on. As a result, he was an intelligent and informed young man, though socially immature. Robert O'Bannon, Sr., recalls that his brother rarely complained about his state. Looking out a window one time, he saw Robert and some other boys playing ball in the yard and longed to be with them. Lewis, seeing how his longing grieved his loving mother, Lillian, never again spoke of what he was missing and remained high spirited. His young life came to an end in 1920 at the age of nineteen. He is buried in Cedar Hill Cemetery in Corydon not far from his parents—just as he lived.

The O'Bannons were loyal members of the Christian Church (Disciples of Christ) just as Lillian Keller's family had been. Lew O'Bannon's family had never resolved a denominational tug of war conducted by his parents between the Methodists and the Presbyterians, and so when he married Lillian, Lew became a member of the Disciples of Christ.

Lillian's religious views toward alcohol reflected her faith; she was a committed Prohibitionist. Though it is unclear whether Lew O'Bannon shared Lillian's commitment to prohibition, he gave up drinking nonetheless to please his wife and her family.

J.L. "RENNIE" O'BANNON

Lew O'Bannon was not the only member of his generation of the family interested in state or local politics. His brother, Jacob Lorenzo O'Bannon (1860-1920), made several attempts at elected office. Rennie, as he was known to family and friends, was elected from Harrison County to the Indiana House of Representatives for one term between 1897 and 1899. Rennie reportedly struggled with alcohol early in his life, including during his term in the legislature. According to Robert O'Bannon, Sr., Rennie's drinking was problematic enough that the family worried about him and arranged with the manager of the hotel where he stayed to send a telegraph stating simply, "Come to Indianapolis," if he got into trouble.[18]

When the telegram came, Lew O'Bannon made his way to Indianapolis. He later told family members that he held his fist up to Rennie and said, "This is the last time you do this, and if you do it again, there's going to be a terrible fight, and one of us, by God, is either going to be awfully laid up or dead." Lew claimed Rennie never drank again after that and kept his commitments in the legislature. Despite his newfound temperance, he failed to win a second or any subsequent terms in the legislature.[19]

Rennie, unlike his brother, lacked a respect and appreciation for organizational party politics, which greatly hampered his political aspirations. He ran for and lost several bids for the Democratic nomination for his district in Southern Indiana. Robert O'Bannon, Sr., notes, "He probably would have made it if he was humble enough to work with the precinct politicians."[20]

Rennie O'Bannon made three unsuccessful attempts for the Democratic nomination for Congress, the last one being in 1920.

J.L. "Rennie" O'Bannon would never live to see the final results of that Democratic primary. The next week's *Corydon Democrat* reported on the sudden death of Rennie at his New Albany home as he talked on the phone with the primary election returns just coming in. He lost the election but won his native Harrison County.

Lew O'Bannon eulogized his brother in a newspaper editorial, and expressed the family's gratitude to Harrison County voters and others of the district who supported Rennie.[21]

Lew O'Bannon died himself on February 16, 1943 in Indianapolis after a short illness. He had remarried following Lillian's death in 1939 and was survived at the time of his death by his second wife, Effie Knight McCauley (1888-1981). [22]

"I think my father was born with a good brain and proper standards," Robert P. O'Bannon, Sr., said of his father many years later. "I felt it kind of gave him a motivation and a standard for the rest of his life, which I think has carried over to his children and I claim even as far as our newspaper...'Why not the best?' was going on way back in his life, too."[23]

3

A Second Generation

Frank O'Bannon's parents, Robert P. and Faith (Dropsey) O'Bannon, lived their lives in the heart of the twentieth century, "America's century," a time of unrivaled change and advancement in the U.S. The rapid change occurring throughout the century was reaching seemingly all parts of the world, including tiny Corydon, Indiana.

Robert Presley O'Bannon, Sr., was named for an O'Bannon family ancestor, Presley Neville O'Bannon (1776-1850), the first American to plant a U.S. flag on international soil at Tripoli, an act immortalized in the Marine Corps hymn lyric, "From the halls of Montezuma, to the shores of Tripoli." Although politics was never first among aspirations for Robert O'Bannon, or his son, Frank, they both succeeded far beyond Lew's aspirations. Father and son, Robert, Sr. and Frank, were able to claim the distinction that neither ever lost an election.

Robert started at Corydon High School in 1912 and graduated in 1916 but had to wait a year before enrolling at Purdue University in West Lafayette, Indiana. Lew O'Bannon wanted his children to work at least one year before going to college, and so Robert took

17

a job as a "printer's devil" in the back room of the family-owned newspaper. His one-year commitment stretched slightly beyond that into fifteen months. His tasks included setting type and running a stubborn folding machine. Eventually, he worked in the front office, collecting the $1-a-year subscription price for the *Democrat*. Always an idea man, Lew O'Bannon assigned Robert or anyone who worked in the front office to engage in conversation with the local farmers and others who came in to pay their subscription. That conversation would often result in a mention in the following week's paper, such as "John Lohmeyer was a pleasant caller at the *Corydon Democrat* office this week. Mr. Lohmeyer is one of the leading farmers and finest citizens of this community." Lew O'Bannon knew everyone liked seeing their name in the paper.

Though the onset of World War I loomed in the background of his young life, Robert wanted to study mechanical engineering at Purdue. He enrolled in the ROTC at Purdue and attended artillery training at Camp Taylor in Fort Knox, Kentucky. By the time he was old enough to serve, the war was drawing to an end. He never saw combat action abroad. Robert was an unremarkable student by his own account. He relied on his father and his mother's twin sister, Rosamond Keller, to pay for college. Rosamond Keller loaned him most of the money he needed for school, though he still took a job working in the basement of the Woolworth's store in Lafayette. After a year of college and lackluster grades to show for it, Lew sat Robert down and talked him out of working and persuaded him to focus on his studies full time. When he graduated in 1921, he owed his aunt $3,200 and signed a note with her for four and a half percent interest, paying on it every month until it was finally paid off in 1933.

ROBERT AND FAITH GET MARRIED

Robert dated other girls in Corydon, but his interest turned to Faith Dropsey sometime in those first years after he graduated from college. Family legend says he first got up the nerve to talk to her as she carried boxes of dishes back from a luncheon at the Methodist church to her mother's home. As Robert carried the boxes for her, they struck up a friendship that lasted a lifetime.

Faith's parents were very strict and monitored their daughter's activities closely, expecting a formal courtship for their college-educated daughter. Their courtship continued until their engagement was announced in a small item in the August 8, 1925 edition of the *Democrat*:

> The engagement of Miss Faith Dropsey, daughter of Mr. and Mrs. Frank E. Dropsey, of Corydon, and Mr. Robert P. O'Bannon, son of Mr. and Mrs. L.M. O'Bannon, also of this place, was announced at a dinner party last Tuesday evening at the home of Mr. and Mrs. Dropsey. The guests were Misses Mollie Keller, Ruth Shuck, Lina Black and Lillian O'Bannon. The wedding will take place September 2.

The wedding occurred less than a month later on September 2, 1925 at the Corydon United Methodist Church on the town square, with a reception following at the Dropseys' home.

The bride, Rosella Faith Dropsey, was born June 29, 1899 in Corydon. She was called by her middle name, Faith, from childhood until the time of her death. Her parents, Frank E. Dropsey (1871-1949) and Etta (Stevens) Dropsey (1877-1961), were devoted Methodists. Faith's father, Frank Dropsey, became a Protestant in order to please Etta and her devout family, despite having been raised Roman Catholic. Over the years, he became an active member of the Corydon United Methodist Church.

THE DROPSEY FAMILY

Faith's mother, Etta, whom all the children called "Mama D," was a kind, generous woman. She saved small spools from her knitting as early "tinker toys" for her children and grandchildren to enjoy and rewarded good behavior by allowing them inside the formal front parlor she kept in perfect order in their simple wood-frame house. "Mama D" was famous for her fried chicken made from chickens she cleaned herself in the back yard and earned "pin money" at Christmastime by placing an ad in the *Democrat* offering her caramels, divinity, and opera creams for sale. To this day, the Dropsey family caramels are a holiday tradition in the Dropsey and O'Bannon family homes and were a lifelong favorite of Frank O'Bannon.

Faith's father, Frank Dropsey, known as "Daddy D," was a jovial, happy man who loved to play old folk tunes and hymns on his mouth flute. A member of the town's volunteer fire department, he was once described as "the greatest fireman because he had the biggest fireman's hat, and usually was the first to arrive at the scene of a fire." Town legend tells of Frank Dropsey's apparent willingness or quickness with an ax, especially as he put it to the roof of almost any burning structure in town, no matter how big or small the fire.[1]

Later, when "Daddy D" was a grandfather, he would delight his grandchildren by standing below a vent to the bedroom above the living room and playing songs for grandchildren who were supposed to be going to sleep upstairs. On Sunday nights, Faith's family enjoyed listening to the radio as "Daddy D" popped red popcorn, using leftover bacon grease to get the kernels going. "Daddy D" sometimes had tremors or shaking in his hands when he spoke. "Daddy D's" namesake grandson, Frank O'Bannon, would be known for having the same "familial" or "essential tremors" throughout his adult life as well.

FAITH DROPSEY O'BANNON: COLLEGE-EDUCATED WOMAN

Faith Dropsey O'Bannon was an excellent student and took to heart her parents' lessons to value every dollar, save every penny possible. Her parents' frugality made it possible for her to attend DePauw University at Greencastle, Indiana upon her graduation from Corydon High School. After she graduated from DePauw in 1920 (where she was a classmate of noted anthropologist Margaret Mead), Faith taught in schools for five years at both Petersburg and Warsaw, Indiana. Following marriage, she joined Robert in Philadelphia where he had accepted a position as a salesman for the Henry Vogt Machine Company.

Robert and Faith O'Bannon welcomed their first child, a daughter, Jane, in 1925. Two years later, after having relocated to Louisville, Kentucky, a second daughter, Rosamond (1927-2005), was born.

As the 1920s drew to a close, Robert faced a tough decision of whether to accept a promotion from the Henry Vogt Machine Company to open a new office in Dallas, Texas or Los Angeles, California, or leave the company and return home to Corydon to assist his father, who had suffered his second heart attack. Faith also felt the call to return home to be near her beloved parents who still lived in Corydon. Robert reasoned that if he took over the *Democrat* from his father, he could run the paper with his "left hand" and sell life insurance or real estate for his real income. He'd soon learn that the newspaper was a full-time calling by itself—though his father had promised he could pursue other interests as well, knowing Robert had no real desire to be a newspaperman.

ROBERT AND FAITH RETURN TO CORYDON

In 1930, Robert and Faith O'Bannon returned to Corydon and Robert took a job working at the *Democrat*. He helped take the business in new directions, printing physician directories and stationery for doctors and other professionals in Indianapolis. He even approached his former bosses at Henry Vogt and successfully landed contracts to print many of their brochures. Eventually, furniture companies and other interests in nearby Tell City, Indiana and Louisville, Kentucky were added as the "left hand" job of the *Corydon Democrat* became a full-time enterprise.

Settled into their new lives in Corydon as young parents, Robert and Faith counted on their extended family and the frequent company of their grandparents, both the O'Bannons (who lived just a block from Faith and Robert's first home on Farquar Street) and the Dropseys (who lived a few more blocks away on Walnut Street). The family grew again when Frank Lewis O'Bannon was born on January 30, 1930 in Louisville, Kentucky. Two other O'Bannon children followed in the growing brood, brother Robert Presley O'Bannon, Jr. (1931-2002), and sister Margaret O'Bannon Fawver (1934-2004). A sixth child, a daughter, died at birth on September 7, 1936.

Robert and Faith O'Bannon had busy lives raising five children and keeping the newspaper a going interest amidst the onset of the Great Depression. Faith was strict but gentle with the children, often requiring mid-afternoon naps on long summer days and on Sundays. Knowing that as the kids got older it would be harder and harder to get them to nap, she agreed that if they remained on the bed and stayed quiet, they could read instead of sleep. As a result, all of the O'Bannon children were voracious readers throughout their lives, and Frank O'Bannon took his love of reading into public policy every chance he got.

Upon the 1943 death of Lew O'Bannon, Robert was named publisher of the *Democrat*. As a community leader, Robert was active, as was expected, in many organizations, including the Methodist church. He was commander of American Legion Post 123, and involved in the Pisgah Masonic Lodge, Scottish Rite, and the Knights of Columbus. Faith devoted her time to Sunday school and vacation Bible school at the church, along with Girl Scouts and Boy Scouts. Jane remembers that her parents were generous and patient, allowing the children to have their friends over to their house. A vacant lot between Robert and Faith's house and Lew O'Bannon's home facing Elliott Street served as an active playground for all the neighborhood kids. The kids were irritated when their parents announced a few years later they planned to build a bigger house on the lot.

To make ends meet, the O'Bannons kept a milk cow or two, which the children, especially the boys, Frank and Bobby, were expected to tend. The depression that swept the United States in the 1930s was all around the O'Bannon family, but the O'Bannons kept afloat as the *Democrat* survived the downturn. Rosamond recalls that when a stranger, or what was then called a "hobo," would occasionally show up at the O'Bannon doorstep, Faith would offer some spare food or clothing to help. Faith made cream, butter, and cottage cheese from the cow's milk the boys collected. The *Democrat* continued publishing in those lean years, though it could hardly pay anyone a living wage. The realities of the Depression era served to stoke the political fires of Lew and later his son, Robert O'Bannon, both devoted "Roosevelt Democrats." Lew O'Bannon kept a photograph of President Franklin Delano Roosevelt (1882-1945) prominently displayed in his home.

For many years, Robert O'Bannon and a woman he hired as a bookkeeper were the only employees the newspaper could afford. Robert would even accept a batch of sausage or other bartered items in exchange for the subscription or advertising bill local farmers accumulated. Paper grew harder and harder to get, and more expensive, but the paper survived by adding in revenue from other printing jobs. Despite these struggles, Robert felt blessed by the income the newspaper provided and was generous, but private, about his giving to others. When he retired, he didn't want to accept his Social Security checks, but they kept coming anyway. He was convinced he didn't need them and that Social Security was meant for the indigent. He finally decided to give the proceeds of each of the checks to people he met in need. In earlier years, after a fire swept through the inside of Robert and Faith's home, Robert hired a single mom from town to clean and scour the house. When she finished, he gave the woman the entire insurance settlement check, refusing to take her protestations into account. "It was way, way more than she expected to make, but he turned over the entire insurance check to her because he thought she had done a good job," said Frank's cousin Diane (Dropsey) Miller.[2]

Jane Parker recalls that their parents "brought home to us the seriousness of the way things were going during the Depression and the war. But we were all in the same boat, we all lived in a small town, and we all knew everyone else was struggling."[3]

"But there was safety in numbers; we could all do something for each other, and count on each other. During the war, large families who weren't too sugar crazy had plenty of everything because you had everyone's ration points," Rosamond said.[4]

On Sunday, December 7, 1941, the O'Bannon kids were with their parents down the street at Lew and Lillian O'Bannon's house when by the evening, the radio began carrying reports of the Japanese attack on Pearl Harbor.

Jane recalls her father being very excited. "He was vowing to go down the next day, which was a Monday, and sign up for the war. He wanted to enlist...He was probably into his forties by then, too old to serve, but he was fired up and upset...We all were."[5]

Frank O'Bannon would tell reporters almost sixty years later on September 11, 2001, that he felt the same way that day as he had as a boy on Pearl Harbor Day.

The O'Bannon children grew up in a household where ideas were discussed, and opinions were allowed and respected.

"His family was real, I have such respect for them," Judy O'Bannon says. "They can argue ideas, and they don't take it personally. In my family, if I had said 'What you just said is illogical,' someone would have taken it personally, and you would have felt just awful...They knew the difference between personalizing everything. None of them had a big ego, and their self-esteem was large enough that they did not feel like people were attacking them. They were comfortable with who they were."[6]

ROBERT O'BANNON ENTERS POLITICS

When Robert O'Bannon decided to enter politics in the 1950s, Indiana Democrats were about to hit a dry spell, breaking a string of electoral successes the party had enjoyed in the two previous decades of the Great Depression and World War II—the Roosevelt years. Aided by years of GOP corruption, Democratic governor Paul V. McNutt (1881-1955) had shrewdly adopted the parts of FDR's agenda that were popular in conservative Indiana and distanced himself from the rest, and despite high aspirations, was never tapped by FDR for a spot on the Democratic ticket.

McNutt ushered in an era of Democratic success in Indiana, becoming the first of three Democratic governors in that era, followed by Governor M. Clifford Townsend (1884-1954) and Henry F. Schricker (1883-1966). Schricker became the first two-term governor in Indiana history, serving two nonconsecutive terms from 1941 to 1945, and again from 1949 to 1953. McNutt, Townsend, and Schricker were masters of the emerging political patronage system in Indiana—a system that may have benefited Frank O'Bannon and his brother Bobby as teenagers. Both won jobs with a state contractor in the hot summer sun of 1951 to help pave the new road between Madison and Vevay.

Democrats approached Robert O'Bannon about running for the local state senate seat in 1950, and because of political infighting among Democrats in adjacent Floyd County, his first attempt at political office was successful, as he outflanked other Democratic candidates from the more populous towns of the senate district that covered Crawford, Floyd, Harrison, and Perry counties. It was a rare moment—most Democrats in the larger communities of New Albany and Jeffersonville were used to calling the shots. But another group of Democratic fathers there turned to a respected businessman and young father from adjacent Harrison County as their compromise candidate.

For Robert, it took only a day or two to decide it was the right thing to do. Faith, insulted at even the suggestion that her husband would be asked to interrupt his work and his family life to run for office, required more convincing. Before it was done, however, Faith became an incredible political asset, helping him engage people with her friendly, affable style. "Faith was the driving force of that duo," Judy O'Bannon says. She describes her mother-in-law as a smart, bold, opinionated woman who "...had the timing of a great comedian." Mrs. O'Bannon notes that though "she was more colorful than Robert," she was restricted as a woman, "but she moved fast and was energetic, probably a lot like the differences between Frank and me."[7]

According to Jane Parker, her father's political ambitions were a surprise to his children, although they were quite clear to which party they owed their loyalty. "...It never occurred to us that he was interested in anything political. That was just not something we really discussed."[8]

His interest grew, though, and the state senate suited the stately and reserved Robert O'Bannon. He quickly became a state budget expert—but mostly by accident. Party and legislative leaders were looking for a new member for the State Finance Committee and were scanning the legislative directory for possible candidates. Someone noticed that O'Bannon was a newspaper publisher and assumed he knew something about finance and budgets. Before he was done, Senator O'Bannon became a strong advocate of state aid to higher education and transportation, leading the effort for the 1963 legislation that hiked cigarette taxes to pay for toll bridges to span the Ohio River between Indiana and Kentucky. In politics, Governor Matt Welsh (1912-1995) was one of Robert O'Bannon's favorites. Robert struggled more to get along with the governor that followed, Roger D. Branigin (1902-1975). Branigin's style was more aggressive than the patrician Welsh—the latter gentleman's approach more closely matching Robert O'Bannon's personality.

Once Robert was elected, Faith traveled often to Indianapolis to see her husband, sitting with other Democratic wives in one area, while Republican wives sat in another area. Jane Parker recalls accompanying her mother to listen to debates.[9]

David Allen, an aide to Governor Branigin (and later to Frank O'Bannon), recalls Robert O'Bannon as "the personification of a truly gentle man," but not one to be pushed around. Allen said Governor Branigin once commented about Robert O'Bannon behind his back, "He may be small in stature, but he certainly wasn't going to be bullied by a governor."[10]

Frank O'Bannon's parents would greatly influence his life. "Frank and I were both taught by our parents what good and responsible people do," Judy says. "We saw that in our parents, and we were of the nature where that fit us well. When they told us what good people did, we wanted to do that."[11]

Frank O'Bannon himself remembered his father's commitment to public service just days after his own election as governor and long after his father had died. "Dad was one of the fairest men I ever met," he told the *Indianapolis Star* in a post-election profile. "He never took advantage of owning the newspaper. He believed if you have power, you never abuse it."[12]

During his political career, Robert P. O'Bannon continued his active involvement in the community, driving to meetings all across his district. When he retired from the senate in 1970 after two decades of service, long-time *Indianapolis News* political writer Edward Ziegner wrote, "He has served under six governors, and with hundreds of legislators from both parties, and has had the respect of all of them."[13]

Robert P. O'Bannon, Sr., was eighty-eight years old when he died June 16, 1987, and is buried in the O'Bannon family plot at Cedar Hill Cemetery in Corydon. Having outlived Faith by about three years, he remarried briefly before the end of his life, with Mildred Kepner O'Bannon of Corydon surviving him.

Faith O'Bannon was eighty-four years old when she died on January 23, 1984. Her passing was lovingly reported in the *Corydon Democrat* by longtime editor Randy West under the headline: "Faith O'Bannon: A Life Well-lived," along with tributes from many friends and political colleagues of Robert's who had the opportunity to know her.

Frank O'Bannon described his parents in simple terms. "They were just good, decent people who I still think about every day. I try to be like them."[14]

The O'Bannon family plot is located at the historic Cedar Hill Cemetery in Corydon. The markers for the O'Bannon family reflect their simple nature. Robert P. O'Bannon, a state senator for twenty years, and his father, Lewis O'Bannon, a one-time candidate for lieutenant governor, are both buried here, with only their names carved into the markers. It reflects the people resting there: prominent, but simple.

4

Frank O'Bannon Grows Up

"I can tell you Frank O'Bannon was a cute little fellow," recalls Fred Griffin about the darkly handsome young boy whose family he had known all his life. "Frank had piercing eyes. You could tell he was always taking everything in." Griffin notes that Frank and brother Bobby "were always getting into things."[1]

It does seem that it was evident very early that Frank O'Bannon's life was destined to be something special.

Frank, early on, demonstrated a thoughtful, aware disposition. An October 1947 article in the *Pantherette*, the student newspaper, reported on Frank O'Bannon's Boy Scout trip to Belgium, Holland, and France.[2] The student paper quoted a remark he made which was quite thoughtful for a seventeen-year-old teenager: "The Jamboree of Peace was a success and very worthwhile. It was truly a challenge to World Peace, maybe our generation can achieve it."[3]

Frank O'Bannon would demonstrate his emerging leadership many times as an adolescent, including one important instance in which he saved his brother, Bobby, from drowning in the Blue River in the summer

29

of 1946. O'Bannon's act of bravery won him notice in April 1948 as *Jack Armstrong Magazine* named him their seventh "All-American Boy," an award made each month by the magazine's publishers. The magazine reported that O'Bannon was also awarded medals by the American Red Cross and the Boy Scouts of America.

Corydon, like most American cities and towns in the 1940s and '50s, was heavily influenced by the patriotism and sacrifice of World War II. In Harrison County, the flag-draped casket of each veteran who died in battle lay in state in the main hallway of the Harrison County Courthouse. Jack and Goldye Miller, owners of the Corydon Sales Store on the town square, took up the ambitious task of displaying the photograph of every man from Harrison County serving in the war. By the time Frank O'Bannon reached Corydon High School, however, World War II was coming to an end, and young men and women in his high school class could begin thinking about a future that included something other than the horrors of the Great War.

At school, Frank was a popular boy and a good student. He played basketball from the time he could dribble a ball all the way to a starting role for the Corydon Panthers. Known for his speed and a beautiful outside jump shot, he was a starting guard on a team coached by Paul Brackemyer. He had known most of his teammates his whole life, including Bill Baker, brothers Frank and John Cook, Huston Ernstberger, Bob Frakes, brothers Bob and Fred Frederick, Ray Glenn, Jack Kirkham, Jack McDonald, Bill Orwick, Doug "Charley" Robson, John Lee Saffer, Glenn Sharp, and Frank Timberlake. Basketball rivalries were as intense then as today, with tiny Corydon struggling to be competitive against the much larger schools from New Albany, Jeffersonville, Seymour, and Madison.

During his senior year at Corydon, the Panthers had a noteworthy season, earning a mention on the sports pages of the *Louisville Courier-Journal.* Sportswriter Bob Owens featured Corydon in his *Hooping It Up* column noting, "Coach Paul Brackemyer has developed a sectional tournament threat at

Corydon."[4] He noted that the team had overcome its apparent height handicap to defeat several worthy opponents including Tell City, Salem, Scottsburg, Vevay, Orleans, West Baden, Austin, and French Lick. The team's losses were to big-school challengers the Panthers seemingly always struggled with: Jeffersonville, Brownstown, and New Albany.

Predictions that Corydon would fare well in the Jeffersonville Sectional Tourney were premature, however. The Panthers won their first tourney game, defeating Charlestown 50-38, with Frank O'Bannon scoring twenty-six points, but New Albany would put an end to any Regional hopes for Corydon.

O'Bannon was named to the Sectional All-Tourney Team by the *Louisville Times*, because, as the *Democrat* reported, "As a senior and captain of the Corydon team, he has been one of the mainstays of the Corydon team for the past three years."[5]

Frank O'Bannon would meet many of the men he would later know through his career in politics on the basketball court. About basketball, Frank O'Bannon wrote many years later that "Indiana and basketball are inexorably linked…I miss playing basketball…but fifty years after I pulled on a jersey, I can honestly say that I do not miss the game. It never left me."[6]

He added, "My own basketball career came to an abrupt, if timely, end in college. Having starred, if only in my mind, on my Corydon High School basketball team, I left for Indiana University and a very comfortable seat on the old Fieldhouse bench. I quickly learned that my attention would be better focused on journalism and law. But I never lost my love for the game, and I never forgot what I learned on the court about cooperation, dedication, determination, teamwork, and fairness."[7]

Frank demonstrated leadership off the basketball court as well, being elected president of the senior class of 1948, fifty members strong. His best friend, Tom Miller, was elected vice president. As class president, he spoke at the commencement exercises for the class on May 14, 1948. The school newspaper, the *Pantherette*, poked at his success a bit in their May 1948 edition. In those days, students traditionally wrote a "prophecy" about the possible futures of the class members and had a little fun at their expense. For O'Bannon, they predicted:

> Frank O'Bannon is the only member of the class who did not amount to much. He is still found loafing around Ding How (a local teen hangout) playing the pin ball machines. Occasionally, he gives lessons to would-be barbershoppers thus managing to eke out a living.

Singing barbershop was one of O'Bannon's youthful passions. He and brother Bobby joined friends Chesney Davis and Miller to form what they originally called The Delinquent Four. The group later changed its name to a less threatening Peach Fuzz Four and sang at various events around the community. Two of the group's members, Miller and Davis, would join some older fellows to sing at the Harrison County Lincoln Day Dinner for the county Republican organization, while Frank and Bobby would sing in a quartet for the Harrison County Jefferson-Jackson Day bean supper for the county's Democrats. Frank and Bobby also later joined some of the adult men in town to form the Corydon Men's Barbershop Chorus that performed throughout Southern Indiana. In the spring of 1948, The Delinquent Four traveled as far as Frankfort, Kentucky and "presented three harmony numbers as part of the Parade of Quartets."[8]

Fred Griffin taught business and typing classes at Corydon High School for many years; he still beams with pride over Frank O'Bannon and the other members of the Class of '48. "During his high school days, Frank was president of the class one year, and the next year, Tom Miller would be president," Griffin said. "They were the same age and grew up in the same area of town. They were the best of friends, even though one was a Democrat and one was a Republican. I asked Frank how they could be good friends and be opposites in politics, and he said, 'Well, we never talk about politics.' That's the kind of guy he was. They just wanted to be friends and that came first."[9]

Miller would go on to become president and chief executive officer of the Indiana National Bank in Indianapolis. Prominent in Republican politics, he remained lifelong friends with his Democrat schoolmate from Corydon. Griffin was rightfully proud. This small town deep in the Indiana hills produced a remarkable generation of young men and women.

Frank O'Bannon seemed destined to become a leader. He did not always seek leadership roles, but they found him anyway. From the time he was a boy until he was a man, Frank O'Bannon made the best of every opportunity that came his way, including going to college and eventually law school. According to Jane Parker, Robert and Faith O'Bannon's children never questioned that they would go to college. "The only discussion was about where you were going and what you were going to major in."[10]

All of the children followed their parents' wishes. Jane attended DePauw and Indiana universities; Rosamond attended Miami University of Ohio, and then studied two years at the Traphagen School of Fashion and Design in New York City; Frank, Bobby, and Margaret all attended Indiana University.

THE PASSING OF GENERATIONS

Bobby and Frank O'Bannon's lives would remain intertwined for most of their lives. During most of their early life, Frank and Bobby were best friends. From his membership in the same fraternity and his stint in the air force to his career as a lobbyist and government affairs professional for the Indiana Telephone Association, Bobby seemed content to follow the lead of his brother.

According to Jane Parker, Bobby was more musical than Frank. Both of the O'Bannon boys sang in the church choir for years, but "Frank slept in the church choir," Jane said. "You'd look up there and he'd be sleeping, and he knew that. He thought that was funny...He couldn't get away with that when he was governor!"[11]

In December 2002, Bobby O'Bannon died at his home in Florida at the age of seventy-one, following a short illness. His brother, Frank, took his death especially hard. Jonathan O'Bannon recalls that upon hearing that Bobby had passed, his father retired to his bedroom and wept. In response to reporters' requests the next day, Frank released this statement about his beloved brother and friend: "In his professional life, Bob was a leader in community and state development. His leadership in the Indiana Telephone Association was innovative and long-lasting. His deep interest in the state's economic development made him active with the policies of several state administrations, including those of Governors (Otis) Bowen, (Robert) Orr, and (Evan) Bayh. Bob and I were close friends all through life, and we will miss him greatly."[12]

Jane Parker describes the youngest of the siblings, Margaret, as an active and outgoing woman, particularly devoted to her church and community. In 1957, Margaret married Keith I. Fawver (b. 1933) of Corydon. They later relocated to California, and she worked many years as a teacher in elementary schools in Orange, California. She died unexpectedly in July 2004 at the age of seventy, less than a year after her brother Frank died. Though she passed from this life far from Indiana, her family brought her home to Corydon, and she was buried in the O'Bannon family plot at Cedar Hill Cemetery.

Rosamond (named for her great-aunt Rosamond Keller) had a deep love of art all her life, working in water color, pastels, and ink, and creating white-layer collages. Several of her pieces were displayed through the years at the Speed Museum in Louisville. She taught art classes for generations of students in Corydon as her primary source of income. She supported herself and three daughters after her husband, Robert (1910-1975), died unexpectedly. Earlier in her life, she worked as an illustrator for L.S. Ayres & Co. in Indianapolis. Active throughout her life, she and her daughter, Leah Porter, started a reading club in the last years of her life. Although Rosamond would live the last thirty years of her life as a widow, she remained in Corydon and was an upbeat and intellectually engaged woman. She kept her life full and busy with activities that interested her and educated and enlightened others. Following a short illness, Rosamond died in October 2005 at the age of seventy-eight.

Fred Griffin, an avid Harrison County historian, made it his business to know the families of Corydon and Harrison County. He knows just about where everyone has placed their loved ones at Cedar Hill. For many years, he served on the cemetery board—along with Robert P. and later Frank O'Bannon. In fact, it was Frank O'Bannon's curiosity about whether any further space existed in the family plot that brought him to Griffin's home one Sunday afternoon in late August 2003.

After attending services at the Methodist Church, Frank and Judy, along with the troopers, stopped by for a short visit at Griffin's house. Frank inquired about the number of graves remaining in the O'Bannon family plot. Griffin recalls Frank being unusually quiet during the last visit and noted that he "looked tired." It was the last time he would ever talk to his friend.[13]

It's a Wonderful Life

Even early on, Frank O'Bannon's life demonstrated extraordinary meaning mixed in among the seemingly ordinary and simple life he pursued. Expected to attend college, O'Bannon chose Indiana University for his undergraduate and law degrees and committed himself fully to being a successful student.

Slowly but surely, the times were changing when a baby-faced O'Bannon entered Indiana University in the fall of 1948. The post-World War II generation nudged the nation forward socially and intellectually and was especially influential in advancing opportunities for African-Americans in society. Those changes were reaching Bloomington as well. O'Bannon's class, too young to serve in World War II but old enough to enjoy the benefits of post-war America, participated in the many changes.

Americans who had fought to liberate oppressed "others" around the world were finding it harder and harder to reconcile the racial inequities still at home. Until 1950, Indiana University participated in "gentleman's agreements" with other schools—most of them in the south—by refusing to field integrated athletic teams. Basketball was one of the last sports to integrate, in part because of fears of close physical contact between the players during the course of a game. That was about to change.

FRANK O'BANNON AND THE HURRYIN' HOOSIERS

Frank O'Bannon was number 15 on the 1949-50 Indiana University freshman basketball team, the first Indiana team to include a black player. The team picture reveals why he never played in a game. Much smaller than his teammates, O'Bannon sat front and center in the team photo but saw his action on a practice team. It must have been a tough adjustment. He was used to a lot of playing time at Corydon. At Indiana University, it didn't matter; the skills that made him a star at Corydon made him just average at Bloomington.

In later years, it made O'Bannon uncomfortable when others would declare that he had "played" basketball at Indiana. He may have been a member of the team, but he didn't play much, and he often corrected folks if they assumed otherwise.

The IU team O'Bannon joined featured the gifted Bill Garrett (1929-1974) of Shelbyville who made history as he led the team in scoring and rebounding and became the first African-American "star" in the respected IU program. Legendary IU coach Branch McCracken (1908-1970) led the effort to recruit Garrett to Indiana, and both he and IU president Herman B Wells (1902-2000) received hate mail from around the country for Garrett's presence.[14] O'Bannon was in awe of men like McCracken and worked hard to please him.

O'Bannon had met President Wells before enrolling at IU through his father and mother, but it was as a freshman that he mustered the courage to direct a personal concern to him. Wells addressed the IU freshmen in the fall of 1948 and told of the school's history and the state's history, referring several times to the "Constitutional Oak" in

Corydon, Indiana, under which the state's forefathers had gathered to create a new state constitution. "At eighteen years old, it took all the courage Frank could muster to tell the great Herman B Wells that it was an elm, not an oak," said Chuck Coffey, a friend and later a campaign aide to O'Bannon. "But he did it."[15]

FRANK BECOMES A FIJI

Elsewhere in college, O'Bannon stayed active in the Phi Gamma Delta Fraternity. He was one of sixteen men in the freshman pledge class of 1948. At the Fiji house, he first served as secretary and later as president in his senior year. His first run for fraternity president was unsuccessful, however, losing to John M. Kyle, a Republican who went on to become a successful Hamilton County attorney. Kyle teased O'Bannon many times over the years whenever he'd see a newspaper article that noted O'Bannon had never lost an election. "Haven't you ever lost an election, Frank?" Kyle would ask him with a wink, reminding him of his unsuccessful bid for fraternity president in 1950.[16] Two years later, O'Bannon started his winning streak in earnest, being elected president of the house for the 1951-52 school year.

Budd Weed, a fellow pledge class member, remembers O'Bannon as "a level-headed guy, a real nice guy," who "...was very good at getting people to work together." Fraternity pledgeship in this era entailed a level of hazing. At the Fiji house, this included dumping freshmen pledges off on their own in rural areas of Monroe or Brown County and forcing them to figure out how to get back to Bloomington. "We really had to pull together on those road trips," Weed says.[17]

Donald E. Lambert, or "Monk," met O'Bannon as a fellow freshman rushee. He remembers O'Bannon as "a clean-cut, good-looking young man with a distinct Southern Indiana drawl." Lambert said. "I liked him immediately."[18] Lambert left the Fiji house in 1950 when he withdrew from IU to enlist in the U.S. Air Force. O'Bannon stayed on to graduate, participating in the ROTC and earning an air force commission. Their paths would cross again, however, far from home when a mix-up left

Lambert who was en route to an air force volleyball tourney without money or accommodations. Someone advised him to check in with the volleyball project officer who turned out to be O'Bannon. O'Bannon quickly offered to help his old friend, and the two bonded again during the ten-day tournament, with O'Bannon offering him a place to stay in his off-base apartment.

William "Bill" C. Reed, Jr., pledged the Fiji house two autumns before Frank O'Bannon arrived. "Corydon, Indiana? Most of us had never even heard of it, but we had this freshman whose name was Frank O'Bannon, and he was a very good basketball player," Reed said. "Frank was a pledge at the Fiji house and was assigned to a room with Davies Robertson and myself...It didn't take long for us to find that Frank O'Bannon was a wonderful person. Davies and I were both veterans of World War II, and so we were not that much for ordering our pledge (Frank) around, and besides, with that smile that Frank had, you couldn't help but like him." It didn't take long for O'Bannon to win over the entire house. "Everyone understood very early on that this freshman, Frank O'Bannon, was destined to become a star."[19]

Fraternity brother Rod Howard concurs. "Frank was a true gentleman and commanded respect from everyone he came into contact with in those days."[20]

Thomas Hoadley pledged Phi Gamma Delta the year before Frank O'Bannon arrived at Bloomington. "I knew him instantly as a small-town boy, like me," Hoadley said. "Phi Gamma Delta at Indiana was not a party fraternity. No beer or girls were allowed in the house." The house attracted some of the best athletes on campus with excellent grade point averages. "If you were a top athlete with a high grade point average from a big city high school, you were asked to pledge. Small-town boys with excellent records were not always asked to pledge. I wondered why Frank and I ever made the pledge class!" Hoadley said.[21]

Frank's younger brother, Bob O'Bannon, also pledged Fiji and served as president the year after Frank had graduated from IU. Fraternity brother Robert Williams, M.D., was closer to Bob than Frank, though he was Frank's roommate in the Fiji house for a short time. "Bob was more outgoing and became a close friend of mine," Williams said.[22]

"Both of those guys were great," said William Boaz, one of Bob's rush classmates. "But Frank was the more serious of the two." Boaz first met Frank during a Boy Scout camp in the mid-1940s.[23]

In his sophomore year, O'Bannon was one of three Fiji men named to the Skull and Crescent Society, founded in 1922 to "foster an active school spirit by cooperating with other organizations and individuals; to promote higher scholastic attainments among members of the Sophomore Class, and to unite sophomore fraternity men into a smooth-working service organization."[24] He was also a member of the Jackson Club, Pre-Law Club, and the Arnold Air Society, a uniformed campus cadet corps for men seeking officer's appointments in the U.S. Air Force.

Pete Obremskey was an undergraduate freshman during O'Bannon's first year of law school, which he began after he completed his air force stint. "He was the counselor to the freshmen, the shoulder to cry on during pledge training," Obremskey said.[25]

The 1952 IU *Arbutus* yearbook shows all of the senior men wearing a suit and tie, including Frank O'Bannon, a government major, looking less baby-faced than he did four years earlier.[26]

UNITED STATES AIR FORCE

Following graduation from IU, O'Bannon was off to Northern California to the air force. He was assigned to the Hamilton Air Force Base near San Rafael, California. Although it has since been deactivated, at the time, Hamilton AFB was a busy and important part of the U.S. Air Force command in the western United States. The base was home to the 78th Fighter Group and the 82nd, 83rd, and 84th Fighter Squadrons during the period O'Bannon was stationed there.

Athletics were a major part of the social life for the men stationed there. O'Bannon was active on the Hamilton AFB "Defenders" basketball and volleyball teams. He earned All-American status for volleyball.

O'Bannon achieved the rank of second lieutenant. His assignment to the "Special Services" included duties such as notifying military families who had lost a loved one about veterans' benefits available to them. "...He was particularly well suited to do that, a man of religion, a good choice for that job," said friend and former senate staff member George Fleetwood.[27]

The job was no easy assignment. According to Judy O'Bannon, it served as preparation for situations he would encounter later in life. "It may look like he had an easier job, because he didn't have to go overseas and all, but he had a very sensitive job, and I think that was something that he could do because he was a listener, and he was sensitive to other people. It also helped him in some of the difficult situations he would be involved in with clients, and later in state government as well."[28]

Following his air force service, he returned to Bloomington to enroll in law school. After O'Bannon was discharged in August 1954, he returned with Lambert to Bloomington. They lived in the Phi Gamma house.

Lambert recalls the outstanding intramural volleyball team from the Fiji house. They lost only one match in two years. "Frank was a natural athlete, well coordinated, and loved all sports," he said.[29]

Phil Gutman was also in the air force in those days in California. A couple of decades later, he and O'Bannon would walk similar paths again as both served as members of the Indiana State Senate. "One thing about Frank, he was always a very straight arrow," Gutman said. "He was always courteous...He was always very kind and accommodating where people were concerned, even back in college. Back in those days, we had some pretty raucous Hell Weeks, and it didn't matter what fraternity you belonged to. Even during those times, Frank was always very kind, concerned about other people."[30]

By the fall of 1955, starting his second year of law school, O'Bannon and Lambert rented a basement apartment from a geology professor. "On many occasions, Frank would let me read his law briefs and give him my opinion as to what the jurors' verdict would be. Fortunately,

Frank never took my advice, because I was almost always wrong!"[31] The two kept in touch after graduation, occasionally sharing visits in Corydon and Indianapolis.

Though many of O'Bannon's fraternity brothers were from Republican families, they readily supported his statewide candidacies in later years, writing checks and voting for him. It was the kind of thing one Fiji man did for another.

These friendships were important to Frank O'Bannon, and he held them dear all his life. Judy O'Bannon says, "If you were Frank's friend, you were his friend forever and ever. He still had that close sense of friendship with all those kids he went to high school with and with the people he knew from college...Friends would call him up, and he would love to talk to them and catch up. He never forgot those people, and I think that comes from being raised in a small town where he had a closeness, a connection to people that was real and lasted his entire life."[32]

Frank & Judy: Partners for Life

FRANK AND JUDY'S BLIND DATE

Frank O'Bannon's boring date with a sorority woman in the fall of 1956 turned out to be the best move of his life. Carolyn Bassett Lambert, one of Judy Asmus's sorority sisters, came back to the house complaining about her date with O'Bannon. "He took me to Crane Naval Depot, and we played bridge, and it was just so boring." Strange as it may seem, the description of Frank as "boring" and "serious" caught Judy's attention. Unhappy in her relationship with her less mature boyfriend, Judy declared to her friend, "I'm ready for boring!" Carolyn agreed to set Judy up on a date with Frank, in part to avoid going out with him again.

They set up the blind date for just before Christmas break. "We went to get a Coke, and the first time I saw him, he was standing in his award jacket that he got for being an All-American volleyball player in the air force. We went out in his brand-new, second-hand car," Judy said.[1]

O'Bannon's car, a Ford Interceptor that had served its time previously as a police car, still had the spotlight attached to the windshield and another luxury for its time: air conditioning. Judy says, "I spent the whole first date teasing him and making fun of his fancy new car, saying, 'Eeeww! What does this button do? Or that one?' That was nice and graceful of me, wasn't it?" But Judy's teasing did one thing, it broke the ice between them and allowed them to share some laughs, in between their very serious conversations about religion, politics, and philosophy. After that first date, Judy bought short-heeled shoes so she would be shorter than Frank.

She was certain their relationship would last. "I knew, I *knew* I would marry Frank the first time I saw him," Judy said. "Partly because we thought so much alike, so I was prepared to like him. It was a rather matter-of-fact thing for me," she says.[2]

Frank and Judy hit it off and continued to see each other. Typical dates involved a trip to the library to study for classes. "It was a cheap date, one we could afford!" Judy says.

Judy was as ambitious a student as Frank was, signing up for two classes that met at the same time because she was unwilling to wait and take one of them later. Frank's days were spent completing his law school requirements and preparing to take the bar exam. "He would put on his glasses to try and 'wow me,' because he knew that I thought he looked so intellectual when he put those on," Judy said. "...It took me forty years of marriage to understand that he was trying to be funny, to make me laugh, but I took him seriously all the time in those days."[3]

The courtship was old-fashioned in many ways, due to the couple's conservative Protestant upbringing and the era in which they lived. Neither one of them was particularly demonstrative, especially in public. "We did not talk sweetsie-sweetsie to each other all the time. He was kind and thoughtful, and it never would have entered his mind to speak a harsh word to me. Very considerate, always," Judy said.[4]

During those cheap dates at the library, Judy noticed Frank's habit of underlining almost every line of text he read (a habit he would keep, underlining almost every line of proposed bills in the state senate or every line of his speeches and briefing materials as governor). He used a small ruler to underline the words. When he and Judy and

Rosamond signed up for a speed-reading class "just for fun," he was very competitive. "Rosamond was in our class, and she would read at an incredible level, something like eleven thousand words, and I was way back at nine thousand words, and Frank would be way back from that. He was very competitive, and he always wanted to do better than us." Judy believes this was when she began to understand who he was as a person and how he would approach almost everything in his life. "He couldn't read as fast as Rosamond or me, but he never missed a comprehension question in that reading class. All of his life, that was how he operated. He was slower, where I would just jump in and make some snap decisions and then have to go back and apologize, or just wallow in the mess I had made. He never had to do that. He was slow, studied, focused, and wise, always."[5]

Frank O'Bannon also moved deliberately when it came to making his relationship permanent with Judy. He proposed in April 1957. "I thought Frank was moving kind of slow...I mean, I knew on the first date we were going to be married, but he took his time. When he finally did propose to me, I did not tell my parents right away because Frank wanted to go talk to my father and ask for his permission," she said.

Judy's father, a quiet but direct man, offered a simple, non-poetic response: "I guess you're old enough to decide that for yourself now, aren't you?"

Judy remembers the proposal as being strange. Although he was hemming and hawing around a bit about what he wanted to do with his life, Judy knew where Frank was headed with his remarks but was determined to make him ask outright for her hand. "Finally, he said, 'I'm moving to Corydon, and would you like to marry me?'" Judy accepted, knowing it meant moving away from the larger communities where she had spent most of her life and adjusting to life in a small town. But Frank wanted to be a county seat lawyer and work at the newspaper. Frank wasn't thinking about public service at the time; according to Judy, all he wanted to do was be a lawyer in his beloved Corydon.[6]

FRANK AND JUDY GET MARRIED

The couple wed on August 18, 1957 at Fairview Presbyterian Church in Indianapolis, just two blocks west of the home that would become the governor's residence where they would one day live. The ceremony was conducted by Dean Bowden, one of Judy's favorite religion professors at Indiana University. Their honeymoon took them on a car trip to Door County, Wisconsin, just north of Green Bay. It lasted until Democratic Party politics interrupted—the first of decades of such interruptions of their personal life for the work of the party.

Frank's mother called the couple informing them that Frank was to be elected IDEA treasurer. The IDEA, or Indiana Democratic Editorial Association, gathered each August at French Lick, Indiana, and Faith O'Bannon expected her son to be there. Judy was unperturbed by the abrupt ending of her honeymoon because they "were running out of money anyway," but she recalls her new role required some adjustment. She sat at the end of the head table in her missionary outfit her mother had sewn for her, and when she was introduced as "Mrs. O'Bannon," Judy looked for Frank's mother and missed her cue.

Having such a prominent seat at a Democratic event stirred guilt in Judy; she worried someone might know that she had voted for Republican Dwight Eisenhower (1890-1969) in 1952. By 1956, however, she had "reformed" and voted for Adlai Stevenson (1900-1968) for president "because by then, I had been given a list of people who I was supposed to vote for."[7]

It was only the start. As a young lawyer and businessman in Corydon, Frank helped Judy to understand that it was important to shop as often as possible at the stores that advertised in the family's newspaper. "My first reaction was, 'What do you mean I have to go to his hardware store? How do you know they sell stuff cheaper than the other one?' And Frank said, 'These are our advertisers. You don't turn your back on your friends; that's how a community helps each other out.' Frank saw it as community building, not just back scratching," she said.[8]

Judith Mae Asmus O'Bannon

Born April 30, 1935 in Oak Park, Illinois, Judy was the second of four children born to Charles Herman Asmus and Blanche Mae (Betts). The Asmus family lived in tiny Downers Grove, Illinois. Judy's older sister, Elsie Louise (Asmus) Brenneman, was born five years earlier than Judy and passed away in 1993. Her younger brother, Charles Theodore Asmus, and sister, Christine Margaret (Asmus) Bible, were born twelve and fifteen years, respectively, after Judy.

In Downers Grove, Judy remembers living within walking distance of a city dump near the high school, a favorite place to explore as a small child. "I liked to explore; I loved that kind of thing…I had a big imagination, something I got from my mother," Judy said. "She was into a lot of things; she ran the Girl Scouts, the Brownies, sewed all of her own clothes, and she loved to garden and can vegetables. I loved to sit and listen to her and her friends talk as they snapped beans or pressure packed something."[9] Judy was determined to be successful at whatever she tried, just as her mother had always been.

"If you've seen me, you've seen my mother," Judy likes to say. "We were best buddies. When she died, I said, 'People are going to think I'm just weird, but now that my mother has died, she's more in my skin than ever.'"[10]

Judy's father, Charles Asmus, worked for Western Electric Company for most of his adult life, moving with the company work assignments, eventually taking the family from Illinois further west to Lincoln, Nebraska, where Judy spent her childhood.

Charles Asmus was raised by a Presbyterian minister who had to move around to make a meager living. Sometimes, his pay consisted of cabbages or other garden harvest. Judy's father was determined to make a more reliable living for his family. To prepare, he attended the University of Nebraska, where he played on the Cornhuskers' football team and was an accomplished Golden Gloves boxer. "We thought he did everything right, and my mother told us he did everything right, so we respected him and listened to him always," Judy said.[11]

As a girl, Judy survived scarlet fever, spending long periods of time bedfast. Her father and grandfather moved out of the house during those months to a hotel in order to keep working. "People couldn't come to our house. They left the groceries at the curb, and if you used anything, you had to burn it afterwards. My sister couldn't go to school for a great deal of that time, so my sister and my mother, who were both good readers, nursed me and read to me," Judy said.[12]

Judy loved the stories, but she wasn't always a good reader. As a very young student, she learned how to memorize her spelling words and other assignments, without ever actually learning how to read herself. Exasperated, her mother promised her that if she turned an F in English into an A, she could get a doll she longed for from the Sears catalog. The doll, which cost $10, was enough motivation, and Judy got her A, but her parents could not afford the doll. Undeterred, the ambitious young Judy decided to send postcards out to her mother's friends asking for work. At twelve, Judy set out to work and earned enough money to buy the doll. She said, "I think of kids today age twelve, and how that would never interest them now! But my mother set up a baby bed and a high chair, and I played dolls with that baby doll until my brother was born, and I put him in that baby bed, too."[13]

Her brother, Charlie Asmus, remembers his older sister being an incredible influence on his life. "Judy is not only an inspiration to her family, but to others as well. As a child, she was my hero. She made me feel important...She put aside time for me. I think it is this quality that has such an effect on others. She can make people feel good about themselves and then is able to encourage them to share these feelings with others."[14]

JUDY'S LEADERSHIP SKILLS EMERGE

Judy's ambition did give her special opportunities for a young girl. In seventh grade, she taught Bible school at the Presbyterian church for the younger children when the teacher's son became ill with chicken pox. "There must have been some wonderful adults in that church, because it stuck with me that they let me do many things. Here I am a kid in junior high school, and that was the age to catch kids like me. They are idealistic, they want to identify, they want to belong and join things, and I wanted all of those things, too," Judy said.[15]

In 1949, the Asmus family moved again, this time to Indianapolis to the Butler-Tarkington neighborhood, not far from the respected Shortridge High School. Her father's new job was to help set up a new Western Electric plant in Indianapolis that would eventually produce thousands of telephones for homes across the nation. Judy continued her active involvement in the church and dove into school life at Shortridge, one of the nation's great high schools with activities and clubs of all kinds, including a third-floor art gallery and a daily student newspaper, the *Echo*. Though Indianapolis was much larger than Lincoln, it still had that small-town feel. When Judy made Phi Beta Kappa, other parents stopped her and her mother to congratulate them as they shopped for groceries at the Atlas Supermarket on College Avenue.

Frank highlighted the differences between Judy's high school experiences and his in a funny story he enjoyed telling audiences. "Judy's class had Duke Ellington play at their senior prom at the Indiana Roof Ballroom. For our senior prom, we had records down at the American Legion!"[16]

By the time Judy graduated from Shortridge in 1953, Frank O'Bannon had already completed his bachelor's degree at IU and was in the air force.

In college, Judy lived at Maple Hall her freshman year and later pledged Kappa Kappa Gamma Sorority, being elected vice president in her senior year. She also participated in the Westminster Foundation, a campus religious organization, and the student senate (as the representative of the YWCA) during the 1955-56 school year. That year, the senate blocked efforts by faculty members to impose a $10 parking fine for students and passed a resolution opposing discrimination in the Bloomington community against any minority groups on the IU campus.

Judy expressed an early interest in the emerging civil rights movement in the U.S. "But there was a lot of apathy...The students in the Y groups were not apathetic; that's why I liked them," she said. During her junior and senior years, Judy attended eighteen leadership seminars and conferences for undergraduates across the country. Her interest in international affairs was also growing, and she applied for a post-graduate scholarship opportunity which would have taken her to Kiel, Germany after graduation.[17]

As her senior year drew to a close, her future plans were being influenced by her new boyfriend (and soon fiancé), Frank O'Bannon. Everything seemed to change. Instead of taking the scholarship opportunity that would have taken her to post-World War II Germany, she took the advice of a professor and applied for a Rockefeller Scholarship and won. The Rockefeller Scholarship paid for one year of graduate study wherever the student enrolled, and Judy had her sights set on Yale University "because that was where all the existentialists were, and I loved all that existential thought, all that nebulous thought and discussion where no one can prove you wrong."[18]

Going to Yale, however, presented a major dilemma: She would have to distance herself from or break up with Frank O'Bannon, who had proposed marriage. Yale immediately seemed too far away, especially with her fiancé determined to go home to Corydon.

For Judy, getting married was part of being a good woman. "I wanted to get married and be a good wife. I think women in my era were programmed to do what 'good women' do, and I think it was productive for us to do so, but it could also be counterproductive."[19]

In the end, Judy's Rockefeller Scholarship paid for a year of study at Louisville Theological Seminary and covered the young couple's living expenses as Frank finished his bar exam and got his law practice started. Judy commuted twenty-two miles each way from her home in Corydon to attend classes at the seminary.

"At the seminary, they said, 'We've never had a Rockefeller scholar, and we've never had a woman.' I hadn't even thought about that."[20]

The seminary, at that time, was located in the heart of downtown Louisville at the corner of First and Broadway. Judy joined her fellow students for lunch, one of 170 enrolled at the time, most of whom were friendly and supportive during her first semester there. During her second semester, with all As to show for her work, some of her classmates began to resent her presence, and the friendliness faded. "The first semester I was cute; the second semester the whole tone changed," she said.

She received angry letters at the seminary after the *Louisville Courier-Journal* article "Bachelor bride? First woman enrolled in seminary's Bachelor-of-Divinity program here" was picked up by United Press International and published in newspapers across the country.

"The letters would say, 'Paul said women should be quiet in the church, what are you, so presumptuous to think you're going to stand up in church and preach?' I wanted to write to every one of them and go through this whole explanation with them."[21]

Judy had no plans to "stand up in church and preach," as the letters claimed. "I was programmed by the times; I would never have assumed to do that. I was just a woman," she said.[22]

The *Courier-Journal* article described Judy as "a blond, twenty-two year-old newlywed" and noted that since the scholarship paid for all her expenses, she "just can't afford to stay at home" and noted "she will do her own housework and cook dinner every night." She told the reporter that she and her then twenty-seven-year-old husband, Frank, enjoyed reading and discussing ideas. "I have a very understanding husband," she added.[23]

6

County Seat Leader and Father

THE O'BANNON LAW PRACTICE

After passing the bar, Frank O'Bannon started on his new career as a young lawyer and businessman. A January 14, 1959 display advertisement in the *Corydon Democrat* featured the picture of a serious-looking Frank O'Bannon and said:

> Announcing, Frank L. O'Bannon opens law office at 303 N. Capitol Ave., Corydon, formerly the Office of C. Bliss Eskew. Business: The General Practice of Law. Education: Corydon High School - 1948. Indiana University, A.B., 1952. Indiana University School of Law, J.D., 1957. Membership: Indiana State Bar Association. Harrison-Crawford Bar Association.[1]

One of O'Bannon's future law partners, Ron Simpson, joined the firm after more than a decade of teaching and coaching seventh- and eighth-grade students at Corydon Junior High School. Simpson attended law school part-time while teaching a variety of students, including a young Polly O'Bannon, Frank and Judy's oldest daughter. He also taught Andy Funk, son of Frank O'Bannon's first law partner, Art Funk. Andy sadly died in 1972 of an anemic blood disease.

By 1979, Simpson had finished law school and was invited to become a partner in the Hays, O'Bannon, & Funk law firm, which Art Funk had formed a few years earlier when he suddenly found himself the sole proprietor of Blaine Hays, Sr.'s law firm. Hays had recruited Funk to Corydon from Indianapolis when his son died, leaving no successor. Shortly thereafter, Hays himself died, and Funk needed help. Hays' firm had many prominent Harrison County clients. Funk approached Frank O'Bannon and "Hays, O'Bannon, & Funk, Attorneys at Law" was born.

Funk's client list worked well with O'Bannon's interest in anything that avoided having to argue in court. "For Frank, I think he always preferred writing a letter to having to speak in court," Simpson said. O'Bannon focused his work on probate, estates, wills, and real estate law, adding in some local school boards and the town of Palmyra. He also assisted local farmers and other landowners who faced eminent domain sale of their land for the completion of Interstate 64 through Harrison County.[2]

Simpson was eager to help bring in his share of business. The types of cases O'Bannon would avoid were Simpson's bread and butter. Simpson took criminal defense work, divorces, bankruptcies— anything to help pay the bills. By 1984, the Hays name was dropped, and the firm became "O'Bannon, Funk, & Simpson." That name would remain until an inmate in the Indiana Department of Corrections discovered a rule that prohibited persons holding executive office from having their name on law firms and filed a complaint in the summer of 1996 against O'Bannon and Simpson (in the midst of the O'Bannon for Governor campaign in 1996), a complaint that was later dropped when Simpson had O'Bannon's name dropped from the firm's sign, letterhead, business cards—even the local phone book. Simpson's two-year stint as a deputy prosecutor in Harrison County had created an enemy in the inmate.

At the same time Simpson was starting his local political career, his law partner Frank O'Bannon was starting his second decade as a state senator. Both Simpson and O'Bannon were Democrats. Funk, on the other hand, was active in Harrison County Republican Party politics, but he and O'Bannon never clashed. Born just a month apart, Art Funk and Frank O'Bannon were very similar men. One of them, though, was a better attorney in Simpson's opinion, and that was Art Funk. "Frank did not like public speaking in his early years," Simpson said. "He was much better in situations where he could sit folks down and work as a counselor at law."[3]

Perhaps it was one of O'Bannon's early cases that convinced him that civil and government law was more to his liking and interest. As a young attorney, he took one divorce case. The case dissolved when the husband and wife opted to reconcile and decided that meant they didn't need to pay the lawyer. But O'Bannon never sued anyone for an unpaid fee. Simpson jokes that was only because he wasn't always sure why folks had come to see him and whether to charge a fee. Some folks came to see him about the newspaper, others about the savings and loan, and still others about state government or legislative business. "Frank would rather eat a loss; he never, ever worried about money," Simpson said.[4]

The three lawyers relied heavily on two trusted employees, Eunice Wiseman and Dwanna Trobaugh, who worked for the firm for decades. Frank offered Simpson, his young colleague, some good advice he always remembered: "Don't be afraid to turn someone down. If you do not feel comfortable with what they are asking you to do, or you think it is beyond your ability, I know it is a hard thing to do, but you should turn them down. There will always be other cases that will come along, and you want to do your best for everyone."[5]

The more deeply involved in state government O'Bannon became following his election to the state senate in 1970, the more he counted on the endorsement of local voters to keep his senate seat (though his challengers never got close), and the more some folks talked behind his back. Simpson said, "Some folks would say, 'Oh, Frank's just that nice because he wants me to vote for him.' But I never believed that about him at all. His niceness, his willingness to help people was just a part of who he was."[6]

In fact, O'Bannon recruited Simpson into his first foray into politics. He helped Simpson, who was still a teacher at the time, land a spot on the local board of zoning appeals. O'Bannon strongly encouraged Simpson's decision to run for county prosecutor.

Just as O'Bannon's standing among Indiana Democrats continued to grow, so seemingly did Funk's place among Indiana Republicans. On a first name basis with both Governor Otis R. Bowen, M.D. (b. 1918), and Robert D. Orr (1917-2004), Funk earned a gubernatorial appointment to the Indiana Toll Bridge Commission. By 1988, though, he chose a "neutral" position as his law partner and friend, Frank O'Bannon, prepared to seek the Democratic nomination for governor.

"It was a different world then than it is today," Simpson said. "People could be on opposite sides of politics and still sit down and talk to one another."[7]

Art Funk was convinced, though, that his friend would become governor. "He really thought Frank was going to be elected in 1988. He was surprised, like we all were, when Frank joined up with Evan Bayh. But Frank was a realist...I think in our hearts, we always remained partial to Frank," Simpson said, comparing O'Bannon's move to the 1960 Democratic partnership that matched the more senior Lyndon Johnson (1908-1973) for the vice presidential nomination with a younger, new politician named John F. Kennedy (1917-1963). Art Funk would not live to see his friend and partner become governor, passing away following a stroke in September 1990.[8]

Frank O'Bannon never got rich being a lawyer. It wasn't that he didn't work hard. Like his father, Robert P. O'Bannon, who cobbled together work as a newspaper publisher, savings and loan director, insurance salesman, and state senator, Frank added lawyer to his father's list of crafts to provide for his growing family. At best guess, however, O'Bannon probably never made more than $30,000 or $40,000 a year from his law practice. Acceptable for its time, it was still not the stuff to make him a wealthy man. His wealth, it seems, always came from the people he called friends.

Simpson and Frank O'Bannon stayed in touch over the years, with the O'Bannons welcoming staff from the law firm into the governor's residence in Indianapolis and at "the barn" west of town for holiday parties. O'Bannon sometimes missed "the old days" when he could look out his office window and take in the entire Corydon town square. "He would call me up every now and again from Indianapolis when he was governor and he'd say, 'Hey, what are ya doin'?' And I'd say, 'Oh, I'm just sitting here looking at this sleepy little town.' And he'd say, 'I'm doing the same thing.'"[9]

YOUNG MARRIED LIFE FOR THE O'BANNONS

Thursday nights in 1960, Gordon Pendleton and Frank O'Bannon could be found in one place: in front of Frank's black and white TV, tuned to NBC to catch their favorite show, *Not For Hire*. The show lasted only one year, but Gordon's friendship with Frank lasted decades, starting in grade school.[10]

After graduating from Ball State University, Gordon returned to his native Harrison County and took a job teaching business education at Corydon High School. He and his wife, Christine, rented the apartment on the second floor of the *Democrat* building after Frank's sister Rosamond and her husband, Bob Sample, moved out to their new house. Up on the third floor, Frank and Judy were making their new home and welcomed their first daughter, Polly, to the world. For Frank and Judy, it was their second home in Corydon. Their first was a small apartment they rented from Melba Hickman on Capitol Avenue. "It was one of those apartments up off the sun porch, and you had to go through five doors with those locks on them to get in, and by the time you got up there, the ice cream would melt," Judy recalls. "We lived there just a year until I started looking around for something else, and I liked the newspaper building. It was built in 1837, and I told

Frank, 'This is really interesting. Let's move up here!'" Her happiness
with the new place diminished, though, as she became pregnant with
their first child, and she discovered the hard way that Frank O'Bannon
did not share her father's interest, or talent, with building things or
construction. "My father had always done construction things around
the house, so I didn't think it was any big deal, so I had them deliver
drywall to the third floor, and when Frank saw that, he took off and
went golfing. I was so mad at him," Judy says, noting, "I never asked
him to do anything like that around the house again, because it was
just not his thing. He was so bad at that. I would get really nervous later
on when he was governor and we would go to a Habitat for Humanity
event, and he would hammer nails, and I would just pray that he would
not hit his finger in front of everyone!"[11]

Judy quickly made friends with the newlyweds downstairs and
joined Gordon's wife, Christine, in thinking "the boys" were silly
in their devotion to their favorite TV shows. The couples became
close friends, though, with Gordon and Frank enjoying a quiet
friendship. "He was a very good listener, and he always wanted your
opinion," Gordon said. "He didn't try to overwhelm you with what
he knew."[12]

O'BANNON AS A WRITER

During those days, O'Bannon also dabbled as a columnist and
photographer for the *Corydon Democrat*, writing an occasional sports
column titled *Hanging 'Round the Rim, by E. Sturdley*. E. Sturdley was a
character created by radio comics "Bob and Ray" that Frank O'Bannon
enjoyed. He also wrote the newspaper's editorial in November 1963
following the assassination of President Kennedy. He tried to capture the
overwhelming grief young and old felt in those cold days as JFK's "New
Frontier" came to a violent end—"his song half sung" as O'Bannon put
it. He wrote, "In the three short years of his national administration,
the young forty-six-year-old leader had become a dynamic symbol of
the emerging era of great scientific and political changes, which, due

to enlarging complexities, are transforming the world." Kennedy had "ushered in a new excellence of the political art which was necessary in a fast-moving world. He symbolized the visionary idealist who sought excellence but realistically was directed by pragmatic actions dictated by logic." He added that he hoped Kennedy's death "may serve the good of reducing the popular notion of hate-filled groups and move us toward a higher civilized state of being."[13]

THE CORYDON SAVINGS AND LOAN

In addition to the *Democrat,* Frank's father and grandfather had started and developed the Corydon Savings and Loan. Eventually, the savings and loan's board decided to seek federal insurance for its meager but growing $1 million in assets. As a member of the board of directors, Frank sought out Gordon Pendleton's help. All Gordon knew about the savings and loan was the balance in his savings account there. The O'Bannons were committed to operating a sound and trusted institution and saw federal insurance for the assets as an appropriate, if not overdue, step.

Frank decided to concentrate on his law practice and asked his good friend Gordon Pendleton to run the savings and loan. Gordon says O'Bannon's support never wavered even when Pendleton had to make tough decisions. Sometimes, when Pendleton made a decision people didn't like, they would complain to O'Bannon, who simply said, "Well, Gordon is the manager of the bank. I'm just a member of the board. I can't override him."[14]

THE O'BANNON FAITH

Those early married years in Corydon were a time of learning and transition for Frank and Judy. Judy returned to Corydon to be a housewife after just one year at seminary. She said, "I was not a woman's rights advocate, and I did not want to fight that battle, and the scholarship ended after one year, so I left."[15]

While her departure from the seminary in Louisville was met with barely a notice, it represented a painful and difficult period for Judy. Her desire to study religion and engage in lay leadership in the church was not diminished, however. Back in Corydon, the O'Bannons attended the United Methodist Church. A request for an adult Sunday school teacher seemed like a good fit for Judy. It wasn't. When she inquired, she was told the teaching position "required the dignity of a man." Told no one would come to a class taught by a woman, Judy withdrew her request, and Frank took the assignment instead. The pain Judy felt was deep and real. She turned her pain outward for a time, acting in a snide way toward Frank and others, including asking difficult questions in the Sunday school class she knew might stump her husband. It didn't take long for Judy to see the wrongness of what she was doing. "It was a prideful reaction, a reaction to my pain," she said. She decided to change and instead support Frank in his teaching, even offering to make the coffee for the class. Over time, Judy's role would increase as the pastor and members of the church grew to know and love her, eventually allowing her to run the Sunday school—a volunteer activity she held for about twenty years. Frank was named to the parish counsel and was a faithful member of the choir.

Fellow church member Callie Zimmerman remembers one time when Frank O'Bannon's attitudes were viewed as perhaps a step too progressive for one member of the church. "At one of the meetings, Frank asked this question, 'Do you think that the time will ever come that a woman could serve as our pastor?'...One older lady spoke up and said, 'No way, I cannot accept that. I wasn't raised that way.'"[16]

O'Bannon's prediction was right. Before long, the United Methodist Church *was* ordaining female pastors, including women who have served in the pulpit at Corydon United Methodist Church.

Judy says the church was the center of the couple's social life in those days and helped solidify their relationship to each other and with God.[17]

Frank's life grew busier, and his law practice expanded. Wednesday afternoons would find most of the offices in downtown Corydon closed (allowing merchants time off so they could be open on Saturday mornings). The *Democrat,* the savings and loan, and the O'Bannon law office were no exception. Frank took that time, often, to enjoy golf at the then-nine-hole Corydon Country Club, knocking the ball around with Pendleton, Funk, Simpson, and local realtor and Republican state representative Joe Harmon.

Judy admits she was a lousy cook in those days. "Poor Frank, I would come home from school and try and cook something, but I think Frank would have eaten better if I had just stayed away...I worried and apologized a lot in those days, being concerned if I wasn't home in time for his dinner. I did what 'good women' did in that period, everything I could to make a peaceful, wonderful home for my husband."[18]

During her years as first lady, things were very different with a staff to clean the governor's residence and even more staff to help her coordinate her active schedule and travels. She enjoyed the help, "but people forget there were thirty years or so in there that I was a mom, and I took care of my husband and my kids and did all my volunteer work. I didn't think it was suffering. I thought it was fine, a wonderful life, and I had so many opportunities because of that."[19]

Judy recalled those early married years once in a moving and memorable speech during a statehouse meeting for Healthy Families workers, a statewide community-based program the O'Bannons championed to help reduce child abuse and neglect. (In fact, Prevent Child Abuse America presented a special award to Governor O'Bannon to recognize his efforts to fully fund the Healthy Families program in all ninety-two counties.) Judy, with tears welling up in her eyes, told the child welfare advocates, parents, legislators, and others gathered that day that she understood what it meant as a mother and a parent to struggle with a child, to try and do what was right.

POLLY, JENNIFER, AND JONATHAN

For Polly D O'Bannon Zoeller (b. 1959), her memories of those early years living above the newspaper office are limited. As a small child, she recalls the many steps in the *Democrat* building and a small courtyard in back. Her memories are more vivid of "the little yellow house" the O'Bannons moved to west of town. Polly's middle name, just the letter D with no period, is in memory of "Mama D" Dropsey, her beloved great-grandmother. Jennifer Mae O'Bannon (b. 1961) soon followed, as did Jonathan Lewis O'Bannon (b. 1965) in those years before the family moved to a rambling ranch-style home on Woodland Avenue.

The O'Bannon children didn't realize it at the time, but they now tell of an idyllic childhood spent running in the woods, playing hide and seek, throwing dirt balls, and riding skateboards and bicycles up and down the hilly roads and driveways on the four-acre O'Bannon parcel.

"I think we had a very careful, easy lifestyle when we were kids. When I look back on it now, I see the ease and innocence of it, and it was pretty nice. I mean, we would get on our bikes and be gone all day. There were no cell phones in those days for our parents to keep track of us; things were very different then," Jennifer recalls.[20]

The O'Bannon kids said they witnessed only one argument between their parents, a momentary disagreement about what time to leave for an event. An instance like that was so rare that it scared the kids into tears, thinking their parents would divorce. Forming their own relationships later, they began to understand how rare it was for a couple to avoid arguments and disagreements over the course of so many years. "When I was dating the woman who would become my wife, Soni, we would have an argument and I would just say, 'That's it,'" Jon said. "It didn't seem normal to me to have this kind of argument."[21]

Frank and Judy O'Bannon were considered strict but fair parents by their kids—all three of whom can never recall their father raising his voice at them. He saved for them a punishment they hated worse: The Lecture.

"By the time Dad was done talking to you about what you had done wrong, you just wanted to go out and jump off a cliff, you felt so bad," Jon said. "I remember when I got in a fight with a kid once and he said, 'That's the most animalistic thing a person can do.'"[22]

Jennifer said their mother would sometimes join in "The Lecture" that almost always took place in the "better" living room behind closed doors. "…Sometimes, I would think, 'Why can't they just be like other parents and just ground me or spank me?!' But that's the way they were, thankfully," Jennifer recalls.[23]

The O'Bannon kids also grew accustomed to their father's attitude, handed down from his father and grandfather, that they could expect no special privileges. When Polly was elected Homecoming Queen at Corydon Central High School, her father hesitated to run her photo in the family-owned newspaper. Jon's photograph rarely appeared in the paper even though he played on athletic teams at the high school.

Frank was also hesitant to offer jobs to his teenage kids at the *Democrat,* for fear he'd be accused of showing them special privileges. He eventually relented on that when co-publisher Denny Huber wanted to hire one of his kids to help sweep up in back. The O'Bannon kids eventually did "everything but write for the paper," Jon recalls.[24]

Polly and Jennifer would never work at the paper as adults, but Jon was named the publisher of the *Corydon Democrat* following his father's death in 2003. Polly went to college and eventually married Tom Zoeller, brother of Masters and U.S. Open golf champion Frank "Fuzzy" Zoeller, Jr. She and Tom had three children, and she worked full-time as a kindergarten teacher, a job that made her father very proud.

As teenagers, the O'Bannon kids tested limits like most kids but had an unspoken rule that grew out of their own wish to never disappoint their father. That rule hung over their young lives effectively. "I don't ever really remember him saying, 'If you get into trouble, you're going to make me look bad'…but you just knew that you had to do your best not to make any trouble. I mean, if you did get into anything, the first thing that would go through your mind is, 'How will this affect Dad?'

It was even that way with my kids many years later," Polly said.[25] There were other tough moments. Jennifer remembers a high school civics teacher labeling all politicians as "crooks," but then quickly adding her father as an exception to that rule.

As each of the kids became old enough to drive, they had to share a 1966 Plymouth Valiant and a high-top Ford camper van Frank had bought secondhand for each of them to knock around town.

Jennifer O'Bannon was eager to flee the confines of Corydon and took her chance when it was time to leave for Indiana University. "I just never felt like I fit in, so I was eager to get away from there," Jennifer said. Away she went, first to Chicago and then to New York City where she worked for Saks Fifth Avenue as a fashion merchandiser. "I can remember the Saks store was closed for inventory on Election Night in 1988, and we were there late into the night, but I kept sneaking away to a manager's office to call back to Indiana to find out how things were going," Jennifer said.[26]

As their father's role in the state senate increased and the children grew older, both Frank and Judy spent more time away in Indianapolis, especially for the first half of the year. All three kids served as senate pages on more than one occasion, enjoying their father's work up close. When he was gone to Indianapolis, "we missed him, but we knew he was coming back soon," Jennifer said.[27]

Polly sums it up this way: "We always knew we shared our father with all of the people of Indiana, but we never felt neglected."[28]

THE BARN

In 1963, the O'Bannons purchased a one-hundred-acre tract of land west of town on what was the old Julius Slaughterback farm at the edge of the state woods and park (the woods was later renamed for Lew, Robert, and Frank O'Bannon). When they purchased the land, the only structure on the land was a small cabin which was built in 1830. It contained bunk beds used by a spelunking club that enjoyed exploring the ancient underground caves on the land. For many years, the cabin was all that stood on the land.

Judy had the idea once that it would be fun for the family to spend the weekend at the cabin. Frank and Judy planned to sleep in the back of their station wagon, and the kids and their friends would have a sleepover inside the cabin. They spent one night with a wheel well poking them in the back and plans moved forward quickly for a new home that would fit the whole family.

Judy had seen a Perry County barn built in 1866 that was for sale but had to be moved from its current site. The original plan was to use the barn wood for construction at the new site, but Judy soon formed another idea. "When we did all the engineering and rigging and they took down each one of those logs, one by one, that barn became a very real, very living thing for me. I knew we had to put it back up, so we moved every single thing, numbered every log, every nail, every rock, and we tried to put it back just as it was."[29]

The barn served as an important touchstone for O'Bannon when his life as governor became busy and complicated. He said, "You know one of the best things about this place? At night, when I turn out the lights and step outside, the darkness and the silence is almost perfect. I like that. You can't find many truly silent, dark places anymore."[30] His rural Harrison County home allowed him to commune in his own way with nature. He became an avid observer of nature, sitting for hours with his binoculars trained on the land around his home.[31]

The cabin project got off the ground in 1987, and the barn work followed in 1995. Frank and Judy were proud to show off their home. The marble countertops in the kitchen had a previous life as tables used to set type for the *Corydon Democrat*. In the kitchen was a tall chair O'Bannon used while presiding over the state senate as lieutenant governor, along with black and white portraits of O'Bannon's parents, Robert and Faith O'Bannon. The furnishings and decorations were eclectic and interesting. Judy says, "I love seeing things that no one else thought had value anymore and bringing it back to life and newness."[32]

O'Bannon told the AP's Mike Smith that a typical day included going for a walk and that he enjoyed watching the bats swoop in at night to take their turn at the pond in front of the house. Reading was a lifetime passion for O'Bannon. "We're just blessed with so many books here. We have Judy's mother's library, and it has a lot of nature and natural history, everything from rocks to insects to butterflies and birds and mammals."[33]

Frank and Judy approached living at the barn in different ways. "Dad put chairs around the cabin, inside and out, just around in different places that he thought would be good for sitting. He'd say, 'This is a good place for birding because there are a lot of bushes, or you can look out over the pond here.' Those two would go down to the cabin, and Dad would sit and read, and Mom would fix something, or dig a pond!" Jon O'Bannon said.[34] Judy kept herself happy by doing, while Frank enjoyed being still.

"…I remember him smiling and looking at me and saying, 'Some days you just have to take time and sit,'" Polly said.[35]

In November 2001, Home and Garden TV, or the HGTV cable television network, broadcast an hour-long special titled *Barns Reborn*. In it, they detailed the work of families all across the country who had transformed barns into new homes. The O'Bannon barn in Harrison County was featured in one of the segments, opening with Frank and Judy seated on the front porch of their barn home.[36]

"When we can get away for a day or so, it is a complete change in the way you approach problems, and it is certainly relaxing and at the same time invigorating," the governor said in the national broadcast.[37]

State Trooper Alex Willis, who joined the governor's security detail in 1999, said, "I think he enjoyed going home a lot. That's where he had the opportunity to relax…When they went to the barn, they had a little more peace and quiet there."[38]

Another security detail member, Trooper Larry Gershanoff, agrees, adding, "There would be a lot of times he'd want to take the long way, down some back roads in Harrison County, and he'd like pointing out a house or some place where he'd been, or where he once worked. He really liked doing that."[39]

Getting completely away from it all was nearly impossible as the O'Bannons never took an entire week off from their duties without at least one or two phone calls, faxes, or e-mails from the statehouse back in Indianapolis. They didn't mind—they knew it went with the territory. O'Bannon said modern technology allowed them to have some privacy while still be "in instant contact with whatever problem or event…might come up."[40]

For Judy, restoration of the barn and cabin was not just about the building; it reflected a commitment to historic preservation—a commitment that led to her appointment to the national board of directors of the National Historic Trust Foundation. "This isn't just about saving buildings; it's saving lifestyles, our histories, our story, the story that our barns tell about how people grew up in an agrarian society," she said. The marks and imperfections of the barn were part of the attraction because "people rubbed against them and they have left their marks when they did their dance with life. I love that!"

The barn home played host to the O'Bannon family every Christmas. In 2000, the O'Bannon-Kernan campaign hosted one of its largest fundraising events at the barn. The event stretched on into the night, with Frank and Jon O'Bannon and Joe Kernan sitting up on the front porch sipping Scotch and talking politics deep into the wee hours of the morning.

Of the barn, the governor said, "It's a great home to have and it really is much more of a home than a house…"[41] The barn represented the meaning of "the good life" to Frank and Judy O'Bannon.

FRANK THE FATHER-IN-LAW AND GRANDPA

Tom Zoeller and Soni O'Bannon had the incredible good fortune to marry into the amazing O'Bannon family—and have loved every part of it. Tom and Soni couldn't have asked for more in a father-in-law.

"He was down to earth, and he never put himself on a plateau above anyone else," Tom Zoeller said. "I would always beat him on the golf course, easiest match I ever had, but I still miss every one of those days now that he's gone."[42] Tom later got the "political bug" himself, serving terms as Floyd County coroner and sheriff.

When Frank was elected lieutenant governor in 1988, he took Tom aside for a moment and warned him about getting involved with businesses that would seek him out due to his father-in-law's position. Frank worried that it could call his honesty into question. "He said, 'Tom, I've always run my campaigns and office to have the utmost respect for honesty, and I want that to continue without a blemish.'"[43]

One of the greatest titles Frank O'Bannon ever gained in his life was the one he didn't have to do much to earn: Grandpa. Throughout his tenure as lieutenant governor and governor, observers often referred to him as "the friendly grandfatherly type," and his political campaigns, not to mention his kind manner and folksy speech, just served to reinforce that image. But for six Indiana kids, they held the exclusive right to truly call him their grandpa.

The oldest O'Bannon grandchild, Beau Zoeller, is the son of Polly and Tom. His red, curly-top hair is familiar to many who have watched the O'Bannons over the years, as he made frequent appearances on TV with his grandfather.

"My earliest memory of my grandfather is probably of hiking with him in the woods at their barn, and going up to a dried-out creek bed and looking at all the different types of rocks in Harrison County," Beau said.[44]

Beau recognizes the unique influence of the governor's office on their lives. "I learned and experienced so many things other kids do not get to. It was amazing meeting so many famous people and all of Indiana's politicians. We visited every different kind of city and town you can imagine, and these are all places I probably never would have visited otherwise."[45]

Beau's younger sisters, Chelsea and Demi, were much younger during the years their grandfather was governor. Chelsea says one of her fondest memories was of her grandfather riding his four-wheeler around with "…his hair flying all over the place."[46]

Demi also recalls riding the four-wheeler with her grandpa, including one time when he ran it into a ditch and couldn't get it out.[47] She describes "staring contests" that she and her grandpa would engage in to pass the time while riding around on the O'Bannon-Kernan campaign bus.

Both girls have great love and respect for their grandfather. Chelsea said, "I consider him a true hero. I will miss him forever and will remember him always as an awesome grandpa!"[48]

Asher O'Bannon Reed, Jennifer's son, had the good fortune to spend everyday time with "Granny and Papa" during the years they lived in the governor's residence after his mother's return to Indiana. Asher's memories are filled with laughing at silly jokes and stories his grandpa liked to tell him.[49]

Asher literally grew into adolescence during the O'Bannon administration but still never lost the wonder of seeing his grandpa on TV or the excitement of the state police helicopter landing on the parking lot at Hinkle Fieldhouse at Butler University—especially when Asher was at recess at the International School (at that time located across the street from Hinkle). He, like his cousins, remembers his grandfather's sense of humor and treasures the time he got to spend with him.[50]

A FIRM FOUNDATION

The family, friends, faith, and community that surrounded Frank O'Bannon from the time he was a young boy until he became a grandfather was reflected in almost every aspect of his life. His intense loyalty to his family and friends was evident in all that he did. His loyalty and commitment to Indiana were never questioned. He received every opportunity that presented itself in the same humble, simple way. It was never Frank O'Bannon's goal to change the world—but he did seek to engage it and live in it as a grateful child of God, and in doing so, he came to know what a wonderful life it truly could be.

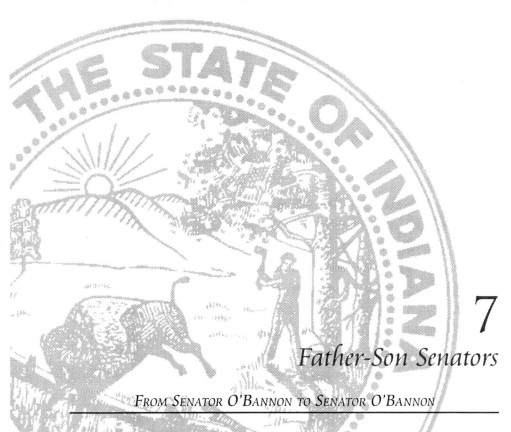

7

Father-Son Senators

When Robert P. O'Bannon decided he was ready to retire in 1970, after serving two decades as an Indiana state senator, the choice to succeed him, at least in the minds of many in his district, was rather obvious. Forty-year-old Frank O'Bannon was the choice for many, but not all. After all, when one person has held the seat for twenty years, others anticipate a day when it may be their chance. Robert O'Bannon knew his son Frank would make a fine senator. Frank had already engaged himself politically over the years, staying active in Harrison County Democratic politics, the Indiana Democratic Editorial Association, and serving as the Harrison County chairman for both the campaigns of U.S. Senator Birch Bayh and U.S. Representative Lee Hamilton.

State Representative Bill Cochran believes O'Bannon felt an obligation to run. "He was dedicated to public service, and he felt like that was his calling."[1]

Judy O'Bannon, like her mother-in-law, Faith, was not that excited about the prospect of her husband entering politics but supported his efforts regardless.

It is clear Frank O'Bannon did not spend a lot of time developing great "master plans" for his life with constructed visions of him at the top of state government or even as a state senator. Instead, O'Bannon approached politics as he had all aspects of his life: When opportunity presented itself, he rolled up his sleeves and got to work.

Frank O'Bannon liked to tell reporters later, while in the midst of raising millions of dollars for statewide gubernatorial campaigns, that his first campaign for state senate cost him only $1,700—all of it out of his own pocket. The 1970 O'Bannon campaign included the basics: yard signs, bumper stickers, even cigarette matchbooks emblazoned with his name—a political "no-no" in later years as tobacco use and smoking became more and more controversial (even in counties in which tobacco was still grown as a cash crop).

A campaign brochure sounded familiar themes that he would return to throughout his political career, citing "his concern for the progress of this area (related to the)…Ohio River bridges, natural resources development, flood control, and water supplies, educational advancements, along with municipal, county, and civic projects." The brochure told voters that Frank O'Bannon would listen to the people of Indiana and that he sought to preserve the natural resources and beauty of Southern Indiana. He proposed improvements for the Wyandotte Caves-State Forest complex in Crawford and Harrison counties and a greater industrial base for Southern Indiana, but noted, "It cannot be developed unless state leadership creates an equitable tax climate which is inviting." Finally, he advocated better highways in the region, declaring, "Adequate transportation facilities will be the backbone of economic progress for tourism and industry."[2]

A display ad bought by the O'Bannon campaign in the family's own newspaper listed what Indiana needed "to move forward again" including tax reform to relieve increasing local property taxes, state support of education "without petty politics," efficient state administration to give services to citizens, and in a nod to the percolating turbulence in American politics in the late 1960s and early 1970s, he called for state leadership against "crime, drugs, civil disorders, and 'radical' law-violators."[3]

In the weeks leading up to the election, O'Bannon and Nelson D. Kennedy, the Democratic candidate for state representative, issued a statement charging Republicans with raising property taxes, enacting a scheme that resulted in a $32 million loss of sales and income tax money to the local government of Indiana.[4] They criticized Republican governor Ed Whitcomb (b. 1917) for not fulfilling his campaign promise to fund 50 percent of public schools' costs from sources other than property taxes and promised to do everything they could to rectify the situation.

The Republican nominee, Gary Becker, ran a vigorous campaign—including the purchase of a display ad in the newspaper owned by his opponent's family, the *Corydon Democrat*. Under the heading "Twenty Years Is Enough," he painted a picture of an inherited O'Bannon legislative dynasty. Becker said that "public office should be earned, not inherited!"[5]

Despite Becker's appeals for a change, O'Bannon won his first race easily, polling an impressive 5,267 votes to Becker's 3,242 in Harrison County alone.[6]

UNBEATEN IN HARRISON COUNTY

Frank O'Bannon never lost an election in Harrison County (with the exception of the 1988 Democratic Primary for governor after he had already withdrawn from the race). In each race, he remained friendly and cordial with his opponents, and they treated him likewise. To do otherwise would not have fit the times, the spirit of the community, or the nature of O'Bannon and the other fine people who also sought public office.

His 1974 opponent, Republican Dale W. Mitsch, a local farmer and mortgage banker from Georgetown, Indiana, sought the senate seat after becoming concerned about the formation of a Conservancy

District in Clark, Crawford, Floyd, and Harrison counties. Mitsch said his education and work as a farmer qualified him for the position, noting that being a successful farmer "is by no means a small accomplishment in this day and age."[7]

The 1974 election occurred in uncertain times—in the shadow of Richard M. Nixon's (1913-1994) resignation as president just weeks before on August 9, 1974. Regardless, O'Bannon wanted a second term as state senator, a job that paid only $6,000 a year.

"I have had an interest in government, both local and state, for many years prior to even running for office. I feel there is an obligation for people to be involved in the governmental process," O'Bannon said in a candidate profile published just prior to the 1974 vote. "My education has been in government and law. I enjoy serving and making what small contribution I can as far as making the democratic system work."[8]

O'Bannon's second term priorities were increased state funding for schools to reduce the burden on local property tax payers, repeal of the county local option tax on individuals, state funding of city police and firefighter pensions, "accelerated completion" of I-64 and I-265, expanded development of both IU-Southeast at New Albany and the Ivy Tech campus at Jeffersonville, and early construction of the Clark Maritime Center near Jeffersonville.[9]

Just prior to the 1974 election, O'Bannon won the endorsement of the Mental Health Association of Indiana because of his commitment to funding community mental health centers. The mental health advocates believed enhanced community mental health centers would reduce admissions to state hospitals and "make it possible for some patients to continue to work or live at home while receiving treatment."[10]

O'Bannon went on to win his first reelection challenge with little trouble, besting Mitsch throughout the senate district by a vote of 24,395 to 12,950—including an impressive win in Harrison County, 6,201 to 2,836. He won his subsequent races easily as well, with O'Bannon defeating Republican Daniel G. Crecelius in 1978, and having no opponent file against him in 1982 or 1986, his last two races for reelection to the senate.

After the 1974 race was over, O'Bannon invited Mitsch and his wife, Zelpha, to ride with him to Indianapolis so they could observe senate proceedings. "In those days, politicians had a more kindly disposition towards their opposition than today," she said.[11]

STATE SENATOR FRANK L. O'BANNON

As a senator, Frank O'Bannon did not make frequent trips to the microphone on the senate floor, both because he did not enjoy public speaking and because he was a person who learned more by listening than talking. Over time, he developed a style that would serve him well. He asked more questions than he gave answers, a rare quality in a politician and one that allowed him to possess an incredible blend of experience, knowledge, and awareness about state government.

In seeking a second term, O'Bannon touted his success in adding openness and integrity to the legislative process. "I have worked for and supported changes which make the state legislature open and accountable to the public, such as making all committee meetings open to the public, all committee votes publicly recorded, ethics guidelines and financial disclosure established for legislators and state officials," he said.[12]

Gordon Englehart, who covered the statehouse for twenty-five years for the *Louisville Courier-Journal*, said, "His father was a much revered Southern Indiana gentleman, and Frank was from the same mold. He was well liked by everybody. He was low key, never pushed for publicity. His arguments on the floor of the senate, even in intense issues, were never ranting, raving, or theatrical. He was always the same: genuine."[13]

In a 1988 draft speech, O'Bannon wrote down why he enjoyed being a legislator: "I think I have benefited so much from my years as a state senator because when you're in the legislature, you never lose sight of the community that elected you to serve. You continue to live there, and you continue to represent the values of reaching out to others for ideas, of building consensus, of working for common goals. You never fall into the trap of believing that you can shut out your natural allies along the way. In short, you live the life of a Democrat."

Frank O'Bannon was part of an interesting group of freshmen senators arriving for the start of the ninety-seventh General Assembly on January 12, 1971. Among the new senators that year were Democrats Adam Benjamin, Jr., of Gary; Joseph G. Bruggenschmidt of Jasper; Philip H. Hayes of Evansville; Don M. Park of Muncie; P. Merton Stanley of Kokomo; Tom J. Teague of Anderson; and W. Wayne Townsend of Hartford City. New Republican standouts that year included Robert D. Garton of Columbus and Walter P. Helmke of Fort Wayne. Teague was recruited to run in the Democratic primary in May 1970 while finishing his tour of duty in Vietnam. Another senator who would be a major influence on Indiana politics in this era, John M. Mutz of Indianapolis, joined the senate in June of 1971 to complete the term of a senator who resigned.

Park recalls, "There was a big swing that year...in the composition of the Senate, especially for the Democrats since we were still in the minority, but we gained several members." The make-up in O'Bannon's first session was twenty-nine Republicans and twenty-one Democrats (up from just fifteen in the previous session).[14]

Park came to know and admire O'Bannon. "Frank's personality, his whole demeanor, his integrity was just beyond reproach."[15]

Townsend, a Blackford County Democrat who served three previous terms in the Indiana House before being elected to the senate, had the advantage of having known Bob and Faith O'Bannon before he knew Frank O'Bannon. "Frank and his father were peas in a pod. Bob O'Bannon was a very soft-spoken, studious person who did his homework well, who measured his words carefully. He never spoke ill of anyone," Townsend said. "They were the genteel kind of person you would love to have in your neighborhood, always looking for the best in people. I never heard Frank O'Bannon say an unkind word about anyone..."[16]

Garton, a Columbus Republican said that Frank was a "solid" and "trustworthy" man but he was not a particularly spectacular orator. "He could still be very effective at the microphone, but he did not speak that often."[17]

Upon arrival for the 1971 session, Frank O'Bannon quickly aligned himself with Senator Robert J. Fair of Princeton, Indiana. A lawyer and former FBI agent, Fair was eleven years Frank O'Bannon's senior and had one term under his belt by the time he arrived. Frank admired his demeanor and gentlemanly approach to the process. Fair served many years as the minority leader among senate Democrats, and one session as senate president pro tem in a short-lived Democrat majority.

O'Bannon also gravitated toward a more gregarious Southern Indiana politician, Senator Jimmy Plaskett of New Washington, Indiana. Plaskett, a World War II veteran and former Clark County sheriff and surveyor, joined the senate in 1963. An outspoken and opinionated man, Plaskett could be loud and was known to carry a gun, even while on the senate floor or in committee meetings. Because of his experience, and perhaps because of his age (Plaskett was of Robert O'Bannon's era), Frank O'Bannon was drawn to him and tried to learn from him.

THE O'BANNON STYLE AND PHILOSOPHY

Doug Davidoff, an *Indianapolis News* political writer, wrote a profile of O'Bannon in late 1987 for his expected 1988 run for governor. In it, he captured O'Bannon's reputation as a state senator: "O'Bannon's leadership style, which concentrates on consensus building within the 20-member Senate Democratic caucus is something of a campaign problem many people mention, including O'Bannon himself. O'Bannon works in the background to keep his caucus together. The security of the caucus allows other Democratic senators to get out in front on key issues like utility reform, license branch reform, and education. O'Bannon admits he is less than forceful and more of a consensus builder."[18]

During his first terms in the senate, O'Bannon rarely, if ever, broke with his caucus and worked hard "earning his stripes" as a senator and in earning the trust and friendship of his fellow senators. In his first session, he successfully pushed Senate Bill 263, which formed the beginning of what would become the Indiana Department of Environmental Management, out of committee. After many weeks of discussion and dueling amendments, O'Bannon used some "down-home Hoosier" wisdom to convince members of the senate's Committee of Environment and Ecology to move the bill to the senate floor for a vote. "This bill takes a big step—maybe too big—but we're down to the last day to do something. I believe in any type of change, a person has to learn to crawl before he walks," Senator O'Bannon said. "I think we need to move it today and make changes that have been talked about for weeks and weeks with no one really getting together on one change. In order to get it out for discussion and perhaps change for the better, I move that the bill pass with the minor amendments to it."[19]

O'Bannon's senate work reflected the varied nature of his interests. "He was interested in a lot of things, education, property taxes, natural resources, but the reality is that due to his position in leadership, and because he was from a rural, Southern Indiana district, a senator from there was not really going to get out in front on issues...He didn't introduce too many bills, but the ones he did introduce were pretty substantive. He played a big role on a lot of the law subcommittees and code revision type of things where a lot of lawyer-type, detail stuff occurred," said fellow senator Mike Gery of Tippecanoe County.[20]

Gery said O'Bannon, despite his low-key style, "commanded respect. You knew that when he spoke to you, or when you asked him a question, he was going to give you an honest answer. What more can you ask for than someone to tell you what they really believe, and help you?"[21]

Fellow Democrat Park agrees. Park roomed with O'Bannon at the Indianapolis Athletic Club and said, "Frank became friends with everybody. Phil Gutman, Larry Borst, or Leslie Duvall, he could get along with all of them. They just liked Frank. He was always open with them, never lied to anyone...That built up his credibility and that carried over to the house, too."[22]

O'Bannon's ability to get along with all kinds of people made him a natural choice for caucus leadership, a position he would earn under Fair.

Although O'Bannon was not a prolific author of bills, he wrote Senate Bill 9 with Republican State Senator Duvall of Indianapolis, during the noteworthy 1973 session. A rewrite of the state's death penalty statute, the bill became necessary after the U.S. Supreme Court declared in June 1972 that existing state statutes covering executions were unconstitutional.

"Frank is credited with renewing capital punishment because it came out in the recodification process for the Criminal Code," said Bob Kovach, a Democrat senator from Mishawaka.[23]

The bombastic Kovach, in almost every way the polar opposite of O'Bannon in terms of personality and style, joined the senate after pulling off a coup in the Democratic primary in 1976. A city councilman at the time he was elected senator, Kovach later was elected mayor of Mishawaka by denying State Senator Phil Gutman's mother-in-law, the powerful Margaret H. Prickett, a fifth term as mayor of that city. Kovach would go on to be one of O'Bannon's closest and certainly most colorful advisers, serving as legislative director during his gubernatorial terms.

Gutman, a Republican from Fort Wayne, lauds the cooperative work of senators in the 1970s. "Things were never all just black or all just white," Gutman said. "It was a matter of where you could get twenty-six votes. I think Frank understood that. If you get caught up in your ideology, you just become a roadblock at times to progress. The democratic process, after all, in my view, is a roadway of small steps, incremental progress toward the goals we all share. I think a good legislator understands that you take what you can get, and recognizes that you sometimes have to take what you can get and try again for more of what you want later."[24]

O'Bannon adhered to the political philosophy that government exists to help create freedom. David Dawson, then a statehouse political correspondent for Gannett News Service wrote in a May 1988 column that O'Bannon believed that government served a role in protecting communities and individuals from dominating political and economic forces that can inhibit their freedoms, while not unduly restraining those forces. "That view puts all public policy decisions onto a scale: Will the good achieved by government action outweigh the potential bad it can cause?" O'Bannon used this "scale" to explain why he originally had voted against allowing a constitutional question to be placed on the ballot regarding the formation of a state lottery. However, in a subsequent session, he voted for it. He told Dawson he became convinced that Hoosiers wanted a lottery, despite his own personal reservations about it. "Government runs on the consent of the governed," O'Bannon said.[25]

Asked about his political philosophies during a nationally broadcast interview on C-SPAN in September 1985 for a special *States of the Nation* program, he expressed concern that politics was moving into an era where it was impossible to talk about real solutions for state revenue issues, including the need to raise taxes or cut spending. He worried that legislators were "playing word games." The revenue issue created inertia in spite of a deepening financial deficit. "When we say 'raise taxes,' everyone clams up and politicians won't touch it. I'm not saying that raising taxes alone will solve the problem; it will take a combination of factors. But when you're down in the hole...we then do something about it. It's political suicide unless we all agree to try and do a program where we cooperate and do things in partnership rather than being at each other's political throat. We govern by crisis anyway, and the crisis is here, but the crisis may not be large enough for anyone to want to do anything."[26]

O'Bannon remarked on the difficulty of progressive movement in government, "When you want to put in a new program, you have to sell it from the perspective of a real need, not a real want...That real need has to be big enough so that it can overcome the negative side which is raising revenue, and you have to keep that balance."[27]

As a senator, O'Bannon rarely got angry at fellow legislators; instead, he tried to understand them and their goals. However, one thing consistently roused his ire: when he felt someone had been dishonest with him, such as slipping provisions into a bill or a conference committee report without fully informing all participants. When a reporter asked him about the rare moments he had become angered, O'Bannon said sternly, "They just don't do it again, that's all."[28]

Jackie McElfresh, a senate secretary for O'Bannon, said she caught a glimpse of some of this anger when a young senate intern decided to forgo participating in the Pledge of Allegiance, which opened each senate session. "Frank was angry. He took him in the office. When the intern came out, he stood there and said that was the first time he'd ever been scolded without being yelled at. Frank told him he could leave during the pledge, but if he stayed, he was going to participate and not stand there like a bump on a log."[29]

Garton recalls only one or two dust-ups with Frank O'Bannon. One was over a seemingly simple proposal to change where legislative assistants were going to sit. "When I told him what our plans were for where they would sit, he said, 'I am not going to do that, and if you do that, I'm going to hold a news conference and complain about it publicly,'" Garton said.[30] The move would have caused O'Bannon to break his word to a Democratic senate staff member—it was something he hated to do.

8

State Senator Frank O'Bannon

A DEMOCRATIC MAJORITY

At the start of the centennial session of the Indiana General Assembly in January 1977, Democrats found themselves in the majority for the first time in more than a decade. With an upstart group of senators elected in the first post-Watergate Senate election, Democrats won the majority with a group of nine new members: Julia M. Carson of Indianapolis; Katie B. Hall of Gary; Douglas A. Hunt of South Bend; Mathias "Matt" A. Kerger of Hammond; Louis J. Mahern, Jr., of Indianapolis; Dennis P. Neary of LaPorte; Robert E. Peterson of Rochester; James W. Spurgeon of Brownstown (returning to the senate after having served from 1957-63); and Thomas J. Wheeler of Shelbyville. (Democratic senator Robert J. Bischoff of Lawrenceburg joined the legislature later in 1977 following the death of Senator Wilfrid J. Ullrich of Aurora.)

The "Watergate babies," as they became known, melded well with a dynamic group of existing senate Democrats. They helped elect Senator Fair as the senate president pro tem in a close race against Senator Townsend.

One of the deals made to secure Fair's win was the promise that O'Bannon would chair the Senate Finance Committee, bypassing Townsend who had experience on the house Ways & Means Committee during his previous three terms in the lower chamber. "I'm guessing Frank wanted to be majority leader, but Bob wanted someone he could really trust to lead the Finance Committee, and Frank and Bob had a very close relationship," Gery said.[1]

Townsend agrees, "Bob had more comfort with Frank in that position than he did with me." Townsend retained a seat on the Finance Committee and made state finance a focus of his legislative tenure.[2]

As chair, O'Bannon appointed Townsend head of the taxation subcommittee and Senator Stanley as chair of the budget subcommittee. Senators Gery, Hunt, Mahern, and Richard were also named to the powerful committee.

O'Bannon admired Fair and believed he was a great legislator. His style greatly influenced O'Bannon as a legislator and later as governor.

Gery said, "Bob Fair…knew that the key to life in politics is balance, and he had a tremendous understanding of the political process. He could give a good speech, though he didn't do it very often. He had a lawyer's mentality to be reasonable, to be rational; he got along with everybody. He was just the consummate politician, totally honest; he would be straight with you. He didn't open his mouth and give a lot of extra information to people if they didn't ask the right questions. I think he was as good as anybody I have ever met in the process."[3]

Freshman Senator Graham Richard's seat on the Finance Committee led later to a seat on the even more powerful joint House-Senate Budget Committee in which he came to know Frank O'Bannon well. "The most memorable experiences for me were really the kind of informal, one-on-one times when he did what I would call 'mentoring without a message.' Frank was not the kind to lecture you or come up to you and put his arm around you and say, 'Now, son, this is what you need to do.' He waited for you to ask him something, and then he gave you advice and he would tell stories. It was never condescending."[4]

Another new senator, Julia Carson of Indianapolis, lucked out, leaving a majority in the house and joining the senate for its first majority in more than a decade. She worked with O'Bannon and others in the "new majority" to advance issues that had waited on the back burner amidst Republican stonewalling for years. One of the most important of those issues for Carson and O'Bannon was the first ever state funding for home healthcare that involved training relatives to care for patients so they would not have to go to nursing homes, thus saving money.

O'Bannon also helped Carson, she said, on bills improving standards for domestic workers, an issue near to her heart as the daughter of a single mother who worked for years as a maid. Carson sought O'Bannon's help also in changing state law on racial definitions for citizens who were of mixed race. "He…showed me how to get one-stop service on legislative issues, how to get some of those things through," she said.[5]

It was a heady, if not short-lived, time for the senate Democrats. Their majority would only last until the next election when Republicans regained control for the 1978-79 session. Graham Richard, who, at age twenty-eight, was the youngest senator ever elected in the first one hundred years of the legislature, describes himself and his colleagues as "firebrands," propelled by anti-Nixon Watergate sentiment and social concerns like education and urban problems. "We'd come through the whole civil rights and Vietnam issues of the 1960s and many of us got involved in that."[6]

The new Democratic majority in the senate (with a Republican majority in the house) produced some of the biggest fights ever between the legislative and executive branches, with the legislature passing the Equal Rights Amendment and sunshine, or "open door," laws that opened legislative hearings and other government meetings to public view. Before these changes, legislators would take testimony in public then kick the public out of the room for the discussion and the vote on pending bills.

The Democratic majority in the 1977-78 session also flexed its political muscle a few times. Robert D. Orr, as lieutenant governor, presided over the senate during most of this era. Orr jokingly groused many years later that O'Bannon and Fair caused occasional flare-ups on the senate floor that led Democrats to appeal Orr's ruling to the full body of the senate. When they did so, Orr had to step down from his position as president of the senate in the rostrum and turn the proceedings briefly over to President Pro Tem Fair.[7]

But even amidst an environment that tempted some Democrats to get too partisan, "Frank provided leadership across party lines. From him, I learned that it was better to build trust and relationships and work across the aisle...Frank gave me a lot of good advice on how to shepherd tough legislation through," Richard said. Richard was later elected to two terms as mayor of Fort Wayne beginning in 1999 at the encouragement of then-Governor O'Bannon.[8]

O'BANNON BECOMES MINORITY LEADER

At the start of the 1979 session, senate Democrats were back in the minority and had a new leader. Fair, who had lost the 1976 Democratic primary for governor to Secretary of State Larry Conrad, declined to seek another term and planned to finish out his term in 1978, moving on to become director of the Indiana Bar Association.

Townsend ran against O'Bannon for minority leader when Fair departed. "It was a very, very close vote. We thought we had it done at one point," Townsend said.

The challenge did not create ill feelings that lasted long, though. "I didn't feel any tension," Townsend said. "Frank and I were a bit different in our style and approach to things. Frank's more studied approach was probably more to his advantage in that situation. I was probably a lot more confrontational than Frank was in those days. We got along."[9]

O'Bannon's approach was similar to that of his father and his predecessor. "Frank was a consolidator," Townsend said. "Some of the members were a little impatient at times, and instead of Frank letting them duke it out, he'd look for ways for them to work it out, to compromise."[10]

Longtime *Indianapolis News* political columnist Edward Ziegner wrote a profile of the Democrats' new senate leader, O'Bannon, and returning house Democratic leader Mike Phillips of Boonville, describing them as "the sort of people Democrats don't have to apologize for." He added, "Theirs is a tough job…and it is the task of O'Bannon and Phillips to make a record for their party in the next election, to try and get the GOP majority to make some changes in key legislation…The new Democratic minority leaders do their work well, and in this period of the legislature, provide by far the most effective voice the party has had."[11]

Ziegner also addressed the inevitable comparison between Frank O'Bannon and his father. He said the elder O'Bannon served with "so much skill, honesty, and ability that lots of people doubted son Frank could measure up to father Robert. But he has."[12]

O'Bannon said he was just doing what the loyal opposition should do: calling the Republican legislative majority, and the Republican governor, to task on their agenda. "The point we've been trying to make is, 'Hey, you're not being honest on the whole program. You can't do both.' I think the surplus should be used for roads, for schools, for an adequate budget…but there's no need to raise taxes, and hopefully, we've made that point…"[13]

O'Bannon, described as "a middle-of-the-road Democrat" was concerned about the "ultra-conservative" and "regressive" Republicans currently in charge. "My biggest disappointment has been that some of the bills have been regressive, a step backward, some symbolic, but some very substantial, like repeal of the direct primary, like repeal of the bipartisan career personnel program, working on the recessions, on the ERA, and on taking away pre-election reporting on campaign (fundraising)," O'Bannon told Ziegner.[14]

"It takes a minority as well as majority to make a quorum to do business," O'Bannon told the *Louisville Courier-Journal*'s Englehart. As he "puffed away on one of his ever-present pipes," O'Bannon added, "We had the traditional responsibility of being the loyal opposition. We will speak for people concerned about Democratic Party principles—but most importantly, we will concentrate on decisions we think are best for the whole state."[15]

Louis Mahern, an Indianapolis Democrat from a safe, working-class eastside district, could afford to be more liberal and outspoken than O'Bannon. Mahern was elected caucus chair when O'Bannon became minority leader and sat next to him on the senate floor for the next eight years. He learned a lot from the quiet man from Corydon.

"Some of the senators would just twist themselves into a pretzel to try and please all these various constituencies with every vote. Frank, on the other hand, just kind of went along and was much more interested in the process, and how the process worked, and what was the right thing to do. Frank was never this ambitious rascal of a guy who was trying to get ahead to the very next office."[16]

Mahern especially enjoys recalling the day when O'Bannon showed up for work on a Monday morning in the senate wearing a new brown, houndstooth sport coat. "He asked me, 'Hey, Louie, what do you think of my new jacket?' And I said, 'I think it looks real nice, Frank; that's a nice jacket,'" Mahern recalls. With expert comedic timing, O'Bannon whispered to Mahern, "'Two dollars. It cost me two dollars! Judy found it at a junk store on the east side!' He just thought that was so funny that here he was on the floor of the state senate with all these guys wearing expensive suits, and he's wearing a $2 sport coat, and no one knows it!" Mahern said.[17]

O'Bannon counted on fellow senators Mahern, Gery, Kovach, Neary, and Jim Lewis (of Charlestown) to help him keep the senate Democrats together against a strong Republican majority.

While O'Bannon and Mahern led the Democratic caucus, Townsend began focusing on his planned 1980 run for governor, in which he lost the heavily contested Democratic primary to businessman John Hillenbrand of Batesville. Townsend was more successful in his second bid, becoming the 1984 Democratic nominee (almost denying Governor Orr a second term).

John Whikehart, who served as staff director for the senate Democratic Caucus from 1988 to 1991, recalled O'Bannon enjoyed widespread respect and admiration among his fellow senators. "He had the personal qualities that made it virtually impossible for his caucus to go against him—they did not want to disappoint him once a direction was set."[18]

Tom New, the son of two-time state treasurer and one-time gubernatorial hopeful Jack L. New of Greenfield, was no political novice when Frank O'Bannon hired him as a staff analyst in 1984. He recalls, "It was in the senate that Frank O'Bannon felt most at home during his many years of state service. Frank loved the senate; he loved the camaraderie, the give and take, the compromise, and most of all, the consensus building. For Frank O'Bannon, the democratic process was as important as the policy outcome itself."[19]

John Hammond, III, an executive assistant to Republican Governor Orr, recalls an unusual move O'Bannon allowed during the 1988 session (which was to be O'Bannon's last term as a senator). He permitted Hammond to address members of the Democratic senate caucus on a highway construction issue, although O'Bannon did not support the Orr administration's position. "That kind of cooperation is not always present among house Democratic leaders."[20]

REDISTRICTING ISSUES

Redistricting always played a key role in the efforts of both parties to maintain or gain control of either body of the legislature, and O'Bannon was focused on it throughout his legislative service. In 1980, he hired a young George Fleetwood to join the senate staff in a more political role than would probably ever be allowed today.

"The Democrats had put together a pool of money to hire somebody to run campaigns for the legislature, and this was the first time anyone had ever done this," Fleetwood said. "Their interest was the 1981 reapportionment that would follow the 1980 census. They wanted to make sure there was a majority in one house or the other, and Representative Mike Phillips and Senator O'Bannon, the two respective leaders for the Democrats, were the ones who were doing the hiring. I ended up coming in to interview with both of these guys."[21]

Fleetwood stayed on the senate staff for eight years—well into the dry patch of the 1980s for Democrats as the Reagan Revolution swept

Indiana Republicans to big majorities in the senate and the house for much of the decade—as well as a stranglehold on the governor's office from 1968 to 1988.

Redistricting battles created a rare flash of anger from O'Bannon. O'Bannon led a mini-walkout of the Democratic members during discussions about redistricting in 1981, angering Garton. "I went up to John Mutz, who was presiding at the time as lieutenant governor, and told him that he could order them back into the chamber and force them back here," Garton said. "John Mutz said to me, 'Do you really want a state trooper to go up there and carry Frank back in here?' I thought about it some more and realized that John was right, and we worked it out."[22] O'Bannon expressed concern about the emerging role of computer technology in creating legislative districts that may not take into consideration the need to keep communities of shared interest together.

According to Fleetwood, O'Bannon would "get involved in the issues that his constituents cared about, a lot of issues related to natural resources and the environment, but he did not carry a lot of legislation by himself; he did not put his name on a lot of bills…His primary focus was keeping busy being the Democratic leader in the senate."[23]

An Era of Dramatic Change: The ERA

Historian Justin E. Walsh writes, "The (legislative) sessions that convened between 1971 and 1978 were the first ones to consolidate the dramatic changes of the 1960s."[24] Those changes included court-ordered reapportionments of legislative districts that substantially reduced the representation of rural Indiana counties, and the eventual elimination of troublesome multi-member districts in more urban areas that essentially locked out equal representation for some minority communities. One of the most obvious changes was the move to annual sessions of the General Assembly beginning with O'Bannon's second session in 1972.

The growing concern for the rights of women related to employment became a major issue almost immediately. This became increasingly more important as women not only needed to enter the workforce to raise the financial stability of families amidst recessions and growing inflation rates, but also because of the rising divorce rate that saw, for the first time in American and Hoosier culture, the increase in the number of single-parent homes headed by women.

Senator Garton took an early lead on the issue and sponsored a bill during his first session in 1971 banning discrimination in employment against women. Garton's legislation sought to amend the state's 1961 civil rights act and passed easily in both chambers (despite opposition from the only female member of the senate, Senator M. Joan Gubbins, a staunchly conservative Indianapolis Republican). Enacting the law did nothing to relieve the legislature of the struggle, however, to pass the Equal Rights Amendment to the U.S. Constitution that came up in sessions repeatedly between 1973 and 1979.

When Democrats won the senate majority in the 1976 elections, Senator Teague of Anderson sponsored legislation to make Indiana the thirty-fifth state to ratify the ERA. Authored by U.S. Senator Birch Bayh of Indiana, enactment of the federal ERA ensured a lively debate in the Indiana Senate after members of the house approved the measure. The language of the ERA was simple enough.

Section 1. Equality of rights under the law shall not be denied or abridged by the United States or by any state on account of sex.

Section 2. The Congress shall have the power to enforce, by appropriate legislation, the provisions of this article.

Section 3. This amendment shall take effect two years after the date of ratification.

Simply worded or not, emotions ran high on both sides of the debate—and national news media attention on the senate debate in Indiana only fueled the fires. The senate took up its final debate on the issue on Tuesday, January 18, 1977 "as six Indiana State Police troopers were stationed in the senate chambers all day to control the milling citizens who thronged to the statehouse to witness the historic vote."[25]

Senator Gubbins led the debate against passage, warning senators that the ERA would open the door for "homosexual marriage, increased sexual deviancy, female soldiers, and motherless children."[26]

Senator Marlin K. McDaniel, a Richmond Republican, argued against the ERA because it further eroded state power and granted more power to the federal government. "The so-called Equal Rights Amendment will result in no specific benefits for women and will, in fact, create a number of difficult problems because of its emphasis on 'unisex,' where sexes are merged into one."[27]

Senator Duvall, an Indianapolis Republican, argued the ERA caused the state to "abdicate responsibility in the delicate relationships between men and women."

Senator Charles E. Bosma of Indianapolis (father of Brian Bosma) carried his Bible to the senate podium and quoted it in support of male superiority, "drawing hisses from ERA supporters in the (Senate) gallery."[28]

Senator Bosma said, "The woman was created for the man...the husband was to be the ruler of the wife" and that the ERA was "not in accord with rules the Creator laid down for the universe...It is an attack on the family unit."[29]

Supporters of the ERA limited their comments to just three speakers, led by Senator Teague. Teague urged senators to act to "eliminate historic patterns of discrimination in this country."[30]

The final vote was razor-thin, 26-24, with O'Bannon voting with the majority. Twenty-three Democrats and three Republicans made up the majority, with five Democrats joining nineteen Republican senators in opposing the measure.

The vote "prompted shouts of joy from ERA supporters and cast a stony silence over the opposition group which had festooned themselves with red 'STOP ERA' signs," the *Indianapolis Star* reported.[31] Senators had received encouragement for their votes from big names like First Lady Rosalyn Carter (b. 1927)[32] and beloved and respected Notre Dame president Father Theodore Hesburgh (b. 1917).[33]

The vote left Senator Teague "quietly sobbing" at his senate desk, the *Star* reported, as Teague declared it "Indiana's finest hour."[34]

The conflict was not over, however, as the subsequent General Assembly, controlled by Republicans in both chambers in the next session, rescinded its previous approval of the ERA. The U.S. Supreme Court never ruled in the matter of whether a state can actually rescind its previous approval of a constitutional amendment. It didn't matter anyway—the ERA eventually failed to get the approval in three-fourths of the states required for its passage.

ABORTION RIGHTS DEBATES

Abortion rights issues often surfaced in the ERA discussions as well. Indiana had banned abortions in most instances since 1905 (despite a 1967 passage of a bill in both chambers to legalize abortion, later vetoed by Democratic Governor Roger Branigin). Abortion rights specifically came roaring to the front again, however, after the U.S. Supreme Court offered its January 1973 ruling in *Roe v. Wade,* overturning laws banning abortions in Texas and Georgia. The ruling said state laws prohibiting abortion violated a woman's right to privacy guaranteed by the U.S. Constitution and ruled that an unborn fetus was not protected under the Fifth and Fourteenth amendments to the Constitution. The ruling, which restricted a state from outlawing abortions during the first three months of a pregnancy, also wiped out Indiana's existing law.

The high court limited states to restrictions only on where abortions could be performed during the second trimester and prohibited states from outlawing abortions during the second trimester in instances where the pregnancy endangered the life or health of the woman. Following the federal ruling, a three-judge federal panel also outlawed Indiana's abortion law, written in 1905, declaring it unconstitutional as well. Indiana's law had forbidden anyone from administering drugs or procedures to produce a miscarriage (or abortion) unless it was an attempt to preserve the life of a woman.

Legislators acted quickly to restore the legal framework in which a pregnancy could or could not be terminated as the state stood for the first time in almost a century without any restrictions on abortion. During the closing months of the 1973 session, the General Assembly produced a compromise bill between varying house and senate versions that replaced as many of the restrictions allowed following the court's action, especially with respect to the trimester distinctions in the high court's ruling.

Senate Bill 334, passed in the 1973 session, required that abortions be performed in a licensed hospital, out-patient clinic, or other medical facility during the first trimester, and only in a hospital during the second trimester; and permitted abortions only to save the life of a mother during the third trimester. The bill also required parental permission for abortions for unmarried women under the age of eighteen. SB 334 and Senate Joint Resolution 8, which urged Congress to call a constitutional convention to amend the constitution and specify life begins at the moment of conception, became law without the signature of Republican Governor Otis Bowen, the state's first medical doctor to be elected governor.[35]

Few legislators spoke in favor of abortion rights during the 1973 session, including Frank O'Bannon. His Southern Indiana district remained conservative territory, and he reflected their views as a senator and later as a gubernatorial candidate. O'Bannon's public position on abortion was best described as pro-choice, but not pro-abortion. He opposed late-term abortions and any public funding of abortion services. He also supported restrictions on allowing abortions without informing the parents of a young woman under the age of eighteen and supported limited waiting periods.

By the time O'Bannon became governor in 1997, Indiana's existing abortion law was little in question, and he repeated often that he did not favor changing the existing law and at the same time, did not favor further expanding restrictions. Abortion rights debates, however, raged on during nearly every legislative session since, including the 1997 session when legislators passed two bills: House Enrolled Act 1185 known as the "partial birth" abortion bill, and House Enrolled Act 1160 known as a "feticide" bill. O'Bannon signed the "partial birth" abortion ban although noting he had reservations; he believed that the bill simply affirmed what already existed in Indiana law. O'Bannon vetoed the "feticide" bill because he believed it would make it possible to prosecute a doctor for murder for performing abortions that were "indisputably necessary to preserve the mother's health."[36]

EQUITY IN FUNDING INDIANA'S SCHOOLS

Senate Democrats in the 1970s era also emphasized the need for more parity under the state's complicated school funding formula. As Marilyn Schultz, a former Democratic house member from Bloomington, described it, "Democrats had been quite concerned about providing equal funding and equal access to educational opportunities for all students. We wanted to make sure that we were on the road to better funding for our urban school districts, and that we were closing the gap between rich and poor."[37]

One of the important early steps was providing any sort of funding, for the very first time, for school corporations that wanted to offer a kindergarten program. Kindergarten and early childhood learning would remain a priority for O'Bannon and many other Democrats.

Democrats worked to ensure funding levels remained steady for urban school districts, despite their often declining property tax base. That was particularly important to school districts in Indianapolis, Fort Wayne, Gary, South Bend, Evansville, and other urban areas where challenges to helping students be "classroom ready" were greater than in other areas, all the while the assessed value of local property continued to decline amidst "white flight" and heavy suburban growth witnessed between the 1970s and 1990s.

PROPERTY TAX BATTLES

As Walsh writes, "(Governor) Otis Bowen's insistence on property tax relief dominated each long session from 1971 through 1977, engendering the most continuous and acrimonious conflict between the executive and legislative branches during the decade."[38]

Bowen's proposals were built around the idea of raising sales and other taxes in order to freeze property taxes paid by homeowners and businesses. Bowen said he pushed the proposals because of his growing concern about property tax rates that were rising faster than inflation and creating a disincentive to owning a home. "My position was that property taxes should be reduced, but the amount of reduction had to be made up from a broader base of taxes, such as sales tax or the income tax. I felt this was an urgent issue and one that I was elected on."

Senate Democrats were united in their opposition to Bowen's plans, voting as a block against each of them and when joined by five Republicans, created four consecutive tie votes on Bowen's plan in March 1973. Bowen's lieutenant governor, Robert Orr, made history that day as he cast four consecutive tie-breaking votes in favor of the plans. Orr's tie-breaking votes were the first cast by a presiding lieutenant governor in the senate that decided the final outcome of a bill since 1851.[39]

Bowen's proposal was not at the finish line yet, however. On April 6, 1973, senators voted 22-28 to reject the conference committee report that had already been approved by house members and was being used to reconcile the differences between the house and senate versions. Again, Bowen's plan was in doubt.

Eleventh-hour support by two Democratic senators, however, ultimately saved the proposals and changed the future make-up of the Democratic caucus in the senate. One of O'Bannon's mentors, Jimmy Plaskett, and another member of the Democratic caucus, Senator Robert E. Mahowald of South Bend, "defied party leadership"[40] and joined twenty-three Republican senators in supporting the sales tax proposal on subsequent votes, and with a fifth tie-breaking vote from Orr, the legislation passed.

Mahowald and Plaskett were punished by Democrats for their votes when they sought reelection in 1974. Party officials recruited Kovach, who enjoyed heavy support from labor unions and other traditional Democratic supporters, to challenge and defeat Mahowald in the Democratic primary in Elkhart and St. Joseph counties. Plaskett likewise lost his Democratic primary in Clark, Jefferson, Scott, and Washington counties, to eventual senator James A. Lewis, Jr.

OFF THE SENATE FLOOR

Outside of the statehouse, Frank O'Bannon and the close-knit group of Democratic senators typically held forth at the Indianapolis Athletic Club at the corner of Vermont and Meridian streets, a few blocks northeast of the statehouse. In the 1970s, downtown Indianapolis had yet to begin its reemergence as a destination location with restaurants, shopping malls, and hotels, and so legislators spent their free time at the Claypool Hotel, the Columbia Club, or the Athletic Club, depending upon their party affiliation.

The Athletic Club was chosen as "home base" on purpose, and not just because of the club's long ties to the Democratic Party. The Claypool Hotel was much closer to the statehouse but had more of a "party" reputation with lobbyists on every floor. The Columbia Club on Monument Circle was the sole domain of Republican legislators.

For Frank O'Bannon, the "off times" in the senate were perhaps as enjoyable as the "on times." The Athletic Club had its own swimming pool and indoor basketball courts, put to heavy use by the Democratic senators who enjoyed playing ball.

"Frank was a pretty social animal. He loved to spend time with people talking," recalls Senator Gery. "I can tell you that he would miss meals and just as soon have a Scotch or a beer."[41]

O'Bannon also enjoyed smoking his pipe as often as he could. His pipe and his eyeglasses would be gone by the time he ran for statewide office, but in the early years, he was easily identifiable by both.

O'Bannon always rented Suite 802 and shared it with other members of the legislature over the years—including Donald Park, Tom Teague, Bill Cochran, and Bob Kovach.

After a long session day, "802," as it was referred to, was often the place to be—and a few friendly Republicans sometimes made their way up to the eighth floor as well. Poker and euchre games went on all night long, along with a ready supply of beer and other libations. A Harrison County farmer gave Frank and Judy a giant, one-hundred-pound bag of popcorn at the start of one session. Frank and Judy brought in an air corn popper—at the time a new contraption—and popped popcorn throughout the session.

"Up there in the Athletic Club, Jimmy Plaskett lived next door to us, and Tom Teague was up there," recalls Park. "Seems like we always had a gathering going on. Whenever people wanted to get together, they'd say, 'Can we use your living room?' and we'd move out so they could have the space. We even had some Republicans who had a meeting in there one time. We had a great time."[42]

The good times included throwing Plaskett a surprise birthday party. "I remember Frank said, 'Jimmy's been in the senate a long time, sixteen years, and he's got a birthday coming up. We should do something nice for him.' Well, he'd known a lot of governors in that period of time, so we had a birthday party for him up there, and by golly, we had Branigin, Welsh, Bowen, and Whitcomb, all four of those governors in the room together. Now, I'm not sure where or when you would have had all four of those governors in the same place at the same time, but we sure did for Jimmy Plaskett's birthday."[43]

Judy O'Bannon participated in the fun, especially in later years after her children had grown to an age where they could be with a babysitter or family member at the house in Corydon. In the early days, when the O'Bannon kids were too young to be left with a sitter, Judy was lonesome and missed Frank when he would leave each Sunday evening to return to Indianapolis during session.

"When you are in the legislature, during the session, your total mind is here, and we didn't have cell phones, and we didn't have e-mail back then, so he'd call once a week, and when you call once a week, what do you say, 'Hi, how are you doing?' You don't talk about everything in that space," she said. "Then when he came home on the weekends, during session, they'd work through to Friday and go back on Sunday night. On Saturday morning, they'd have those Third

House breakfasts. Saturday afternoon, you tried to hold on to whatever business you had because you had to have a way to make a living once the session was over. Sunday morning, you'd go to church, every week; he never missed a week."[44]

Thankfully for Judy, the Assembly Women's Club offered her a chance to get involved at some level with the events that dominated her husband's professional life. She would take the Greyhound bus up to Indianapolis every other week or ride with Viola Wathen, Republican house member Richard Wathen's wife. Judy explained that during that time, party association was much less of an issue once the campaign was over. When her children were older, Judy would go up to Indianapolis and stay for much longer, enjoying the camaraderie and experience of those involved in state government.[45]

9

Becoming a Politician

Republicans throughout the statehouse trusted and admired O'Bannon, even though he was a fiercely loyal Democrat. Governor Bowen said of Frank O'Bannon and his father, "Both of them were very quiet and easygoing and quite sincere. They were never rude, never mean politically, but they *were* politicians."[1]

Political opponents appreciated O'Bannon's ability to see both sides of an issue fairly. "O'Bannon seemed to understand the role of the governor and the difficult position he often found himself (in), especially when it comes to legislative relationships," William J. Watt, a top aide to Bowen wrote. "Occasionally, observers reasoned that the governor should have given the General Assembly more explicit instructions and outlined a more extensive agenda in his messages to the legislature and in public statements about its progress. Frank O'Bannon's reaction to (Governor) Bowen's State of the State message concisely stated the problem: 'When he gives a complete legislative program, he is criticized for being a dictator. When he gives a speech, he is criticized for a lack of leadership. He can't win.'"

Watt noted that relations between the governor and senate Democrats seemed to improve under O'Bannon and with the departure of Senator Fair. "Relations between the governor and Senate Democratic Leader Robert Fair never flourished. Mutual respect existed between the two, but little real warmth ever materialized." Two Democrats in the senate helped to bridge the gap, Adam Benjamin and Frank O'Bannon.[2]

It wasn't that O'Bannon could not be tough. In 1984, responding to Governor Robert Orr's State of the State address that focused on the formation of a utility study commission, O'Bannon said Orr borrowed heavily from the Democrats' agenda and spoke mostly in partisan terms in preparation for that November's election. "I think it's still mainly words. Sometimes I think we elected a dictionary rather than a governor in 1980," O'Bannon said.[3]

The state's auto license branch issue had continued to grow as a sore spot for Indiana voters, while Orr and the Republicans struggled for a way to respond—especially after Townsend and his running mate, Ann DeLaney, rode that issue to within a hair of unseating Orr and Mutz in the 1984 election. At the time, Indiana allowed the party of the governor to control the license branches stretched out across the ninety-two counties—a political patronage system that stretched back more than fifty years in Indiana history. By 1985, Indiana Republicans could count 1,300 of their own faithful as on the payroll in the state's license branches with contributions flowing from branches to the state GOP in excess of a reported $1 million a year. In addition, audits, investigations, shortages, indictments, and convictions had flowed forth from some who found it difficult to run the party's "cash machine" honestly. The license branch issue, while failing to catch Governor Orr in the 1984 race for reelection, was a key factor in the 1988 race yet to come.

FRANK'S GOP FRIENDS

Senator Walter Helmke of Fort Wayne, a Republican who became a personal friend of Frank O'Bannon, saw the challenges O'Bannon had to overcome as a senator. "Frank, unfortunately, had a stammer when he spoke, and he always had that quiver in his voice," Helmke said. "When he was in a social setting, there was no problem, but it seemed very uncomfortable for him to go to the microphone."[4]

Helmke's wife, Roweena, and Judy O'Bannon would spend their free time exploring thrift stores and antique shops in Indianapolis and surrounding communities while their husbands debated in the senate.

Senator Lawrence Borst of Indianapolis knew O'Bannon well as both a senate colleague and as an opposition leader during O'Bannon's later terms as lieutenant governor and governor. He recalls with a laugh that "there were five or six young Democrats who came in, and they were all very, very capable. The thing that I remember is that they would show up during the day, and then they'd always play basketball together in the evening. They would go out and eat, and in the majority, we Republicans would be sitting there trying to figure things out, having bills..."[5]

Being in the minority was a struggle at times, "with lots and lots of down time. As I've often said, being in the minority is like being a spectator with a really good seat," said Senator Mahern.[6]

Senator Gutman, who successfully removed the lieutenant governor's power to appoint committees and assign bills to committees in the senate during his tenure as senate president pro tem, remained friends with the O'Bannons even during some tough days near the end of his political career. "Frank and Judy were always good friends, and that never changed."

Helmke believes political relationships with those of the opposition party were more accepted than they are in more partisan times today. Legislators felt more open to be friends with one another off the floor of the chamber.

THE TOP-RANKING DEMOCRAT

For a time in the 1980s, being minority leader of the Democrats in the Indiana Senate meant Frank O'Bannon was the most powerful Democrat left standing at the statehouse. Otis Cox won an unexpected term as state auditor in those lonely days, but Evan Bayh had yet to steal the show with his amazing 1986 run for secretary of state (defeating Robert O. Bowen of Bremen, son of the former Governor Bowen). In Washington, things were no better for Democrats. Ronald Reagan (1911-2004) ushered in the first of three terms of GOP control of the White House and a surprising shift to Republican control of the U.S. Senate in 1980, a shift that elevated U.S. Representative Dan Quayle (b. 1947) to the Senate and sent home one of the nation's best-known senators, Birch Bayh (b. 1928).

In 1982, Frank O'Bannon, by chance, was seated next to U.S. Senator John Glenn (b. 1921) of Ohio at an off-cycle Democratic Party event—an invitation he had received as the top-ranking Democrat in Indiana. O'Bannon greatly admired Glenn and the two hit it off. O'Bannon was tapped to head Glenn's 1984 presidential campaign in Indiana, a rare primary declaration for O'Bannon.

Glenn's campaign had high hopes for states such as Indiana where they believed his hero status to be an asset in appealing to traditionally Republican or independent voters. Glenn visited French Lick in August 1983 and Indianapolis in 1984, but by May 1984, the time of the Indiana Democratic Primary, the race was mostly over—with Democrats settling on former Vice President Walter F. Mondale (b. 1928) to challenge President Reagan for reelection.

END OF AN O'BANNON ERA

On March 7, 1996, members of the Indiana Senate voted unanimously for a resolution honoring Lt. Governor Frank O'Bannon, who on that day, ended a forty-six-year O'Bannon family run in the state's upper chamber representing Southern Indiana. "You embody what I think we all want to be," State Senator Kathy Smith, a New Albany Democrat, said during the O'Bannon tribute. All fifty senators signed the resolution and presented him with the senate president's chair he had used during his eight years as lieutenant governor.

For his part, O'Bannon was humble as always in accepting the honor, calling it "overwhelming." He added, "To be part of this body that sets the policy to make Indiana the best it can be has always been a great pleasure." He recalled the progress of the senate since he first joined it in 1971 and said, "I think the good that is here is the good in each member of this legislature. And I say the good is overwhelming."[7]

POLITICAL ADVISERS AND MENTORS

The list of individuals who can be counted as Frank O'Bannon's political and personal mentors throughout his rise in state politics is long, as one would expect from the quiet man who took in information anywhere he could and enjoyed the company of all types of people. Without a doubt, his personal and political values were formed mostly through the influence of his parents, Robert and Faith O'Bannon. Later in his political career, his wife, Judy, would serve as perhaps his most influential political and personal influence—as well as being an incredible political asset to him.

In earlier years, men like George Fleetwood, who served as O'Bannon's chief of staff in the senate, and Tom New, who went from a senate staff position to chair O'Bannon's 1996 and 2000 campaigns for governor, had great influence upon him. John Goss, who quit his job to take on the task of trying to help elect Frank O'Bannon governor in 1988, and David Johnson, who volunteered to help with the John Glenn campaign, also quickly became trusted advisers. Robin Winston, who went from being "county coordinator" on O'Bannon's statewide campaign in 1996 to being his choice as chair of the Indiana Democratic Party, and Pat Terrell and Cindy Athey, key staff members on the '96 and 2000 campaigns, were all key advisers.

Winston said O'Bannon "had a larger quality about him, a larger vision than I did on some things. I will tell you this, the greatest quality that this man gave me, and I tell people this all the time, is that he made me a better person, absolutely a better person."

"Personally, I owe a great deal to Frank O'Bannon," New said. "He was more than just my boss; he was my mentor; he was my friend. He gave me the opportunity of a lifetime...One of my deepest regrets, however, was that I never properly thanked him for these opportunities, or the trust that he placed in me. I always thought I had time to do that."[8]

Two of O'Bannon's most influential friends and advisers were Republicans—his law partner, Art Funk, and his best friend from high school, Tom Miller, who became a successful Indianapolis banker and a leader in the Republican Party.

At home, Harrison County Democrat Herb Woertz, Jr., a retired tobacco company executive, became an O'Bannon adviser and accepted the position as chair of the Harrison County Democratic Central Committee. Two of Woertz's favorites were Frank O'Bannon and Lee Hamilton, and he chaired both of their campaign committees in Harrison County. Woertz was one of the Corydon faithful who had to swallow hard and accept Frank O'Bannon's decision many years later in 1988 to abandon his own campaign for governor in order to run for lieutenant governor on a ticket headed by Evan Bayh. When O'Bannon was elected in 1996, Woertz's health was failing, and he was resting in Florida. Regardless, he was one of the first to call O'Bannon in his private suite at the Hyatt Regency after hearing on the national news that O'Bannon was projected as the winner. Although he had just spoken to Vice President Al Gore (b. 1948), O'Bannon told Woertz that he didn't consider his win official until he heard it directly from Herb. Upon his death in August 1997, at the young age of fifty-eight, O'Bannon grieved his death and said he "always valued Herb's counsel and his friendship. He was not only a political friend; he was also a close personal friend."[9]

In Indianapolis, Bill Schreiber quickly became O'Bannon's friend and supporter. Active in the then-struggling Marion County Democratic Party organization, Schreiber encouraged O'Bannon to run for governor. Schreiber's youngest son, Ben, recalls, "We all went to the Marion County Jefferson-Jackson Day Dinner in 1987, and our family sat with the O'Bannons…My dad was one of those who did not jump the ship when Evan Bayh got into the race. He stayed loyal to Frank O'Bannon…"[10]

Schreiber, a frequent analyst on WTHR-TV, Channel 13 and on *Indiana Week in Review* on statewide public television, was committed to O'Bannon's campaign when he tried again in 1996, joining the lieutenant governor's staff to help O'Bannon with political issues as he prepared to run for governor. One of Schreiber's earliest tasks on the campaign was to help O'Bannon find media advisers and pollsters who could help a Democrat win in traditionally Republican Indiana. The 1996 campaign was ultimately one Bill would never live to see. A painful shoulder prompted him to consult his doctor, and he learned he only had a short time to live because of the onset of cancer in his lungs and bones. He died January 11, 1996 before the O'Bannon for Governor campaign was even launched.

At a statehouse memorial service, Frank O'Bannon and Evan Bayh both spoke. "I remember Frank O'Bannon said my father was magnanimous in victory and resolute in defeat. They were friends. I think Frank viewed him as a confidant, someone he could trust. My dad felt the same way. That came from their years together in Democratic politics. They all sort of had to band together," Ben Schreiber said.[11]

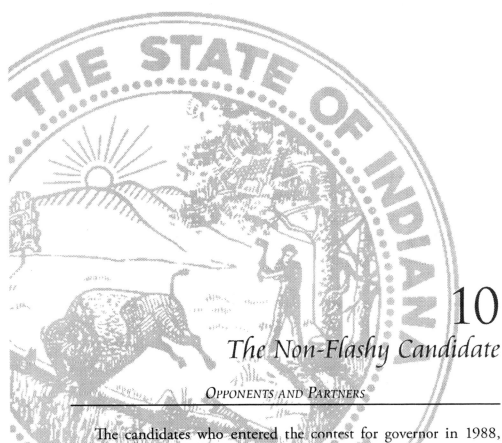

10

The Non-Flashy Candidate

OPPONENTS AND PARTNERS

The candidates who entered the contest for governor in 1988, including Frank O'Bannon, let where, when, and how they announced their intentions reflect the kind of candidacy they brought to the race, *Indianapolis Star* columnist Pat Traub noted at the time.[1]

O'Bannon got in early, May 16, 1987, just two weeks after the 1987 legislative session ended. He went home to Corydon to emphasize his roots deep in Hoosier history and his long record of service to Southern Indiana.

Evan Bayh waited until the 1987 Municipal Elections were over in November before he stepped up on the front porch of the Bayh family homestead in Shirkieville in the northwest corner of Vigo County, the same porch from which his father, Birch, launched four campaigns for the U.S. Senate.

Two-term Kokomo mayor Steve Daily was officially the first candidate in the race, starting in January 1987, and stayed far outside of Indianapolis to reflect what he hoped voters would see and embrace: a non-Indianapolis candidate.

The only Republican in the fray, Lt. Governor John M. Mutz got officially a one-week start on Bayh, taking the stage at the center of the statehouse on November 7, 1987, reflecting his years of service to Hoosiers from that building, staying true to outgoing Governor Orr who was ending eight years in office.

In his announcement, the then fresh-faced and just thirty-one-year-old Bayh banked on his famous last name and the culture of change he sensed in the air, noting, "My paper résumé does not go on and on for page after page. But what I believe state government needs today is a fresh approach and that it will truly take a new broom to sweep the statehouse clean."[2]

Mutz geared his announcement directly at Bayh and emphasized his experience in state government. Acknowledging Bayh's incredible statewide use of paid and earned media in his just-completed 1986 run for secretary of state, Mutz cautioned voters that "Indiana cannot afford to let image makers decide its choice for chief executive. The times do not permit it. The ever-escalating demands of a changing world allow no substitute for a proven record of experience and leadership. I am not interested in slick campaign commercials."[3]

Bayh put Mutz's experience and years of Republican rule at the center of the debate. "During the last eight years, those who now come before us touting their experience have given Hoosier taxpayers the two largest tax increases in the history of our state. They have raised state spending in real terms by 38 percent. They have dramatically increased the number of state employees. During the same period of experienced leadership, we have seen virtually every criteria of evaluation of our education system decline, per capita income of the average Hoosier has eroded (and) by their own admission, the condition of our roads and bridges and highways has reached the critical point," Bayh said.[4]

For his part, Daily stayed away from the "inside I-465" debate raging between Mutz and Bayh. At the end of 1986, Mayor Daily decided against seeking a third term as mayor and had taken a pass on the idea of running for Congress as well. What interested him was governor; his desire was to reform the way state government dealt with local units of government. "I think I decided to run for state office in part out of frustration, part out of anger, and part out of ambition."[5]

Daily attempted to ward off other potential candidates from the ranks of Indiana's other Democratic mayors, including Win Moses of Fort Wayne, Pete Chalos of Terre Haute, or Michael Vandeveer of Evansville. He also viewed his age, thirty-nine, as an advantage over other older candidates such as the 1984 Democratic nominee, State Senator W. Wayne Townsend, and Senate Minority Leader Frank O'Bannon.

Daily did not hear the coming thunder of the Bayh for Governor campaign until it was too late. "If I had a clue that Evan was going to run, I don't think I would have attempted to run. We saw Evan as a bright young guy with a great future, just winning a big seat," Daily said. "I thought that, quite frankly, I better get in now, and I am sure that Frank (O'Bannon) had some similar thoughts. I am sure there were a lot of people looking at Evan and thinking that he was the future of the Democratic Party in Indiana. At the time, I was only thirty-nine years old, but Evan made me feel like an old man."[6]

O'BANNON, BAYH TRADE ENDORSEMENTS

Bayh's campaign was a serious challenge from the start. Besides winning Townsend's endorsement after he decided not to make a third run for governor, former governor Matt Welsh and the United Mine Workers were there from day one. Additional top union support was forthcoming. But Bayh had not locked up all the key endorsements. At his May 1987 announcement in Corydon, O'Bannon featured Congressman Lee H. Hamilton and two former gubernatorial aspirants in his fold, former secretary of state Larry Conrad and former state treasurer Jack New. Dozens of members of the legislature also came on board, including house Democratic leader Mike Phillips of Boonville.

"I supported Frank early on, and I endorsed him...I had become a supporter of Frank O'Bannon to the distress of Evan, I think," Hamilton said. "Of course, I had been very close friends and a good supporter of Birch Bayh's, but I had agreed to be a co-chair of Frank's campaign. I was trying to play a helpful role to him. Evan clearly, though, moved ahead in the race."[7] Hamilton added, "...I was one of them who was saying that Frank is in line; it's Frank's turn, and Evan should wait."[8]

Hamilton's endorsement was based on his long history of friendship with O'Bannon dating back to their years at the IU Law School in Bloomington.

"Evan was disappointed that I had done that because of my influence in the ninth district and the southern part of the state," Hamilton said. "They were a little concerned about that, and as it turned out, they needn't have been because Evan was very successful at building his own base."[9]

THE O'BANNON CAMPAIGN ENGAGES

O'Bannon emphasized jobs as his number one issue, as the state's economy continued its slow and sluggish climb out of the recessions of the 1980s. But he also was concerned about growing scandals emerging in the aging Republican machinery that had ruled the Indiana governor's chair since 1968. "I want to talk about public morality. It's time for a change in Indiana. I think it takes new leadership, and I think it takes experienced leadership," he said.[10] He noted problems the Orr administration had had with the Department of Corrections and Bureau of Motor Vehicles. While he avoided directly blaming Orr or Mutz, he did say the problems were the result of too many years of one-party rule. "They act like they own the government," he said.[11]

O'Bannon saw the benefit of getting an early start, according to campaign aide and adviser David Johnson, after witnessing how much a lack of money had hurt Townsend's 1984 campaign in the closing days.

"He knew it was going to take almost two full years to get it done as a Democrat," Johnson said. "No Democrat had done that before, but I think he knew that was what it was going to take."[12]

The *Corydon Democrat* first reported on O'Bannon's interest in a gubernatorial candidacy as early as January 1987. Editor Randy West revealed the formation of an exploratory committee for 1988 quoting O'Bannon as saying he had made "a personal commitment" to run. The story noted he spent the previous weekend calling more than 125 Democrats, including 92 county chairs and members of the Indiana Democratic Central Committee to tell them of his plans to run. O'Bannon said he had thought about running for more than a year and estimated he would need to raise between $2 and $3 million to be successful. O'Bannon said he hoped his candidacy would appeal to a "broad cross-section of the Democrat Party" and that he would work to "pull the party together."[13]

The May 17, 1987 formal kickoff of the O'Bannon campaign was a classic Corydon event. Emphasizing the town's significance to Indiana history, they built the announcement around a celebration on the town square using the Hurley D. Conrad Memorial Bandstand as its base. The O'Bannon family invited all local residents to attend.

The day's events included craft stands on the town square, scheduled tours of the state historic sites around town, chicken dinners, and a concert by the Harrison County Community Band. A free, four-page souvenir edition of the *Democrat* was offered (paid for by the O'Bannon campaign) and included profiles of Frank and Judy O'Bannon, their children, and a narrative on the O'Bannon family history in Harrison County. The newspaper emphasized the greatest strength he had going for him: experience.

The special edition newspaper quoted O'Bannon's announcement speech with as "strident" or "political" a remark as he would ever make about his more youthful, less experienced opponent, Evan Bayh: "To be successful as governor, you must understand state government and have judgment that is shaped by experience. If you're going to succeed, you must have a record of achievement. I have that. You must demonstrate that you can *hold* office as well as *run* for office."[14]

He added this upbeat theme, "We must show the ability to lead in a new, creative way, and we must have a candidate who can unite the Democratic Party. I think that's one of my assets that has been evident in my leadership in the senate."[15]

Polly Zoeller's son, Beau, O'Bannon's first grandchild, was just eighteen months old at the time and appeared in the publication riding along giggling in a wheelbarrow being pushed by Grandpa Frank.[16]

The kickoff rally on a perfect spring-like day on the town square attracted hundreds. O'Bannon told the crowd, "Some people say I'm not flashy enough to run for statewide office. Well, I don't want to be flashy! I want to be steady and reliable." He said Hoosiers deserved a "seasoned" candidate and addressed the idea that a Democrat could not be elected governor of Indiana, telling the audience that since 1932, eleven men had been elected governor, six Republicans and five Democrats. "We're going to even that score," he declared.[17]

He drew heavy applause as he said, "Most of all, we need to give Indiana that fresh start I spoke about a moment ago. I know it might be fashionable to deplore all of the things that have happened under recent Republican administrations, but that would not be fair or accurate. Good things have happened in Indiana, especially when Democrats and Republicans have put aside political differences and worked together. But it is fair to say, I believe, that the Republican leadership of this state is getting complacent. There is not a freshness in the air. New ideas are not usually welcome. There is a lack of energy to tackle the challenges that must be met. Too many Republicans have come to think that vast areas of this state are their own personal property. They feel that what is good for them is what is good for the State of Indiana, and that is simply not so."[18]

Finally, he sounded themes in this his very first statewide campaign that would be with him throughout his career in public life in Indiana. He said, "We all pay a lot of taxes. We all have the right to expect a fair return on that investment. It is time to ask ourselves: 'What are we getting for our taxes, our investment?' Where are the educational and employment opportunities for our young people? Too many young people are unable to find decent jobs in Indiana. Why? Where are the programs that ease the burden of our elderly citizens when they need care in their homes? Where are the programs that encourage families to stay together through tough times rather than split up and drift apart? It has been said that the character of a state can be judged by how it treats those who live in the shadows of life, the young, the elderly, the disabled, all who are in true need of help. Give me a chance to point a beacon of hope and rehabilitation in the direction of those who live in the shadows of our state. A compassionate state government can make all the difference in the world in bringing people out of the shadows and into the sunshine."[19]

State Representative Paul Robertson, a Democrat from nearby DePauw, likened O'Bannon's background to that of Abraham Lincoln, who said, "I shall study hard, and perhaps my time shall come."[20]

Former secretary of state and onetime gubernatorial hopeful Larry Conrad (1935-1990) said, "Frank has mastered the art of political compromise in Indianapolis and that simply means he would rather get something done than nothing at all...He gets the job done. His tools are fact and reason. And, Ladies and Gentlemen, you can't argue with that at all. Frank is a very serious person. I believe that if we were out to hire a governor for the State of Indiana, we would hire Frank O'Bannon."[21]

INSIDE THE *O'BANNON* '88 CAMPAIGN

The 1988 O'Bannon campaign was counting on a key group of supporters and advisers, including Judy O'Bannon; John Goss; George Fleetwood; Tom New and his father, Jack L. New; David Johnson and his wife, Anne Nobles; Carlyn Johnson; State Senators Mike Gery, Louie Mahern, Bill McCarty, Bob Kovach, and Dennis Neary; State Representatives Mike Phillips and Bill Cochran; campaign stalwarts Bill Schreiber and Chuck Coffey; former state Democratic chair Don Michael; 1980 Democratic gubernatorial nominee John Hillenbrand; Jack Wickes (who would challenge U.S. Senator Richard G. Lugar, R-IN, in 1988); and longtime East Chicago mayor Robert Pastrick.

Chuck Coffey, a former reporter for WHAS Radio in Louisville, Kentucky, traveled with him and worked as a speechwriter. O'Bannon told Coffey that if he could not raise an adequate amount of money for his campaign, he would see that as a sign he should not run.[22]

Cochran said getting O'Bannon to see himself as gubernatorial timber was not easy. "He was that type of person who never saw himself as the guy, as the leader."[23]

Donna Imus said she wasn't that impressed when she first saw O'Bannon in action in 1988 at a Democratic event in Clay County. "He was the keynote speaker, and he talked for five or maybe ten minutes at the most...He was very uncomfortable, it seemed to me..."[24]

O'Bannon had a lot to learn about campaigning at this level. His senate campaigns had been relatively easy for him. The race for governor would prove to be a whole different matter.

The possibility of an Evan Bayh candidacy troubled many powerful Democrats including longtime O'Bannon family friend Mayor Pastrick. Pastrick said Democrats were torn between the two who were both from well-liked political families. "...We wanted one of them as a governor candidate and one as a lieutenant governor candidate. However they worked that out between them, we were going to support it."[25]

Thirty-six-year-old John Goss resigned as deputy mayor of Bloomington to be the manager of the O'Bannon for Governor campaign. Frank's personal style presented quite a hurdle for a race like this one. "Frank is not a slick Madison Avenue type," Goss said. "It's a challenge to educate voters on O'Bannon's style of leadership, but it's worth it."[26]

Goss committed himself fully to the cause. He accepted Judy's invitation to move with the O'Bannons into their new, larger apartment at Lockefield Gardens, just west of the statehouse along Indiana Avenue in order to conserve precious campaign funds.[27]

In the summer of 1988, Goss tagged along in back of the O'Bannon van to the Democratic National Convention in Atlanta, Georgia.

At the convention, Lesley Stahl of CBS News interviewed O'Bannon. The convention ended on a high note, with Massachusetts Governor Michael Dukakis (b. 1933) nominated for president, with U.S. Senator Lloyd Bentsen of Texas (1921-2006) his running mate against the Republican ticket of Vice President George H.W. Bush (b. 1924) and his Hoosier running mate, U.S. Senator Dan Quayle of Indiana.

On the way home from the convention, Goss suffered an embarrassing "incident." He rode in the back of the van where he could catch up on some much-needed sleep. "They stopped at a rest park near Chattanooga, Tennessee to get some gas, and they're being real quiet opening their doors slowly to not wake me. Well, I woke up anyway and decided that I needed to use the restroom, so I went inside the gas station…When I came out, I saw the back of the van pulling out of the station and back onto the interstate headed north."[28]

Goss took off running after the van in cut-off jeans with no shoes and no wallet. He didn't catch the van, or the O'Bannons' attention as they sped north.

"The lady in the Visitors' Center said they had had kids left behind there often, but never an adult," Goss said sheepishly. He was eventually reunited with the O'Bannons thanks to a minister who gave him a ride—but not before Frank and Judy were more than an hour away.[29]

THE EVAN BAYH FACTOR

While the O'Bannon campaign didn't lack for enthusiasm or commitment, it did lack the organization and the fundraising ability that Evan Bayh seemed to demonstrate immediately.

Bayh's campaign relied heavily on strong connections Evan had made through running his father's last statewide campaign in 1980, as well as work he did on behalf of '84 nominee Townsend—and most importantly, the fact that he was less than two years removed from his impressive win in the 1986 race for secretary of state. "Evan Bayh…

was in office at that point, and he was quite strategic about putting together all of the pieces of a campaign structure," David Johnson said. O'Bannon's campaign remained simple, key contact names kept on 3x5-inch index cards, rather than the computer databases and call centers Bayh had. "What Evan Bayh had was certainly nothing like what candidates have today, but he was so far ahead of what Frank O'Bannon had. He was way, way ahead of the pack…He just knew what it took."[30]

Despite a good start, good endorsements, and the good will that comes from eighteen years as a trusted state senator, the specter of an Evan Bayh candidacy was having an effect on the O'Bannon camp's efforts.

"Some of the Bayh supporters, particularly the union guys, wanted to get Evan in the race…," Goss said. In spite of O'Bannon's proven union voting record (rated 94 percent by the Indiana AFL-CIO), the unions saw Bayh as a sexier candidate, more likely to win against the Republican. Some of the larger contributors waited to see how the primary would end up before committing.[31]

Money would clearly be a deciding factor in what was to transpire. O'Bannon was quite aware of the importance of having enough campaign money but remained confident that voters would support him once they came to know him.[32]

THE NAÏVE O'BANNON CAMPAIGN

Judy O'Bannon looks back now and describes their 1987-88 effort as almost naïve. "If we had been more experienced in campaigns, we would have seen the writing on the wall earlier," she said. Judy said the two of them would leave Democratic Party events scratching their heads, stumped by how Democrats in Lawrenceburg, Gary, South Bend, Seymour, or Evansville could all be saying the same thing: They liked Frank O'Bannon, but they thought Evan Bayh was the candidate who could win.

The O'Bannons developed deep respect for Bayh's campaign ability. Bayh's presence at Democratic events attended by both O'Bannon and

Daily clearly demonstrated the difference. The O'Bannons would always show up early and stay to the bitter end. Somehow, Bayh's campaign was more sophisticated at almost every turn, arriving at Jefferson-Jackson Day Dinners sponsored by county Democratic organizations or other events when the crowd was at its maximum. The deeper into 1987 they got, the stronger the talk of Bayh's potential candidacy for '88 grew. By year's end, Bayh's campaign coffers topped $773,702, while O'Bannon had $367,768 on hand. In any other year, O'Bannon's total would have been a positive start for a Democrat in the twenty-year rut in which the party found itself. But this was a different time, and change was in the air. Democrats weren't going to nominate "the next person in line" this time—and even those closest to Frank O'Bannon began to see that the campaign was not going to succeed.[33]

Sunday, January 17, 1988, one week after a damaging public poll showed him trailing Bayh badly, O'Bannon spent the day calling on his friends and other Democratic leaders across the state. The notes he wrote on a legal pad that day reflect the reality that was becoming more and more true. Next to Jack New's name, O'Bannon had written in quotes, "Why can't we get a deal?" and "No fight."

Many of his longtime friends supported O'Bannon but questioned whether he could do it alone. Others were starting to suggest a Bayh-O'Bannon ticket, in some order.

O'Bannon made a call that Sunday to a man who knew Indiana politics extremely well, Larry Conrad. Conrad told him to "do what's best"—and O'Bannon seemed to be moving toward a decision of what was "best" for the Democratic Party.[34]

THE MEETING

Jane Parker, Frank's oldest sister, lives on a well-kept suburban street in Plainfield, Indiana. Her comfortable home was perhaps the last place anyone would suspect a major political meeting would occur—but it became the cradle of the one of the great political partnerships in Indiana history.

"Frank said they wanted to be somewhere where nobody knew who they were," Jane Parker recalls about the random call her brother placed to her on a Thursday evening, asking to use her living room to meet with Evan Bayh. "Frank came first...they were here all afternoon. I just sat in the other room while they met—I think I got them cookies and some coffee and that was it."[35]

As Frank O'Bannon and Evan Bayh sat side by side for more than three hours on that cold January afternoon in 1988, they came to understand each other.

Evan Bayh left the meeting with even more respect for Frank O'Bannon. "Frank really came across as someone who cared about the state and who cared about the Democratic Party," Bayh said. "...He wanted to do what was best for both, even if that meant subordinating his own ambitions...I think we were able to concur that we were compatible with one another and that we had some very similar views about what was good for the State of Indiana. It was just a very amicable meeting, and my overwhelming recollection or memory is that Frank O'Bannon was a man who cared very deeply about the greater good more than he cared about his own narrow self-interest."[36]

POLLING

The Bayh-O'Bannon meeting had come about after days of secret conversations between Bayh's campaign manager, Joe Hogsett, and O'Bannon's manager, John Goss. Both had kept the lines of communication open over the last half of 1987 as the campaign for governor wore on. For Goss, such communication made sense as more and more tangible signs emerged indicating that Frank O'Bannon was going to have a terribly difficult struggle on his hands if he wanted to even compete seriously for the Democratic nomination for governor.

The *Indianapolis Star* broke new ground for its time in January 1988, when it began publishing its own public opinion polls. Prior to that time in Indiana, for the most part, newspapers and television stations simply reported the results of polls given to them by political campaigns and parties. In this instance, the *Star* set about finding out for itself how voters felt going into 1988.

The results were clear: Evan Bayh enjoyed a huge advantage not only over both of his Democratic challengers, O'Bannon and Daily, but also in a head-to-head race with the presumptive GOP nominee, Lt. Governor Mutz. The poll published in the *Star*'s January 10, 1988 edition found an incredible 60 percent of Democrats polled favored Bayh, while O'Bannon gathered the support of just 8 percent, and Daily 5 percent. In a head-to-head match-up with Mutz, Bayh also held a statewide lead, 38 to 28 percent, over the older and more experienced Republican. O'Bannon and Daily both trailed Mutz when placed in head-to-head contests with him.

Goss told the *Star* that Bayh's popularity did not scare them and added, "It is still very early, and this race is far from over. Several hundred thousand dollars of television will bring any candidate's name up. It will take a significant media campaign for any candidate to make any significant gains."[37]

What was clear, however, from both the public poll the *Star* published and the one O'Bannon commissioned himself was that O'Bannon started out way behind Bayh—despite months and months of tireless campaigning across the state and nearly two decades of work in the state senate. O'Bannon tried to put the best face on it but gave a typically honest answer: "I think we still have a long way to go. I think polls are important to show what people know at a particular time," and said he saw hope in the number of undecided voters that the race may still be open. "We've said all along that the name identification's not going to go up until you go on TV. We still feel there's a race to be won," he told the *Star*.[38]

O'Bannon's own polling, however, showed troubling results as well. Among Democrats, Evan Bayh's "net positive rating" was at a whopping 54 percent while O'Bannon was back at 7 percent, with 73 percent of those asked unable to recognize his name. Polls showed voters thought government experience, Bayh's perceived weakness, was important, but it was a "Teflon" issue for him. Voters (particularly Democrats) didn't care about that; they liked him anyway.[39]

In summary, O'Bannon's pollsters told him, "We are in a long-shot position, and we are short on name recognition and funds to develop the necessary campaign for name recognition. A lot of personal contact has been made and that should be helpful. The campaign speech and themes are jelling, and the candidate delivery is continuing to show improvement. The challenge is formidable, and Bayh starts from a position of greater strength because of his prior statewide race."[40]

Hogsett recalls hearing word within days of the *Indianapolis Star* poll that it would be a good idea for him to call Goss and see what he had to say. The pressure for a meeting between the two had been building for months.

"I am sure that people were thinking by the fall about how we could put this all together, and do that in a way that makes all of us a winner," Hogsett said. "I think the most accurate way to put it is that I never sensed any disagreement at some stage of the campaign that Frank O'Bannon and Evan Bayh needed to get together. The only disagreement was what alignment would that partnership take. I ultimately have to credit Frank O'Bannon for making the decision…"[41]

"We could see the writing on the wall. I mean, we didn't have any money, and the other guy had a couple hundred thousand more than us," Judy O'Bannon said. "With Evan in the race, we knew we would have to reconsider."[42]

After the discussion with Bayh, O'Bannon began to privately ask friends and advisers what they thought he should do. David Johnson said, "He did not want to disappoint people who had supported him for office, but he was also very concerned about what was best for the Democrat Party." At his core, O'Bannon remained a fiercely partisan person, loyal to the Democratic Party to the end. "He believed in his political party, and he thought this was the best thing for his party. (His withdrawal) was an act of tremendous grace and courage," he said.[43]

Senator Louis Mahern, who was among those backing O'Bannon over Bayh, said O'Bannon's move was exactly right. "I thought it was gracious for him to drop back, and it was very smart politically," Mahern said.[44]

An internal O'Bannon campaign memo, titled "Project 88-206," had already laid out for O'Bannon what the stakes were in the 1988 campaign calling the 1988 election a "crucial" one for Indiana Democrats. "Every effort must be made to select and then elect our nominee to the office of governor. The very viability of the two-party system at the state level in Indiana can be correctly called into question if another Republican nominee continues the string of unbroken election victories from 1968 through 1984."

The memo emphasized the importance of avoiding the "intra-party bloodletting" that had plagued Indiana Democrats in previous election cycles. "The Democratic Party cannot afford the luxury of self-destruction," and said the Democratic candidate must not focus on what the Republicans are doing, and instead focus solely on "MOPI," money, organization, polling, and issues.[45]

O'Bannon told political columnist Brian Howey, "Ultimately, the decision was mine. I felt that really, what we were talking about was changing administrations and the party. And by far the best thing that could happen was not to have a primary fight. I felt I could bring the strengths I had along with those of Evan Bayh to give us the best chance to win in 1988. I think that was accomplished, and I feel real satisfied that that was the right decision."[46]

For Bayh, the advantages of blending the two campaigns was obvious. "The advantages were several and significant," Bayh said. "First, I always believed that primaries are best avoided in terms of the expenditure of money and the sort of inevitable bad will that is generated, even if the two candidates get along. There is always friction that is created between the supporters of the two, and that kind of thing, so to unify the Democratic Party was a very important step…And number two, I was young at the time, and I looked even younger, so I looked at this as a very good thing to have someone like Frank with his experience and gravitas by my side. I think it helped us present the right combination of youthful energy and seasoned experience."[47]

After a few more telephone calls between the two campaigns, on Thursday, January 21, 1988, Frank and Judy O'Bannon strode across the south atrium of the statehouse toward the secretary of state's office for their planned meeting with Evan and Susan Bayh. A few moments later, Bayh and O'Bannon would enter a jam-packed statehouse news conference to the delight of the many Democrats who managed to cram into the room. It was official, the fifty-seven-year-old O'Bannon would end his campaign for governor and instead be the choice of the now thirty-two-year-old Bayh as his running mate for lieutenant governor.

Immediately, other Democratic hopefuls for lieutenant governor, including State Representatives B. Patrick Bauer of South Bend and Stanley Jones of West Lafayette, and State Senator Douglas Hunt of South Bend, indicated they would end their campaigns and support the Bayh-O'Bannon ticket. O'Bannon said he had considered carefully what to do given the growing strength of Bayh's candidacy and determined that a negative campaign would be required to try and compete with Bayh.

"Frank himself, more than anyone else, realized that Evan enjoyed enormous name recognition, in no small measure due to his father's name, and held a statewide office," Hogsett said. "He knew that it was going to take him an enormous amount of money to get his name recognition up to where Bayh's was, and then he would still have to try and mix it up to get the race engaged. I think he could see that he was going to have to mix it up pretty seriously, and that was just never part of his personality."[48]

O'Bannon's 1987-88 gubernatorial campaign did not falter for a lack of trying. John Goss believes O'Bannon gave it his all. "Frank certainly learned to or became a better speaker and a better campaigner over the course of that fall." Goss said he believes their barnstorming strategy was successful. "It was starting to pick up some momentum, but I still think we made the right decision around the first of the year to team up with the Bayh campaign."[49]

To describe Democrats in Indiana as jubilant at the Bayh-O'Bannon announcement would be an understatement. State Senator Carolyn Mosby of Gary declared it "the happiest day of my political life. For the first time ever, I really believe we Democrats can control the statehouse." State Representative Earline Rogers of Gary (who would go on to succeed Mosby in the senate) took fellow Democrats aside and persuaded them to sing and dance in the statehouse halls following the announcement.[50]

"I could not find a single Democrat in the state of Indiana who was not exuberant that Evan Bayh and Frank O'Bannon, in whatever order it was in, had gotten together," Hogsett said. "Frank's move brought together an unbelievable level of unification among Democrats that was truly needed…Frank brought a level of experience that negated very effectively the Republican notion that Evan Bayh was too inexperienced or too young to be governor. From the very beginning, Evan and Frank made it clear that they were a team, that they were running as a team and intended to serve as a team."[51]

Judy's disappointment at having to shutter the O'Bannon for Governor campaign was perhaps greater than Frank's—or at least it tended to show more—right up until the joint announcement of the merged campaigns. She feared that they had waited too long, and now the chance for Frank to be elected governor of Indiana was slipping away. Two years of work and effort to reach out to Democrats all across Indiana was hard to put aside. Judy had wanted her husband to run four years earlier, in 1984. "I thought that was his year…," she said. "…But somehow, his mind wasn't there yet."[52]

Goss confirms that many of Frank's friends resisted the idea of him quitting his campaign and joining Bayh.[53] However, Goss wasn't convinced O'Bannon's closest friends and advisers had it right, so he tried again. He talked to Frank and Judy, and they finally reached a decision to approach the Bayh campaign about working together.

George Fleetwood, who had worked for O'Bannon in the state senate and was advising him on his gubernatorial campaign, said,

"Frank was not a man of great ego. I think he felt that if he could help Evan Bayh become governor, and the Democrats could win the office, that this would be a good thing for the state of Indiana, from his perspective."

The move to shut down his own campaign fit into what Fleetwood often saw in O'Bannon. "Being governor was not like this lifelong ambition of Frank's," Fleetwood said. "I mean, being a father, being a lawyer, running a newspaper, being a good Christian man, those were the kind of things that he wanted to define himself as, not being a state senator, not being lieutenant governor, not being a governor."[54]

Senator Mahern agrees. "Frank didn't lust after power the way other people did…Frank did not have to be the governor in order to validate his life."[55]

Frank O'Bannon approached the idea of running for lieutenant governor with gusto. He based this decision, like others, on the question of: Could he make a positive difference? In Indiana, the lieutenant governor was blessed at that time with possessing a meaningful, valuable role in the administration. As head of the Department of Commerce, he would be in charge of important aspects of economic development and tourism. He would also be head of the Department of Workforce Development, commissioner of agriculture, and presiding officer in the state senate, a role that particularly appealed to O'Bannon. For O'Bannon, every part of the job description seemed a good fit. One fact emerged: Frank O'Bannon wanted the job.

Johnson was convinced Bayh and O'Bannon were ultimately a very good fit. Beyond the balance and expected "gravitas" O'Bannon brought to the ticket, Johnson felt "…the two of them really understood each other from that basic political level."[56]

O'Bannon, it seems, never harbored a doubt that he had done the right thing. "I think it was one of the best political decisions I have ever made in my career, and not just for me, but for the strength it gave to the Democratic Party," he said.[57]

STEVE DAILY: ODD MAN OUT

In one day, Steve Daily quickly became the "odd man out." Reports at the time indicated Bayh and O'Bannon had attempted to reach out to him to determine if there was a role for him in a potential Bayh-O'Bannon administration.

Daily says he recalls hearing directly from O'Bannon that he was planning to withdraw, but if Daily ever considered dropping out at that point, it didn't show publicly. Describing himself as a "pit bull terrier," Daily dug in and told the largest crowd of reporters he had ever drawn that his campaign would go on.

"Right now, I am interested in being governor of the state of Indiana," he said.[58]

With O'Bannon's withdrawal, Daily declared himself the most qualified Democratic candidate remaining in the race.

"I think at that point, everyone expected me to drop out and wanted me to drop out. I heard a lot of that," Daily said. "I know, in retrospect, I probably could have salvaged my political career if I had gotten out at that point, but at the time, that didn't matter that much to me."[59]

Daily's campaign was crippled by the Bayh-O'Bannon announcement, as he struggled to not only get reporters but Democratic voters to listen to his agenda and move on from the question: When do you plan to exit the race? In the end, Daily stayed on the May primary ballot, and it was no contest. Bayh rolled up 493,198 votes to Daily's 66,242.

GOP CASTS A WARY EYE

Republicans were worried about the new Bayh-O'Bannon ticket and the prospects of a united Democratic team but didn't let on publicly about their concerns. Privately, Republicans knew it was trouble.

"We would have preferred to run against Frank O'Bannon," Mike McDaniel, Mutz's campaign manager, said. "(The partnership) was troublesome, certainly...The big difference for us would have been that Frank O'Bannon had a voting record, and Evan Bayh had no record at all...Everyone knows that you can go through a person's voting record and make something out of almost any vote. O'Bannon had literally hundreds of votes we could look at. He was there in the senate when they had to make some hard decisions, and I am sure there would have been a lot of fodder there for the campaign."[60]

Republicans also preferred O'Bannon because he was untested statewide. "Frank O'Bannon had not run statewide at that point; he was not known," McDaniel said. "Evan Bayh had just won the secretary of state's race, and of course, everyone knew his father, Birch Bayh...Frank O'Bannon would have had to spend the first half a million dollars or so that he raised just introducing himself to the voters, telling them who the heck he was."[61]

Bayh and O'Bannon had good geographic balance. With O'Bannon, "You had someone who could probably deliver a good part of Southern Indiana, which is always very important for the Democrats," McDaniel said.[62]

McDaniel added that beyond O'Bannon bringing vast institutional knowledge and geographic balance to the ticket, "You have to add in a high likeability factor. Frank O'Bannon has always had that. People have always liked him. I think the world of the guy."[63]

A GOP CHALLENGE GONE AWRY

Indiana Republicans were not going to roll over without a fight, however. Under the leadership of Chairman Gordon Durnil, the Indiana GOP was used to winning elections. Durnil delighted in reminding Lincoln Day audiences across the state that the party had won twenty-five of twenty-six statewide races over the last two decades. But there was no question they were worried about the prospect of the young Evan Bayh ending their twenty-year hold on the governor's office. Their concern bubbled over, it seems, in a strange and ultimately harmful effort to try and deny Bayh even the chance to run. After months of bad-mouthing Bayh as an alleged "carpetbagger" returning to Indiana for political opportunity, Durnil and other Republicans began to question whether Bayh met the state's constitutional requirement to hold the office of governor.

They pointed to Section 7, Article 5 of the Indiana Constitution that provides for the qualifications of those who serve in the executive branch.

The constitution said, "No person shall be eligible to the office of Governor or Lieutenant Governor, who shall not have been five years a citizen of the United States, *and also a resident of the state of Indiana during the five years next preceding his election…*" (emphasis added). The Republicans pegged their argument to whether Evan Bayh had been a legal resident of Indiana for the five years prior to the November 8, 1988 election—which would be November 8, 1983.

From the start, it was an odd effort, but one most Republicans were absolutely determined to pursue. Eventually, even Governor Orr and Lt. Governor Mutz joined the challenge, with Mutz challenging Bayh to release five years of his federal tax returns. Republicans were convinced that one or several of those returns would show Bayh listing Washington, D.C. or Virginia as his residence, not Indiana.[64]

Bayh stood firm, rolling out all sorts of evidence of his "Hoosierness." "The standard is one of intent, where one intends to reside…There is no question I have been a resident of Indiana all my life. I lived in Washington roughly from July 1983 and back in September 1984 to campaign for Wayne (Townsend)," Bayh said.

The next day, Bayh told a packed news conference, "I have paid taxes every year in Indiana. I have voted ever since I was eighteen years old in Indiana. I registered with the Selective Service in Indiana. I went to college in Indiana. I am living here with my family. Unquestionably, I have always been a resident of the state of Indiana."[65]

To most insiders, the residency challenge looked and smelled like fear on the part of the Republicans. To "Joe and Martha Hoosier," it just looked ridiculous that anyone would even try to argue that Birch Bayh's son was not a Hoosier.

For McDaniel and many Republicans, still today, they believe the challenge was legitimate. "…Evan Bayh had clearly not lived in Indiana," McDaniel said. "There is no question about that. He grew up in D.C., he really had, and we had plenty of evidence that he had not really lived in Indiana."[66]

"In retrospect now, there is no question in my mind that we would have been better off if we had played the 'carpetbagger' issue during the campaign as opposed to acting like the big guys who want to keep the new young guy out of the race," McDaniel said. "Clearly it spilled over onto the campaign. That is all water over the dam now, but it all had an effect."[67]

Hogsett believes the residency challenge absolutely backfired on the GOP. "There is no question that they miscalculated," Hogsett said. "It is an open question as to whether or not by November those issues still resonated, or were still determinative to the outcome. But I think that gave...Evan Bayh enormous amounts of free publicity that he would not have normally generated during this otherwise rather uneventful period of time in the campaign season of January, February, and March."[68]

Hogsett said the challenge also "played very well into what was an ultimate Bayh-O'Bannon theme, that it was really time for a change. Whether or not there was legal merit to the Republicans' question about the constitutional eligibility of Evan Bayh, I think it ultimately came across in many circles as evidence of their willingness to do anything to maintain their power..."[69]

WISH-TV statehouse reporter Jim Shella said history indicates the residency challenge was "a colossal mistake. What came out of that was this message that they were afraid of Evan Bayh. They tried to make the argument that Birch Bayh's son is not a Hoosier. The public said, first of all, that you can't tell me that Birch Bayh's son is not a Hoosier, and second of all, why are you so afraid to run against him anyway? I think they may have lost that race then and there."[70]

The residency challenge played out from September 1987 into the first half of 1988 on two fronts—first via the Indiana State Election Board at the request of Governor Orr, and the other in the courts, where Bayh went seeking a declaratory judgment that he met the constitutional requirement to serve.

O'Bannon's own gubernatorial campaign, as early as July 1987, kept a close watch on the residency challenge and did their own "political calculus" on the issue.[71]

Publicly, before joining Bayh's campaign, O'Bannon said little about the residency issue. After joining Bayh, he said he doubted the challenge would be successful. "There is no question that his intention was always to be a resident of the state of Indiana, in my mind. I think Evan would be successful (in a court challenge)."[72]

The residency challenge ultimately prompted the newly formed Bayh-O'Bannon team to come to an unusual agreement: O'Bannon would leave his name on the ballot for the Democratic nomination for governor for the May 1988 Democratic primary as a backup should Bayh later be determined ineligible to run. In that case, Hogsett said, the team would have become the O'Bannon team, with the Bayh camp doing all it could to ensure O'Bannon won the May primary and the November election. In that scenario, however, Bayh would also have been ineligible to run for lieutenant governor, since the constitutional residency requirement for that office is the same as it is for governor. The issue was resolved, however, just before the May primary, with a Shelby County judge (and later the Indiana Supreme Court) affirming Bayh's residency status and eligibility. The ruling came too late, however, to remove O'Bannon's name from the ballot, and he polled 34,640 votes statewide for governor—a figure that was meaningless next to Bayh's impressive total. The 1988 Democratic primary would be the only time O'Bannon lost a vote in his home of Harrison County. Although closer than any other county in the state, Bayh still won Harrison County nudging O'Bannon 2,967 to 2,046.[73]

From there, Democrats went forward with an unfamiliar feeling of confidence as the race was set. Bayh invited Daily to serve as the chair of the state Democratic Convention in June, where the united and excited Democrats nominated O'Bannon for lieutenant governor, John Rumple of Tippecanoe County for attorney general, and Mary Peterson of Lake County for state superintendent of public instruction.

The Republicans, meanwhile, continued forward with a ticket dominated by Marion County, as Mutz selected Marion County prosecutor Stephen Goldsmith of Indianapolis as his running mate, along with Indianapolis resident H. Dean Evans for state superintendent of public instruction. Only Attorney General Linley E. Pearson, who sought reelection, was from outside Marion County, but he was still widely viewed as an Indianapolis candidate because the duties of his office kept him in the capital city.

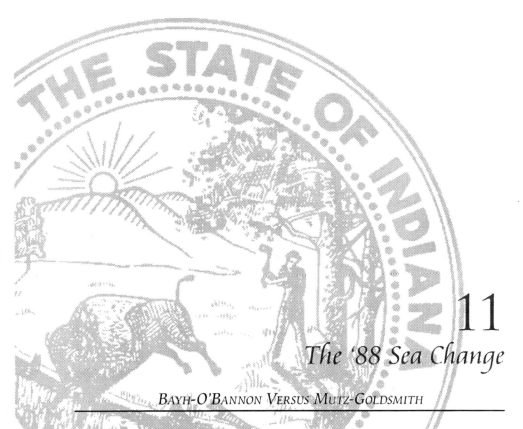

11

The '88 Sea Change

BAYH-O'BANNON VERSUS MUTZ-GOLDSMITH

For its time, the 1988 campaign set records in money spent and in nastiness. Indiana Republicans were determined to hold on to the governor's office, and their best hope was an energetic and hard-working lieutenant governor, John M. Mutz, who had a résumé and background that mirrored O'Bannon's. A difference, however, was that Mutz had worked his way up in Indiana Republican Party politics through the Republicans' most important county: Marion County. He fought tough races for his senate seat (after losing an earlier house bid) and won the 1980 Republican primary for lieutenant governor. (It was only the second time that primary voters nominated candidates for the second spot on the ticket. Since 1980, lieutenant governor nominees have been selected at state party conventions.)

After almost eight years as Orr's number two man, internal GOP polls showed him with high name identification. Despite that, media polls released early in the year showed Mutz trailed Bayh and ran the risk of ending the Republican dynasty at the statehouse.

Although Mutz won the nomination easily after Indianapolis Mayor William H. Hudnut, III opted out, Mutz knew that many Hoosiers had begun to think about making a change, but he did not want to distance himself, as many had advised, from Governor Orr. According to his campaign manager, Mike McDaniel, "Mutz said, 'I'll have none of that. He's been too good to us.'"[1]

Mutz faced tremendous pressure in selecting a running mate that would help him as much as O'Bannon was helping Bayh. Many Republicans wanted the job, including several state legislators and mayors and State Treasurer Marjorie H. O'Laughlin, but Mutz focused on the up-and-coming ambitious Marion County prosecutor, Stephen Goldsmith. Goldsmith had built a résumé as a law-and-order county prosecutor who had focused attention on the importance of child support collections. He was also well known in the state's largest media market of Indianapolis and, as a result, was viewed as a positive addition to the ticket that Mutz could not pass by.

In spite of these qualifications, grumbling began quickly among Republicans because of Goldsmith's strong-willed manner, and rumors circulated that the "Mutz-Goldsmith" team was anything but a team.

Shella said of the Goldsmith pick, "...I think they thought they had to pick him because they felt he was the only guy who could help them on Election Day...But as it worked out, I think they were disappointed, and Goldsmith was not much of a team player."[2]

Goldsmith had a lot to learn about certain aspects of the lieutenant governor's job, especially the role of commissioner of agriculture. Joint appearances with O'Bannon meant he had to prepare. "I didn't know anything (about agriculture) when I started," Goldsmith said. "And Frank knew a lot. I went through kind of a quick crash course to learn all I could."[3]

Campaigns at most every level in 1988 took on a "gotcha" feel, starting with Democratic presidential hopeful U.S. Senator Gary Hart (b. 1936) of Colorado being washed from the race by allegations of marital infidelity, and plagiarism charges being leveled against other candidates, such as U.S. Senator Joe Biden (b. 1942) of Delaware and the Reverend Jesse Jackson (b. 1941). The issue of whether a candidate had ever smoked marijuana also became a big issue in 1988—at least for some voters.

When Bayh disclosed in February 1988, in response to a reporter's question, that he had in fact smoked marijuana once while a student at Indiana University, the Republicans pondered whether to pounce.

"Campaigns were very different then," McDaniel said. "This was before we had the 'attack mode' campaigns. I really wanted John (Mutz) to go after Evan Bayh on that issue. Someone had a picture of Evan from when he was in college when he had long hair down to his shoulders. He looked like Sir Lancelot…I wanted to run an ad that featured that picture." Mutz would have nothing to do with that.[4]

Mutz did air one provocative ad that featured a "Bayh detector" instead of a lie detector to run comparisons between his campaign promises and those of Bayh. McDaniel told reporters after the election that the original version included a reference to Bayh's admitted one-time marijuana use, which was later dropped.

Ultimately, the contrast between Mutz and Bayh was not favorable. While lacking Mutz's experience in state government, Bayh seemed to have a confidence and natural ease to him that generated energy and excitement among already hopeful and excited Democrats, interested Independents, and terribly worried Republicans. Bayh seemed destined for greatness. He answered every question put to him with ease and comfort. He railed against twenty years of Republican rule but did it in a way that did not annoy or put off Hoosiers. Mutz and the others were older than him, but he exuded an incredible confidence that belied his age. Bayh also successfully "stole" the right flank from Republicans, consistently hitting on his plans to lower state spending, cut taxes, and be "a true fiscal conservative."

McDaniel says that Mutz, although a great problem solver, was hindered publicly by discomfort with some aspects of campaigning. "…John worried that some of what we asked him to do would come off as phony, and as a result, he was uncomfortable at times." He believes voters misinterpreted his discomfort as aloofness.[5]

As the campaign entered the summer of 1988, Indiana Republicans were jubilant, if not distracted. Republican presidential nominee George H.W. Bush selected Indiana's junior Senator Dan Quayle as his choice for vice president. Excited Indiana Republicans hurried to Huntington, Indiana to greet Bush and Quayle as the 1988 Republican campaign got underway on Hoosier soil. In Indiana, despite his continued popularity among Hoosiers, Quayle's presence did little to help Bush, who already had Indiana wrapped up, and any hope that Quayle's presence on the national ticket would help the Mutz-Goldsmith campaign quickly faded.

As the campaign wore on, Bayh and Mutz exchanged a barrage of "comparison" television ads. At the time, most observers thought it the nastiest campaign for governor they'd ever seen.

O'BANNON'S ROLE

O'Bannon barnstormed Southern Indiana for the Bayh-O'Bannon ticket with enthusiasm, using a van borrowed from Judy's parents. He went anywhere and everywhere the Bayh campaign said he was needed. As a candidate and a public speaker, he continued to improve. Goss said the campaign had worked with O'Bannon from an early point to try and improve his presentations, including helping him focus his remarks down to one to three major points, instead of the dozens of topics in state government he knew well and could and would hold forth on in earlier speeches.

They brought in Ron Powell from Bloomington to help O'Bannon improve his sometimes-hesitant speech pattern. "I think he helped Frank realize with some video work and other things the items he needed to work on. Frank improved tremendously...," noted Goss.[6]

O'Bannon was initially sensitive to accepting help with his speaking style, but he grew to know he needed to improve. Marilyn Schultz, a house member who had worked with O'Bannon, recalls raising the public speaking issue with him directly. She and her husband, Republican house member Richard Good, were early supporters of

O'Bannon's campaign. When Frank asked them what he could do to improve his chances, Schulz suggested he find a professional speech coach to help with presenting himself and his ideas.[7]

Schultz said, "I could just tell that he really thought I had crossed over the line on that one...I think it is hard for anyone to get that kind of feedback."[8]

Goss said there was also the issue of the shaking or essential trembling in O'Bannon's hands and sometimes in his voice. As a solution, they decided to keep his hands busy holding something.[9]

Indianapolis Star reporter Joe Gelarden profiled the contrasts between the two candidates for lieutenant governor in his final report before the election. He noted Goldsmith's energetic, forceful speaking ability but sensed his "nervousness" during a joint appearance with O'Bannon in Lake County—friendly territory for a Democrat. O'Bannon, however, spoke in "a careful, soft style."[10]

O'Bannon refused to engage in any attacks on John Mutz, someone he knew well from their service together in the state senate. During an October debate between Goldsmith and O'Bannon, Goldsmith took several shots at O'Bannon's running mate, Evan Bayh. O'Bannon finally replied, "I'm not going to bash John Mutz the way Steve is bashing Evan Bayh."[11] O'Bannon insisted that his campaign remain issue-based.

O'Bannon told Gelarden he was not bothered by the fact that the campaign's focus was entirely on Bayh. "Ego is an occupational hazard you can't afford."[12] He also noted that he had once underestimated Bayh's political abilities, but had come to know how good Bayh really was. "Once we joined our campaigns, I knew the Republicans would underestimate him, too," he said.[13]

O'Bannon, in the final days of the '88 campaign, sounded confident and pleased in a radio interview with Bob McIntosh of New Albany in which he discussed the Bayh-O'Bannon plan for leadership in Indiana focusing on important issues like education and the economy. "We have stayed on that positive note, and I think that has got the message around the state of Indiana that Evan Bayh and Frank O'Bannon can provide good leadership for Indiana for the next four years."[14]

On Election Day, Bayh-O'Bannon rolled to a comfortable win, taking away about one in every four Republican votes and becoming the first Indiana Democrats in two decades to win the state's top offices. The final tally, Bayh-O'Bannon's 1,138,574 to Mutz-Goldsmith's 1,082,207, was less important than the fact that the once unbeatable "dynasty" of the Indiana Republican Party had finally met its match.[15] For Indiana, it meant that the state was returning to its historic tradition of being a more evenly divided two-party state. Previous stories about the death of the Democratic Party in Indiana were gone, and Frank and Judy O'Bannon were thrilled to be along for the ride.

Bayh and O'Bannon were inaugurated on January 9, 1989 before more than 3,000 overjoyed Democrats in the south atrium of the statehouse, at the doorstep of the governor's office. The event was preceded by a long but incredible night of dinners, dances, and fireworks for more than 3,500 win-starved Democrats who partied late into the night at the Hoosier Dome (later renamed the RCA Dome), a block away from the statehouse. Of the 350 tables on the floor of the dome, six were occupied by Harrison County friends and family of Frank and Judy O'Bannon. Judy greeted them all, near tears, thanking them for all they had done. She wore earrings and a necklace belonging to Frank's departed mother, Faith Dropsey O'Bannon, telling one group, "She would have just loved all of this!"[16]

At age thirty-three, Bayh became the nation's youngest governor. Joseph H. Hogsett of Rushville, Indiana, a trusted Bayh adviser, was also inaugurated as the state's new secretary of state to complete the term Bayh was vacating to become governor. The new young governor was introduced by his proud father, former U.S. senator Birch E. Bayh, in an emotional ceremony.

O'Bannon took the oath as recited by his friend U.S. Representative Lee Hamilton and in his remarks warmed up the crowd by reminding them, "Well, I stand here as living proof that you can take the capital out of Corydon—but you can't keep Corydon out of the capital."[17]

He described the day as "a day for celebration and ceremony" and "a happy day" but seemed determined to prepare Hoosiers for the change that the state's first Democratic administration in two decades would bring. "Of course, we will have to deal with change. Every generation of Hoosiers has had to deal with change. In talking about change, the author Jacob Ronowsky wrote that 'human beings are not merely figures in the landscape, but the shapers of the landscape.' The key challenge that Evan Bayh and I face is to shape the landscape in such a way that we do not lose the essential spirit that has made Indiana such a great state."[18]

THE TRANSITION

In the weeks between Election Day and the inauguration, droves of Democrats who had longed for decades for a chance to work in state government scurried to get their résumés into the transition office. Evan Bayh continued to make history as he moved to wipe out the state's antiquated and unpopular political patronage structure that Republicans had worked for decades—one that required state workers to get endorsements from their local county or district party chairs and required the donation of 2 percent of their wages back to the Republican Party. Bayh created the state's first merit system for most state positions, a system that put emphasis on job skill, experience, and ability, rather than political affiliation. He also instituted an executive order creating a collective bargaining agreement for state employees after multiple attempts to get such approval via the General Assembly failed. Bayh and O'Bannon quickly signaled that state government was going to be run differently than in the past.

O'Bannon put John Goss and Tom New to work immediately on developing staffs and programs for the Department of Commerce and the Department of Workforce Development, the latter department still under the control of the lieutenant governor, though it would later be moved under the governor. New focused on policies to match the campaign promises and initiatives, including the sensitive matter of how to handle foreign investment in Indiana given the controversy the Subaru-Isuzu economic deal in Tippecanoe County had ignited in the Bayh-Mutz match-up. Bayh wanted to be certain the jobs promised would be delivered. O'Bannon would later focus on the same theme as governor.[19]

Recruiting new people for the administration was not difficult— résumés flooded the mailbox daily. Goss eventually recruited talent from across the state, especially from the ranks of city administrations he had encountered during his work as deputy mayor under Bloomington Mayor Tomilea Allison. Others from the ranks of city halls in Indiana who joined up were Craig Hartzer from South Bend, D. Sue Roberson from Richmond, Betty Cockrum and Thayr Richey from Bloomington, and Matt Reuff from Elkhart.[20]

Longtime Bayh friend and adviser Bill Moreau headed up Bayh's transition effort, which produced one of only a few moments when Bayh and O'Bannon publicly disagreed. Moreau recalls reporters asking for copies of the cover letters and résumés submitted by all of the people who had expressed interest in working in the administration. Moreau and the Bayh team decided they should release the information and planned to do so. When Moreau contacted Lt. Governor-elect O'Bannon to instruct him to do likewise, he met with a moment of resistance. O'Bannon said no, worried that it could damage or hurt those who had applied for jobs in confidence, some not wanting their current employers to know they were looking for another job. It was a rare glimpse of light slipping between Bayh and O'Bannon publicly.

Lt. Governor O'Bannon Takes the Reins

At the Department of Commerce, Hartzer came aboard after having served as deputy mayor of South Bend and recalls O'Bannon immediately put his imprint on how business was to be conducted. Under O'Bannon, economic development efforts would be more inclusive. "He was reaching out to folks on both sides of the aisle. He was very thorough and very systematic in his approach...It was very much focused on economic development being a locally driven activity. He brought everyone to the table," Hartzer said.[20]

Bringing everyone to the table meant creating a point system for awarding community development block grants that flowed through the state from the U.S. Department of Housing and Urban Development. Help for local communities would focus on "capacity building and technical assistance" recognizing the highly regionalized nature of the state's economy.

Local Economic Development Opportunity, or LEDO, grants quickly became a strong focus of the O'Bannon team, along with Community Development Block Grants that eventually became part of the "Community Focus Fund." Although O'Bannon did award a $16,500 grant to the Corydon Chamber of Commerce during his first few weeks in office to support the community's successful "Main Street Program," locals back in O'Bannon's hometown of Corydon remember that he refused to play favorites with Harrison County. Darryl Voelker, head of the Harrison County Economic Development Commission, recalls O'Bannon winced at the idea of calling a good prospect for new jobs for Harrison County once he learned officials there were competing for the jobs against two other Indiana communities. He did finally relent and make a call after a Harrison County firm announced it would leave the state, taking several jobs with it. "He was not up for helping one Indiana community compete against another, but he was always very, very helpful in all other ways," Voelker said.[21]

As the state's second highest ranking official, O'Bannon remained remarkably accessible. On two separate calls Voelker recalls making to O'Bannon's statehouse office, O'Bannon himself answered the phone announcing, "Lieutenant Governor O'Bannon's Office," when his secretary, Lois Stewart, was out to lunch.[22]

O'Bannon maintained his simple style as the state's second most powerful leader, becoming known for going to others' offices for meetings, rather than summoning others to his third-floor office. One of those he called on was State Treasurer Marge O'Laughlin, a prominent Republican.

"I remember after he was elected lieutenant governor…I ended up dealing with him directly quite a bit," O'Laughlin said. "Frank called and asked if he could come by my office. I had been head of the Indiana Housing Finance Authority, but that had been Governor Orr's decision, and Governor Bayh wanted to replace me with Frank. Frank came down to my office and asked me if I would stay on as vice chairman and work with him…His style was so endearing, there was no 'Mr. Imperius' and being summoned up to his office."[23]

O'Laughlin said O'Bannon's approach won her over easily. "We were allies on that board, there is no question about that," she said. "I worked with him, not against him…I don't ever remember a time when…any partisan politics that got in the way of the relationship that he and I had."[24]

Bayh also asked O'Bannon to represent him often on the three-member State Board of Finance, consisting of the governor, auditor, and treasurer, leaving him outnumbered by Republicans O'Laughlin and State Auditor Ann G. DeVore.

Not surprisingly, O'Bannon's love of Indiana and its history meant that he gravitated a lot toward the tourism and rural development issues in his LG job description and quickly focused on the value of promoting the state's little known or hidden historic treasures as a means of opening up small, rural communities for potential tourism. As a result, he went on frequent tours around the state, often with Judy, to visit and promote the smaller communities and their assets, like Bradstreet Sluggers Baseball Bat Factory in Jeffersonville, Indiana, makers of the famous "Louisville Sluggers" baseball bats.

"Tourism is about a $4.4 billion interest in the state of Indiana and what we are emphasizing in tourism celebration are some of the more out-of-the-way places, not just the bigger attractions," O'Bannon said.[25]

New recalls one trip Lt. Governor O'Bannon took in 1992 with him and fellow LG staff member Greg Porter (who was later elected to a seat in the Indiana House of Representatives) to a farm in southwest Indiana where film director Penny Marshall was filming a scene for her film *A League of Their Own*, involving actors Tom Hanks and Geena Davis. Davis's character was milking a cow as Hanks tried to talk her into joining his all-female baseball team.

"The original cow used in that scene was very, very pregnant," New said. "But the cast and crew, being from Los Angeles, did not realize this. Lt. Governor O'Bannon was quick to point out the cow's condition, but the director, Penny Marshall, did not seem too concerned. The lieutenant governor persisted and warned them that it looked like the cow could give birth at any moment, but they went ahead with the shoot."

New said O'Bannon left the set frustrated but not before "we heard this most ungodly sound coming from the barn, and it seemed like all hell was breaking loose as the cow began to give birth. Frank just looked at Greg and me and said, 'Dammit, I told them!'"[26]

O'Bannon was also interested in foreign trade and its potentially positive impact on the state's economy. He told Hoosiers they were involved in a global economy and must "be competitive with our products in a worldwide market." Furthermore, he noted the opening of markets in Eastern Europe and more markets in Japan and Western Europe.[27]

LIVING ON THE OLD NORTH SIDE

Once elected, Frank and Judy O'Bannon searched for a new home in Indianapolis, settling on an unusual giant Queen Anne Victorian home in the shadow of Interstates 65 and 70, deep in what was then cautiously referred to as "a neighborhood in transition."

According to Judy O'Bannon, they both liked older buildings and wanted to be downtown near the statehouse. As an added bonus, the house was around the corner from the Central Avenue United Methodist Church, a struggling yet historic downtown congregation that welcomed the arrival of the O'Bannons and other new families into the neighborhood. The house itself was adjacent to a three-story walk-up apartment building that had long ago been transitioned into low-income housing, with most of the residents' rent being paid by Section 8 from the U.S. Department of Housing and Urban Development (HUD).

The O'Bannons' new neighborhood proved quite a learning experience. "We found out so much about ourselves, about living amongst different people, about expectations of other people, and what brought opportunities to everybody and what maybe didn't," Judy said. "We learned that we could have fun and laugh with folks we might have thought we had nothing in common with."[28]

Frank described the experience this way, "We have seen the commonality of the human experience. The kids in that neighborhood want the same things the kids in Corydon want."[29]

The O'Bannons would, before it was all said and done, become deeply involved in the lives of the families living in the low-income housing. Judy advocated on their behalf and attempted to lead the residents to advocate for themselves for better living conditions. She made late-night phone calls to the owners of the building making sure they knew that the families were struggling in the oppressive summer heat with no air conditioning.

Frank and Judy also reached out to Susan Williams, the Indianapolis city councilor who represented the historic Old North Side, a neighborhood consisting of an interesting mix of some of the city's most expensive homes and some of the city's most dilapidated.

The interest the O'Bannons expressed in the housing mess over their backyard fence was not just about increasing the value of their property or improving the looks of their neighborhood. Williams describes Frank as an atypical politician with "a deep humanitarian spirit." She says, "He just did not think that people should have to live that way." O'Bannon was "deeply offended" that a Florida landlord made a large profit while his tenants lived in deplorable conditions in Indiana.[30]

Williams planned out strategies with Judy over the O'Bannon kitchen table and in between helped Judy and Central Avenue UMC members with gift baskets for the holidays, which eventually grew into the annual SantaLand event the O'Bannons hosted for years for low-income Indianapolis families. "Judy got her hair cut over there at the apartment house, so she was very comfortable, and she knew a lot of those folks," Williams said.[31]

In subsequent years as governor, O'Bannon backed efforts by State Representatives John Day of Indianapolis and Brian Hasler of Evansville to assist renters in getting back deposits paid on apartments, a warranty provision for the working and livable conditions of rental property, and the right of renters to keep their personal property that some landlords seized in situations where rent had fallen behind.

Frank grew so frustrated with the condition of the apartments and the continued negligence of the landowner and HUD that he snapped photographs documenting what he saw in the buildings and then sent them anonymously to WISH-TV, Channel 8 and their "I-Team Investigators" for an important series of reports on housing struggles for low-income Hoosiers.

Frank O'Bannon kept another secret. Judy still fights back tears as she recalls the night Frank comforted a small boy on their porch who came over and said, "My mom is in there crying because somebody beat her up."

"Here you have the lieutenant governor of Indiana, out in the street with this family, in the middle of the night, with the police cars and ambulances all around, and he's trying to comfort this boy, just like any good neighbor would do," Judy said.[32]

A TRIP TO RUSSIA

In July 1990, O'Bannon led a delegation of thirty-four Indiana business, community, education, and agricultural leaders to Russia, Ukraine, and Poland just after the fall of the Berlin Wall. A videotape sent back to Indiana from the trip showed Lt. Governor O'Bannon and then South Bend Mayor Joe Kernan strolling through Red Square in Moscow and observing the changing of the guard at Lenin's Tomb.

O'Bannon said the goal of the trip was fact-finding and making long-lasting professional business contacts. "The most important thing is that we have already made some very direct contacts here with folks who will represent Indiana in an ambassador-style function, who have familiarity with our state, and have already visited us," O'Bannon said. Many of those contacts were scheduled for subsequent visits to Indiana as well.[33]

O'Bannon met with two members of the Supreme Soviet inside the Kremlin and found the business leaders he met enthusiastic and eager to learn more about how to operate in the shifting Soviet economy that was just beginning, under the leadership of Soviet Premier Mikhail Gorbachev (b. 1931), to embrace a market economy.

"The people feel open to speak candidly about the strengths and weaknesses they find, and the challenges and interests that they have going forward," O'Bannon said. "This was just not that evident in the past several years..."

One of the Soviet officials drove five hundred miles to meet with delegation members, and the Indiana delegation members were the first foreign individuals many of the business people had ever met. "We find they are very hungry to learn...how our decentralized system of democracy works in our country," O'Bannon said. "If you look at the great task they have in front of them, of reforming their government, and to reform their whole economic system, they have a lot of work ahead. They look at it with great enthusiasm and hopefully we can help them be successful."[34]

Kernan, who was spending his first extended period of time with O'Bannon, was especially pleased to meet the four members of the newly formed "Notre Dame Club of Moscow," alumni from the university based in his hometown of South Bend.

Managing the Partnership

Leading state government is heady, intense business and often attracts driven, aggressive, and doggedly earnest individuals who truly want to make a difference. The Bayh-O'Bannon team was no different than any others who have worked to make the governor-lieutenant governor relationship work. There is no question Evan Bayh and Frank O'Bannon enjoyed a close personal friendship and working relationship. Frank O'Bannon refused to ever express any unhappiness or frustration in his eight years as lieutenant governor, so it is hard to gauge if he ever actually felt many of those feelings. What those around him do know is that he was determined to support Bayh's choices as governor. He was firmly and totally loyal to Governor Bayh.

Tensions would, however, occasionally arise between members of the Bayh and O'Bannon staffs.

John Goss summed it up this way, "It was tense and difficult at times. Frank was a gentleman and a statesman. He made that relationship work. That meant being quiet when he might have had another opinion. It meant letting the governor take the lead on some of the announcements...It was okay with Frank in his own mind. I think the rest of our team was more upset about it than he was..."[35]

Bayh acknowledges some of those staff tensions existed but said that he and O'Bannon remained close. "I think there are inevitably some jealousies or challenges that come up between the two staffs. But, look, if there was ever any sort of problem at all, Frank and I would sit down and talk about them and work that out. I just had a tremendous amount of respect for him, and I hope he felt the same way."[36]

Conflicts between staff members intensified when Bayh sought a more active role in making economic development announcements. Frank O'Bannon understood, even if some of his staff didn't, that it was only natural given that Bayh was the boss, and he would lead the ticket for the Democrat's reelection campaign in 1992.

Judy O'Bannon said Frank kept one goal in mind: How could his work help Evan Bayh be a successful governor? "When he would talk to other lieutenant governors around the country, he would quickly realize that he had much more of an opportunity to participate than some of them had," Judy said. "When Governor Bayh wanted to make some shifts in how the Department of Commerce was handled, he did that in a positive way. They worked together; there was no shutting each other out, no speaking ill of each other. They just worked it out. I know Frank thought he had been treated right."[37]

Bayh was extremely pleased with the role O'Bannon played in his administration. "Frank was exemplary," Bayh said. "Obviously he worked well with state legislators because that was where he had spent his career in public service. Administering the Departments of Workforce Development, Commerce, Tourism, and Agriculture, in all the things he did, he was a tremendous goodwill ambassador around the state. Frank was just a very steady individual and a very good partner."[38]

PRESIDING OVER THE SENATE

With his election as lieutenant governor, Frank O'Bannon assumed a new role in an old setting. As lieutenant governor, he would serve as president of the senate. The role of senate president had been somewhat diminished. Principally, the lieutenant governor retained the constitutionally granted authority to preside and cast tie-breaking votes, but little else.

The reduction of power did not mean O'Bannon's eight years in the seat at the front of the room came without some fireworks. The first memorable moment occurred when "beer baron" legislation was revived that would allow wholesale beer distributors in the state to form special districts or areas for distribution, requiring retailers to purchase beer from their area distributor, rather than any vendor they wished. As a senator, O'Bannon had backed the bill. Opponents argued the bill would create monopolies for a few small beer distributors.

Under Governors Bowen and Orr, the legislation had languished, but under Governor Bayh, supporters (particularly Democrats) thought there was a possibility of new life. Governor Bayh initially supported the idea of special territories or districts for beer distribution but decided late in the process to oppose the legislation. Bayh sent his legislative director, Ann DeLaney, to inform Lt. Governor O'Bannon that the governor would like him to vote against the bill if it ended in a tie in the senate.

"Frank said, 'I can't do that. I'm not voting against this bill. I have given my word to these folks. I have to vote for this,'" said Jim Maguire, who served in the 1989 session as senate parliamentarian. "Well, the tie vote came down, and Frank did vote yes on it, knowing that the governor said he would veto it."[39]

Despite O'Bannon's vote in favor of the bill, Bayh later vetoed it, placing the lieutenant governor in an awkward position.

O'Bannon also broke a tie that has continued to offer long-term benefits to the state. He voted in favor of a bill that would expand the FedEx hub at the Indianapolis airport against opposition from UPS.[40]

THE VOTING BOARD STANDOFF

Late in June, on the eighth day of a contentious Special Session in 1993, O'Bannon presided over the threatened shutdown of state government if a budget deal was not brokered by June 30. Governor Bayh had proposed an increase in the state's cigarette tax to make his budget plan work—Republicans opposed the plan.

As the senate finally took up the measure, the voting board showed twenty-eight, mostly Republican, votes as "no" and twenty-one, mostly Democrat, votes as "yes." Normally, that would be that. But O'Bannon surprised everyone in the room and in the statehouse when he immediately called a recess and refused to shut down the voting board and record the vote.

O'Bannon felt the rather dramatic action might prompt renewed talks.[41] He decided he had "to be prepared to stay here until in the morning."[42]

Garton was stunned. "It was unbelievable...I was shocked, absolutely shocked, because he and I always talked...If he was going to take us on or vote against us, he would tell me what he was going to do..." Garton approached Frank when he saw he intended to keep the machine open and told him they had to talk. Frank responded, "'No, I am not leaving this podium, and I am not leaving this machine.'"[43]

Reporters covering the proceedings were just as stunned; O'Bannon's move became the lead story on TV and in newspapers across the state for the next forty hours. Reporter John Ketzenberger said, "I think people were surprised that anyone would do that at all and surprised that Frank O'Bannon was the one orchestrating it."[44]

O'Bannon vowed to keep the machine open all night, and Garton faced growing pressure from members of his caucus to do something. Some assumed O'Bannon, eventually facing the need to use the restroom, would have to release control of the board and allow the defeat of Bayh's proposal to be recorded. O'Bannon vowed to stay put, however, even receiving visitors on the rostrum, including his wife and Democratic House Speaker Mike Phillips.

As the standoff wore on with O'Bannon refusing to budge, reporters and senate members took to impromptu games of euchre.

"I remember that at some point in the evening, everyone agreed to call it quits and the state police were posted, and the next morning, things continued...," reporter Kevin Corcoran recalls. "...No one expected Frank O'Bannon to do something like that...It was as risky as moves go, but it was not something that hurt him at all. (People learned that) Frank O'Bannon would do something that you would not expect."[45]

Almost forty hours into the standoff, however, it was clear O'Bannon was not going to succeed in changing any votes.

Republicans had tired of the effort and used some maneuvering of their own to regain control. Garton said Senator Joe Harrison of Attica reminded him the senate conducted its business using *Mason's Manual for Parliamentary Procedures*. "In *Mason's Manual*, if the presiding officer frustrates the body, it can take charge of itself," Garton said.[47]

"I remember that before the session started, we were all still milling around, and I went up to the state troopers and I said to them, 'You have no authority to arrest anyone in this chamber. This is an independent branch of government,'" Garton said. "They looked at me with the strangest look because they didn't know what was going to happen next. And it was tense, it really was."

What followed were two quick speeches from the floor of the senate, including one by Garton where he ordered the machine closed and the vote recorded. "I could hear Frank behind me saying, 'We're still in recess! We're still in recess!' I couldn't turn around, and I kept asking, 'What is the vote?'" Garton said.[48]

The vote was the same as it had been forty hours before—Bayh's plan was defeated 28-21.

Mike Smith recalls, "…There was this big question about who was really in charge of the podium. The kid, this clerk (who operated the voting board), looks around, and he really didn't know what to do. Garton looked at him with this look I will never forget and said, 'Close the voting board.' And this kid just closed the board right away."[49]

The tax increase defeated, Republicans later would gloat that they "saved Governor Bayh from himself" as the cigarette tax increase was not passed—allowing Bayh to later remind voters often that there had been no general tax increases in the eight years he served as governor. The final budget, passed days later, included a new provision for riverboat gambling as a means of adding new revenue to the state budget—a threshold some Republicans had vowed they'd never cross over. Perhaps the showdown had worn some of them down or perhaps the prospect of an unprecedented shutdown of state government spurred some to compromise. Whatever the reason, O'Bannon knew the fight had been contentious. "…It was getting very, very difficult to even talk rationally, and I think you have seen some statements made in the last couple of days that were not rational," O'Bannon said.[50]

Mary Dieter wrote in her *Louisville Courier-Journal* column, "On its face, the tactic didn't work. Despite persistent rumors that some Republicans were close to switching their votes, none did so before O'Bannon—unwilling to take a political ploy so far that a young clerk would have to be arrested—called the whole thing off. But the scheme did succeed in doing something perhaps more important. It brought Republicans back to the table so that real negotiating—toward a compromise between the parties, not a take-it-or-leave-it proposition—could proceed."[51]

Dieter added, "…of all the politicians in Indiana, only O'Bannon could have pulled off what he did. And not just because he was in the official position to do so: his reputation for honesty and trustworthiness, as well as his long experience in the senate, enabled him to be a catalyst for compromise."[52]

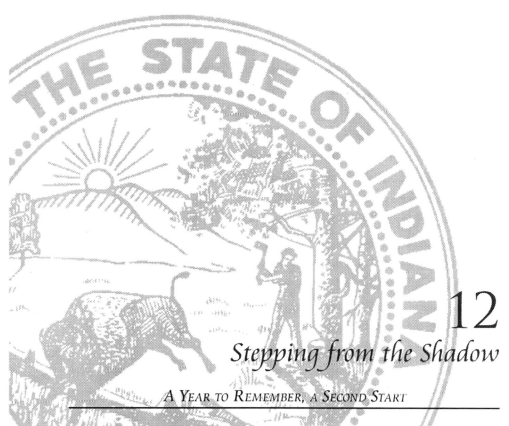

12

Stepping from the Shadow

On January 30, 1996, Frank and Judy O'Bannon went home to Corydon to celebrate Frank's sixty-sixth birthday—and to try for a second time what they had done once before in 1987. This time, however, Frank O'Bannon made the announcement that he was running for governor with the benefit of almost eight years in the state's second highest office and more importantly, a clear path to the Democratic nomination. O'Bannon asked those gathered inside the Harrison County Courthouse that day to see how the strong foundation of the O'Bannon's barn, added with modern essentials, including "smart wire" for the Gateway 2000 multi-media computer O'Bannon loved, symbolized Indiana's crossroads at the close of the twentieth century.

He declared, "I'll be able to sit in the rustic woods of Harrison County with our grandkids on my lap and surf the Internet—visiting new places and new ideas and old truths. Our barn is a symbol, not only of the foundations we've built in the past, but also of our capacity for change and our focus on the future. We have, as a state, built a strong foundation. We built it with the values of hard work and common sense, and with the drive to innovate and find better ways of doing things." That said, O'Bannon added, "With a thankful heart and a deep commitment to the people of Indiana, I declare that I am a candidate for governor of Indiana!"[1]

The slight shake and quiver in his voice that reporters had noticed when he said those words all those years ago in 1987 was gone. This was a new, more confident Frank O'Bannon who was about to begin one of the best years of his life.

O'Bannon's announcement speech emphasized themes that would come back again and again during his years in public life: improving public schools, creating well-paying and sustainable jobs, building first-class highways and transportation systems, keeping communities safe from crime, and a common sense approach to state government that emphasized progress over partisanship.

His speech relied most heavily, however, on citing the accomplishments of the Bayh-O'Bannon administration, a move that reflected a shrewder political wisdom than most people ever gave him credit for. Frank O'Bannon's 1996 campaign message was that voters would know what to expect from O'Bannon as governor, and that was the same leadership they saw with the Bayh-O'Bannon administration. Former secretary of state Joe Hogsett said the O'Bannon campaign "very shrewdly juxtaposed the conventional wisdom about the two major political parties. Republicans in Indiana had typically been successful by running on very conservative platforms, conservative in the sense that, 'We like things the way they are now, and we'll keep things mostly the way they are now…' Democratic candidates traditionally presented themselves as reformers, these progressive candidates who were going to come in and change government and make it more vital. Valid or not, that was the conventional wisdom…I think what you saw in 1996, in effect, was the Democratic nominee for governor saying, 'The way things are now is pretty good, and if I'm elected governor, I'd keep things the way they are now and in the direction we've been going for the last eight years.'"[2]

O'Bannon's calculus was right. Republican nominee-to-be Stephen Goldsmith, only weeks removed from his 1995 campaign to win a second term as mayor of Indianapolis, approached the race with "new ideas" about privatization, playing well into O'Bannon's calm, stay-the-course strategy and message.

From Corydon, the O'Bannon team headed by airplane for a noon rally in the Statehouse Rotunda with Governor Bayh in Indianapolis. To the shouts of "eight more years!" O'Bannon asked Indianapolis Democrats to "...stand with me. We'll make Indiana first in the nation in top-notch schools, first in high-paying jobs, and first in communities safe from crime. Stand with me, and we'll make a better future for every family in Indiana."[3]

He started the campaign with $2.3 million in the campaign bank account—normally a respectable amount, but this campaign would set records for spending exceeding $18 million by both campaigns.

A CHALLENGE AVOIDED

While the path to the Democratic nomination for governor was officially clear for Frank O'Bannon in 1996, he narrowly avoided what he would have hated most: a primary battle. As the Bayh administration was entering its final years, most Democrats assumed Lt. Governor O'Bannon would seek to succeed the popular two-term Evan Bayh. Few knew that the O'Bannons themselves had to decide if they wanted to go forward with the 1996 race.

"When he was first elected lieutenant governor, people would say to him, 'You would have made a fine governor,' or 'You can run next time,' and I was thinking no way!" Judy said. "I thought Frank would be too old after that, and he would probably want to retire by then."[4] She says Frank did not spend his days as lieutenant governor sitting around thinking about running for governor. People urged him to run, and he thought it was important to make up his mind quickly.

One of the many who encouraged O'Bannon to run was his former senate colleague, Louis Mahern of Indianapolis, the last Democrat to mount a serious challenge to Goldsmith. Mahern's 1991 campaign for mayor had raised a record amount of money for a Democrat in Indianapolis—only to be dwarfed by what the ambitious Goldsmith raised among Republican donors. Mahern advised O'Bannon to commit himself entirely to the race and begin a physical exercising regimen that would not only make him physically stronger as he campaigned across ninety-two counties but also give his mind needed energy and respite during the darkest days of a grueling campaign.

One person who thought O'Bannon's deliberation of whether or not to be a candidate in 1996 was going too slowly was Baron Hill (b. 1953), at that time a former member of the Indiana House from Seymour, Indiana, who came within a whisker of defeating Republican Dan Coats (b. 1943) in a special 1990 election for the U.S. Senate seat vacated by Dan Quayle when he became vice president of the United States.

"I went and told Frank I was thinking about running (for governor in 1996), and I think he was pretty much stunned," Hill said. "I didn't think, at the time, that Frank was doing what needed to be done in order to be elected…So I flirted with the idea for awhile."[5]

Hill soon backed off. "Frank actually picked up the ball and began to run with it. He really got with it. When I saw that happen, I thought I wasn't the man who could do it," Hill said.[6]

Governor Bayh's support was never in doubt—he backed O'Bannon.

O'BANNON THE CANDIDATE

Frank O'Bannon knew something important going into the 1996 race for governor: He knew himself. He understood his strengths and his weaknesses. He knew where he needed to grow and change. He knew campaigns took an incredible amount of money in order to be successful. And he knew, as difficult as it would be, he would have to reach beyond the loyal cast of family, friends, and supporters who had helped him get this far. He knew his 1996 campaign had to be so much more than he ever had imagined when he ran for governor the first time in 1987-88.

"He thought it was a privilege not only to be elected, but it was a privilege to seek elective office, to be a candidate," said longtime campaign and political adviser David Johnson. "Once he had stepped forward to ask people for their vote, and often for their money, he felt you had a strong obligation to be the very best candidate you can be. That included understanding what your limitations were and getting people to help supplement for that."[7]

O'Bannon and campaign manager Tom New decided early on that he would hire outside consultants. New and Johnson recommended O'Bannon consider only firms that had helped Democratic candidates win in 1994, a disastrous year for Democrats across the country as Republicans regained control of the U.S. Congress for the first time in four decades. "He went with people who had a track record of winning races in states like Indiana. Those were the people he wanted to work with. That is not a small point. Candidates often go with their hearts or with people they know already and like and trust," Johnson said.[8]

The campaign hires included Washington, D.C. experts, pollsters Fred Yang and Geoff Garin and media consultant Frank Greer. Rachel Gorlin also came on board from Washington, D.C. to serve as the campaign spokeswoman. O'Bannon aide Bill Schreiber contacted Yang and Garin because he believed their work in helping Florida Governor Lawton Chiles (1930-1998) win reelection in 1994—a rare Democratic victory that year—could be translated to Indiana.

Gorlin had never worked on a political campaign in Indiana before and wasn't particularly interested in doing so in 1996 either. She agreed to meet O'Bannon, however, on one of his trips to Washington, D.C. "There was something about him that I liked. He just seemed like someone who would be worth making the effort to try and help get elected," she said. She quickly saw his ability to connect with people. "That's something someone just has, or they don't, there's no training for it," Gorlin said. "His style was folksy, but he was actually a sophisticated person and political thinker."[9]

Garin said he liked what he saw from the start with O'Bannon. "Frank seemed like a nice, very easygoing person," he said. "He was very smart, very careful about things. So we knew that we had a very skilled, substantive, and able candidate to work for."[10]

The stakes were high—and outside consultants coming in to help were taking a chance. Every poll had O'Bannon trailing badly, as the *Cook Political Report* summed up the upcoming 1996 race in Indiana: "The race to replace popular but term-limited Governor Evan Bayh *could* develop into a real barn-burner, or if the national political field tilts sharply in the Republicans' favor again, a walk for the GOP (in Indiana). Indiana today is marginal for Democrats, and the ceiling for them in a statewide race here is fairly low—they probably could hope to pull off a single-digit victory at best."[11]

The pundits had reason to doubt O'Bannon at the start. Yang and Garin did their first "name ID" poll for O'Bannon in November 1995 just as municipal elections wrapped up across the state (and as Goldsmith skated to a second term in an easy win over Democratic nominee Z. Mae Jimison). The poll was conducted by telephone among 805 registered voters in Indiana—and the results were not promising. At first pass, Goldsmith led O'Bannon 48 to 32 percent.[12]

PACKAGING FRANK O'BANNON

The entire crew knew they were starting from behind, but all felt confident that if voters only *knew* O'Bannon better, they'd like him.

Garin said, "The conventional wisdom was that Steve Goldsmith was going to get elected governor and that Frank O'Bannon somehow was not going to be able to fill Evan Bayh's shoes. But we always had a lot of confidence from the time that we did the first poll for Frank. He had a very powerful story to tell as a candidate, a powerful case to make as a candidate, and…people reacted to him very well personally when they saw him or heard him."[13]

Media consultant Greer began planning immediately for ads that would introduce Frank O'Bannon to Indiana voters. Doing so meant heading south—to Corydon to direct the taping of the first O'Bannon campaign ad. While cameras rolled, O'Bannon talked to pressroom employees at the *Democrat* as that week's edition rolled off the press and joked with others in the front office. On the sidewalk outside the office, Greer taped O'Bannon talking and joking with longtime newspaper employees and friends Ruby Rooskby and Eunice Wiseman and resident Cecil Fravel. Harrison County Sheriff Clyde Sailor and others showed up to create close-up shots of O'Bannon talking with police officers. Harrison County Council Attorney Gordon Ingle and his wife, Darla, came by with their then three-month-old daughter, Anna, for the requisite "baby shot" with O'Bannon.[14]

Frank O'Bannon, in spite of serving as lieutenant governor and a state senator, needed to get his story out to the public, Greer believed. Furthermore, people perceived Indiana to be a "fairly conservative" Republican state, and Frank "had been in the shadow of Evan Bayh." So they set out to develop his identity and appeal to a more bipartisan base. They also worked to portray his personality, "his sort of down-to-earth, common-sense Hoosier style…These were going to be his great strengths…He really did tap into what I think Hoosiers ultimately think of themselves. But he wasn't flashy," Greer said.[15]

In addition, O'Bannon's uncontested Democratic primary was a huge advantage. Greer suspected the two Republican candidates for governor, Goldsmith and former state GOP chairman Rex Early, would likely "go negative" on one another. "We decided to do 'early media' that year. The theory was that while those two were being very negative, we could be very positive," he said. "The first spot we ran was about his history, his grandchildren, and it had everything from putting together that barn, running a family newspaper, and coming out of a small-town culture and having traditional Hoosier values. It had all of that."[16]

New and Johnson, having known O'Bannon for longer, were uncertain how well O'Bannon would do on TV, a key component of any modern statewide campaign. Greer was insistent that O'Bannon speak directly to voters in at least one of his ads. As lieutenant governor, however, O'Bannon had never spoken directly to voters in any of the

Bayh ads, and all the campaign had to go with was O'Bannon's speaking style before larger audiences. Given the challenge O'Bannon sometimes faced as a public speaker, there was cause for concern. One report at the time still described him as "a tortured public speaker." Time spent worrying about that, however, was unnecessary.

"None of us had ever really seen him on TV before, and television is a very intense medium, and we just weren't sure," Johnson said.[17]

It was O'Bannon himself who insisted on making his first ad for the fall campaign in which he spoke directly to the camera.

Despite miles of video shot of Frank and Judy O'Bannon at home in Corydon collected for introductory or biographical ads, it was Goldsmith's tax proposal that prompted O'Bannon to want to speak directly to voters. And he did. The result was more than anyone expected.

"For some reason…there was something about looking into that camera that was easier for him," Johnson said. "He acted like he was just talking to a person, one on one. He was warm and comfortable, and he had that twinkle in his eye that Joe Kernan talks about. He was devastatingly good."[18]

Johnson thought the TV ads worked so well because they portrayed the real Frank O'Bannon. "The thing is, there are some people who are incredible, have tremendous skill, but that just does not come through on television. With Frank O'Bannon, however, the TV camera lens captured him very, very well, and I think it was a combination of skill and discipline and some extraordinarily good Frank O'Bannon luck."[19]

The spring ads helped O'Bannon—as Goldsmith and Early traded barbs and O'Bannon took the high road. But they also helped Goldsmith. A May 1996 poll just as primary season wrapped up found O'Bannon's numbers up seven points, to 39 percent. But Goldsmith was also up slightly and remained in the lead in a head-to-head match-up, 50-39. In none of O'Bannon's ads did he identify himself as the Democratic candidate, but he began to strongly make the case that he was the natural successor to the popular term-limited Governor Bayh.[20]

One of the most memorable ads of the campaign, based on feedback and polling response, featured not Frank O'Bannon but Judy O'Bannon. Seated on the porch swing of Bobby Small's Lockerbie Square home in Indianapolis, Judy spoke directly to the camera about her husband, their forty-plus years of marriage, and her conviction that "growing up in a small town, helping run the family business, gave (Frank) those common-sense Hoosier values…Frank is a good, a wise, and a kind man, and I know he'll be a great governor."[21]

It was classic Judy O'Bannon, and it worked—well. Many Hoosiers were seeing Judy for the first time, but it was clear they liked what they saw.

Governor Evan Bayh also cut an ad for O'Bannon from inside his statehouse office (a practice that would be disallowed in future campaigns). The ad ran in the final weeks of the campaign, with Bayh saying, "I know Frank O'Bannon very well, because I have worked side by side with him for eight years. Together, we have made a lot of changes in Indiana…I know we can trust Frank O'Bannon to keep Indiana moving forward. He's hard working, he's honest, and he cares about the people of our state. Frank O'Bannon will be a great governor."[22]

In another ad, Frank O'Bannon again appeared on Small's front porch with his shirt sleeves rolled up and said to the camera, "You see this? It's a property tax bill for a Hoosier family, and if you ask me, it's too high!" It was an optimistic ad, typically filled with promises of what he would do as governor, and before his time was through, O'Bannon would fulfill all of the promises he made that afternoon on those front steps.[23]

ENGAGEMENT

Goldsmith officially opened his fall campaign ads just before Labor Day on a negative note, firing away on O'Bannon for allegedly voting to raise taxes thirty-eight times while a member of the state senate. O'Bannon fired back with an ad that declared "under Goldsmith as mayor, taxes and fees have gone up. He increased spending by a billion dollars and forced the city deeper in debt. Steve Goldsmith. Negative ads. Not telling the truth. How can we trust him to be governor?"[24]

Goldsmith's move was unusual since perception and polling indicated he had the lead. The O'Bannon and Goldsmith campaigns were beginning to see that the conventional wisdom that Goldsmith would be swept into office as Indiana returned to its more natural Republican roots was not holding true. A July 1996 O'Bannon poll showed the beginnings of the shift. That poll, again of more than 800 Indiana voters and tilted slightly toward more Republican voters than Democrats or Independents, found Goldsmith's edge trimmed to 46-38. By September, Goldsmith's slow but steady slide continued—that poll found Goldsmith leading by a 44-40 count, a lead matching the poll's margin of error. Public polls at Labor Day showed a similar result—the race was fully engaged, and O'Bannon was a contender.[25]

O'Bannon did not leave Goldsmith's attack ads with no reply; he fired back as "comparison" ads flew back and forth between the two at a record pace. O'Bannon's response TV ad, titled "Real," featured black and white photos of Goldsmith floating over headlines of newspaper editorials criticizing the negative tone of the GOP campaign. The language of the O'Bannon ad was tough and removed, perhaps for all time, any doubt that Frank O'Bannon could get tough. He called Steve Goldsmith "desperate" for resorting to "false, negative attacks," and maintained that his record as lieutenant governor included tax cuts and a balanced budget while criticizing Goldsmith's record as mayor with increased spending, taxes, and debt. Finally, he added, "The truth is that under Goldsmith as mayor, taxes and fees have gone up. He increased spending by a billion dollars and forced the city deeper in debt."[26]

O'Bannon's response ad ran statewide—while Goldsmith's original "attack" ad ran only in Indianapolis and, interestingly, in Chicago (reflecting a failed GOP strategy to cut into Democratic strongholds in northwest Indiana). "We immediately produced a response ad that indicated Goldsmith was lying about Frank O'Bannon's record," Yang said. "We put that ad up everywhere in Indiana. So here is the situation, if you are a person in Evansville or Fort Wayne, you are seeing an ad that says Steve Goldsmith is lying about Frank O'Bannon's record, and our version that demonstrates O'Bannon's real record as a fiscal conservative."[27]

The immediately negative tone of the race was difficult for the O'Bannon family and loved ones to watch. It was the first time Frank O'Bannon had ever been directly challenged in such a pointed manner for any office he had ever sought. For the Southern Indiana politician known as "the gentleman from Corydon," Frank O'Bannon began to prove doubters wrong and demonstrate he had the stuff to give as good as he was getting.

Jennifer O'Bannon said watching the television ads about her father would sometimes be difficult, especially because as the campaign wore on, they seemed to be on the air constantly. "The ads are horrifying to experience, but if you are an educated, or informed person, you realize that this is just part of the game. But they can get your ire up, that's for sure…I was afraid it was just going to be difficult to win if people base their votes only on ads on TV."[28]

"Dad would always say that if you don't want people to say bad things about you, then sit at home and do nothing. No matter what you try and do in this world, someone is going to try and take offense or criticize you on it," Jonathan O'Bannon recalls.[29]

O'Bannon addressed the negative tone of the ads himself in one TV ad where he spoke directly to the camera and said, "If even half of what Steve Goldsmith says about me in his negative ads were true, I'd have to stop my grandkids from watching TV. But I think most Hoosiers see through the misleading attacks, and to me, this election is not about politics as usual, it's about how we keep Indiana moving forward," he said.[30]

TAXES FALL FLAT

The Goldsmith campaign ads on O'Bannon's tax votes in the state senate were part of a poorly conceived approach. Goldsmith's claim that Frank O'Bannon had voted for thirty-eight tax increases during his tenure in the state senate quickly fell flat. The problem was, some of the "tax increases" were actually enabling legislation for local option taxes, or increased fees. The actual votes to raise any taxes had been done at the local level, not in the senate. One of Goldsmith's ads said, in part, "O'Bannon voted to raise your taxes at least thirty-eight times, higher taxes on everything from gasoline to food, from cars and boats to haircuts. Frank O'Bannon never met a tax he didn't hike."[31]

At the same time he was calling O'Bannon's votes, even for fee increases, "tax increases," Goldsmith said his own fee increases as mayor were just that, fee increases, nothing more.

It was a charge the O'Bannon campaign expected from Goldsmith, and they responded immediately, following the "rapid response" model perfected by the Clinton-Gore campaign in 1992. O'Bannon's campaign benefited from many young, energetic staffers, including Steve Bella, who worked on gathering the information used to fire back at Goldsmith; Kevin Waltman, who woke up early every morning and faxed out news releases and called radio stations one by one, offering tapes of O'Bannon's remarks for morning "drive time" news programs; and Jeff Coyne, who drove O'Bannon wherever he needed to go across the state.

"Firing back" included a rare public display of O'Bannon's anger.

"You always remember when the 'nice guy' shows a flash of anger," political columnist Brian Howey said. "Frank O'Bannon had long cultivated good relations with the statehouse press corps, inviting them to his near north side home each summer. In September 1996, those relationships paid off."[32]

Howey said O'Bannon "stood before the microphones, looked into the eyes of the statehouse press corps, and exhorted reporters to confront what he called 'distortions.'"[33]

"Goldsmith went overboard with that tax stuff," Dieter said. "I still remember the press conference—reporters were fairly livid that he was trying to make us think a vote to enable a locality to impose or raise its local option tax was a vote in favor of a tax increase. But he wouldn't characterize his own fee increases as tax increases."[34]

Reporter John Ketzenberger said Goldsmith's claims about O'Bannon's voting record "didn't pass a straight-face test...The reaction was immediate. People were really surprised that they had basically tried to lie on that issue. It was a subtle point...but that they tried to pull that off sent a signal to all of us who were covering this campaign."[35]

Goldsmith admits the approach fell flat and was not helpful, whether it was a difference between actual votes for tax increases or authorizing legislation. "...There are plenty of theories, but in conclusion, it just didn't do much good," he said.[36]

The damage was done, and with the O'Bannon campaign loudly crying foul, Goldsmith pulled the ad that included the line, "Frank O'Bannon even voted to increase taxes on hot dogs! Hot dogs!"[37]

Jim Shella of WISH-TV was surprised by the withdrawal of the ad. "What struck me was, if you're Goldsmith and you're going to make that argument, you have got to stick with it. For them to immediately back down and change the spot, that really appeared amateurish."[38]

THE CONFRONTATION

Campaign ads prompted a surprising, impromptu one-on-one debate between Frank O'Bannon and Steve Goldsmith in the closing days of the 1996 campaign as the two appeared at an Indianapolis event. It was a classic, unscripted moment that voters and reporters say they long for, and cameras from WISH-TV and WTHR-TV and a WIBC Radio News microphone caught the confrontation on tape.

It started when a reporter asked O'Bannon about Goldsmith's ads as Mayor Goldsmith stood just steps away.

"As soon as he pulls his negative ad, I will pull my response ad," O'Bannon said.

Goldsmith stepped up to interrupt. "And will you commit that neither you or anyone speaking for you will..."

Then O'Bannon interrupted, shaking his head, saying, "No, no, I'm not at that point!"

Goldsmith replied, "Well, when you're at that point, call me."

"All right, then you don't want to pull your ads, that's what you're saying. All I want to do is run an ad that is not distorted and follows the Code of Fair Campaign Practices (from the League of Women Voters). If he'll read that, that's what I'll do," O'Bannon said.

It was Goldsmith's turn to shake his head, as he thrust his hand toward O'Bannon. "Just shake my hand and pledge right here and now that there will be no negative ads by you or anyone speaking for you for the rest of the campaign."

O'Bannon responded with disgust and reached out for Goldsmith's hand and said, "I'll tell you what, I *am* going to talk about your record."

Goldsmith said he was comfortable with O'Bannon talking about his record, but called on him to remove any ads featuring "anonymous voice-overs" making "nasty remarks about me."

"There won't be any nasty talk. All of that was started by you in September, and I had to answer it because you were doing it all over the TV," O'Bannon said.

As Goldsmith began to walk away from O'Bannon, he added, "You've got an offer, let me know if you want to accept it."

O'Bannon was not done. He replied after Goldsmith, "Well, you never accepted my first offer (back in May)!"[39]

Some O'Bannon campaign insiders believed Goldsmith's campaign planted the question and their candidate nearby on purpose to try to remove some of the "nice guy" shine off O'Bannon. Whether true or not, the O'Bannon campaign was thrilled. Worried at times that their candidate could be too flat or worse yet, boring, it was one of those classic and wonderful moments when O'Bannon spoke forcefully, clearly, and stood his ground.

In a post-election interview with John Stehr from WTHR-TV, when asked about the confrontation, O'Bannon said, "Once you get into politics, and get into a campaign, one of the guiding principles I have learned is…You can't take it personally. If you do, it's going to kill you. You have to do the best you can in a campaign, with good issues and talking about the future. If you win, you move forward. If you lose, well, you say you did the best you could."[40]

A FOCUSED APPROACH

Focus groups conducted with specifically selected groups of voters were key to planning the ads used in the campaign. Yang and Garin provided the campaign's most accurate polling results, more accurate than any media polls, and certainly more accurate than Republican polls.

O'Bannon's campaign had enough money to also allow Yang to conduct focus groups by showing them advertisements from Goldsmith's campaign and similar ones from O'Bannon's. "Polls are incredibly valuable because you get the numerical values, quantitative values of how you are doing, but focus groups are very valuable because you get people telling you why they feel the way they do, and you just get more qualitative information about how the campaign is progressing," Yang said. "The difference for me is expressed like this, a poll is like a black and white TV and focus groups are color TVs."[41]

In fact, it was through a focus group that the campaign decided to use Judy in an ad as well, Greer said. Hearing a brief comment about the O'Bannons having been married for more than forty years, "everyone in the room...really responded favorably to that," Greer said. So they had Judy do an ad talking about their marriage.[42]

Garin believes, "...If you're painting the tableau of what it was like to be part of this campaign, and Frank O'Bannon's political life, the picture is incomplete without Judy in it."[43]

O'Bannon did not engage in the specifics of polling data, leaving that instead to Tom New and David Johnson to worry about. "...Frank, unlike some of the candidates we work for at times, was a fully formed person and he had been at this for a while. He was not looking to be molded," Garin said. "Part of what was Frank's charm is that what you saw is what you got. He really dealt with the bottom line."[44]

Gorlin felt O'Bannon's sincerity and the degree to which he loved Indiana would help him be elected governor. Voters participating in focus groups were giving similar responses. "Geoff Garin showed the groups Goldsmith's ads that were already on TV because of his primary with Rex Early, and some footage of Frank. It was fascinating to see the participants' dislike of Goldsmith surface as they discussed their reactions to even his bio spot. Even more encouraging, they really warmed to the footage of Frank, although they knew very little about him at the time," she said.[45]

O'Bannon had limits to what he would do, however, to get elected and wasn't afraid to set them. Garin recalls one prominent Democrat with access to O'Bannon during the heat of the '96 campaign who was pushing him to be more aggressive in his approach and be tougher on Goldsmith. "This person was worried that Frank was being too nice and taking the issues too seriously to get elected," Garin said. "He quoted Everett Dickson to Frank by saying, 'Before you can be a statesman, you have to be a politician.' Frank got a good laugh out of that. Frank wanted to be both, and...he thought he could be a good statesman and a good politician...he didn't think he had to trade in the one for the other."[46]

In the end, O'Bannon surprised himself as much as he surprised Goldsmith and the Republicans, particularly with his ability to raise, for its time, a record amount of money for a Democratic candidate for governor. Another surprise was the success he had speaking in his own advertisements.

"...Frank was not a great orator and was not that slick; he wasn't a kind of a modern image of a blow-dried candidate, and a lot of people didn't think he could come across well and communicate well," Johnson said. "I don't think people knew that he could communicate rather well on television and speak to people in their living rooms in a way they would be comfortable with...Frank was coachable, yes, but there was a lot of inherent talent that allowed him to connect with people in a meaningful way..."[47]

RAISING THE MONEY

Consultants advised O'Bannon to start asking for money first among those he knew best. Even though he was lieutenant governor, that did not mean that people would automatically support him, and some of them might not think he could win, so early money from his family and friends was very important.

As part of the process, he also met the expectation that he sit in a campaign office and face down the dreaded process of "cold calling" prospective donors—many people he had never met before—in telephone calls that began with O'Bannon introducing himself to the prospect and ending with him asking for a specific dollar donation, knowing that without that, donors who could give $10,000 might just send $500. Ellen Hurley, Mike Edmondson, Deidre Murphy, and Megan Murphy were assigned campaign staff jobs to help O'Bannon raise the money.

Edmondson said O'Bannon was good at the calling but had to be pushed along to keep at it. The political consultants on board wanted the calls to be quick and successful—a simple proposition: more calls completed meant more possible campaign donations.

"We were hired as basically what they called 'Rolodexers,'" Edmondson said. "What he did, every day, was get on the phone and call people for money. Our job was to identify people he could call for money. He would start off with his personal contacts…we would call these folks, and he would ask them for a contribution, but he would also ask them if I could come by and meet with them and go through their Rolodex and identify other people that they think could help the campaign as well."[48]

Beyond O'Bannon's own personal contacts, call lists were created from donor lists kept by the Indiana Democratic Party, Evan Bayh's list, and various other past Democratic candidates, along with "known anti-Goldsmith" contributors from Rex Early's campaign.

Some of those they called were not regular contributors to political campaigns but were people who believed in and supported

Frank O'Bannon. Others may have needed convincing or would have said no to anyone other than Frank O'Bannon himself. The calls were not easy. Almost all of the calls were considered "cold calls," made to people O'Bannon had never met before but were considered "good leads" for a possible donation. In the end, most of the calls were successful.

"There were some who said they had committed already to Steve Goldsmith, but I cannot recall anyone at all ever being rude to him," Edmondson said. "He wouldn't have held that against anyone anyway. If they told him they weren't going to support him, he was okay with that."[49]

O'Bannon still loathed the process, Edmondson believes. "Anyone who knows Frank O'Bannon knows that is not his style to enjoy getting on the phone and asking people for money," Edmondson said. "...But he realized that it was something he just had to do, he had to raise the money. I mean, at that point, in 1996, we were running against a man who could just raise boatloads of money."[50]

Robin Winston, who joined the 1996 O'Bannon campaign as the county coordinator, believes New's "disciplined approach" to the campaign was a key for O'Bannon. "You had this sixty-six-year-old man coming in there, on time, every day, making those calls knowing that many of those would be rejections, but he got in there day after day and did what he had to do...They underestimated, really, how competitive Frank O'Bannon was."[51]

O'Bannon trusted New and the small circle of advisers around him. "His campaign management style was to follow Tom New's doctrine, and that is a marathon style," Winston said.[52]

Despite his willingness to let campaign advisers, pollsters, and media consultants have a major say in how the campaign progressed, he remained "fiercely independent," Winston believes, and relied most heavily on his own judgment and that of Mrs. O'Bannon, New, Johnson, and Athey. O'Bannon was never interested in campaign events where he'd simply announce an idea or a program that lacked "meat on the bones." Winston adds, "He wanted whatever he did to be extensively researched, he wanted it to be documented to make sure it wasn't 'fluff,' his favorite word toward me...He wanted it to have substance."[53]

That stance would become extremely important as the campaign wore on. O'Bannon refused to release any advertisement, for example, without documenting the facts and statistics behind each claim in the ad—consistent with the League of Women Voters' campaign guidelines.

O'Bannon was never happy with the amount of money required to run a statewide race in Indiana, whether it was among gubernatorial hopefuls or legislative candidates. He further disliked Indiana's long tradition of failing to disclose campaign finances at critical points. "Good disclosure shines a light on the process. It discourages corruption and helps us all make better choices," O'Bannon said.[54]

O'Bannon urged the General Assembly to pass legislation requiring contributors giving more than $1,000 to disclose whom they worked for and what they did for a living, requiring campaigns to disclose their finance reports by September 1 and post their finance reports online, and requiring that contributions for more than $1,000 in the last twenty-five days of a campaign be reported within two days of receipt.

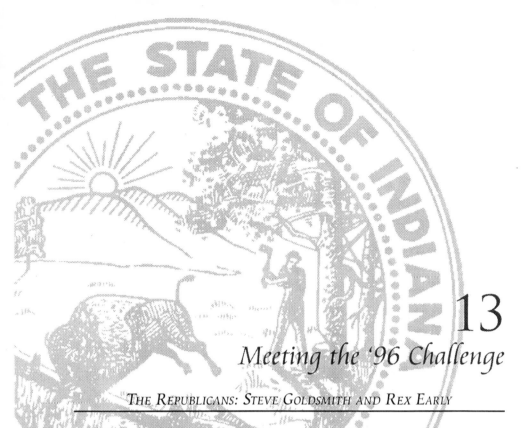

13
Meeting the '96 Challenge

One could hardly call Indianapolis Mayor Stephen Goldsmith disadvantaged in his 1996 run for governor, enjoying higher name recognition, poll numbers, and more money than anyone else running for governor that year. But his path to the Republican nomination for governor was a difficult one, one that ultimately may have cost him the race. In late 1995, as many as five Republicans had their eye on the "open" seat for governor in 1996 with Evan Bayh constitutionally barred from seeking a third consecutive term. In the race with Goldsmith were Senate President Pro Tempore Robert D. Garton of Columbus, Indianapolis insurance executive J. Patrick Rooney, Bluffton newspaper publisher George Witwer, and Rex Early.

Rooney and Witwer were the first to fold their campaigns as party regulars and others began assembling around their favorites, mostly Goldsmith and Early. Garton ended his campaign just before the start of the 1996 legislative session.

"One of them had the money (Goldsmith) and the other one had the organizational support (Early)," Garton said. "I said to myself and my family, 'Okay, we climbed the mountain and found that the campfires were all banked.' So we went home and forgot it."[1]

The departure of Rooney, Witwer, and Garton left Goldsmith and Early paired up in what turned out to be one of the ugliest gubernatorial primaries in Indiana in decades.

Early counted heavily on the organizational support of "party regulars" he had come to know as their state chairman. He also banked on any "anti-Indianapolis" sentiment he could find. Though he now lived in Indianapolis, he was identified closely with other parts of the state (such as the Knox County area) and was running against the sitting mayor of the state's largest city.

The GOP primary took on more than a divisive tone; it turned mean. "Goldsmith had plenty of money, and Rex was trying to appeal to the old-line, the more 'hail-fellow, well-met Republican fellow' of his youth," Ketzenberger said.[2]

The bad blood continued throughout the spring of 1996 with Goldsmith and Early running weeks of negative TV ads at one another.

The divide created among Republicans was wide, so wide that Goldsmith made an extraordinary move: After securing the nomination, he threw open the choice of his running mate for lieutenant governor, asking delegates at the State Republican Convention in June to nominate his partner. His move broke with what had become standard operating procedure for Indiana gubernatorial candidates: The candidates tell the convention who they want, not the other way around.

AP's Mike Smith said, "I don't know of any other candidate or nominee who has had to go to such lengths to try and heal the party wounds. A lot of the reporters were convinced that the wounds were too deep, that they would never heal completely, and that is really how it all turned out."[3]

WISH-TV statehouse reporter Jim Shella said, "...I think Rex and a lot of party people did not like the fact that Goldsmith was not paying proper homage to the party. I think part of what happened in that primary is that he sent the message to the party that he didn't need them, and in fact, he probably did."[4]

If Goldsmith's move to open the Republican convention *was* meant to heal any wounds, it failed. Delegates selected Witwer to run with Goldsmith as there stood no chance that the party could heal the divide and combine the Goldsmith and Early campaigns into one as Bayh and O'Bannon had done eight years earlier. Goldsmith's handling of the situation, and the remaining resentment from Early supporters, revealed serious problems for the party and its nominee that were not going away. Worse yet, an open rumor circulated among reporters at the time that Goldsmith had ordered Witwer to "steer clear" of him, and the hope of a coordinated campaign between the two was never a reality.

Today, Goldsmith is reluctant to talk at length about the 1996 Republican primary battle, one that he describes as "very negative." He agrees that the primary was a factor in the final outcome for 1996: "It was just that it was a very difficult and a very negative primary, and it did not end at the primary…it went on."

In fact, some believe as much as Bayh was a positive factor in O'Bannon's favor, Early was equally a negative factor for Goldsmith's chances.

MAKING THE RIGHT CHOICE

Frank O'Bannon had an advantage in selecting a running mate for lieutenant governor in 1996. After seven and a half years in that office, he understood better than anyone the importance of the job and the qualities that would make a good partner. He wanted a full and true partner, both in the campaign and if elected, in office. His choice was watched closely at the time—not only for any additional political help he could give his own campaign, which still trailed Goldsmith in the polls, but for the judgment it would indicate in his decision making. He found an old Notre Dame baseball player fit the bill, and he hit a home run.

But it was almost a partnership that didn't happen.

Joe Kernan was fifty years old in 1996 and just starting his third term as mayor of South Bend, having won a tough Democratic primary in May 1995 over a popular St. Joseph County Democrat, Richard Jasinski, and a more-spirited-than-normal Republican challenge that fall from Carl Baxmeyer.

Publicly, Joe and Maggie Kernan expressed nothing but enthusiasm for the O'Bannon campaign—but that did not necessarily mean Joe wanted to be on the ticket. Privately, Kernan wasn't interested.

"It became apparent to me that Frank might ask me to run with him," Kernan said. "In March and April of 1996, I began to think about whether it was something I wanted to do or not. I sat down with Maggie and with friends. We sorted through it, and I made the decision that I did not want to do it…I had just been reelected mayor, I loved being mayor, I loved South Bend, and I didn't want to leave."[5]

O'Bannon was not deterred. He had met Kernan six years earlier on a trip O'Bannon led to Eastern Europe as lieutenant governor and worked closely with him in 1994 on a statewide environmental policy reform panel. Most important, O'Bannon liked him.

To help convince Kernan, he sent in a mutual friend to grease the skids—Bob Kovach, a former state senator and former mayor of neighboring Mishawaka. Kovach knew both O'Bannon and Kernan well and was a skilled negotiator. However, Kernan stood tough and told Kovach he did not want to run.

Kernan did not want to be asked to run and face the decision of whether to say yes or no to someone he liked and respected. Several more weeks went by with a variety of Democrats reaching out to Kernan, including O'Bannon's campaign manager Tom New.

South Bend Tribune political columnist Jack Colwell helped stoke the Kernan fires, asking the mayor several times about whether he was interested in running. Finally, as the Kernans went to Indianapolis for the dedication of new memorials for veterans of the Korean and Vietnam Wars, O'Bannon saw an opening and asked to meet with Kernan face to face.

"Frank picked me up at the Embassy Suites in Indianapolis, and we went to Aesop's Table on Massachusetts Avenue," Kernan recalls. "We had dinner…and I explained to him why I was happy doing what I was doing and this was not on my list of things, it was not something I had been dreaming about. I had no ambition for it. I told him that so he would know where I stood…He did not ask me to run, but I did want him to hear it from me."[6]

As the dinner ended and the two prepared to part, Kernan said, "Governor, you know where I stand on this. But if you ask me to run with you, I will."

Kernan said he decided to say that, despite his expressed lack of interest in running for the number two spot. "I came to that decision because of my friendship, respect, and my trust for him. If that was what he decided would be best, then I would run," Kernan said. "He dropped me off at the hotel and I told Maggie about our conversation and she said, 'Oh, that's great, it's over with now.' That was Memorial Day night. That Monday night, at about 11:15 p.m., the phone rang, and it was Frank asking me to run with him."[7]

Judy O'Bannon said Frank finally settled on an unusual means by which to make a final decision on a running mate. "He said, 'I will come up with my idea, and you come up with yours, and we won't tell until we both tell at the same time.' So we did that, and we both said 'Joe Kernan' at the same time. Right then, he went to the phone and called Joe Kernan and asked him to run."[8]

Judy believes Kernan's military experience and his work as mayor of South Bend won him Frank's respect. "Frank knew about his experience in the war. You have to say, the guy has got guts. He had survived that not only physically…but he also had the mental strength to get through that. He had emotional and spiritual strength beyond anything I can imagine …he came out of all of that whole and enriched."[9]

Kernan served eleven months as a POW near Than Hoa, North Vietnam. "What stood out for Frank was that he had withstood this terrible time in his life, and come out so well, so able," Judy said.[10]

Publicly, Frank O'Bannon was clearly pleased that Kernan had agreed to join the team. Privately, he was thrilled—and so were Indiana

Democrats, convinced O'Bannon had made the best choice possible. "Joe's common-sense Hoosier values will make him a strong partner, and I'm proud to have him on the ticket," O'Bannon told reporters.[11]

The Democratic State Convention

Inspired and motivated to hold onto the power they had wrestled away from Republicans just eight years earlier, Indiana Democrats gathered for their state convention on June 8, 1996 at the Indiana State Fairgrounds. Kernan's nomination by O'Bannon was approved unanimously. The convention also nominated Marion County Prosecutor Jeff Modisett for attorney general, and retired teacher Ann England of Richmond for state superintendent of public instruction. O'Bannon's convention speech was described by one reporter as "gentle," while Kernan's remarks were labeled "fiery."[12]

Kernan's role was to call attention to stark differences between O'Bannon and his Republican opponent. In his convention speech, Kernan said that Goldsmith's privatization efforts reflected "his fundamental lack of faith in people. He's given up on the men and women who work for the city of Indianapolis. I think he's also given up on himself to provide the leadership necessary to provide the services to his customers and is willing to shuffle off both the responsibility and the accountability to the private sector."[13]

Campaign and state party officials hoped Kernan could add another $500,000 to campaign coffers by raising funds separate from O'Bannon. He met that goal, and then some, coming up with donations exceeding $750,000 just one year after raising money in his reelection campaign for mayor.

The Dog Days of Summer

The normally quiet summer days in any statewide campaign took a different path in 1996, as O'Bannon and Goldsmith struggled to find much to agree upon. They even argued over how to conduct a campaign aligned with a code of fair practices written by the League of Women Voters. The day after the May primary, O'Bannon was first out of the box with a statehouse news conference and a letter to Goldsmith outlining a ten-point plan he hoped the two of them would follow in the campaign before them. Among the planks in the plan were pledges against personal attacks, use of distorted facts, or the leveling of unfounded accusations, and the requirement that the two campaigns preview their TV and radio advertisements to the news media before they air, providing documentation for all of the claims made in the ads. Additionally, O'Bannon asked Goldsmith to join him in a campaign spending cap of no more than $5.8 million per campaign.

For O'Bannon, it was an open admission that Indiana Republicans are rarely, if ever, out-financed by their Democratic counterparts.

But the Goldsmith camp smelled a rat. The cap proposed by O'Bannon would include funds the two used in the just-completed primary. For the unopposed O'Bannon, primary spending was considerably below what Goldsmith had expended in his bitter defeat of Early. Goldsmith called O'Bannon's spending cap "a political gimmick" and the two continued to trade campaign letters.

One fact the two did agree on: the need for up to ten debates between the two of them in each of the state's then ten congressional districts. It was a short-lived agreement. In the end, the two campaigns could only come to terms for three debates.

THE DEMOCRATS RETURN TO CHICAGO

The last week of August 1996 was a typical, sweltering week in Indiana as the final days of summer's heat and humidity held on just a bit longer. These dog days would also prove to be a pivotal part of the '96 race for governor between O'Bannon and Goldsmith, shaping up to be the closest and most-watched statewide race in the country that year.

For Indiana Democrats, it was an incredible week that included a quick campaign stop by President Bill Clinton (b. 1946) to Michigan City, Indiana, en route to the 1996 Democratic National

Convention in Chicago (the first visit by Democrats there since their fateful 1968 Chicago convention). The convention was one Democrats relished as Governor Evan Bayh delivered the keynote address, and O'Bannon and Indianapolis congressional hopeful Julia Carson spoke to the crowds gathered at the United Center. O'Bannon turned down his first invitation to speak on Wednesday because he wanted to be in Michigan City to greet President Clinton. His Republican opponent, Goldsmith, had done him one better, having not one, but two speaking opportunities before the already-completed GOP Convention in San Diego, California.

O'Bannon dubbed himself "a C-SPAN star" since his speech was at 4:15 p.m. on the last day of the convention, Thursday, hours before any major network or cable coverage had begun. He borrowed from Ronald Reagan's famous 1980 debate remarks when he asked Americans if they were better off now than they were four years ago. O'Bannon noted that Indiana's economy, economic opportunity, and personal responsibility were all moving in the right direction under his leadership and that of outgoing Governor Bayh.

WISH-TV's Jim Shella reported from the convention that O'Bannon "appeared relaxed, confident and took good advantage of the opportunity" but did little to separate himself from Bayh's record; he seemed a bit overshadowed by Bayh and his keynote slot.[14]

Shella asked him whether he hoped some of Bayh's popularity would extend to him, and O'Bannon replied confidently, "Sure, sure! I shouldn't be running unless I am very proud of our record of the last eight years, the foundation we have laid…I am very proud to try and take it to the next level."[15]

Overall, O'Bannon was beaming. "It was just a wonderful opportunity to talk about things that are important to people, whether it's education, jobs, or the environment, and talk about things that will move Indiana and the country forward," O'Bannon said. "It was just wonderful, just wonderful."[16]

THE BRAWL

Back home in Indianapolis, things were about to turn bad *and* ugly for Indiana Republicans. The week began with an event that many believe contributed mightily to the ultimate end of a promising campaign by Goldsmith. Buried on page C-4 of the *Indianapolis Star* on the same day Clinton, Bayh, and O'Bannon's images and words were emblazoned on the front pages was a story about the arrest of two men after "scuffling" with a group of off-duty Indianapolis Police Department (IPD) officers. Before the week was out, the "scuffle" was transformed into a "brawl," moved to page one, and became the top story on all local TV news stations, as witnesses came forward to describe brutish and allegedly drunken behavior by the off-duty officers.

The witnesses told a tale of the officers allegedly beating two men, uttering racial epithets at blacks involved or nearby, and making sexually crude remarks to women. It was not the first time such complaints had been lodged against IPD officers, but unlike other times, when accusations against the police had faded quickly or been written off as "just more black-white politics," more credibility seemed attached to these accusations, perhaps given that most of the witnesses were white.

The witnesses included three young Westfield ministers who had been enjoying milkshakes on a hot summer night at the downtown Steak 'n Shake at the same time the IPD officers were throwing back drinks at Ike & Jonesy's, a downtown pub just around the corner.

The witnesses painted an ugly scene. The Rev. Timothy Kemp told reporters that as he and his wife and two other couples left the Steak 'n Shake, they heard a loud group of men walking north on Meridian Street between Maryland and Washington streets. Kemp's sister-in-law, Kim Collingsworth, told the *Indianapolis Star*, "They were yelling. I heard one yell, 'Go home niggers!'" She said the group then noticed a black man in a convertible stopped in traffic to talk to another man, and the brawl broke out between the off-duty officers and two handcuffed men.

Reverend Kemp told reporters, "(The man) was yelling, 'I didn't do it! I didn't start it! They came after me!'" Kemp described the scene as "the most unfair thing I ever saw in my life. They (the police) were half-drunk. I told one cop, 'You guys are a disgrace.' I mean, he was blowing Budweiser in my face."[17] Construction workers working nearby on the new Circle Centre Mall repeated the claims that officers used the "nigger" word and threatened those who tried to intervene on behalf of the two beaten men, saying the police officers present called the brawl a "police matter." The situation took its first steps toward Mayor Goldsmith as reporters learned the off-duty officers had spent part of their evening in Goldsmith's private suite attending an Indianapolis Indians baseball game at Victory Field. With every new report, the situation seemed to get worse.

The Goldsmith administration responded poorly as reporters and others began to spot blood in the water. The mayor did label the growing accusations against the officers as "troubling" and pledged: "The public needs a thorough review. It raises serious questions on the conduct of our officers, and we will review it."[18]

But his assertions also came with what some reporters saw as curious moves on his part.

John Ketzenberger recalled, "Once the police brawl happened in Indianapolis, the turning point for me in my mind...was about two days later; there was a news conference. I asked Goldsmith about the brawl, and he said something like, 'I can't do anything about that. That is up to the public safety director to deal with.' And I'm thinking, this is the guy who says he is going to take charge, and now he's trying to distance himself. They just handled that really badly."[19]

WISH-TV's Shella believed the O'Bannon camp was wise to steer clear and let the story play out, confirming what he believed: "From beginning to end, I think the 1996 campaign was all about Steve Goldsmith. Now that is not meant to take anything away from Frank O'Bannon. I mean, what he did was keep pointed straight ahead and do what he had to do. But I think at some point, the O'Bannon people were quite comfortable with letting Goldsmith be the story."[20]

Goldsmith's handling of the IPD situation was *the* story for the critical opening weeks of the fall campaign for the Indianapolis area media (which is read and viewed by a huge portion of Hoosier voters).

The whole fiasco reminded voters that the Republican candidate was an urban mayor and playing out in front of them were some of the worst urban problems the 1990s had to offer including boiling police-community relationships that seemed inextricably tied to the sad state of race relations in America.

"The police brawl really hurt Goldsmith," reporter Kevin Corcoran said. "He did not handle this well, and you had this guy who wants to be governor who as mayor is saying that he cannot control his own police department, or do anything about it."[21]

Goldsmith told reporters at the time that "the campaign and city issues keep colliding because of the conscious effort by Democrats to make that occur. That has been very difficult because I have done what I think is right in a bipartisan way."[22]

The O'Bannon campaign, however, never ran a single ad addressing the police brawl issue.

Senator Mahern, who lost the 1991 race for mayor to Goldsmith, believes the explosion of a law-and-order issue in the campaign was pure poetry. "John F. Kennedy used a quote once that said, 'He who seeks to ride to power on the back of the tiger, sometimes ends up inside the tiger as its meal,'" Mahern said. He said the quote fit Goldsmith, who he believed "had ridden the Indianapolis Police Department" and law-and-order issues throughout his political career. "It just really hurt Goldsmith because he was a guy who wants to run the state of Indiana, and it appears that he cannot even control the cops in his own city."[23]

Looking back, Goldsmith believes the issue was terribly distracting to his campaign. "I don't think the event was overplayed; the event was rather important, really," Goldsmith said. "I think it was overplayed, though, as it related to the campaign…unfortunately, it was very disruptive."

THE DEBATES

O'Bannon and Goldsmith met for three face-to-face debates, one each in Greencastle, Crown Point, and Evansville. For O'Bannon, the original ten-debate proposal came at a time when he was far behind in the polls, and more appearances with Goldsmith in high-profile debates were to his benefit. Goldsmith's team probably saw it differently and were not that worried about limiting the exchanges to three given Goldsmith's reputation as a glib and always well-spoken public figure. O'Bannon's camp succeeded, though, in adding Libertarian nominee Steve Dillon to the mix. Dillon's presence helped eliminate the "head-to-head" comparisons that a debate between just O'Bannon and Goldsmith would have highlighted and provided a buffer period in the debates for O'Bannon to prepare stronger responses.

In the first debate at DePauw University at Greencastle, expectations for the two candidates varied widely. As statehouse reporter Norm Cox reported on WRTV-TV, O'Bannon had to overcome what many saw as an inability to express his ideas clearly and forcefully. Goldsmith had to avoid falling into "technocrat" speech and boring audiences with pat answers that sounded too bureaucratic. O'Bannon prepared diligently, Johnson said, staging mock debates with younger opponents, and exceeded expectations widely. At the Greencastle debate, O'Bannon was animated and jovial, often addressing the camera directly. Goldsmith seemed uncertain as to whether to address the camera or the small audience assembled there. O'Bannon's choice made sense, and it played to his strength, his grandfatherly, friendly style that came through so well on camera.

The biggest confrontation of the night came when Goldsmith returned to his theme that O'Bannon had voted more than thirty times as a state senator to increase taxes. O'Bannon shot back, "The real question is false, misleading ads. He painted a completely false picture. Those votes were to help Indianapolis build a convention center, a domed stadium, or a baseball park. [Mayor Goldsmith] used those taxes to do those things; he didn't turn them down. So if you're trying to paint a picture of a tax and spend liberal, you're looking at the wrong person if you're looking at me."[24]

For Judy, the debates were some of the most nerve-wracking parts of the campaign. "Those things were just terrible," she said. "...He applied so much pressure to himself to not let everybody down."[25]

Corcoran, covering the 1996 race for the *Times of Northwest Indiana,* said, "People thought that Goldsmith was this better speaker, he was more entertaining, in some ways, but in other ways he was less so. He was always hot or cold. I think people always thought that he could run circles around Frank O'Bannon...in a head-to-head race, in a competition or a debate, maybe he does. But the campaign was more than that."[26]

"I don't think people cared that much about the debates," Goldsmith recalls. "I don't think it was what Frank was best at. It was not like he was awful, but it was just not what he was best at. I don't think the debates back then made that much difference to the people of Indiana. It helped me a little bit, I think."[27]

RECORD SPENDING

In what seems like small numbers today, the two 1996 candidates for governor of Indiana set records for their spending levels—quickly blowing through the roof on earlier hopes by O'Bannon to limit the influence of money on the race. By October, media reports showed the race costing both sides more than $18.5 million combined, making it the most expensive gubernatorial contest in the U.S. in the 1996 campaign cycle.[28]

The pace broke the previous record set by Bayh and former lieutenant governor John Mutz in 1988—and would eventually be overcome by even larger sums spent in the 2004 gubernatorial election. Of the $11.6 million spent by Goldsmith, $2 million was used to dispatch Early, the other $9.6 million blasted at O'Bannon (including expensive ads on Chicago TV that made no difference in suppressing O'Bannon's impressive vote totals in traditionally Democratic northwest Indiana). O'Bannon raised and spent just under $7 million—a record for its time for any Indiana Democrat.[29]

POLL WATCHING

No one questioned that O'Bannon started from behind in 1996, meaning that he had to run a near-perfect campaign if he expected to defeat Goldsmith.

He went out and did just that.

The final public poll offered in the 1996 race, from the Public Opinion Laboratory at Indiana University-Purdue University at Indianapolis (IUPUI), showed O'Bannon ahead 45.5 percent to 40.4 percent for Goldsmith (among the nearly 900 statewide voters polled). Nine percent were still undecided.

Internally, O'Bannon's campaign advisers saw reason for optimism. Their final poll, taken the weekend before the November vote, found O'Bannon holding a narrow but consistent 45-42 lead over Goldsmith. Still within the margin of error for the poll, but consistently, the numbers were encouraging. "I thought we had a good chance to win, but I did not think for sure that we were going to win until the last weekend," Yang said. "Even that last weekend, the last poll showed O'Bannon ahead, but knowing how Republican Indiana is in general, and knowing that Bill Clinton was going to lose to Bob Dole in Indiana, we were just worried that a lot of the Republicans were going to pull the Republican lever."[30]

O'Bannon and his campaign expressed their cautious optimism publicly, with campaign spokeswoman Rachel Gorlin noting, "A poll is meant to be a reflection of what people are planning to do, not what will happen if they don't do it."[31]

"We felt confident that he was going to win, and I think Steve Goldsmith's pollster was also confident that Goldsmith was going to win," O'Bannon pollster Garin said. "When you do this, there is an art to this, and you set out to make an educated guess of what the composition of the electorate is, and sometimes, your heart can get in the way of your head. And like it or not, we're in the head business, not the heart business, in terms of saying where a race is at any given moment..."[32]

Up until the end, Goldsmith remained optimistic, saying the IUPUI poll did not match his own numbers and that "the momentum has pretty consistently moved in our direction in the last few weeks," he told statehouse reporter Mary Dieter of the *Louisville Courier-Journal*.

In fact, Republicans were still not convinced they would lose even as exit polling by the national television networks showed O'Bannon was the winner.

When Shella reported on the air that CBS News was projecting O'Bannon would win, the Republicans gathered around him at Goldsmith headquarters were incensed.

"As soon as I had the exit polling, I went on the air and said as much. Well, the Goldsmith people, as Mike McDaniel likes to say, were acting like their hair was on fire. I was looking at them thinking, 'Can you people not read? What part of this do you not get?'" Shella said.[33]

In the end, it would be Goldsmith's poll numbers that were wrong, so wrong in fact, that Goldsmith made an unusual move after the election was over—summoning reporters who were interested to come to his campaign headquarters to see his polling data for themselves.

Goldsmith said his pollsters made mistakes and noted, "They had done a lot of Republican polling in Indiana, but things were changing a lot in Indiana at that time. The unions were doing a really good job on getting out the vote. I think they were missed, and they missed the voters' intent, and I think they missed the fact that because we had a Republican primary and split the vote up."[34]

COORDINATION WITH CARSON

Goldsmith and the Republicans also miscalculated the impact Center Township Trustee and former state senator Julia M. Carson would have in 1996 (and in subsequent years), as she made her first run for the U.S. House of Representatives. Winner of a tough

Democratic Primary where she was outspent in TV ads by veteran Democrat Ann DeLaney, Carson had created and mobilized one of the nation's strongest ground campaigns and ran a circle around DeLaney. Pollsters often missed her voters and more importantly, missed the intensity with which they would approach the 1996 election. African-American Democrats in particular were truly excited about the prospect of electing only the second African-American to represent Indiana in the Congress.

Carson and O'Bannon had a personal history. Both had served in the Indiana State Senate and knew and respected one another.

"Frank did not shun me. A lot of politicians shun me because I'm so radical, but Frank did not do that. He would campaign with me. We went to black churches together and I would introduce him there," Carson recalls.[35]

She noted that O'Bannon related well with African-Americans, despite being from a small Southern Indiana town and speaking with a noticeable southern drawl.

"I think Frank had the persona that would allow for almost instant acceptance," Carson said. "He was very smart, and so is his wife, and they got into the hearts of people of color. He spoke in a kind of simple way, and he was not a pretender, he was a genuine kind of guy. People could see that."[36]

Judy adds, "It was a team deal, and you cannot underestimate that. Frank always said, 'Never underestimate Julia Carson. When she is on, and she is before an audience, she is just superior.'"[37]

While the O'Bannon campaign focused heavily on Marion County, Goldsmith took the unusual task of investing nearly $2 million for television advertisements on Chicago TV to reach counties in Northwest Indiana, including populous Lake County.

"A big strategy of Goldsmith's was to try and drive up this big Republican vote there because it has the second highest Republican vote total in the state, after Marion County," Corcoran said. "...It didn't get them anything. That was a big, hard lesson for the Republicans to learn."[38]

ELECTION DAY

Frank and Judy O'Bannon didn't vote on Election Day 1996. They had already cast absentee ballots for Harrison County. Instead, they spent Election Day in Indianapolis visiting polls, conducting interviews for radio and TV, and thanking campaign workers. Frank O'Bannon had his camera in hand, clicking pictures of campaign volunteers.

Reports from around the state were encouraging. Extra voting machines were ordered for polling places in Democratic strongholds such as Lake and Vigo counties, the O'Bannons were told, surely encouraging signs.

Pollsters working in Indiana on behalf of three national television networks, ABC, CBS, and NBC, were conducting "exit polls" at key precincts. Although unscientific, voters were still asked how they had voted for president and for governor. The results continued to add encouragement as they showed both Republican presidential nominee Senator Bob Dole (b. 1923) of Kansas and Frank O'Bannon of Corydon enjoying a good day among voters in Indiana. Only O'Bannon's good day would last into evening.

In the end, it was, as the *Indianapolis Star* said, "swift and stunning," as the too-close-to-call race wasn't that close at all.[39]

AN EARLY WIN

Even as the votes rolled in, O'Bannon remained characteristically reticent—cautiously waiting to claim victory until 11:05 p.m.—just in time for his remarks to be carried live on the late television news across the state. "I'm honored, and I'm humbled, and I accept your public trust," O'Bannon told the elated overflow throng gathered in the 500 Ballroom of the Indiana Convention Center.

Crowded behind him on the stage were all the O'Bannons—a beaming Frank and Judy right up front. "They're all behind me, the whole family. It's like Thanksgiving and we didn't have to cook!" O'Bannon told reporters.[40]

O'Bannon wasn't the only one reluctant to claim victory too quickly.

Campaign manager New refused to declare victory, even after Marion County, Goldsmith's home turf, came in with a comfortable margin of victory for O'Bannon.

For some connected to the campaign, it had been an uncertain outcome until the end. For O'Bannon, he filled the waiting time with phone calls from friends and supporters, and appropriate for the tension of the night, he read a *Goosebumps* book to grandson Asher Reed.[41]

O'Bannon's sisters Jane Parker and Margaret Fawver were also surprised at the early finish.

"We were all sitting around here that night waiting for the election returns to come in and we weren't worrying too much, and all of a sudden, they said he'd won, around six o'clock in the evening!" Jane Parker said. "We scurried around to get dressed and get ready so we could get in there to Indianapolis. We were not planning to go downtown that soon…We said, 'We better get going. We better get our glad rags on and get to Indianapolis.'"[42]

For Jane, the oldest of Robert and Faith O'Bannon's children, it was a proud night and the culmination of a long but fun year. She and her husband, Ted, a Republican-turned-Democrat, had toured around in the hot sun attending parades in Hendricks County and elsewhere in mostly Republican counties that Frank and Judy could not reach during the demanding schedule in the closing days of the campaign—anywhere they were needed, their van covered with "O'Bannon for Governor" signs.

Frank's sister Rosamond Sample drove up to Indianapolis from her home in Corydon for the evening's festivities. "I remember we were just horribly excited when he won in 1996," she said. "…I don't know that I was surprised that he won, though. I didn't entertain the thought that he was going to lose, which was somewhat naïve, I guess. I just always felt he was a more agreeable public character than most and that would help him win."[43]

Rosamond is not sure whether Frank's father, Robert, ever knew his son was interested in running for governor or not. Confined to a nursing home for the last months of his life, when Frank and Judy visited Robert O'Bannon in 1987 and told him what they were planning, Robert, unable to speak clearly because of a stroke, uttered a sentence that Rosamond believes was, "Well, better you than me."

Ironically, it was Robert O'Bannon who had perhaps first planted the idea of running for governor in his son's mind. "I remember once when we were coming back to Corydon from Indianapolis and Frank was driving because his father was older and not driving much then," Judy recalled. "Robert said to him, 'Son, you might want to think about the governor thing. I used to think it was well beyond any capacity any of us would have, but the more I am around it, the more I see there really are interesting situations to be looked at, to work on, and it doesn't take someone out of the ordinary to do it.'"[44]

The final tally, known days later, showed the width and depth of the win—O'Bannon polled 1,087,128 votes to Goldsmith's 986,982. Libertarian nominee Steve Dillon received 35,805 votes. It was not a landslide, but a solid win for a Democrat in a state that polled almost identical numbers—but in reverse—in the Clinton-Dole race at the top of the ballot.

O'Bannon won half of the state's ninety-two counties, including all-important Marion County, Goldsmith's home, by a vote of 146,092 to 127,207—the first Democrat to do so in decades—and against the sitting Indianapolis mayor.

Harrison County did not disappoint—O'Bannon 9,398; Goldsmith 4,228. In fact, O'Bannon won all of the Ohio River counties.[45]

Exit polling showed O'Bannon did well not only in all Southern Indiana counties, but also among black voters, according to polls of 1,555 voters conducted by Voter News Service, a cooperative effort of the Associated Press, ABC, CBS, CNN, and NBC. The exit polling also showed the primary issue for voters had been what it always seems to be: the economy. Among those who ranked the state's economy as good or excellent, O'Bannon enjoyed a 16 percent edge over Goldsmith—a key edge in a race as tight as this one.[46]

Also caught off-guard that night by the early finish was Governor Evan Bayh. He was at the governor's residence with First Lady Susan Bayh and their one-year-old twin sons, Beau and Nicholas, preparing to go downtown for the Democratic rally at the Convention Center.

Bayh press aide Steve Campbell remembers seeing the news flash on the TV that O'Bannon was being declared the winner. "Governor Bayh was wanting to wait to do any interviews until later so he could congratulate Governor O'Bannon first," Campbell said. "It's 6:20 p.m. and Governor Bayh came downstairs and he said, 'Steve, try to get the governor-elect on the phone.' So I called Cindy Athey, and I told her, 'Governor Bayh wants to talk to Governor O'Bannon,' and so she puts Governor O'Bannon on the line, and Bayh says to him, 'Governor, this is the governor, congratulations!' I remember thinking that was the funniest moment to hear them referring to each other as governor."[47]

For Goldsmith, the night held a surprisingly quick finish.

At 6:01 p.m., network news programs declared O'Bannon the winner. The Associated Press and local news reports followed within moments.

His own polls dead wrong, Goldsmith faced no other choice than to call O'Bannon at about 10 p.m. from his suite at the Westin Hotel and congratulate the lieutenant governor on his victory.

Lots of phone calls came in as O'Bannon waited for returns to come in their nineteenth-floor suite at the Hyatt Regency Hotel, including one from Vice President Al Gore.

After taking Goldsmith's call, O'Bannon emerged from a private room in the suite and asked everyone but family to meet him a few moments later across the street at the Convention Center. The walk from the Hyatt to the Convention Center was an O'Bannon family stroll—ten-year-old grandson Beau Zoeller in charge of holding an elevator for the family to ride. A row of TV reporters and cameras from around the state were soon in tow—and a few thousand of their newest and dearest friends waited to cheer their arrival at the 500 Ballroom.

Following his brief remarks that night, O'Bannon showed a rare glimpse of his competitiveness as he pumped his fists firmly and shouted, "Yes! Yes!" to supporters who crowded the stage.

ASSESSING GOLDSMITH'S LOSS

Just a block down the street, dejected Republicans left the Westin Hotel after Mayor Goldsmith publicly conceded. Republican strategists attributed the loss then to the influence of outgoing Governor Evan Bayh, perhaps even in defeat, underestimating the political strength of Frank O'Bannon.

"I think some people always underestimated Frank," Goldsmith acknowledges. "He had been in Evan's shadow. Governor Bayh's impact was important and complicated. I don't think people understood at the time the significance of his influence; Hoosiers were satisfied with the direction of the state, they liked their government."[48]

Mike McDaniel, serving as Republican State Party Chair in 1996, agrees they terribly underestimated O'Bannon. McDaniel said they predicted O'Bannon would lack the stamina to campaign vigorously statewide, or could raise the money needed to run a competitive campaign, and as a result, not be able to attract the national media and strategic assistance that could make the difference. In the end, O'Bannon had all of those things in spades, while it was Goldsmith who struggled to connect with Hoosier voters.

AP's Mike Smith described it this way: "Frank O'Bannon lacked the polished political style, rapid-fire speech, and smooth television demeanor that Stephen Goldsmith had…What he had in the end, however, were the votes."[49] Goldsmith started out the clear frontrunner, Smith noted, "but he was tagged for firing the first TV attack ads, was dogged by a controversial shakeup in the Indianapolis Police Department, and O'Bannon raised and spent millions himself."[50]

WISH-TV's Shella summed it up well during election night coverage when he quoted one Republican as saying, "Had I known it would have been such a long night of looking at the floor, I would have worn a better pair of shoes."

MOMENTUM FOR O'BANNON

In the weeks leading up to that incredible night, many had sensed that if there was such a thing as political momentum, the O'Bannon-Kernan ticket seemed to have it. Reporters Mike Smith and Kevin Corcoran remember interviewing a confident Goldsmith just days before the balloting. They found him seemingly certain of a win. No doubt he had reason to be: His pollsters told him he was going to win.

The reporters were not convinced. For Corcoran, Goldsmith's campaign seemed only able to operate as if it were ahead with all the breaks going their way. Their faith in pollsters seemed nearly absolute, but as the police brawl incident indicated for most observers, things were not breaking Goldsmith's way.

In contrast, Smith and Corcoran noted a very different scene when they arrived one afternoon to ride along on the O'Bannon campaign bus. In the parking lot of the Landmark Center in Indianapolis, O'Bannon was outside the bus clicking pictures with a small "point and shoot" camera. Both found that unusual and reflective of the kind of guy he was and the sincerity of his campaign. He didn't send a campaign aide out to click the picture or jump in the picture himself; he wanted to shoot the pictures himself which he said he would one day put in a scrapbook for his grandchildren.

Political columnist Brian Howey noticed the sag hitting the Goldsmith campaign late in the going as well, and the mayor's relations with reporters continued to be poor. "A few days before the election, you could feel the air rushing out of the Goldsmith campaign," Howey wrote. "I went up to the Allen County Republican bean dinner, and Goldsmith showed up late, spoke, and then left early. (Later) I ran into him and his wife, Margaret, in the halls of the Scottish Rite Cathedral. Mrs. Goldsmith glared at me. 'You're gonna pull this thing out, aren't you?' I asked. Goldsmith responded, 'Do me a favor and never write anything about my humor again.'"[51]

Cochran experienced some of Goldsmith's lack of humor in the closing days as well. "Steve was either in a good mood or he wasn't" and would often "question the premise of every question you would ask him …if Frank O'Bannon ever thought I asked a dumb question, he kept that to himself. Steve Goldsmith was not that kind of candidate."[52]

O'Bannon's campaign made use of campaign volunteers in an era when most modern campaigns struggle to find things for them to do. The O'Bannon "ground-pounders" were a presence wherever the candidate went. Robin Winston's job was to make sure volunteers were out passing out literature, putting up yard signs, walking parade routes, and attending county fairs and town festivals in Indiana communities, big or small, Republican or Democrat. As the campaign drew to its frenzied and nervous finish, the TV ads weren't going to sway that many more voters. It was going to take some old-fashioned one-to-one connections to make it happen. Winston asked the ground-pounders to call their family members and friends the weekend before the vote and make sure every one of them planned to vote for Frank O'Bannon.

Reporters noticed another big difference between the two campaigns as the waning days wore on. When the O'Bannon-Kernan bus tour took off across the state, it was loaded down with family and friends of each of the candidates, as well as other statewide candidates. Getting a seat on the bus was a premium, as those gathered munched on home-baked cookies, buckets of chicken, and potato chips. (At day's end, a few beers were also known to be popped open.) At each O'Bannon-Kernan stop, at least thirty to fifty enthusiastic supporters were present. Advance work had paid off, and volunteers and supporters alike were there to create the vision of a groundswell.

Reporters quickly contrasted this with Goldsmith's approach— usually traveling alone with one aide, and few if any crowds gathered at the unplanned stops. Goldsmith's running mate, George Witwer, rarely, if ever, campaigned directly with Goldsmith. The Indianapolis mayor was sometimes met by confused café patrons who didn't know the Republican nominee had planned to stop by. Stops at county GOP headquarters were equally ineffective, reaching already sold folks, instead of undecided or independent voters.

The O'Bannon campaign also reached out to volunteers in a particularly aggressive and personal manner. Appointing "county coordinators" in all ninety-two counties, the campaign conducted daily phone banks (in the days before the state's Anti-Call List was instituted) beginning in late summer. O'Bannon and Bayh also recorded specific phone messages for identified Democrat or "leaning Democratic" voters in which they asked each one of them to come out and make a difference.

Specific, customized direct mail pieces were sent to thousands of voters, including one just for female voters. The mailing, sent to thousands of Hoosier women, outlined O'Bannon's views on childcare, school performance, and classroom safety, and his commitment to public safety. Emily's List, a national fundraising political action committee that supports only candidates it believes uplift women and children, paid for the mailing and others. Specific outreach efforts also targeted African-American voters, members of organized labor, and gay and lesbian voters.

GOTV, or Get Out The Vote, efforts by Indiana Democrats in 1996 were inspired—helped along by volunteers from organized labor, women's groups, black churches and community groups, gay and lesbian organizations, and many, many off-duty state employees worried about the prospects of a potential "Governor Goldsmith." As Indiana Democratic insider Ann DeLaney writes in her book *Politics for Dummies*, GOTV efforts "are a very important part of any campaign. A candidate who convinces a majority of potential voters that she is the best candidate still loses if she fails to get those supporters to come out and vote."[53]

Judy admits there were moments when the campaign was tiring, and she thought, "This isn't for me, but then we'd look around and see all of these active, involved young people, who were committed to the campaign and committed to Frank, and you rapidly felt like this was a team deal. A lot of people had committed themselves, had cleared their calendars, some had even burned bridges as far as an occupation or sometimes political friendships."[54]

Rachel Gorlin, the campaign spokeswoman, said the victory was not based on any one issue. "I think the voters took the measure of these two men, and they wanted someone they could trust to lead this state for the next four years," she told the *Corydon Democrat* on election night. "I don't think they were comfortable with Stephen Goldsmith."[55]

Lots of post-election analysis would follow. Mary Dieter's take in the *Louisville Courier-Journal* was typical. She too noted the race had not come down to one factor, but many. She wrote, "…The race pitted a beloved Statehouse veteran with enormous people skills but a frequently twisted tongue against a brash, self-assured policy wonk who exhibits little patience for those less gifted."[56]

She noted that Goldsmith and his campaign likely underestimated their opponent, whom she dubbed "a southern gentleman whose slow-paced, tortured speech belies his intelligence and political savvy."[57]

IUPUI Pollster Brian Vargas, whose last pre-election poll predicted the outcome correctly, noted for Dieter's story, "You put all of those things together and you've got a victory, and a rather decisive one, in many respects, given where he started from."[58]

A HAPPY HOMECOMING

After months and months of campaigning, fundraising, and traveling to every corner of the state and back again—the O'Bannons were eager for a little rest and relaxation after the '96 campaign. Demands grew by the hour and day, however. The O'Bannons began to notice quickly there was a difference between being lieutenant governor and governor-elect. There was an administration to form, a legislative agenda to finalize, and so much more. It seemed like the phone rang constantly, with one more thing to consider and coordinate in the few short weeks between the election and the inauguration.

One call Frank O'Bannon was pleased as punch to receive was from Bill Clinton, forty-second president of the United States. Clinton phoned O'Bannon at the barn in Corydon to congratulate him on his win and reached him just as Frank came in from a short walk outside in the woods. Family members strained to sit close enough to hear the president's words to him but couldn't and settled on clicking a photo of a smiling Frank O'Bannon dressed in blue jeans and boots, seated on the floor talking on the phone with the president of the United States.

Despite calls and well wishes from the famous, the O'Bannons could not and would not forget the lifelong family and friends in Corydon and throughout Southern Indiana who had always been there for them.

About two hundred Harrison County faithful showed up at the courthouse square just one week after the election and waited in windy, 30-degree temperatures for their chance to shake the hand of their old friend, Frank O'Bannon, now the governor-elect of Indiana.

It was an important event for Frank O'Bannon.

"These are the people who influenced my life," O'Bannon said.[59] "Growing up in Corydon and Harrison County and here in Southern Indiana, it's really what I'm all about," he said from the bandstand on the courthouse square. "Our campaign was well run, but bigger than that was the support of the people in a way that we couldn't have asked for. When you come to say what the town of Corydon and Harrison County has done for me, it's made me and molded me in many, many ways. You can talk about buildings, you can talk about the schools, but the big things...are the people."[60]

Frank and Judy O'Bannon stayed until the last person left, shaking every hand they could, posing for pictures, and exchanging countless hugs and well wishes from those who had known them forever. Corydon was the first of several stops that week to thank Indiana voters for their confidence. It had to be "because all of these are people I know...some of them I went to school with," he said. O'Bannon told reporters he was surprised so many people showed up, reflecting his trademark lack of ego, and expressed worry that any of his old friends would have to wait twenty or thirty minutes to shake *his* hand.

Frank O'Bannon's childhood home, Elliott Street in Corydon, Indiana.
PHOTO CREDIT: Melissa McIntosh

Lew M. O'Bannon speaking beneath the Constitutional Elm
during Corydon's Indiana Centennial Celebration, 1916.
PHOTO CREDIT: O'Bannon family collection

Robert and Faith O'Bannon with their children, Christmas circa 1940s.
PHOTO CREDIT: O'Bannon family collection

INSET: Frank O'Bannon as a boy in 1937.
PHOTO CREDIT: O'Bannon family collection

Frank O'Bannon as a member of the
Indiana University basketball team, 1949-50 season.
PHOTO CREDIT: Indiana University/O'Bannon family collection

Senate Minority Leader Frank L. O'Bannon
with his 1970s trademark glasses and pipe.
PHOTO CREDIT: AP Wide World Photos

Frank O'Bannon "works" a parade route, circa 1980s.
PHOTO CREDIT: O'Bannon family collection

Frank and Judy O'Bannon welcome
Secretary of State Evan Bayh to Corydon, summer 1988.
*PHOTO CREDIT: Randy West, **Corydon Democrat***

Frank O'Bannon takes the oath of office as governor,
January 1997, as administered by U.S. Representative
Lee Hamilton. Judy O'Bannon is at the center.
PHOTO CREDIT: AP Wide World Photos)

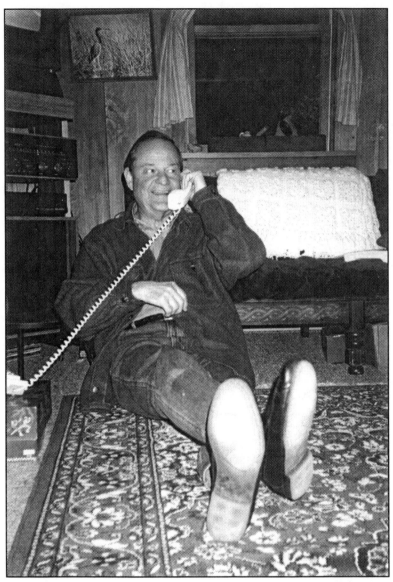

Governor-elect Frank O'Bannon sits on the floor to take a
call from President Bill Clinton, circa November 1996.
PHOTO CREDIT: O'Bannon family collection

O'Bannon family Christmas card, circa 1999.
PHOTO CREDIT: Indiana Democratic Party

Governor Frank O'Bannon delivers his January 2001 inaugural
address before a record crowd at the RCA Dome in Indianapolis.
PHOTO CREDIT: AP Wide World Photos

Governor Frank O'Bannon promotes academic achievement for
Indiana students with Peyton Manning, Indianapolis Colts quarterback.
PHOTO CREDIT: John Phung

Governor Frank O'Bannon at the site of the World Trade
Center attack, New York City, October 2001. Pictured from
left are New York Gov. George Pataki, Gov. O'Bannon, Utah
Gov. Mike Leavitt, and West Virginia Gov. Bob Wise.
PHOTO CREDIT: AP Wide World Photos

The flag-draped casket carrying the body of Governor Frank O'Bannon is removed from a National Guard plane by an Indiana State Police Honor Guard, just after midnight on Sunday, Sept. 14, 2003. Pictured directly behind the casket is Lt. Ray Raney, head of O'Bannon's security detail.

PHOTO CREDIT: AP Wide World Photos

Joseph E. Kernan, Jr. takes the oath of office as the 48th governor of
Indiana, administered by Supreme Court Justice Theodore Boehm
on Saturday, Sept. 13, 2003. Holding the Bible is Maggie Kernan.
PHOTO CREDIT: AP Wide World Photos

Governor Joe Kernan offers a hug to now former first lady
Judy O'Bannon moments after taking the oath of office.
PHOTO CREDIT: AP Wide World Photos

Judy O'Bannon gives a "thumbs-up" at the close of the Indianapolis memorial service for Governor O'Bannon. Standing behind her, from left, are Donna Imus, Pat Terrell, Lois Stewart, and Cindy Athey.

PHOTO CREDIT: AP Wide World Photos

The Frank O'Bannon Elementary School located
at 1317 173rd Street, Hammond, Indiana.

PHOTO CREDIT: Andrew Stoner

14

Becoming Governor O'Bannon

HIGH HOPES

Hopes ran high for the new O'Bannon administration in the jam-packed days between the November 1996 election and the January 1997 inauguration. In those sixty days, O'Bannon "exuded confidence" in the transition to being governor, according to *Indianapolis Star* political reporter Mary Beth Schneider.[1]

The day after the election, Frank and Judy O'Bannon made a visit to the governor's office as guests of Governor Bayh, drawing a throng of reporters and more than a few supporters who applauded loudly. "Put your feet up and make yourselves at home," Bayh told his successor and Mrs. O'Bannon.[2] He vowed to make it "the smoothest and most successful transition in the history of Indiana government."[3] It was; Bayh seemed as pleased as anyone with O'Bannon's unexpected and impressive win.

Bayh had had a somewhat tumultuous relationship with legislators, but as Schneider predicted, "O'Bannon won't have that problem. He already is known and liked by the legislators—virtually all of them, regardless of party."[4]

O'Bannon knew the legislative process and the players especially well and was willing to let state agency heads help drive public policy. Therefore, many in the legislature and state government expected a smooth run with the new governor. One Republican sounded a word of caution however—former state GOP chair Al Hubbard worried aloud that O'Bannon would be hostage to the demands of unions across the state. An obviously still thrilled Frank O'Bannon addressed that issue with a wide smile and said, "I'm pro-labor, and I'm pro-business, and I'm pro-everybody in the state of Indiana."[5] He had reason to be excited. He was at the top of his political mountain. "Everybody wants to be president of the United States," O'Bannon told Schneider. "And I'm not one of them."

O'Bannon asked David Johnson to lead the transition team. They stuffed themselves into a tiny lower-level office provided by the state in the bowels of the statehouse. As they had eight years before, résumés poured in from new people and known commodities. Some of the Bayh team wanted to stay, but others were committed elsewhere or ready to move on.

A House Divided

The 1996 election set another record, producing for only the second time in the state's history a fifty-fifty tie in the Indiana House. The previous tie, less than a decade before, had resulted in a rare "co-speaker" arrangement with committee chairs being shared equally by both parties in a brokered arrangement. In 1995, however, lawmakers passed a bill granting the majority in a tied legislative body to the winning party in the gubernatorial race, or to the winning party of the secretary of state's race in non-gubernatorial election years. In this case, that meant the colorful John Gregg, a state representative from Sandborn known for his butch haircut and handlebar mustache, would become the new speaker of the house. Gregg predicted O'Bannon would enjoy a better relationship with legislators—particularly among Republicans who he said had at times shown disrespect for the younger Bayh.[6]

"It was extremely difficult," Gregg said. "It took fifty-one votes to pass anything...When the numbers are close, the partisanship becomes just tighter than Dick's hat band...We were always hungry for a Republican vote. We were like a skinny dog looking for a big soup bone when it came to that."[7]

Expectations for O'Bannon's relationship with members of the Indiana General Assembly, based on his eighteen years as a senator and eight years presiding over the senate as lieutenant governor, were high, perhaps too high. Political leaders, reporters, and other observers looked to his legislative approach for clues to how he would govern. They also looked to his personality. IUPUI pollster Vargas said, "Many people don't appreciate the amount of savvy that Frank O'Bannon has about state government, that he's been in the legislature, that he can work with these people. I expect him to be somewhat more active in dealing with the legislature."[8]

O'Bannon said he was not concerned about the divided house. "I'm sure I can make it work whatever happens," he said. "Politics is only about 15 percent of what we do in the legislature...I'm confident I can work with the leadership, whatever it is."[9]

O'Bannon genuinely respected the differences between the executive and legislative branches of government and let the legislature, particularly the divided house, work out its own issues.

"What Governor O'Bannon was good at doing was using the office of the governor to articulate to members of both parties in the house and to people around the state the importance of issues," Gregg said.[10]

Representative B. Patrick Bauer of South Bend also gained a new leadership role: chair of the powerful House Ways and Means Committee. "In Ways and Means, you really have to work, and when I was chair, we had some really lean years on the budget," Bauer said. "The Democrats had the governor's office that whole time, so we really had to work hard to balance a very lean budget and work to protect the governor's program. You have to get the budget through that he needs to govern."[11]

In the Midnight Hour

Frank O'Bannon became the forty-seventh governor of Indiana at precisely 12:10 a.m. on January 13, 1997 in the governor's office, Room 206 of the statehouse. State Supreme Court Justice Randall T. Shepard administered the oath to O'Bannon in the presence of his family and a handful of his closest advisers. He would repeat the oath in a public ceremony about twelve hours later on the west steps of the statehouse. Mary Dieter was the only member of the media present. She described a slight glitch in the ceremony when they could not find a Bible to use for the swearing in. Finally, an aide, Donna Imus, procured a Bible and the ceremony continued. "Judy O'Bannon, her smile broad, but her eyes misty, held it for her ebullient husband of thirty-nine years as he carefully enunciated each word of the oath Shepard dictated."[12]

While the highlight of the evening was the private swearing in, the O'Bannons were busy all weekend. More than 1,100 people attended the inaugural dinner at the Westin Hotel, and another 3,200 the ball at the Indiana Convention Center. Demi Zoeller, then just two years old, clung tightly to her grandpa's neck as she joined him and Grandma Judy in the first dance of the night. Frank O'Bannon's youngest sister, Margaret Fawver, was in town from Orange, California. She told a reporter she had not expected her brother to achieve such a high position. "We came for his inauguration eight years ago, and we thought that was the tops," she said.[13]

A Cold, Bright Day

January 13, 1997 was a rather typical winter day in Indiana, except that temperatures struggled to get above the zero mark. Stubborn snow stacks served as perfect white bunting along the edges of the statehouse limestone for the inauguration. O'Bannon's outdoor inaugural was the first since Paul V. McNutt became governor in 1933.

Donna Imus, who helped plan the inauguration, said they decided to hold the event outside because a teacher from Greensburg, Indiana had asked if her fourth-grade Indiana history students could attend the event. Imus said, "I remembered the Bayh inaugurals were crowded inside the statehouse…I knew that Frank O'Bannon was just as popular and would have just as large a crowd. So I reasoned that all of the inaugurations they have had in Washington, D.C., and we're sort of on the same weather pattern that they are, well, they've only had to cancel their outdoor events once or twice."[14]

In retrospect, Imus said she was glad it was so terribly cold that day that many schools canceled. "Even though we had worked on a bus plan, and we were supposed to have twelve thousand kids show up…we still probably would have had logistical problems with all of that…As it turned out, we had a couple thousand hearty kids who showed up."[15]

The fewer than three thousand students who actually made the trip in the cold temperatures warmed themselves inside the Indiana Government Center complex prior to the start of the ceremony. Children in the Indianapolis Children's Choir were bundled tightly in coats, hats, and scarves as they sang "This Is My Country" and "On the Banks of the Wabash." Imus, Cindy Athey, Barbara Lawrence, Pat Terrell, and many others pulled together a beautiful ceremony under a bright, sunny midday sky. Reporters focused on the bone-chilling temperatures and the clouds of mist that formed above everyone's mouths as they spoke or took a breath.

Inside the west hallway of the statehouse, Frank and Judy O'Bannon and their family waited to be introduced to the assembled crowd shivering outside. Dieter wrote, "Even as he waited to be introduced at the inaugural ceremony yesterday, his moment in history, O'Bannon was circumspect. 'It certainly has sunk in, particularly in the last two days,' that he is now governor, he said."[16]

O'Bannon's friend U.S. Representative Lee Hamilton led him in a public recitation of the governor's oath: "I, Frank O'Bannon, do solemnly swear that I will support the Constitution of the United States of America, and the constitution of Indiana, and that I will faithfully discharge my duties as governor of the state of Indiana to the best of my skill and ability, so help me God."[17]

Afterward, he delivered an inaugural speech lasting less than seven minutes (undoubtedly pleasing the freezing crowd gathered). In it, he quoted George Bernard Shaw when he said, "I am convinced my life belongs to the whole community." The quote perfectly fit the simple man from Corydon.

He called the day one of new beginnings. He reminded Hoosiers of their government's foundation. "Forty-three men crowded into that small, one-room capitol building to hammer the terms of how we'd live together. That was our constitution and it guides the future and how we live today. Among the very first words they wrote were, 'All power is inherent in the people.' In other words, the state of Indiana is a people's government."

He declared, "That's why we're here again, to begin once again the people's government. You have given me your public trust and entrusted me with our state's future. I promise you, I won't let you down. Because my goal for our state is one that we all share: to make Indiana the best place on the earth to live, to work, and to raise a family."[18]

He set high challenges for himself and the administration. "Every action that we take in this building ought to pass a simple test: Does it leave our children and our grandchildren better prepared for tomorrow?"[19]

Lt. Governor Joe Kernan and Attorney General Jeff Modisett were sworn in at the same ceremony, Kernan taking the oath of office from his father, Joseph E. Kernan, Sr. Lt. Governor Kernan got a big laugh from the frozen crowd when he accused those present of only clapping in a futile effort to keep their hands warm and added, "We have picnics on days like this in South Bend!"[20]

REFLECTING THE STATE WE SERVE

Frank O'Bannon compiled an impressive, if not immediate, record on keeping his commitment to assemble an inclusive administration. Without exception, women, African-Americans, Hispanic and Latino Hoosiers, and gay men and lesbian women enjoyed tremendous access and opportunities in state government under Governor O'Bannon. O'Bannon personally appointed many minorities to key positions, not only on his personal staff, but also to lead the many state agencies, boards, and commissions. His commitment included key appointments to state and local courts in Indiana when judgeships came open.

On his staff, O'Bannon named the state's first woman as chief of staff, when Margaret Burlingame held that position following the departure of Tom New, who left to head up O'Bannon's 2000 reelection campaign. Other women in key policy positions in his office and administration included women who served as general counsel, press secretary, legislative directors, and top policy advisers. O'Bannon also appointed numerous women to head many key state agencies.

African-Americans were also in key positions in the governor's staff and state agencies, including the state's first black superintendent of the Indiana State Police, Mel Carraway.

O'Bannon's commitment to the inclusion of gay and lesbian staff was real—despite political fallout at times. O'Bannon endorsed state personnel policies prohibiting discrimination against gay men and lesbian women at all levels of state government and won a special award from the Indiana Stonewall Democrats for his work, an award renamed later in his honor. Appointments of gay people and his refusal to sign legislation that would ban adoption of children by gay people won him the scorn of many conservatives, including a radical church group from Topeka, Kansas led by the Reverend Fred Phelps—the same group that later picketed funerals of U.S. soldiers killed in Afghanistan or Iraq. A one-day protest outside the statehouse by the group in 2002 included some of the ugliest and meanest protest signs ever seen at the capital. O'Bannon did, however, sign the Defense of Marriage Act legislators passed that limits marriage rights in Indiana to unions of men and women only.

O'Bannon also felt it was very important to listen to the concerns of Hoosiers. Nancy Milakovic McGann worked for many years in the lower-level offices of the governor's office, making sure the average of just more than 30,000 letters sent each year to the governor received a response. "Governor O'Bannon felt the public had a right to be heard," Milakovic McGann said. "He took the time to respond to them since they took the time to write to him."[21]

FOB MANAGEMENT STYLE

Governor O'Bannon utilized executive assistants for various policy areas, a practice first started by Governor Otis Bowen many years earlier.[22] As opposed to a formal cabinet, the "EA" system counted on those appointed individuals to provide a vital communication link between the governor and the agencies. Important duties of EAs included avoiding surprises, using multiple lines of communication to ensure that the proper information was supplied to the governor, and remembering that "the governor appoints agency heads to lead and manage their agencies. Assisting the agencies, however, is a responsibility of the EAs and the governor's staff."[23]

The main contact points for the EAs and the agencies were the chief of staff, deputy chief of staff, press secretary, and the general counsel. Agency heads frequently talked with and met with the governor on a variety of issues, but those discussions always included representatives of the governor's staff.

Former state party chair Robin Winston said O'Bannon's management system functioned with three circles with different levels of influence. The tightest inner circle around the governor included often Tom New and David Johnson, even though Johnson never officially held a position in the governor's office. New, as chief of staff, and later Margaret Burlingame, Jim Maguire, and Tim Joyce held tremendous influence over the day-to-day operations of the office. Staff were expected to "vet" issues and concerns with the chief of staff, or at least inform him or her, before approaching the governor. Cindy Athey, as the governor's personal executive assistant, was particularly effective at helping control the circle in which the governor operated.[24]

A circle one layer removed included the EAs, agency heads, and most especially, Mrs. O'Bannon. While not a formal part of policy discussions, Mrs. O'Bannon's influence on the governor was great as she and her husband often discussed major issues privately together. Moreover, the governor trusted Judy's instincts and counsel—especially as it related to appointments and staff positions.

A third, further removed circle briefed the governor on more specialized or complex issues, allowing him to benefit from their high level of experience in issues and allowing them valuable "face time" with the head of the team.

In legislative matters, the circle was perhaps tightest. The chief of staff, legislative director, budget director, and the general counsel were most frequently involved in those discussions, waiting to bring the press secretary in at later points in the process. O'Bannon met weekly during sessions with legislative leaders, particularly members of the senate and house Democratic leaders, or members of the Black Legislative Caucus. Lobbyists rarely, if ever, met directly with the governor. Advocates, particularly those for people with disabilities and mental illness, senior citizens, veterans, environmental groups, and public access advocates had regular meetings with the governor to discuss their concerns.

The physical set-up of the governor's office provided very little opportunity for private, deliberative meetings without a great many people knowing who was seeing the governor. The main lobby of Room 206 of the statehouse was wide open, generally, to anyone who happened by, and in spite of moving the press office to the rear of the office closer to the Capitol Avenue doors of the statehouse, many reporters came through the office "via the back way" to just keep an eye on who was coming and going.

O'Bannon was an easygoing, active listener. It was not uncommon for O'Bannon to have spoken the least of anyone in a briefing. It was unstated but understood that the governor was taking in information at the head of the giant conference table in his massive office, but the governor was not necessarily going to decide on a course of action with the entire briefing group present. He often conducted subsequent, smaller meetings with his tighter circle of advisers, where he would make final decisions.

Tim Joyce, who started in 1999 as the deputy chief of staff, had a favorable impression of O'Bannon as a leader from the beginning. As time went by, he felt his initial sense had been correct. "...His strongest suit was his ability to listen...He wanted to hear what your opinion really was..."[25]

At Christmastime, the O'Bannons hosted every member of the staff and their families at a private reception at the governor's residence to show their gratitude for their hard work. The event included a meal and gifts for every staff member—always a book the governor personally selected from some he had read in the previous years.

MEET THE PRESS

O'Bannon enjoyed an outstanding relationship with each and every reporter who covered his administration. That is not to say that reporters did not take their turns slamming him or his performance in sometimes painful ways, but it was always clear that members of the statehouse press corps and "out state" reporters liked O'Bannon the man, very much—and he liked and respected them. While on the road outside Indianapolis, O'Bannon seemed to make a special effort to engage local newspaper, radio, and TV reporters, waving off staff efforts to keep him moving along. It not only was a gentlemanly thing to do, it paid off often. One Terre Haute TV reporter who was just starting out later became a valued reporter at one of the largest TV stations in Indianapolis. It didn't hurt at all that she had talked to and known O'Bannon to be "real" even when she was working her way up.

During legislative sessions, O'Bannon would conduct weekly news conferences where reporters from around the state would gather around the large conference table in his office and ask whatever questions they had for the week.

Most always, these weekly conferences were conducted late in the week for reporters who were working on Saturday or Sunday stories (particularly print reporters). There were few surprises in these sessions, as O'Bannon's press secretaries, Phil Bremen, Thad Nation, and Mary Dieter, would quiz reporters beforehand about what was on their mind that week. Most would gladly give a broad overview of their particular line of questioning—a few did not. Regardless, any information gained was helpful in prepping the governor prior to the sessions. He rarely made headline news in these sessions and impressed many by his rather adept ability to talk about and discuss issues but rarely take controversial or problematic positions that required clarification or backfill. While it frustrated, perhaps, many of the reporters around the table, for those of us in the press office, it was preferable to a governor with a loose or speculative tongue or lack of discipline when on the record.

"It was one of the true frustrations of covering him," Lesley Stedman Weidenbener said. "You would go to an availability and go back and listen to your tape and have no idea on earth where he was on an issue."[26]

Brian Howey put it this way: "I always enjoyed covering a presser by Governor Frank O'Bannon, in part because he wasn't a very good public speaker. But he always spoke from the heart. He tended to ramble. He would call the press in on Fridays, give an opening statement, and then take questions. Figuring out how to get the next question in was always a challenge, because the governor rambled. When reporters thought he had finished an answer, you'd hear a series of single syllable, 'Wha' or 'Why...' and then O'Bannon would resume."[27]

WISH-TV statehouse reporter Jim Shella and Governor O'Bannon continued a weekly practice started under Governor Bayh of conducting individual, weekly interviews with the governor. The segments, rarely edited, ran for their entirety on typically news-scarce Sunday evenings. For the governor, it allowed him unfettered access to address issues. For Shella and WISH, it gave them substantive local news on an otherwise slow news day.

There were differences, however, in how Bayh and O'Bannon handled the longer form interviews. Reporters who covered Governor Bayh complained often about his "pat answers" and unwillingness to answer questions he didn't want to—in short, he was "too slick" some thought, according to Mary Dieter. Ironically, under Governor O'Bannon, some of those same reporters would complain O'Bannon was not "slick enough" and gave longer, more complicated answers, and over time, certainly was not "the king of the sound byte."[28]

Phil Bremen, a veteran reporter who worked several years as a correspondent for NBC News and later as a reporter and anchor at WRTV-TV in Indianapolis, joined the O'Bannon administration in its first few weeks in January 1997 and served the entire first term as press secretary. Bremen did not know O'Bannon personally before being appointed but, as a TV veteran, was focused on helping the governor succeed on TV.

"Most people do not read the paper and most of them do not read it very critically. I knew that we had to get our message across on TV or we were going to fail…Did I know that he was not the world's greatest public speaker? Sure…But I thought that was just who he was, and I did not want to undermine his confidence. I thought that if we just put him out there and let him be who he was that we would be perfectly okay," Bremen said.[29]

The governor remained a newspaperman at heart, whether reporters knew it or not. He never liked hearing about a state agency slow-walking a media request or that he himself (or anyone else) should give a slick or "half answer" to a question. In fact, when he felt staff were protecting him too much from questions, he would quickly cut through that. He also rejected suggestions that he ignore the question asked by a reporter and instead answer the question he wished they asked.

Dieter said she knew O'Bannon was for real and witnessed it at times when he had no points to score, no gain to make. During an editorial board meeting at the *Fort Wayne Journal Gazette*, the editors raised their concern with the governor that the state's Bureau of Motor Vehicles had been unforthcoming with a variety of public records requests they had made over the preceding months.

"He just listened to them and sort of nodded, and I am sure that there was steam rolling out of my ears as we heard what the BMV had been doing over the course of many, many months to not comply with their requests for public records," Dieter said. "...When we got out to the car, I could tell the governor was angry—angry almost to the point of speechless. I said to him, 'Governor, do you want me to call the BMV?' And all he could say was, 'Yes.'"

Dieter worked the phones while en route from Fort Wayne to Indianapolis, and by day's end, the BMV was photocopying the requested records for overnight delivery the next day. "I could just tell that it hurt O'Bannon's sensibilities at a very basic level," she said. "He took the open records law very seriously, and he felt it very, very important to be open and honest with the press, and to sit there and realize that members of his administration had done the exact opposite, really, made him very, very angry."[30]

O'Bannon was committed to an open government, as recognized by the Hoosier State Press Association. During his tenure, he created the Office of Public Access Counselor following a series of reports in Indiana newspapers detailing difficulties many of them had in obtaining access to public records. Attorney Anne Mullin O'Connor became the first public access counselor. She said other states consulted with Indiana on open access issues after the office was established. The key to Indiana's success, according to O'Connor, was the unwavering support of the governor.[31]

Stephen Key, general counsel for the HSPA, remembered O'Bannon's opposition to a 2001 bill that would have exempted state lawmakers from the state's open records law by keeping some of their records, including e-mails on state accounts, private. Key believes O'Bannon avoided the "safe" approach by letting the bill become law and instead vetoed it. Key said the veto was "an example of personal courage and moral conviction that I'll always remember."[32]

During his second term, O'Bannon paved new ground, becoming the first Indiana governor to offer radio addresses every other week on a network of Indiana radio stations operated by Network Indiana, mirroring the approach of presidents Bill Clinton and George W. Bush. The addresses allowed O'Bannon unfettered access to voters to talk about issues of importance at the statehouse. In his initial speeches, O'Bannon focused solely on positive subjects such as the importance of celebrating the birth of Dr. Martin Luther King, Jr., or volunteering in one's community. His positive, high-road approach did not save him from petty criticism, however, as house Republican minority leader Brian Bosma of Indianapolis and the State Republican Party complained to Network Indiana and others that the governor was being granted an unfair advantage (despite the fact that the addresses were initiated at the start of 2003, when O'Bannon was constitutionally barred from seeking a third term in office). For a short time, Bosma and other Republicans offered "Republican Response" recordings for Network Indiana—all of which took on heavily partisan tones and attacked the governor's record. O'Bannon remained committed to his original intent, staying away from partisan issues in his remarks, and continued to record the messages every two weeks until the time of his death in office.

ESSENTIAL TREMORS

Reporters had generally ignored the fact that Frank's voice would quiver and his hands would often shake during particular times he was in public. Some thought these attributes were more pronounced when the governor was nervous or when TV cameras and lights were pointed in his direction. However, for almost all of those years, no one reported on his appearance. At the start of 2000, the governor's office and state Democratic leaders began picking up on rumors that some Republicans were circulating that speculated that O'Bannon's tremors represented the onset of Parkinson's disease, or worse yet, Alzheimer's disease.

Norm Cox, a veteran statehouse reporter for WRTV-TV, reported on the governor's shaking hands early in 2000 when O'Bannon appeared before a special hearing of the House Ways & Means Committee in the north atrium of the statehouse. Without a podium or desk, O'Bannon's shaking caused the papers in his hand to flap gently, something the

WRTV cameras zoomed in on. (Similar video shot later in his term would show his hand shaking strongly when he signed bills at ceremonial bill signings in his office.)

Some members of O'Bannon's campaign team were nearly panicked that Cox's report would be harmful to the governor's reelection campaign. The governor was out of town on state business and unable to address the issue head-on. It didn't matter; Judy O'Bannon took the bull by the horns that day and explained that the governor had a medical condition known as "essential tremors" or "familial tremors." Common in the Dropsey side of O'Bannon's lineage, the tremors were in no way debilitating to the governor or reflective of any diminished capacity.

"I have lived with him for forty-three years, and he has had it the whole time I have known him," Mrs. O'Bannon told the Associated Press after the WRTV report aired.[33]

The administration also quickly made available O'Bannon's personal physician at the Indiana University School of Medicine who confirmed the tremors and dubbed them more an annoyance than anything else. "It is not associated with any kind of brain disease. It is not related to Parkinson's or any other neurological disease. It doesn't affect brain function at all," Dr. Robyn Goshorn told reporters.[34]

Although refuted by physicians and family, the rumors of a debilitating medical condition did not stop. The rumors persisted into 2001 when one WSBT-TV reporter from South Bend called the press office and repeatedly asked the governor's office to "confirm or deny" that the governor had been "diagnosed as being in the early stages of Alzheimer's disease." The reporter declined to name her sources and probably never had any of any repute, for her story never ran.

Her inquiries, though, provided for an awkward exchange between me and the governor in his office when I was sent to explain to him the line of inquiry from the television reporter. "Show her my medical reports. Have her talk to my doctor," the governor said as he turned and walked back toward his desk, flashing a rare moment of either anger or embarrassment about being asked such a delicate and potentially hurtful question. The governor routinely provided the results of his annual physical to reporters from then on, up until and through the time of his stroke and death in September 2003.

Reporter John Ketzenberger believes O'Bannon was hard to rattle and understood the roles of reporters. When asked about how it felt to take so much flak, O'Bannon replied, "'Oh, it's no big deal; it's just part of the process,'" Ketzenberger said.[35]

"Ketz" remembers with fondness another time when Frank O'Bannon was at ease and a good sport with reporters. During the annual softball game between members of the press corps and members of the administration and legislature, O'Bannon (then serving as lieutenant governor) was the "secret weapon" reporters called on for their team to pitch against Governor Bayh's team. "Well, he got shelled. He was not a good pitcher! But it was indicative of the good sport that he was. We had a lot of fun that day!"[36]

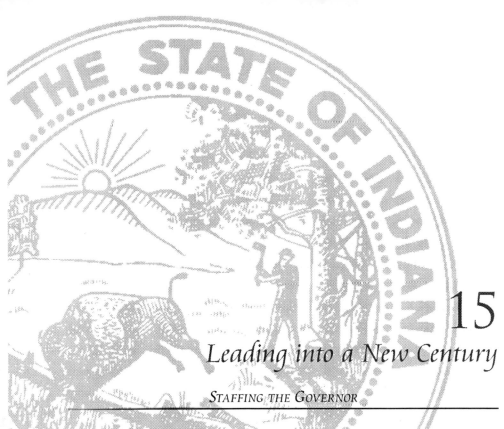

15

Leading into a New Century

Staffing the Governor

As the O'Bannon administration started, a "staffing the governor" document was presented to help new staff understand their duties and define the role of state police troopers who accompany the governor wherever he goes. The communications and press office staff often helped prepare briefing and advance materials for Governor O'Bannon, though executive assistants and agency heads played key roles as well.

Staff was responsible for prepping and briefing the governor before he attended public events. As schedule demands continued to grow, so did the importance of these duties. Schedule requests poured in daily, and several times a week, a team consisting of the chief of staff; the press secretary; Cindy Athey, the governor's executive assistant; and Jonathan Swain, the first lady's chief of staff, reviewed them. The governor's deputy chief of staff or deputy press secretary would also occasionally attend. Athey helped sort out requests for Governor O'Bannon. She had the advantage of having worked with him for many, many years and understood well the events he would like to attend, or needed to attend.

En route to events, Governor O'Bannon often reread briefing materials, especially talking points he would use for his public remarks. His habit was to underline phrases in the talking points. He often underlined almost every word in the document.

Governor O'Bannon was not a difficult public figure to "staff." He was rarely demanding and was exceedingly patient and kind, but was very interested in making sure he was on time to an event. He understood his role in the events he attended. Introducing the governor was rarely necessary—Frank O'Bannon knew someone everywhere he went. That's what thirty-three years in public life in Indiana had brought, a familiarity that Hoosiers normally reserved for members of their families. They treated him like a favorite uncle or grandfather.

Even as governor, Frank O'Bannon acted like a candidate in that he always wanted to arrive on time and often was one of the last to leave. He was patient and open with Hoosiers he met in communities big and small who wanted to connect with their governor—even the ones who would complain to him directly. He saw it as part of the job.

One night, I attended a Governor's Council on Aging dinner with O'Bannon at the Adam's Mark Hotel. It had already been a long night with too many speeches. The event edged near 10 p.m., but as we started to leave, many of those in the audience approached wanting to take pictures with the governor. Some were more aggressive than others in making their requests, but the governor honored each one of them. He quietly waved off my attempts to facilitate his exit. During the car ride back to the statehouse, the governor said to me kindly, "You know, some of those folks just want to take those photos because they think they've met someone famous. And for them, they have. They've met their governor. It's not that they want to have their photo made with me, it's that they want to say they had their photo taken with the governor." A moment later, his classic smirk came over his face, and he said, "Some of them probably think my name is Evan Bayh!"[1]

This was not the first time he was mistaken for Governor Bayh. Following editorial board meetings at the *Fort Wayne Journal Gazette* and *News-Sentinel* one morning during the governor's push for Energize Indiana, the governor asked to make a stop at a Burger King in downtown Fort Wayne to pick up a quick lunch. Standing in line to order food, the governor picked up something for the troopers on his security detail as well, while I waited further back in line. The man standing with me noted, "That guy up there, he looks real familiar, but I can't remember who that is."

I smiled and said, "That's the governor of Indiana."

"That's Evan Bayh?" the man said in all seriousness. "He looks different in person than on TV."

I gently corrected the man, noting, "Oh, well, that's actually Governor Frank O'Bannon."

"Oh, of course! O'Ban-yun!" he said, offering up the most common mispronunciation of his last name.

State Trooper Alex Willis recalls an incident in which the governor decided he wanted to talk firsthand with a guy who had followed him around for the better part of a day with a sign protesting the extension of the Monon Trail north from Marion County into Hamilton County. Willis said he first noticed the man circling the governor's residence near Forty-sixth and Meridian streets before the governor left for the statehouse for the day. His truck was decked out with protest signs saying, "Stop The Monon Trail!" Later, the same man circled the statehouse several times and stopped his truck near the governor's vehicle along Capitol Avenue as the governor exited for the day. According to Willis, the governor became curious about the man and his signs and walked up to him to talk. "He said to me, 'See, that guy just wanted to talk to the governor. Now he can go back and tell his friends that he got to talk to the governor about his concerns.'"[2]

Joe Smith, Jr., recalls traveling with O'Bannon in the state police plane to attend a day packed full of school and church events in Lake County in observance of the Dr. Martin Luther King, Jr., holiday. Smith said O'Bannon lived out the "day on, not a day off" theme for the King Day holiday to promote community development and improve race relations, and he avoided the misstep that other politicians would sometimes make—showing up for a service at an African-American church just long enough to be introduced or speak—and then sneaking out before the service was over.

"He was very comfortable staying for the whole service, and I think he actually enjoyed the services, enjoyed being part of it," Smith said. "He had a good rapport with a lot of the ministers in Indianapolis and Lake County...I think they honestly felt a connection with him, and they knew they could come to him and talk to him."[3]

John Zody traveled with the governor often and helped prepare advance materials. He met O'Bannon earlier during campaigns in the "bloody eighth" congressional district of Southwestern Indiana. Zody keeps as a treasured memento a photo from one of O'Bannon's "Straight Talk Walks" that he would take as a candidate through neighborhoods in various Indiana cities and as another a photo O'Bannon snapped of Zody as he peered out the window of the state police helicopter trying to identify landmarks along the way.[4]

The governor often sought to record memories by either pulling out the pocket-sized digital camera that went almost everywhere with him or the larger, more sophisticated digital camera he kept in a bag. He was especially proud when trips included sweeps over his home in Harrison County. "The governor always proudly pointed out familiar places in Harrison County, evidence that this was home to him," Zody said.[5]

O'Bannon avoided using state helicopters or the state police airplane as often as he could. Sensitive to the cost and the appearance of sweeping in to events in a helicopter or plane, O'Bannon more frequently rode in a state police car. His very last public appearances in Indiana in September 2003 are an example: He was driven from his home in Corydon to Indianapolis to board a National Guard helicopter to view flood damage in southwestern and western Indiana from the air and then returned to the airport and rode back to Corydon by car.

THE DETAIL

The governor of Indiana and his immediate family is provided twenty-four-hour-a-day security from a "security detail" comprised of members of the Indiana State Police. The men and women of the detail work extremely long hours, but also enjoy attending all of the events the governor attends and often meeting many of the people the governor would meet. Lieutenant Ray Raney was in charge of the troopers who made up the detail and coordinated his work through Bobby Small, the governor's executive assistant for public safety, and Cindy Athey.

Raney said, "We had a good relationship from the very start. The governor was just a very kind man, a gentleman's gentleman."

Raney recalls his first weekend at the O'Bannons' barn home at Corydon. "(Trooper) Jay Nawrocki and I were sleeping on the floor in sleeping bags in their living room," Raney said, noting that final plans had not been made on where the troopers would spend their nights in Corydon. "Governor and Mrs. O'Bannon came in and watched movies with us at night on TV. It was a family-type setting, very laid back. We weren't used to being in casual clothes as much as we were with the O'Bannons down at Corydon and other places."[6]

Judy O'Bannon said the adjustment to having a security detail was larger than she had expected. "Most of the time you think (having the detail) is a big help, and you understand, but there are days when you are feeling tired and a little overwhelmed, and it can feel smothering," she said.[7]

Judy remembers with a laugh the first time it "sunk in" that the security detail was going to be with her for a long time. "I was in the department store and planning to buy some personal items, and then I remembered I had the trooper with me, so I thought, 'Well, I'll just wait until tomorrow to buy this,' and then it hits me, he'll be with me again tomorrow, too!"[8] She decided to "get over" her shyness and bought what she needed and was on her way.

Securing the governor's safety at the statehouse and the governor's residence in Indianapolis was rather straightforward. Raney had considerable experience, having worked on the detail for both the two previous governors. The O'Bannons' home in Corydon, however, was a bigger struggle. While the home was set far back from the roadway, down a long lane, leaving clear view of any arriving visitors, the O'Bannon home backed up to hundreds of acres of natural forest in a state park and was difficult to secure.

Eventually, the troopers stayed at a small cabin on the O'Bannon property or a local motel. If the O'Bannons did not leave their home or property, they were left alone. Detail members, however, always went with O'Bannon on his hikes through the woods, bird watching, or on canoe trips.

Trooper Alex Willis, a tall, imposing former Marine, gained a new appreciation of bird watching, something he had never considered before. "I enjoyed being in Corydon, and he taught me a lot about nature," Willis said. "You know, living in the city you don't think about the birds and the trees. Being down there, I gained an education about different types of birds, and turtles and all sorts of wildlife. Just floating down Blue River in a canoe...he would point out a lot of things that you wouldn't see or wouldn't notice since you live in the city."[9]

The governor himself did not view the detail as an imposition—he understood what their job was and let them do it. He did not want to be "over-staffed" and wanted the troopers to be present but at an appropriate distance and never interfered with their work. Over time, he became very close with each of the men (and one woman) who served on the detail. Willis smiles when he recalled O'Bannon liked to sneak away to the China King carry-out restaurant just down the street from the governor's residence or the Hardee's in Corydon, for a quick bite to eat. Knowing Judy did not like it when her husband ate "junk food," he'd smirk and tell her, "The boys were hungry, so we stopped off for some food."

The State of the State

One of the most exciting and tense times of all in a governor's office is the annual January rite known as the State of the State address. The "SOS," as it's referred to by staff, offers the governor a chance to address a joint session of the Indiana General Assembly in the house chambers. The day of the speech, Governor O'Bannon was frequently out of sight, completing last-minute changes on the speech or practicing it one more time. Over the years, the amount of time television stations across the state are willing to give to the speech for live broadcast has continued to shrink, placing tremendous pressure on the governor to keep his speech within the approximate twenty-five-minute frame of TV time provided. Frustratingly, as the O'Bannon administration moved into its sixth and seventh years, some Indiana TV stations declined to accept free satellite feeds of the address for broadcast altogether, instead either broadcasting it on tape delay on another day, or featuring highlights on the late local news. O'Bannon campaign funds were used to pay for the satellite broadcast so that taxpayers had no expense for this broadcast. Indianapolis TV stations, however, ran all seven of the governor's speeches in their entirety, even those that slipped a little past the twenty-five-minute mark.

All staff members had specific assignments on SOS day and into the evening, ranging from ensuring that invited guests got to their seats in the house gallery, to keeping Mrs. O'Bannon and family moving toward their seats or even making sure department heads and other guests, who watched the speech on TV from the governor's personal office, were seated. Copies of the speech were placed on every chair in the house chambers in the last hour before the speech—the real struggle being to keep lobbyists from swiping up all the copies of the speech before legislators arrived. Most legislators, particularly legislative leaders and Democratic leaders, had reviewed the speeches in advance either via e-mail or in hard copy. As a result, there were usually few, if any, surprises on State of the State night.

One year was the exception, and it was a critical mix-up that had to be solved immediately. Going into his first State of the State address in January 1997, just days after his inauguration as governor, O'Bannon's staff had worked feverishly to meet all sorts of new demands, including just figuring out their new jobs.

"There had just been so much to do, and we all had these specific jobs to do, but no one had taken on the role to contact the guy who runs the teleprompter," staff member Donna Imus recalls. "That afternoon, the governor is supposed to begin his final practice for the speech, and to use the teleprompter. It's then that we realize we've never reserved one! We called the teleprompter guy, and even though it's like 2 or 3 p.m. on the day of the speech, I begged him for his help, and he agreed to come down and help us out at the last minute."[10]

Imus and Cindy Athey delayed Governor O'Bannon's arrival from the residence to the statehouse while the teleprompter was hastily set up at the statehouse, so as to not throw off his speech preparations. "Everyone loves Frank O'Bannon, but the comparisons between him and Evan Bayh, as far as being a smooth speaker, were not always flattering to O'Bannon, and without a teleprompter, it would have been him reading the speech from paper, and oh, that would have been a disaster," Imus said.[11]

Governor O'Bannon would start work on the text of his State of the State address several weeks ahead of time, with key policy staff beginning to suggest major themes or ideas. Because the address was the best chance to highlight the governor's legislative agenda each session, the "meat" of the address was almost always known well in advance. O'Bannon worked with just one primary writer on each of the speeches, which over the years included Tom New, Rachel Gorlin, Ron Powell, Cheryl Reed, and Mary Dieter. O'Bannon also conferred closely with the lieutenant governor, accepting major suggestions and additions to the speech. The governor's chief of staff (New, Margaret Burlingame, Jim Maguire, or Tim Joyce), Cindy Athey, and First Lady Judy O'Bannon were also primary advisers—particularly when it came time to settling on particular phrases, examples, or themes to use in the speech.

"The governor sought active involvement from the lieutenant governor," Cheryl Reed recalls. "I think that was a testament to the governor's confidence in him as a leader and as a full, working partner in the administration."[12]

O'Bannon also liked to follow a style of speech seemingly perfected by both President Ronald Reagan and later President Bill Clinton and borrowed heavily by most smart politicians since. To make a point or to emphasize one, it was always valuable to have real-life Hoosiers in the gallery or elsewhere in the room that he could welcome and highlight.

"For the 2002 speech, following the 2001 terrorist attacks, he was very concerned about and interested in having representatives of the Muslim community in the room," Reed said. "He was always interested in including the role of faith in the addresses, but in 2002, it was particularly important."[13]

"The governor was never hesitant to change any speech he gave or to disregard the comments we gave him entirely, and that was true for the State of the State as well," Reed said.[14]

Governor Bayh attended Governor O'Bannon's first State of the State address on January 28, 1997, just days after he had left office— undoubtedly a surreal experience as he moved from the front of the room to the house gallery.

The speech contained few surprises for those who followed O'Bannon's '96 campaign for governor and focused on the enactment of property tax cuts balanced with new money for schools as part of his 21st Century School Improvement Plan, highway construction as part of the Crossroads 2000 program, and five hundred more police officers in Indiana communities. Most of all, the speech reflected the flush economic times in which it was offered.

"We can do all of this and still leave the state with a reserve of a billion dollars," he said, adding that every decision must be measured against the question: "Does it leave our children and our grandchildren better prepared for tomorrow?"[15]

In that first speech, he highlighted Lt. Governor Kernan's recent hip replacement surgery with a hip built by a Warsaw, Indiana company. O'Bannon drew a hearty laugh from all when he said that Kernan's new hip meant, as director of the state's economic development efforts, that "he not only talks the talk, he walks the walk."[16]

O'Bannon's second address, in January 1998, came exactly one year to the day after his inauguration and after weeks of build-up with the governor out on the road highlighting his legislative agenda for the upcoming session. He touted many accomplishments in his first year: more than $300 million in tax cuts, the Alternative Schools program for high school students in danger of dropping out or being expelled, five hundred new police officers on the street, welfare reform and job training, more help for prosthetic devices for injured Hoosiers, and Emily's Law for tougher standards for amusement park rides and operator insurance (which he signed in the presence of four-year-old Emily Hunt of Indianapolis, a young girl who lost her grandmother and was paralyzed in an amusement park ride accident).

The big question going into the speech, however, was whether the governor would endorse a house Democratic caucus proposal to send a $100 "refund check" to each and every Hoosier as part of tax cutting amidst a growing state surplus.

"We stand here in a time of prosperity looking forward to the next millennium," he said. "Hoosier families should not have to wait to share the benefits of this year's higher than expected reserve. After all, it was created largely by their tax dollars. Let's get their money back to them directly. I believe the best way to do this is to send every Hoosier a check," he said, drawing heavy applause from house Democrats. Then he quickly added, "But, I recognize this isn't the only way," this time drawing heavy applause from Republicans.[17]

The words he used next would prove prophetic to the days that would lie ahead in the second O'Bannon term: "My bottom line is simple, I'll sign a tax cut that does not jeopardize school funding, does not increase the base budget, does not create an operating deficit, and does not reduce our reserve below $1.1 billion. Because our state learned a hard lesson in the recession of the early 1980s, you cannot prepare for a downturn when you are already in one. Only in the sunshine can you plan for a rainy day, otherwise you end up soaked."[18]

In the 1999 speech, O'Bannon highlighted his most beloved public policy issue: state funding of full-day kindergarten. His speech came as the state found itself with a record surplus of $2.1 billion. He noted that his legislative agenda built off the success of his early childhood development initiative, "Building Bright Beginnings," launched a year earlier, advocating high-quality, affordable child care and ready-to-learn programs for the state's youngest children.

Introducing outstanding kindergarten teachers from across the state, the governor said, "Though we've made it optional, the benefits of full-day kindergarten are so great that I hope that every community takes advantage of this opportunity. From music to computer skills, the full-day curriculum exposes developing minds to areas of lifelong interest. I want to sign full-day kindergarten into law this session."[19]

Former governor Ed Whitcomb attended the January 1999 O'Bannon speech, but it was former governor Robert D. Orr, a Republican, who attended each O'Bannon speech. Governor Orr's presence became something O'Bannon staff and supporters looked forward to each time. Though physically slowed by his age, Governor Orr remained mentally and intellectually engaged to the end of his life. Governor Orr's loyalty grew from his friendship with O'Bannon when they both served in the state senate (and during Orr's eight years presiding over the senate as lieutenant governor) and his shared interest in Indiana history and government. Like Governor O'Bannon, Governor Orr loved Indiana and loved the formality and tradition of the State of the State address— and his friendly and genuine manner was welcomed and appreciated each year by Republicans and Democrats alike.

First Lady Judy O'Bannon was a welcome guest at each of the State of the State addresses, and Governor O'Bannon always acknowledged her and the lieutenant governor at the start of each of his speeches. During the particularly challenging period of the second term and reflecting how much he had come to rely on those who loved and knew him best, the governor's voice cracked heavily with emotion at both the 2002 and 2003 speeches as he greeted Mrs. O'Bannon, calling her "my partner in life and a tireless worker for the state of Indiana." The O'Bannon children and grandchildren were also often in attendance, including the 2000 speech when grandson Asher Reed decided to sit on the floor of the house gallery at Judy's feet, peeking through the beautiful brass railings as his grandpa's speech went forward on the house floor below.[20]

During the 2002 address, O'Bannon told Hoosiers that "our world has changed and our country is at war. Six hundred men and women of the Indiana National Guard are on active duty in fourteen countries around the world tonight. Our armed forces are on the front lines, and we are all engaged in the fight against terrorism wherever it lives." He noted that Hoosier lives were among those taken in the September 11, 2001 terrorist attacks, and just days before the speech, U.S. Marine Sgt. Jeanette Winters of Gary was killed in action in Afghanistan, the first Hoosier to die in the conflict. The 2002 speech coincided with the birth date of Reverend Dr. Martin Luther King, Jr. (1929-1968), prompting the governor to add that King's life "reminds us of the power each one of us has, and how that power grows when we work together."[21]

The last State of the State address offered by Governor O'Bannon came on January 14, 2003, a speech that reporters said was more hopeful than they expected given the deepening recession that gripped the state's economy and, as a result, state government's checking account.

O'Bannon remained positive, however, and focused heavily on his Energize Indiana initiative, property tax reform, and improvements in public education.

He urged those in attendance to "mark this day on your calendar, mark this day because today is the beginning of a revitalized economy in Indiana, one in which our citizens can find and keep jobs that provide a living wage. Mark this day because it will be remembered as a day in which we embraced tradition but resolved to make it better, when we recognized our strengths and were committed to build on them. A day when we looked at the faltering national economy and said: Enough! It will be remembered as a day when government will say that we have a moral obligation to take care of our fellow citizens who need our help and pledged to do our best for them."[22]

PEOPLE WITH DISABILITIES

One of the most critical public policy issues left as a boiling pot on the stovetop of state government for literally decades boiled over during Frank O'Bannon's years as governor. Still unresolved was the manner in which Indiana planned to provide services for people with disabilities.

While some states, including Michigan and Oregon, had moved aggressively to eliminate large, state-run facilities for people diagnosed with mental retardation, developmental disabilities, or mental illness, Indiana (like most states) continued to rely heavily on state developmental centers and state mental health hospitals. And while thousands of mental health patients had successfully rejoined the community with the help of new and aggressive prescription drug treatments and advances in civil rights laws, persons with mental retardation and developmental disabilities often languished in the state system.

A variety of pressures were building on the system, including a U.S. Supreme Court ruling in *Olmstead v. Georgia* that required states to make additional accommodations under federal Medicaid rules to provide services in the least restrictive setting possible. Another was the unexpected and accelerated closing of several privately run institutions in Indiana operated by ResCare that resulted in a closing process filled with controversy. A multi-month investigation later by reporters Kevin Corcoran and Joe Fahy of the *Indianapolis Star* found several problems with the ResCare closure process—problems that were never again repeated by the state, but provided painful lessons regardless.

In July 1997, the long-simmering pot boiled over for the first time. A hidden-camera report on WISH-TV, Channel 8, in Indianapolis, confirmed in seconds what many had feared or suspected for decades. The hidden camera, worn by a state employee who had grown frustrated at the level of abuse and neglect she witnessed, showed employees of the New Castle State Developmental Center in Henry County openly and frequently verbally and physically abusing the clients. The story was quickly picked up by the national media, especially CBS News and CNN.

O'Bannon visited the site immediately to see for himself, firsthand, the problems the hidden camera had recorded. Staff members were fired or suspended, and O'Bannon ordered cameras installed in the public areas of the center as an additional means of preventing abuse. The facility's seemingly overwhelmed superintendent was replaced, as were senior managers in the Family and Social Services Administration (FSSA) responsible for the New Castle center. Criminal charges were filed against some state workers, though final convictions were difficult to achieve. Adding oil to the fire, an Indiana State Department of Health survey at the facility during the same period cited dozens of instances of abuse or improper treatment and placed the facility on a fast track to losing its federal funding—representing two-thirds of the facility's budget.

O'Bannon called upon Kathy Davis, FSSA secretary, to lead an aggressive process to downsize and eventually close the facility. Davis dove in with a dedicated team from FSSA and throughout state government, personally convening many of the task forces created to address the transition issues presented as residents were prepared to move from the New Castle center to community-based care settings, closer to their families, and hopefully away from the abusive tendencies of state-run facilities.

While the transition process at New Castle moved forward quickly, Davis represented the governor on every front possible—with residents, their families, state employees, and community leaders and members. She withstood many days of criticism from family members or state employees but systematically helped lead a historic transition in the way Indiana would provide care for some of its most vulnerable citizens.

However, the problems at state facilities were not over and would soon engulf other state facilities like the Muscatatuck State Developmental Center in rural Jennings County where similar allegations of abuse and neglect arose. The facility eventually lost Medicaid funding, meaning state revenue would have to replace millions in federal funds to pay for the care of residents. Never before in the state's history had a state-operated facility been decertified by the federal government.

Despite earlier hopes to save Muscatatuck, the governor gave in to the reality that the facility needed to close, costing Jennings County its largest employer. He called upon Katie Humphreys, the new FSSA secretary, to lead that closure process. Humphreys had earned a deep respect from O'Bannon for her previous work in correcting problems at the Indiana Toll Road and for her outstanding leadership in the development of Hoosier Healthwise, Indiana's CHIP program.

While New Castle and Muscatatuck parents and state workers were angry with the governor for the closings, advocates for people with disabilities (particularly John Dickerson and Costa Miller) remained supportive of O'Bannon and his efforts.

The Arc of Indiana, the state's most outspoken organization for people with disabilities, presented O'Bannon and members of the General Assembly with its "2000 Legislative Award" for their efforts to implement components of Senate Enrolled Act 317, or "the 317 plan," as it became known, that pumped the first significant sums of *new* money into the care system for people with disabilities. The "317 plan" set aside $39.3 million in new state funding for services. The result was immediately positive.

"Just three years ago, people with developmental disabilities, or the family member who serves as their primary caregiver had little choice other than institutional care," the governor said. "Now, we're focused on providing community-based care whenever possible. With the help of Arc and others, we're providing a more active form of care that is giving these Hoosiers freedom and independence that they have never before experienced…"[23]

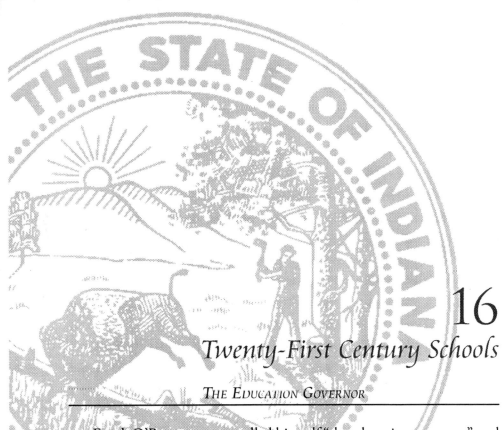

16

Twenty-First Century Schools

THE EDUCATION GOVERNOR

Frank O'Bannon never called himself "the education governor" and seemed at times to shy away from the oft-used title. But there are few issues in which O'Bannon's impact and love shine more brightly than in education including traditional K-12 public schools, but also early childhood learning, full-day kindergarten, post-secondary opportunities for college-bound young adults, and educational opportunities for returning adults needing to recapture skills and abilities for the ever-changing workplace. In short, O'Bannon envisioned an educational system in Indiana for "lifelong learning," a term that many Hoosiers had yet to embrace at the start of O'Bannon's governorship.

A great symbol of O'Bannon's commitment to education stands along West 173rd Street in Hammond, Indiana, a working-class neighborhood close to the steel mills and the busy streets of Chicago and a state away from Frank O'Bannon's hometown near the Ohio River. The Frank O'Bannon Elementary School sits proudly as the largest and newest school in the city of Hammond. It's a school Frank O'Bannon would love. His name is emblazoned on the school sign outside and on a wall inside the front doors of the school, but those aren't the only references to the school's namesake one can find. One small black and white picture of the governor is thumb-tacked up to a bulletin board inside a display case which is dominated by the artistic achievements of the more than four hundred kindergarten through sixth-grade students who attend school here. The students are as diverse as Indiana in the new century—one-third African-American, one-third Caucasian, and one-third Latino or Hispanic. A vast majority of the students at the Frank O'Bannon Elementary School receive free or reduced school lunches, and the school continues to challenge itself to improve its performance on statewide academic achievement tests. It's a lively environment where learning is happening in high-tech classrooms outfitted with the latest audio-visual technology and computers.

Improving Indiana's educational system was at the top of O'Bannon's list when he entered office and remained there throughout his tenure as governor in spite of resistance he sometimes encountered in the statehouse.

TWENTY-FIRST CENTURY SCHOOLS

In his first month in office, O'Bannon launched into a statewide campaign for his "21st Century Schools Plan," an initiative to improve Hoosier public education, make education more affordable, raise student achievement, create public charter schools, ensure safe and drug-free schools, and expand local control of schools. One goal of the plan, free school textbooks, produced a major fight with some legislators— particularly Republicans. O'Bannon felt strongly that free textbooks were an essential component of equality in education and that textbook fees placed an unfair burden on Hoosier families. O'Bannon said, "Our state constitution was one of the first in the country to guarantee a free public education to every child. A free public education must start with free textbooks."[1]

Undaunted by legislative challenges to his priorities, O'Bannon visited Indiana schools frequently, touting the fact that the state was picking up the cost of textbook rental for students whose household income qualified them for free lunches. In previous years, the General Assembly had appropriated only enough to pay for 70 percent or less of the textbook rental fees for free-lunch students. In the state's urban school districts in particular, that was a major expense. At the time, 65 percent of Indianapolis Public Schools students were on the free lunch program, with similarly large numbers in school systems in Clark County, Fort Wayne, Evansville, Gary, Lafayette, New Albany-Floyd County, South Bend, Terre Haute—22 percent of all students statewide. "That forced the hard-pressed school districts themselves to make up the difference, siphoning precious dollars away from other educational efforts," O'Bannon said.[2]

The 1997-98 school year also saw the start of alternative school programs in many school systems across the state, giving expelled or soon-to-be expelled students a second chance to finish high school. The General Assembly granted O'Bannon's request for $15 million in funding for a two-year program—giving schools $750 more for each student who needed to be enrolled in an alternative school.

The governor knew that students who quit school or were tossed out because of behavior or other problems were often set on a course for financial and personal struggle for years to come. "Alternative schools in Indiana have already proven they can turn young lives around," O'Bannon said. "I'm proud that we now are better able to encourage this important work."[3]

That fall, O'Bannon completed his statewide tours of schools by promoting $6 million in new Safe Haven grants to local schools. The Safe Haven program gave children a safe place to go before and after school where they could learn and get help with homework.

The governor also pushed for remediation funds for local schools to help them focus high school students to successfully complete the ISTEP Plus (Indiana Statewide Testing for Education Progress) test before they graduated.

In the weeks that followed the April 1998 Columbine High School murders in Colorado, public school safety received a great deal of attention from concerned parents and educators, as well as the media and legislators. O'Bannon used his already scheduled statewide town-hall forums on public education to revive interest in school safety programs he had previously pushed. O'Bannon urged lawmakers to support his Safe Schools Plan that focused on appointing school safety specialists in every school corporation, creating School Safety Commissions in each county to develop safety plans, and the establishment of a State Council on Safe Schools to receive grant requests for safety funding and review county safety plans.

"Children can't learn and teachers can't teach if they are worried about getting mugged, beaten, or shot," O'Bannon said. He knew Indiana schools weren't immune to the violence. "…If there's one thing the tragedies in other states have taught us, it's that it can happen anywhere."[4]

READY TO READ: FOCUS ON THE BASICS

O'Bannon, a voracious reader throughout his life, believed reading was the foundation for nearly all other learning, "…not just in school, but in all of life," he said. With test results showing a third of the state's third-graders unable to pass the ISTEP reading test, O'Bannon urged lawmakers to pass legislation requiring that every third-grade student be able to read at or above a third-grade level before being passed on to the fourth grade. His plan focused on pinpointing students struggling with learning to read in first and second grade, proper diagnosis of specific reading problems, and working with parents to help tailor individualized reading improvement plans for each student who was struggling.

Dr. Suellen Reed, the state superintendent of public instruction, shared O'Bannon's commitment to helping students struggling with reading problems at an early stage in their education. "…The issue is just that the gap just gets wider and wider because they did not have the basics to build on to start with. Those problems just start to show up more and more and there is the discouragement and disillusionment that students get into and they stop trying."[5]

SCHOOL ACCOUNTABILITY

The O'Bannon administration also focused heavily on increasing and improving the accountability of Indiana schools. As a long-time legislator, O'Bannon understood that Hoosiers were willing to support education and schools, but a near-constant fight had to be waged to answer the pointed question, "Just what are we getting for our money?" To address that, O'Bannon pushed hard in 1999 for expanded "report cards" for Indiana schools using measures to stimulate and track continuous improvement. Beyond that, he proposed initiatives to help reward schools that met achievement goals and provided help to schools and communities where progress was slower.

"It's important to honor and even financially reward schools that make exemplary progress," the governor said. "Indiana must have a strong accountability system, not to punish schools, but instead to pinpoint where improvement is needed and then push to achieve that improvement."[6]

O'Bannon's attention to standards and school accountability won him notice as the National Education Goals Panel named him the chair of its bipartisan group for 2001. The panel, created by President George H.W. Bush in 1990, engaged federal and state officials from both parties in focusing state efforts on supporting increased student achievement, high school completion, teacher education, and lifelong learning.[7]

THE EDUCATION ROUNDTABLE

To help improve accountability, O'Bannon formed the "Education Roundtable," whose job was to "flesh out the accountability plan and serve as a standing advisory body to the State Board of Education on Indiana's standards and accountability systems."[8]

The Education Roundtable would grow in power and influence over public education in Indiana during the course of the O'Bannon administration.

Created through the work of O'Bannon, Reed, and their advisers, the Roundtable sought to bring together divergent groups of Hoosiers that heretofore could find little to agree about on education. Situating O'Bannon, a Democrat, and Reed, a Republican, at the head of the effort was not only wise politically, it assured widespread buy-in from across the state. O'Bannon and Reed both enjoyed a high level of trust and respect from stakeholders in all corners—respect earned from years of having worked for what was best for schools, not just for politics.

Dr. Reed told O'Bannon, "Don't you think it would be good to bring these people together? If they looked each other in the eye, I think the conversation could be elevated considerably, and we could possibly get something done."[9]

To create that eye-to-eye discussion, O'Bannon made a rare move for a governor, but not one that was all that unusual for him. He proposed that he and Reed *jointly* appoint all of the twenty to twenty-five members of the Roundtable, and do so by mutual agreement rather than splitting up the appointments between them, forcing them to seek a group of people with particular strengths and assets. "We wanted a group that would go out and report back to and seek input from their constituencies, and then bring that back to the table so that a broad base of people all across the state would know what was going on," Reed said.[10]

O'Bannon and Reed devoted themselves to the process, keeping their promise to attend each and every meeting of the roundtable for six years. "If we were going to get CEOs and other very busy people to come and commit to this, we had to show that we were committed to it at an equal level," Reed said.[11]

Reed helped salve some initially wounded feelings on the part of members of the State Board of Education—for decades the most powerful group in deciding the path for Indiana's schools. Reed said, "Many of the board members felt the Roundtable was taking away some of their role. It was all for the greater good because there were folks and constituencies represented on the Roundtable that were never represented on the board. They were able to leverage the power in the legislature that we never could get otherwise. We even had legislators on the Roundtable. So I think the board understood that it was their role to offer final approval, and that it was up to the Roundtable to recommend..."[12]

The success of the Education Roundtable became more and more apparent as the work progressed. *Indianapolis Star* education reporter Michelle McNeil attributed the success to the people serving on the board. She said, "There were some very powerful people there, from all sectors, business, education, unions, several groups that had previously been in conflict with one another. It was led by two people...whose passion and concern for education was unchallenged."[13]

FDK

Frank O'Bannon had felt strongly about the value of kindergarten in early childhood since 1964—the year his own daughter Polly was five years old and ready to attend. At that time, no public or traditional kindergarten existed in Corydon. Judy O'Bannon went to work that year with a group of other parents and started the first Kindergarten in Corydon, which was then incorporated into the public school system.

"Both of us attended kindergarten, and we knew the value of getting an early start on education," the governor said. "We didn't have science to back us up then, but we do now."[14]

Knowing his own children benefited greatly from at least a half-day of instruction as five-year-olds, O'Bannon made the concept of full-day kindergarten, or FDK, the centerpiece of his 1999 State of the State address, if not the number one goal of his first term in office. "Science now tells us that the earliest years of a child's life bring opportunities that may never come again," he said. "These are opportunities not only for learning, but also for learning how to learn. What we invest in education early on for our children will pay dividends throughout their lives."[15]

O'Bannon was convinced that full-day kindergarten would improve a student's readiness for school, build a foundation for lifelong learning, broaden the skills and interests of young students, involve their parents more, and provide flexibility for parents and local school corporations concerned about their youngest ones.

The experience of the Evansville-Vanderburgh School Corporation became "ground zero" in the full-court press the O'Bannon administration applied to the need for full-day kindergarten. Evansville had invested as early as 1986 in a full-day kindergarten program and had improved test scores among most of its students, particularly in the important elementary school years. Compared to students in other urban districts in the state, Evansville students had higher high school graduation rates, higher SAT and ACT scores, earned more scholarships and honors diplomas, and had higher marks on report cards for academic performance and conduct.

Almost daily in the last half of 1998 leading up to the 1999 legislative session, the governor, lieutenant governor, and Mrs. O'Bannon fanned out across the state making the case that five-year-olds in Indiana could use the opportunity of FDK to move ahead now and throughout their lives.

O'Bannon's plan called for the state to make available $15 million to local school corporations for the space, staffing, and transportation issues created by expanding kindergarten. He estimated it would cost another $96 million to take the program statewide in the second year of the 1999-2001 budget biennium—all supported by the state's then surplus-rich General Fund, not local property taxes. To gain passage, the governor suggested in his proposal that local officials could use the funds to implement other early childhood education programs, such as supplementing Head Start, Even Start, transitional kindergarten, or transitional first grade.

O'Bannon confronted doubters straight on. "When it comes to state education policy, full-day kindergarten is not 'cutting edge'; it's only catching up," he told legislators at a hearing in late January 1999, urging passage of House Bill 1689 that carried the

FDK provision. He noted Indiana was one of only a dozen states that didn't fund even optional full-day kindergarten in the public schools.[16]

"How can we expect our kids to compete on the SAT with Iowa or Ohio or New Jersey if they are already behind them from the get-go?" O'Bannon asked legislators. "Without full-day kindergarten, both our kids and our economy are at a competitive disadvantage."[17]

Joining O'Bannon at the front of the fight were two important allies, state school superintendent Dr. Suellen Reed and Dr. Phillip Schoffstall, superintendent of the Evansville-Vanderburgh School Corporation. Schoffstall said, "Full-day kindergarten is an integral part of today's total educational program. It is the foundation upon which all future education is built. A kindergarten filled with a variety of learning activities will help the child grow socially, emotionally, physically, and intellectually."[18]

Dr. Reed was equally committed and happy to have the power of the governor behind the idea. "I can tell you, as an educator, it was very gratifying to work with a governor who paid so much attention to these issues, and cared so much about them."[19]

Legislators, it seems, were going to be a harder sell.

"First of all, kindergarten is not mandatory in Indiana, and the governor was going to make it an all-day thing and spend how many millions of dollars to do that? A lot of people asked, 'Why not make it mandatory first?'" said John Ketzenberger, who covered the 1999 FDK debate. "I don't think the public really got it...There was good research and certainly good intent, but the inability to get it through some of the Democrats in the house where they had a majority was startling."[20]

The less-than-enthusiastic reaction of some legislators deeply frustrated the O'Bannon team who had sent the governor out on thirteen separate Education Forums in communities big and small in every corner of the state in the fall of 1998 leading into the '99 session.

In spite of all of Frank and Judy O'Bannon's efforts, Senator Lawrence Borst, the Republican chair of the Senate Finance Committee, rated O'Bannon's ability to rally support for the FDK initiative as "negligible."[21]

O'Bannon adviser David Johnson said some legislators viewed the proposal as perhaps a step too far into the personal choices of parents raising their young children. "For some of the legislators...it was closer than they felt comfortable getting into it."[22]

Despite concerns coming from many quarters, the FDK bill finally began to move in the Democratically controlled house, thanks in large part to the efforts of Democratic Speaker John Gregg and Representative Greg Porter of Indianapolis, the chair of the House Education Committee. Efforts continued, however, to shave off the cost of the program—particularly for the second year of the biennium—in an effort to attract more votes.

Phil Bremen, O'Bannon's first-term press secretary, thinks the governor approached the issue in the right way. "I think the governor had it exactly right: Make it available full-day and allow parents to send their children if they wish. I think he knew that would work in Indiana," Bremen said.[24]

As the long session moved into its final days, however, the fate of the governor's full-day kindergarten proposal was still in doubt.

O'Bannon and Gregg made one more big push—hosting a loud, overflow rally in the statehouse rotunda on April 21, 1999. At the rally, Dr. Schoffstall, the Evansville superintendent, presented the governor with more than 1,700 cards bearing the thumbprints of five-year-olds who attended full-day kindergarten, bringing a wide smile and a trademark "thumbs-up" from O'Bannon. Schoffstall introduced the governor as "one of the greatest advocates for children I have ever known," and O'Bannon himself seemed overwhelmed with the volume and passion of the rally.[25]

"There is no question that all legislators support our schools," O'Bannon said, making certain to avoid labeling opponents as not caring about kids.[26]

"Brain research tells us now that learning begins from day one. We know also that a child's brain grows 90 percent in the first three years of life, and we have to concentrate on that," the governor said. He believed investing in full-day kindergarten would lessen the cost of remediation, decrease the numbers of dropouts and children left behind, and increase the likelihood that more graduates would finish school possessing the skills they would need for the workforce.[27]

Knowing a fight was on to save his plan, O'Bannon continually emphasized the voluntary nature of his program—voluntary for local schools to determine whether they could support such a program and voluntary for any parent who did not think his or her five-year-old child was ready to attend school all day. His move was especially important amidst a counter proposal offered by Senate Republican leaders, dubbed a "cafeteria plan," that would offer local schools a pool of new funds from which they could select to offer full-day kindergarten or fund other needs.

O'Bannon was determined to fund FDK separately and set his outer limit on what sort of compromise he could accept. "No school district should be put into a position to pick and choose safety over a good start for kids, or remediation over a summer school program."[28]

In the days that followed, behind-the-doors biennial budget negotiations progressed with majority Democrats from the house and majority Republicans from the senate driving the process. In a surprising finish that shocked many, full-day kindergarten became an unexpected casualty as a proposed conference committee report left O'Bannon's plan on the floor. The reasons why it was left out prompted immediate and angry disagreement at the time—a disagreement that time has not healed.

Senate Republicans were one major hurdle. Among their caucus, support for FDK was strongest among Republicans representing more urban areas, and those with more moderate political perspectives. Overall, Republicans were leery of handing O'Bannon such a powerful "tool" for his expected run for reelection the next year. Widespread rumors at the time indicated that State Republican Party chairman Jim Kittle heavily pressured his party stalwarts to stand strong against it.

Senator Morris Mills, an Indianapolis Republican, authored the GOP's "cafeteria style" plan. Democrats viewed the plan as unacceptable—fearing local schools would be too budget-pressed to use those funds for other operational expenses and not invest in FDK.

Representative Bauer, the South Bend Democrat in charge of the powerful House Ways & Means Committee (and later elected speaker of the house) and a key player in the house-senate conference committee on the budget, said, "The senate Republicans had the cafeteria plan... We fought over this for three weeks, and finally, it came down to the fact that we gave them some money for some of their things and they would give us 50 percent of the kindergarten funding the first year and 50 percent the second year."

From there, disagreement sets in as to how the proposal failed.

Some think it was a political gaffe on the part of the O'Bannon administration—refusing the 50 percent offer and instead calling the GOP's bluff with an "all or nothing" ultimatum. Worse yet, rumors emerged that the O'Bannon team had failed to fully communicate amongst themselves what was happening in the budget negotiations. Others chalk it all off as a big political gamble—a stare down with the Republicans and a dare to send them back to their districts to try and explain why they opposed spending part of the state's still-flush General Fund on such an important educational advancement. Still others question the commitment of some house Democrats to begin with, saying they favored new money for schools that went directly to teachers' salaries and additional teachers to reduce class sizes, or even other spending or tax cuts, and not new money for a new program.

Everyone agrees on one thing: Republican and Democratic politics played a part.

Mike Smith, who covered the debate for the Associated Press, said, "I think O'Bannon stuck to his guns to the very end on that and to tell you the truth, that surprised a lot of reporters...There was no way that the senate Republicans were going to give him the whole cake on that."[29]

Statehouse reporter Jim Shella agrees and offers a second reason: He believes O'Bannon failed to convince the public they needed it.[30]

Legislators were pleased a budget deal had been reached, meaning no special session would be necessary and the regular session could end on time. "It became obvious shortly after we expressed our euphoria about the fact that we had a deal, that someway or another, something had happened where some others were on a different page," Gregg said. "I can remember some heated conversations with some people, not with the governor, but with some of the people who worked for the governor, and even though we were all kin, we were all of the same party, there was some major disagreement about what had happened. Governor O'Bannon came back down to the statehouse in the middle of the night, and we met. The problem was, as I recall it, that Pat (Bauer) had reached an agreement and we had given our word and all of this was in motion and there was a breakdown..."[31]

O'Bannon and his team were stunned—and angry at the legislators, at themselves, and at the process. The breakdown was painful and difficult to digest.

"I don't think that Frank O'Bannon was well-served by the process," Johnson said. "He had heard a lot about early brain development and early childhood development and had become captivated with that and its potential...By then, he had established the Education Roundtable and was really bringing people together and trying to do something in those areas. The issue has moved quite a bit since then, but there was some real, actual resistance to the idea of full-day kindergarten."[32]

As O'Bannon arrived back at the statehouse in the wee hours of the morning, he made it clear to Democratic legislators that he was unhappy—very unhappy—that the budget did not include funding for full-day kindergarten. Understanding the process and that Democrats felt they had made a deal on the budget, O'Bannon asked Gregg and Bauer to make another attempt to resurrect the plan and put FDK into another bill still pending—a last-ditch effort to save the plan. O'Bannon and Reed showed up the next day at a legislative hearing and made impassioned pleas for the passage of some form of FDK in a new bill, even if it wasn't included in the biennial budget.

The effort failed, with senate Republicans refusing to go along, noting they had offered a cafeteria plan for FDK earlier—and reminded everyone they had a budget deal already agreed to with house Democrats. Shortly thereafter, legislators voted for a new biennial budget that did not include FDK funding and went home, sine die.

The issue of full-day kindergarten was also sine die.

O'Bannon signed the budget regardless of the fact that it lacked its number one priority for the session and took the high road publicly. He told a joint meeting of the Indiana School Boards Association and the Indiana Association of Public Schools Superintendents, "Many people asked me why I didn't veto the budget since full-day kindergarten was not in it. My answer was there were so many other good programs that did pass, and I couldn't jeopardize them. First and foremost among them was the favorable funding for public schools."[33]

His office issued brief remarks just after midnight on April 30, 1999 when the budget passed and FDK was left behind. The release quoted the governor as saying, "This is a very good budget and will do good things for the people of Indiana." A paraphrased paragraph followed, however, outside of quotes that said, "At the same time, O'Bannon expressed anger that lawmakers had turned their backs on his proposal to fully fund full-day kindergarten for every school system and every family that wanted it. They were turning their backs on their own campaign promise as well as on the state's children, he said."[34]

Dr. Reed recalls, "…I think in the end, the truth of the matter is that when we had money and could have spent it on that, we did not have the unanimity of the people to do that. We worked so hard to get that, that later on, when we did have more of a consensus of feeling about the importance of FDK, then we didn't have the money."[35]

McNeil, covering the debate for the *Indianapolis Star*, said, "I think O'Bannon's views were very influenced by the importance of early learning, full-day kindergarten. He had a commitment to funding education if even, politically, it needed to be cut. I think his philosophy was that this was not a place for politics, per se, and that the more resources we could put into early education, and education in general, the better. I thought he was for real on that issue. You could see that he was at some of his best with kids…"[36]

"Significant progress always comes with difficulty," Phil Bremen said. "Typically, in the course of history, the people who are most responsible for it are not around to see it happen. What we have seen is that full-day kindergarten has gone from a statewide campaign that Frank O'Bannon painstakingly engineered to sell people on its value. We had legislators tell us 'I didn't have full-day kindergarten, and I turned out okay.' That argument was gone in 2004…The debate had shifted down to one issue: How to pay for it. That happened because Frank O'Bannon laid the groundwork and got people thinking."[37]

The governor's chief of staff, Tom New, said, "Not being able to see the enactment of full-day kindergarten was a major, major disappointment to Governor O'Bannon."[38]

New said enacting FDK would ensure "all of Indiana's children… the right start, the start they deserve, and the start that Frank O'Bannon wanted for them always."[39]

ACADEMIC STANDARDS AND OTHER ACHIEVEMENTS

Despite his stunning and demoralizing defeat to enact full-day kindergarten for Hoosier youngsters, Governor O'Bannon maintained his focus on improving Indiana schools and began a push for new charter schools in Indiana; full funding for special education programs for local schools; character education programs, including supporting zero tolerance policies for profanity and abusive language among students as a means of promoting a more favorable learning environment (particularly in secondary schools); closing the achievement gap between rich and poor students; improved teacher training; and less regulatory requirements at the state level, to promote more local control of schools.

Academic standards became a major push in the governor's second term, with Indiana earning outstanding praise for its progress. The Indiana Chamber of Commerce, longtime critics of public schools in Indiana, lauded the state's new standards for English as "the very best in the country." The chamber, along with the Indiana Education Information Center, funded a study by the Thomas B. Fordham Foundation to look at state academic standards for students and concluded Indiana's performance was noteworthy among the states.[40] Achieve, another nationally recognized and independent organization that evaluated states' academic standards, assessments, and accountability practices, joined in praising the progress being made in Indiana.[41] Later, the American Association for the Advancement of Science gave Indiana an "A" for science standards that they said were "among the best in the nation."[42]

A RAND think-tank report in July 2000 said Indiana was among the top four states in the nation for raising the mathematics scores, "with gains about twice as great as the national average," and ranked Indiana among the top eight states in academic performance for students from similar racial and socio-economic backgrounds.[43]

By 2001, Hoosier students began scoring higher on head-to-head testing standards reported periodically by the National Assessment for Education Progress, or NAEP. The results were impressive: Among fourth-graders, Indiana students ranked second in math scores, eighth in science, seventh in reading, and ninth in writing. Eighth-graders in Indiana ranked fourth in math, seventh in science, eighth in reading, and eleventh in writing.

O'Bannon pointed praise toward students, teachers, parents, and even his Republican and Democratic predecessors. "Governor (Robert) Orr started us in the right direction when he introduced a statewide education assessment system," O'Bannon said. "Governor (Evan) Bayh then refined the assessments, put in place the state's first academic standards, and improved teacher quality. Since then, we have raised academic standards, and we have also improved the assessment process by bringing real accountability through clearly defined goals and expectations."[44]

The progress being made in Indiana did not go unnoticed by the administration of President George W. Bush following his inauguration in January 2001. Bush had campaigned hard on the need for high standards as a way of improving the nation's schools. In January 2001, O'Bannon was among a small group of governors invited to the White House to discuss public education reform efforts at the state level with the president. O'Bannon reported to Bush about Indiana's effort to increase academic standards, support for quality teachers and professional development, and the emphasis on early reading as a basic skill for long-term success. In January 2003, Bush invited Dr. Reed to the White House for a special ceremony recognizing Indiana as among the first five states to receive immediate compliance with the president's highly touted "No Child Left Behind Act of 2001." The No Child Left Behind Act provided new and unprecedented federal accountability measures for all K-12 schools, school districts, and states—and Indiana was in an elite group of states getting the job done on the state level.

COMMUNITY COLLEGES OF INDIANA

Another major push of the O'Bannon administration was for the creation of a first-ever community college in Indiana.

In January 1999, O'Bannon asked legislators to join the existing Vincennes University in Knox County and the Indiana Vocational-Technical College, or Ivy Tech, into one Community Colleges of Indiana, on twenty-three separate campuses.

Bringing the leaders of Vincennes and Ivy Tech together was no small feat but represented the level of trust and respect leaders across the state had for O'Bannon. If Frank O'Bannon was asking them to come together, they had to at least try. O'Bannon also enlisted the Indiana Commission for Higher Education and his hand-picked commissioner, Stanley Jones (a former state legislator), to develop the partnership over the coming years.

By September, community college campuses were all reporting record-breaking enrollment increases in the range of 17 to 22 percent.

In 2001, enrollment figures showed overall growth above 40 percent at all campuses—"helping provide a bridge for students, young and old, who aren't sure that a four-year university is right for them, but for whom the existing two-year programs weren't a good fit. There is a place in Indiana for all of these alternatives," O'Bannon said.[45]

Gregg believes the community college system, eventually built around the Ivy Tech system and not his beloved Vincennes University, is a major O'Bannon achievement. "You have a system that is working, you have twenty-plus sites around the state where people are going to school, and that will always be a big part of Frank O'Bannon's legacy," Gregg said. "He changed the face of public education in Indiana, and if you look at the five state universities and the regional sites, almost every person is now within a short driving distance of a community college."[46]

Bill Moreau, a long-time adviser to both Governor and U.S. Senator Evan Bayh, also praises O'Bannon's role in helping ensure community colleges were born in Indiana. "It's been controversial, but any change is controversial in Indiana," Moreau said. "...But for Frank O'Bannon, and Higher Education Commissioner Stan Jones, there would be no CCI. To be certain, it caught the Indiana higher ed establishment completely by surprise, triggering some hostile reactions...The sneak attack was necessitated by (Jones') well-founded belief that the initiative would have been killed by the higher ed establishment had it been subjected to a year-long study or some other process in the name of consensus building. There have been several attempts to kill CCI in the cradle."[47]

17
Issues of Challenge

NATURAL RESOURCES AND THE INDIANA STATE MUSEUM

Throughout O'Bannon's terms as governor, Indiana's natural resources enjoyed a strong friend in the governor's office. In Indiana's official state song, "On the Banks of the Wabash Far Away," lyricist Paul Dresser writes about longing for his Indiana home, "where I first received my lessons, nature's school." The words fit O'Bannon's life perfectly. O'Bannon was an early explorer of the woods, streams, and trails of hilly Harrison County—and always lived near the land. In time, bird watching would become one of his greatest personal passions.

O'Bannon was devoted to the Department of Natural Resources, which was viewed by some as an "extra," ripe for budget trimming when state revenues fell flat. He was readily available for DNR-related events, whether it was for a community park, recreation development, historic preservation, or even urban forestry.

Three projects completed during the O'Bannon administration will stand as long-term evidence of the governor's commitment to natural resources: the new Indiana State Museum, the completion of the White River State Park, and the creation of the new Prophetstown State Park.

The state museum project, when completed in 2002, was the capstone of decades of work. The $65-million, 230,000-square-foot facility anchors the White River State Park and provides a vibrant look into Indiana's history and the promise of its future. Its completion pleased many, many Hoosiers—but it perhaps pleased the first lady most of all. Judy O'Bannon had served many years on the museum board of directors (under the appointment of Governor Bayh) and was thrilled the project finally moved forward under her husband's watch.

"There were a whole lot of people who hung tough on the state museum project for a whole lot of years. They believed in it," Judy said. "…They felt it was important, and even when other people didn't think it was important…They did whatever it was they could, whether that was making sure there was money in there from their role on Senate Finance, or some other way."[1]

Frank O'Bannon liked the personal stories of Hoosier history, "and he was very much in awe of what other people in Indiana had done. He saw the state museum as a wonderful way to present in a collective way the many wonderful things that Hoosiers have done over the generations. This is something that (former Lt. Governor) John Mutz agreed with, too. When…John and Frank were running against each other in 1988, they would say: 'Hoosiers don't think enough of themselves,'" Judy said.[2]

O'Bannon and Betty Cockrum, who ran the Department of Administration during the first term, knew the work of completing a state museum and the multitude of other state building projects was an important one. They both settled on the idea of asking Susan Williams, an outspoken and tough-minded member of the Indianapolis City-County Council, to help.

The project was not going to be easy, and O'Bannon told her that. "He knew that things had to change, he knew that some folks had to go away, and he knew that the project where it stood was not going to be funded by Lilly Endowment," Williams said. "…He wanted a museum that people would be proud of and that after they walked out, they would be proud to be Hoosiers."[3]

Williams decided basically to start over, firing the former architect and hiring a new one. O'Bannon's support never wavered for Williams or the project. "The state museum is not the most important thing he ever did in his administration, but it is about the only thing from his administration that will be standing there a hundred years from now," Williams said.[4]

O'Bannon was equally excited about the start of the state's twenty-third state park—the Prophetstown State Park in Tippecanoe County (which Governor Joe Kernan opened in September 2004). The park, a long-term project for former senator Mike Gery, State Representative Sheila Klinker, and others in west central Indiana, was a favorite of O'Bannon's for another reason—because of a specific commitment to include areas that maintained important (and quickly fading) sections of the Indiana prairie, savanna, forest, and wetlands common to the area more than 200 years ago. Completion of the park meant that every Hoosier now lived less than an hour's drive from a state park facility.

John Goss, head of the DNR after Larry Macklin retired, believes the Hoosier Heritage Trust program is also a big part of his legacy. "Well over 300 properties have been purchased and 33,000 acres have been set aside, permanently, into public trust."[5]

CROSSROADS 2000 AND I-69

As a former legislator, O'Bannon focused perhaps more of his energy on transportation issues than did other governors. He knew the value of quality roads, bridges, and highways across the state—not only to legislators, but to the citizens they served. O'Bannon was more supportive of twenty- and thirty-year bonding arrangements to fund needed improvements. The bonding effort led to "Crossroads 2000," the governor's aggressive program to fund more than $560 million in improvements through the Indiana Department of Transportation during a four-year period. The first bonds were sold in early June 1998. Curt Wiley, O'Bannon's first INDOT commissioner, said without the governor's commitment many of the projects would never have gotten off the ground.[6]

Among the key projects moved forward because of Crossroads 2000 was the Hoosier Heartland project across north central Indiana, linking Fort Wayne, Logansport, and Lafayette. Improvements to heavily traveled interstates in Lake County were also completed under Governor O'Bannon.

Another O'Bannon commitment was to build two new bridges to span the Ohio River between Indiana and Kentucky. O'Bannon and his friend Kentucky Governor Paul Patton, also a Democrat, signed a pact detailing how the two states would proceed with the projects. Patton said the pact became known as a "two bridge, one project" agreement calling for a bridge on Interstate 265 on the east side of Louisville, Kentucky, and a downtown bridge from Louisville to Indiana. Patton said the pact reflected "an atmosphere of communication and coordination" that existed between him and O'Bannon and their shared commitment that development and success on one side of the river positively impacted both sides of the river.[7]

The biggest project that took important steps forward under Governor O'Bannon (and later under Governor Kernan) was the completion of Interstate 69 between Evansville and Indianapolis. O'Bannon decided to ride by car from Indianapolis to Evansville along existing winding and narrow state routes to make the announcement that was met with cheers and a few jeers in Evansville on January 9, 2003.

O'Bannon said he knew some, particularly environmentalists, who opposed any new road construction and instead favored a route for I-69 to follow I-70 west from Indianapolis to Terre Haute and then south to Evansville along the route of U.S. 41 in southwestern Indiana. "I have always been an advocate of protecting our precious natural resources, and I pledge to you today that my commitment has not and will not waver as this project proceeds. In fact, I have already directed INDOT to begin work with the appropriate state and federal agencies to get to work on environmental permit and mitigation issues," O'Bannon said, doing little to placate a few "boo birds" present at his packed announcement.[8]

The Republican mayor of Evansville at the time, Mayor Russ Lloyd, Jr., and Democratic and Republican legislators stood shoulder to shoulder with O'Bannon as the announcement was made. "Thank you, Governor, for keeping your promise and selecting a route," said State Senator Greg Server, an Evansville Republican who never shied away from criticizing the governor when he felt it appropriate, noting that he had personally tracked the project for more than twenty years. "I think of all the economic development proposals the governor has put forward, this one will have the longest term effect on southwestern Indiana," Server added.[9]

LIFE AND DEATH DECISIONS

A governor can influence many, many aspects of life in a state such as Indiana, but no other aspect of the governor's job description was as closely guarded and gravely serious as the decisions O'Bannon faced regarding whether a death sentence would ultimately be carried out.

Seven men were executed by the State of Indiana during O'Bannon's two terms, more than the three previous administrations of Governors Bowen, Orr, and Bayh combined. All were by lethal injection. The path to this increase in the number of executions reflected the varied and challenged road the death penalty had taken in Indiana and all states in the final decades of the twentieth century—including a record-setting pace of placing ten men on Indiana's death row in 1985.

Governor O'Bannon considered and denied clemency for each of the seven men. In each instance, he carefully and, perhaps most importantly, privately considered his decisions. He rarely conducted interviews on the subject of the death penalty but made it clear as a state senator and later as a candidate for governor and as governor that he supported the death penalty in certain cases.

In announcing each of the clemency denials, O'Bannon carefully outlined his process for determining whether to grant clemency. He consistently listed five points or "tests" he needed to satisfy himself that the sentence was appropriate.

First, he noted his support for the separation of powers between the branches of government: "I give substantial deference to the laws written by the legislature and the conclusions reached by the courts. Our legislators have clearly demonstrated that the death penalty is appropriate in aggravated murder cases and because the General Assembly has the constitutional authority to establish penalties for crimes, I will not substitute my judgment for theirs."[10]

Second, he noted that "it is not my role to second-guess years of judicial proceedings. Rather, I look to whether there is compelling and credible new evidence that would indicate a grave miscarriage of justice—evidence that was never presented to the courts (or) evidence that can no longer be presented to the courts." He also said he focused on whether "there is some fundamental defect in the judicial process that would erode our confidence in the integrity of those proceedings. If the process was fair, then I will defer to the findings of the court."[11]

"Exceptional circumstances" were also a consideration, such as acts of heroism or compassion conducted by the condemned person that could support granting clemency "even where guilt is clear and the legal proceedings were fair," he said.[12]

Finally, consistent with O'Bannon's respect for state government and its institutions, he said he considered fully the recommendations of the Indiana State Parole Board in making clemency decisions. In fact, he honored the Indiana State Parole Board's findings in each instance, including the delay in the Darnell Williams case occurring in what were to be the last weeks he was in office in 2003.

O'Bannon called death penalty decisions "the weightiest and most difficult responsibility of any governor" and never took any public delight in pounding the pulpit of law and order when the final days before an execution approached and a clemency decision was awaited from him.[13]

Judy O'Bannon believed these proceedings were difficult for Frank. "We never went anywhere the day of an execution, and often the day before, we would also cancel events. He thought it was important that we stay focused on what was happening."[14]

When any of the execution deadlines approached, O'Bannon took sometimes difficult questions from reporters, frequent and emotional appeals via the mail, telegrams, and phone calls, and on all seven occasions, pickets led by death penalty opponents on the sidewalk in front of the governor's residence on North Meridian Street. The picketers' voices and chants could be heard inside the residence. The O'Bannons understood it "went with the territory," as the governor often said. "It is hard to hear people yell that you are a killer," Judy O'Bannon said. "People of good will, and I think most people in public service are of good will, don't always make decisions that we agree with…"[15]

In one interview on the subject, O'Bannon told *Indianapolis Star* political writer Mary Beth Schneider that he had signed up as a law student to witness an execution but never got the call. "I wanted to see… personally what my mind would tell me about an execution," O'Bannon said. His comment drew a quick response from death penalty opponents who criticized him for allowing executions without ever having seen one (forgetting that no modern-day Indiana governor has witnessed an execution).[16]

The direct phone line from the residence to the execution chamber at the Indiana State Prison at Michigan City was always tested the evening of an execution, but O'Bannon never used the phone line and never permanently stayed any executions.

Indiana actively conducted the executions in the first fifty years of the twentieth century, by means of hanging from 1900-1913, then electrocution from 1913-1995, when Indiana's law was changed to require executions by lethal injection. Every person executed in Indiana has been male and 71 percent of them have been white.[17]

Support for the death penalty has remained high in Indiana throughout the decades, as public opinion polls demonstrate, although Indiana's death penalty statute followed an uncertain path throughout the 1970s, as it did in every state. In 1972, a U.S. Supreme Court ruling in *Furman v. Georgia* struck down that state's death penalty, striking down similar statutes existing in all other states, removing 629 inmates from death row across the U.S., eight of them in Indiana (each of whom had their sentences commuted to life imprisonment). As a result, the 1973 session of the General Assembly acted quickly to install a new death penalty statute removing death penalty discretion from juries and making the death penalty a mandatory sentence upon conviction for first-degree murder when aggravating circumstances were present. That statute was invalidated three years later by a 1976 U.S. Supreme Court decision, resulting in seven more men having their sentences commuted to life sentences. In response, the 1976 legislature (with then-State Senator Frank O'Bannon and Senator Les Duvall of Indianapolis drafting new legislation) passed I.C. 35-50-2-9, modeled after a Florida statute allowing for consideration of aggravating and mitigating circumstances presented to a jury.

Then-State Senator Frank O'Bannon's support of the death penalty did not come without personal pain. Among those who registered their complaints with him was his own sister, Rosamond (O'Bannon) Sample, who sent a telegram to her brother at the statehouse telling him of her disapproval of the death penalty.[18]

With new laws in place, Indiana's death penalty appeals process began to take about a decade to complete—resulting in a larger number of death penalty cases reaching their conclusion under Governor O'Bannon than any of his three predecessors in office. Executions did not proceed in Indiana, however, without careful consideration, especially considering irrefutable evidence (often tied to emerging DNA test results) in other states, including nearby Illinois, that clearly indicated innocent individuals had been sentenced to die for crimes they could not have committed. In 2000, Governor O'Bannon asked his friend State Senator William Alexa of Valparaiso to lead the Indiana Criminal Law Study Commission in a review of all aspects of Indiana's death penalty system to reveal whether any bias existed and whether safeguards were in place to ensure that innocent persons were not put to death.

The study took two years to complete, and O'Bannon declared that the report determined Indiana has in place strong safeguards—principally standards for representation in capital cases and a thorough review process by our dedicated Supreme Court—that guard against wrongful convictions of the sort that have occurred in some other states. The study found white defendants were more likely to be sentenced to death than minority defendants and an especially important consideration for some of the state's cash-strapped smaller counties: death penalty cases cost taxpayers about one-third more than cases ending with a life sentence. The report recommended statutory changes signed into law by O'Bannon following the 2002 session, including raising the minimum age for the death penalty from sixteen to eighteen years of age, representing the final chapter to Indiana's infamous place in the international spotlight when sixteen-year-old Paula Cooper of Gary was sentenced to death for her role in the murder and robbery of an elderly Bible study teacher, Ruth Pelke. (Cooper's death sentence was vacated in 1989 in a ruling by the Indiana Supreme Court that it is unconstitutional to execute persons under the age of eighteen. Her sentence was commuted to life.)

In 2003, following successful efforts in overturning death penalty sentences in Illinois, a group of law students and nationally recognized appellate lawyers descended upon Indiana to take up the matter of the pending execution of Darnell Williams of Lake County. On July 28, 2003, Governor O'Bannon took a rare step and granted a sixty-day reprieve to Williams' scheduled execution so that DNA testing could be conducted on blood found on Williams' trousers to permit "all relevant evidence to be discovered." Williams and Gregory Rouster were originally sentenced to death for their roles in the 1987 robbery and murder of an elderly Lake County couple. Rouster's death penalty was vacated earlier by the courts. Governor O'Bannon did not live to see the conclusion of the Williams case, with DNA testing ruled inconclusive as to Williams' involvement in the murder. Subsequently, the Indiana Supreme Court set a new execution date of July 9, 2004 for Williams, but seven days earlier, Governor Joe Kernan issued an executive order commuting the death sentence of Williams to life imprisonment. Kernan was concerned that Rouster was more culpable in the murders but had been spared the death penalty after he was declared mentally impaired.

O'Bannon's views on the death penalty remained strong throughout his public life, causing some tension among his political and personal friends (and sometimes even members of his personal staff) who opposed the death penalty. "We should never be sanguine about our capital litigation system, nor should we cease examining each individual case for errors that could lead to appellate reversal or executive clemency," O'Bannon said.[19]

A FULL-TIME FIRST LADY

Frank O'Bannon kept a very small circle of advisers on issues as important as executions. His closest and most influential adviser on difficult and personal issues such as the death penalty was his best friend, Judy O'Bannon.

Judy approached her role as first lady much like she had approached her entire life—full speed ahead. She viewed being first lady as a great opportunity to use the time and the position to advance important ideas. The Benjamin Disraeli quote "The greatest good you can do for another is not just to have your riches, but to reveal to him his own" sums up her approach to being the first lady of Indiana.

Judy focused on community-building efforts, helping with Scouting, church activities—even the addition of cable television in hilly and TV-antenna-challenged Harrison County. Later, she served eight years as chair of the Indiana Main Street Commission that reached out to Indiana cities and towns, big and small, in an effort to not only revitalize the downtown business districts in these Hoosier communities, but to use Main Street revitalization as a starting point for broader efforts at historic preservation, redevelopment, and community building. As first lady, she hosted the "Communities Building Community" roundtable—a forerunner to her weekly television show on public television stations across Indiana. Originating from WFYI in Indianapolis, the show won the support of the Indianapolis Foundation and other underwriters and has won multiple Emmy awards for local programming.

Communities could benefit from technological advances as long as people in the community made reaching out to others a priority, she believed, but she emphasized the importance of personal interaction.

Judy believed that when we involve ourselves personally with one another beyond what any technology allows, "We can look people in the eye, and we can see who is of comfort that day, and who it is who could use a little more consoling or comfort that day."[20]

At the turn of the New Millennium, more than 160 Indiana communities began to prepare for the future. Seedlings were planted on the grounds of the governor's residence and tended to in part by volunteer gardeners from the Indiana Girls School, a correctional facility for juvenile and adolescent girls who had been arrested and required incarceration, who were partnered with master gardeners as mentors. "We were helping these girls who had made bad decisions to feel that they needed to take responsibility not only just for themselves, but for other people," Judy said. "...We're planting the seeds for something good in the future, empowering them with self-confidence."[21]

Gardening remained a focus of Judy's life and work. She started as a young girl as she used a hoe to open folds in the sun-baked Nebraska dirt for a small flower patch, to her own yard in Corydon, and then later when the O'Bannons lived on Broadway Avenue in downtown Indianapolis. She was convinced gardening could bring people together in a community. "Most of all, we're interested in growing people and friendships and community, and along the way, people get to know themselves better," Judy said.[22]

The arts were an important component of life at the governor's residence during the O'Bannon tenure. Judy guaranteed display space for contemporary Indiana artists in a rotating show of their work in all of the public spaces of the residence, rather than the traditional display of nineteenth- and early twentieth-century Indiana artists' work on loan from the Indiana State Museum. "We had enjoyed for years the wonderful paintings from the 'Hoosier Five,' and I like their art, and they looked wonderful here, but I have a real sense that art is alive and well today in Indiana, and we need to celebrate and appreciate those artists as well," Judy said.[23] In all, twenty-six separate shows were opened in the residence.

Each year the O'Bannons hosted four hundred special needs children and volunteers for "A Day for the Arts" at the residence, benefiting Very Special Arts Indiana (VSA). VSA, an organization working with children with autism, developmental disabilities, mental illness, or other challenges, uses art to help them learn how to express, empower, and communicate their feelings and their lives. To conclude the day, they used handmade paper to create bookmarks that read, "There is no limit to where we can go when we go together," with the reverse side featuring a decoration of the children's making. Each child made a bookmark to take with them and a second one that the O'Bannons could distribute at special events and gatherings across the state for months to come.

GOVERNOR'S RESIDENCE RENOVATION

Judy and Frank O'Bannon became convinced of the need to renovate the governor's residence on their first full day there. Among the hundreds of guests invited to the residence that January day in 1997 to celebrate the inauguration was Greg Bedan, a loyal and generous supporter of the O'Bannon campaign. Judy was troubled to find Bedan was prevented from moving around the residence easily because of the multiple floors and steps impeding his progress in a wheelchair.

"I saw Greg sitting there in the dining room and I asked him, 'Greg, how did you get here?' and he said, 'They carried me,' and that was unacceptable to me," Judy said. "I had been a guest at the residence many times before in the past, and I had seen the ramp there and thought that was really all that was needed. I never noticed that the big ramp got you nowhere. I just thought it was taken care of. I never saw anyone there in a wheelchair, and I was negligent in not seeing that. I worked on it from then on."[24]

It would take six more years and a lot of struggle, but Judy and Frank eventually convinced even the harshest critics and doubters of the need to move ahead with a renovation project that made the residence accessible to all Hoosiers.

To help move the issue along, Judy took the unusual step of stringing Christmas lights to the port-o-let parked in the southwest parking area at the residence. The lights and the port-o-let reminded all that a person in a wheelchair, though an invited guest at the governor's residence, would still have to go outside and use a portable toilet in the parking lot regardless of the weather.

Judy also recruited Greg Fehribach, a successful Indianapolis attorney who works from a wheelchair, to join the Governor's Residence Commission. Fehribach's presence, along with his textbook knowledge of accessibility issues, made him a living, breathing example of why Indiana needed to make this improvement.

A study by Nancy Cira, a member of Judy's staff, found Indiana's Governor's Residence far behind many other states. Alabama boasted the best accessibility, in part because Governor George C. Wallace (1919-1998) was wheelchair bound during his last years in office.

In the end, $1.3 million in renovations and additions were added to the house, including a new elevator that stopped on each floor and new office areas, kitchen areas, and dining areas for the governor and his guests. The O'Bannons, however, would never live in the renovated home. The project, started just off the top of O'Bannon's second term, wasn't completed until 2004, when the O'Bannon administration had already ended. In the interim, the O'Bannons moved in late 2002 to the Harrison House on the campus of the former Fort Benjamin Harrison in Indianapolis. The former nurses' dormitory suited the O'Bannons well—though they scaled back official entertaining during this period. The Harrison House was also made accessible during the period the O'Bannons lived there.

Judy said, "It is a civil rights issue for me. To say we believe in equality and then not to be able to get a bunch of people in the governor's residence, that is inconsistent for me."[25]

18

The 2000 Race

Governor O'Bannon launched his campaign for a second term on March 22, 2000 with speeches all around the state, including Corydon, Indianapolis, Terre Haute, and Evansville. The next day, he and Lt. Governor Joe Kernan visited Fort Wayne, South Bend, Gary, and West Lafayette as well.

The record he chose to run on was exemplary: record low unemployment; second in the nation in rise of household income; lowest crime rate in a decade; no tax increases for twelve years; tax cuts of $1.5 billion; above national average scores for math and reading by Indiana students; the Crossroads 2000 highway program representing the biggest investment in roads and highways in state history; protection for more than 15,000 acres of sensitive natural areas for recreation and wildlife; and national leadership in moving Hoosiers from welfare to work and in providing healthcare coverage for more than 114,000 children under the Children's Health Insurance Program.

In his remarks, O'Bannon promised a positive campaign based on issues and not personal attacks. He said education would remain his number one priority for a second term but emphasized his desire for legislators to pass his Taxpayer Protection Plan that included his oft-repeated request that welfare costs be removed from the local property tax rolls. Less than a month later, the governor rolled out a new sixty-second TV ad titled "Right Values." The themes were familiar, images of O'Bannon as a child in a soapbox derby and a Boy Scout uniform, a quick shot of him in his Indiana University basketball uniform, and mention of his Air Force service. The ad ends positively, "It's all about leadership and Hoosier values."[1]

As in the 1996 campaign, the O'Bannon-Kernan campaign included supporting documents for each of the ads' claims about education, employment, tax cuts, more police on the streets, prescription drug coverage for seniors, and welfare-to-work progress.

The campaign would be the second gubernatorial race in a row to set spending records, with O'Bannon and his Republican opponent spending a combined $19.9 million before they were done.[2]

HOMETOWN PRIDE

The reporters and editors of the *Corydon Democrat* were in an unusual position throughout the time Frank O'Bannon was in public life. They were obligated to cover his campaigns and his movements as governor, as well as cover the opposition. That was on the news pages, and they gave the kind of coverage one would expect when the governor comes from a small town. The editorial page, however, was a different matter, and in 2000, Editor Randy West let his pride show. In his editorial a week after O'Bannon launched his campaign for a second term, he recalled Frank's father, the late Robert P. O'Bannon, and what he would say about politicians as he prepared his weekly editorial, *The Weekly Wheeze*, while seated before a little blue portable typewriter. West told readers that the elder O'Bannon would say that politicians tended to look at things in one of two ways: They would "view with alarm" something they didn't like and "point with pride" to something they did like. "If he were here today, the late Robert P.

O'Bannon…would be very proud" of his son but "If he wrote anything at all, he probably would have called his son 'a Corydon boy.'" West went on to describe O'Bannon as a "servant leader" with the right values and attitude to lead Indiana.[3]

A DIFFERENT CAMPAIGN

The 2000 campaign would be very different from the 1996 campaign for O'Bannon, mostly because his opponent was very different. As much as he disagreed with Mayor Goldsmith on policy approaches, Goldsmith and his team maintained a public and private demeanor that was respectful and straightforward throughout the heated campaign. The campaign of his 2000 opponent, U.S. Representative David McIntosh, for the most part, was populated by younger, less-established, and certainly more ideologically conservative Republicans than Goldsmith's team and had an edge that was not seen four years earlier. McIntosh himself at times struggled to keep the campaign on a high plane, interrupting the governor during debates and drudging up troublesome national issues such as partial-birth abortion during the debates—hardly a state issue that Indiana voters wanted to hear their gubernatorial candidates debate.

Some of the struggle for civility may have been related to how far back McIntosh started. Roles were reversed from 1996, when O'Bannon started out behind. In 2000, initial head-to-head polling found O'Bannon with a commanding lead over McIntosh, who was little known outside his east-central Indiana congressional district. In fact, a November 1998 poll by O'Bannon pollster Fred Yang found the governor leading a match-up with McIntosh by a 55 to 28 percent margin. "That is a huge difference from what we had in 1996…," Yang said. "The big…challenge was to try and get our voters to believe that we were continuing the progress, that Indiana was heading in the right direction, and that we had an effective and strong leader."[4]

The campaign was also very different because of the advancement of technology. "What you see is the sheer impact of technology on campaigns," Winston said. "In 1996, we had a mobile phone or a bag phone that came in a bag about the size of a briefcase...We still pulled off the road and used payphones often. We were not blast e-mailing press releases. We were faxing them and invariably being told they did not get them, and we had to send them again. In 1996, when we did the commercials, they would UPS them into us..."[5] That had all changed by 2000. Ads were sent back and forth electronically.

Just getting the candidate to the campaign stop, fundraiser, or other event advanced tremendously in this time period as well.

"This was before MapQuest, too, so in 1996, Cindy Athey would get on the phone and get directions to an event. Cindy has the most powerful Rolodex in the free world, in my opinion, and if you said to her you needed a number, she would have it," Winston said. In 2000, MapQuest readily called up maps—and moving Candidate O'Bannon (as well as First Lady Judy O'Bannon and Lt. Governor Joe Kernan) was many times easier than before.[6]

The 2000 O'Bannon-Kernan campaign was what one dispirited Republican once referred to as "a three-headed monster." While the governor and lieutenant governor campaigned together often, their ability to draw an audience of supporters and reporters and their speaking skills meant they could double up the possible coverage by going two places at once. Mrs. O'Bannon added a third, almost equally important component.

A gifted public speaker, Winston dubbed Mrs. O'Bannon "the greatest campaign weapon in the world...She gave the campaign that extra thing that it needed, and that was high-touch."[7]

Representative David McIntosh

David McIntosh went to the U.S. House of Representatives as part of the 1994 "Republican Revolution" that swept a wave of conservatives into the House and captured the majority in that body for the first time in four decades. Born in 1958 in California but raised in Kendallville, Indiana, McIntosh represented the then-second congressional district in east central Indiana from his home in Muncie and signed the "Contract with America" promoted by the new U.S. House Speaker, Representative Newt Gingrich of Georgia. In Washington, he was earmarked as a House member to watch. His 1994 Republican primary ended before it started, as his expected Republican opponent, State Auditor Ann G. DeVore, stumbled badly and failed to meet the official filing deadline. In the fall, McIntosh had a tougher go of it but eventually overcame Democratic Secretary of State Joe Hogsett to win his first term.

Indiana Republicans worked hard to attract someone to the 2000 race, a winnable race in their estimation, despite the fact that Indiana voters had never failed to reelect a governor since they'd been able to do so for the first time in 1972. A busload of Republican leaders made a trip to McIntosh's Muncie home during the summer of 1999 as part of a publicity campaign to "draft" McIntosh into the race.

On July 7, 1999, the forty-one-year-old McIntosh made it official by filing a campaign committee with the secretary of state's office, with his statehouse rotunda announcement following shortly afterward on August 31. He defeated remaining contender John Price easily in the Republican primary.

As the campaign started, it had all the markings of a marquee race for both parties nationally. Jim Nicholson, chairman of the Republican National Committee, said in May that the Indiana gubernatorial race was "the highest-priority governor's race we have."[8]

Kentucky Governor Paul Patton, chair of the Democratic Governors' Association, was the keynote speaker at the 2000 Indiana Democratic State Convention and said "an incumbent like Frank O'Bannon will be very high on the priority list." To delegates, he said, "No one in the country is doing a better job than Frank O'Bannon. It is my plea on behalf of the Democratic governors that you continue to show good judgment and ensure that not only Indiana, but the nation will have the benefit of leadership from Frank O'Bannon."[9]

McIntosh's campaign got a good boost going into the summer with the selection of State Senator J. Murray Clark of Indianapolis, a Republican respected on both sides of the senate aisle, as his running mate for lieutenant governor.

The Ads and the Money Chase

O'Bannon and McIntosh set new records for campaign spending in 2000, topping $19 million. O'Bannon campaign manager Tom New said, "This is as strong a position as any gubernatorial candidate has ever been in at this point in Indiana."[10]

There was some initial concern about the comparison between McIntosh, at age forty-one, and O'Bannon, at age seventy. O'Bannon would surpass former governor Orr as the oldest governor in the state's history. Orr was seventy-one when he left office in 1989. McIntosh's campaign banked on some of this—repeating the phrase "a fresh start" in most of his TV ads. McIntosh said, "We have to give people a reason for making a change. This election is a referendum on Governor O'Bannon. Should we continue with him or bring in the new, younger leadership?"[11]

Campaign media consultant Frank Greer and campaign manager New came up with an interesting idea. "We decided to do an ad where we had a senior advocate (Mary Jane Philippe of Greenwood) talk about the good things he had done for older Hoosiers, and at the end, we had her say, 'And he's a nice-looking young man, too!'" Greer said. "His age was more of a concern in 2000 than the other campaign, but it was only because of the contrast in his age with McIntosh. We wanted to make sure that people did not think about that."[12]

Other ads featured O'Bannon in active situations, dribbling a basketball, talking with a group of young students, and even shooting a one-handed basket behind his back and over his shoulder (a trick that took several takes, O'Bannon would admit, and a little help from a second shooter standing off-camera on top of a ladder, dropping the basketball through the net at just the right moment).

McIntosh was as aggressive in the 2000 campaign as he had been in Washington and, at times, showed bad judgment. Over Memorial Day weekend, McIntosh made headlines for being refused the right to appear before hundreds of thousands of spectators in the "Festival 500" parade through the streets of Indianapolis. O'Bannon was in the parade by virtue of being the governor, and McIntosh demanded equal treatment. However, parade officials quickly repeated their policy of only allowing the current governor of Indiana and the current mayor of Indianapolis in the parade. McIntosh and his campaign staff were left appearing on Indianapolis news stations arguing with surprised parade volunteers and staff.

Regardless, McIntosh began to show positive movement in head-to-head polling. Yang's polls showed the May 2000 numbers as close as McIntosh would ever get—O'Bannon leading 49-37.[13]

Later, in June, McIntosh jumped on a troubling report of continued problems at the Muscatatuck State Developmental Center in Jennings County to request a federal investigation of how the state had handled the situation. His claims failed to gain any real traction, though.

In response to McIntosh's attacks, O'Bannon continued to flex his advantage as the incumbent governor, announcing the same day of the congressman's assault on the Muscatatuck issues a $310-million education agenda using gaming revenues to help students and train teachers. The next day, he suspended the state's tax on gasoline, grabbing an even stronger hold of the campaign agenda. McIntosh again seemed out of step when in August he tried to make an issue of single-class basketball in Indiana—a legislative issue that had as many foes as supporters.

O'Bannon, McIntosh, and Libertarian nominee Andrew Horning participated in three debates, including one at the Indianapolis Children's Museum in which the candidates answered questions from the children. A straw poll of the children present had Horning winning—the only election he won that year.

THE GAS TAX

On June 20, 2000, Governor O'Bannon declared an "energy emergency" and suspended the state gasoline tax. At the time, gas prices hovered near $2 a gallon. The law O'Bannon used to suspend the tax, passed in 1981, had never been used and allowed the governor to suspend collection of the tax for sixty days, with the possibility to renew the suspension for another sixty days. O'Bannon left in place the state excise tax collected on each gallon of gasoline, however—funds used to support highway construction. At the time, gas prices per gallon were soaring but only in the Midwest.

The decision to suspend the gas tax was not an easy one—and threatened at one point to create a significant "inside" divide between O'Bannon's advisers in the governor's office and those running his 2000 reelection campaign. Always more conservative or cautious than the campaign advisers, budget and policy advisers to the governor worried that the suspension may not be legal or may not be viewed as legal. Campaign advisers pushed ahead, arguing they would love the opportunity to fight the Republicans on whether the governor's effort to reduce the price of a gallon of gasoline for working Hoosiers was legal or not.

"The storm clouds over gas prices were rising, and people were asking, 'What can be done?'" campaign spokesman Thad Nation recalls. "We had a series of discussions about calling a special session or suspending the gas tax or doing something to help consumers. Fred Biesecker, the governor's general counsel, was asked to go look at the statutes, and Fred came back and said there was one passage in state statute in an energy bill that addresses the governor's executive authority over some of these issues. It was basically in the case of an energy crisis, he could take executive authority. So it was determined that he could suspend the gas tax."[14]

The *Indianapolis Star* reported that gas costs were 30 to 50 cents lower in other parts of the country and came up with a variety of explanations, including slashed prices for the production of crude oil; dwindling oil supplies at U.S. refineries; new environmental regulations requiring cleaner-burning fuel in Chicago, Milwaukee, and other major cities; fewer resources devoted to making conventional gasoline as refineries struggled to produce the new gasoline; and perhaps most importantly, two pipeline ruptures in lines carrying gasoline from Texas to Chicago, and another that stretched from

Joliet, Illinois to Detroit. "By summer, they were repaired, but only approaching full capacity," the *Star* reported. "Price gouging, to varying degrees, likely occurred up and down the production and distribution chain as producers and sellers took advantage of tight supply and continued strong demand."[15]

After acting to suspend the state sales tax on gasoline, O'Bannon wrote to President Clinton and his fellow Midwestern governors urging them to join him in responding to the hardship. "Prices nationwide have risen nearly nine cents per gallon for conventional gasoline over the past two weeks. Here in the Midwest, it's even worse, with price surges of 15 cents per gallon…in Indiana and other Midwest states; some motorists are now paying $2 or more per gallon. This is already causing concern and economic hardships for Indiana residents."[16]

A month later, gas prices in Indiana dropped back to normal levels, but the governor extended the gas tax suspension another three weeks to compensate for higher prices paid by motorists over the Labor Day weekend. Republicans cried foul saying O'Bannon was using the suspension as a means of grabbing votes for reelection. The suspension officially expired on October 25, 2000. The suspension and subsequent drop in gas prices had an overwhelmingly positive impact on the hopes of the O'Bannon campaign.

Republican Mike McDaniel said, "People were hurting out there with some very high gas prices, and the governor did what he could, and we all wondered at the time where he got the authority to do something like that. But when he did that, the public said, 'What do we care or not about whether he has the authority to do this? He's trying to save me some money.'"[17]

Polling would show the move was very wise politically. Pollster Yang found O'Bannon surging far ahead of McIntosh by a margin of 25 points. "O'Bannon's surge was incredible after the gas tax suspension," Yang said. "I would not say that is why he won, because the numbers show he was going to win anyway, but after the governor did the brilliant move of suspending the state's gas tax, he went back up to a huge lead."[18]

Nation was not convinced that the move was necessary to win, but it demonstrated O'Bannon's willingness to take action to help consumers. "We were national on that issue. *Newsweek, USA TODAY,* and clips from around the country were coming in on what the governor had done. This was while the Congress, the president, and everyone else was debating what could be done about gas prices. You had one governor in the Midwest do something about it. Illinois tried to act quickly to do the same thing."

Nation adds the move changed the complexity and the agenda of the race. "For a month basically, during the summer, we were everywhere and everything," he said. "Not a night went by for two weeks that this was not on the news. I remember distinctly Channel 13 did a 'man on the street' story asking consumers about this, and one of them said, 'This is so great, thank you, Governor O'Bannon.' You can't beat that."[19]

McIntosh had few options in responding, initially sounding cautious about the value of the suspension, but then later supporting it. He suggested that it was a temporary fix for tax issues in Indiana and attempted to loop the issue back to what he considered a "long-term" answer for taxes—his 25 percent property tax cut.

State Senator Lawrence Borst of Greenwood, the longtime chair of the Senate Finance Committee, labeled O'Bannon's move "absolutely illegal." Borst said the suspension of the gas tax really was "a $15 to $20 million contribution" to the O'Bannon campaign.[20]

Of the gas tax suspension, Jim Shella said, "I absolutely thought it was gimmicky, but I also think it absolutely worked!...I think it clinched the campaign for him."[21]

A 25 Percent Guarantee

In July, McIntosh made a risky and unusual move, promising voters a 25 percent property tax cut, *guaranteed.* For weeks, he was short on details of how it would be possible to pay for such a cut with a new property tax reassessment system looming on the horizon, one that suggested some homeowners' tax bills would as much as double. When the details finally were delivered on the "guarantee," it failed to impress many, including some Republicans.

"He came out with a guarantee to cut property taxes, and I don't know how many weeks or months that went by, but naturally, the media asked for details, and there were none," Associated Press reporter Mike Smith said. "Naturally, reporters began hounding him over the details of it. I doubt very many people took it seriously, and the use of the word 'guarantee' in a political campaign seemed like a rather poor choice."[22]

As statehouse reporter Lesley Stedman Weidenbener wrote in the *Courier-Journal*, "...The proposal never seemed to resonate, even with voters in Lake County, where reassessment was expected to cause the largest percentage increases for homeowners."[23]

South Bend Tribune political writer Jack Colwell told McIntosh during a public television interview, "Even at the Republican National Convention in Philadelphia, there were some very prominent Hoosier Republicans who told me they wished David had not used the word 'guarantee,' because it is so hard to reach."[24]

Further hurting the McIntosh attempts to make looming property tax reassessment issues the center of the campaign was a flawed campaign TV ad. McIntosh offered up an ad featuring a Muncie homeowner, Will Staton, who said the property taxes on his home had doubled under Governor O'Bannon's tenure.

"O'Bannon was a stickler for research, so when that poor guy from Muncie got on the TV and said that his property taxes had doubled, we immediately dispatched someone from the campaign to Delaware County to do the research," Robin Winston said. The O'Bannon team located Staton's records and found that his taxes had not gone up on his home but had gone down, along with David McIntosh's.[25]

McIntosh pulled the Staton ad from the air.

Stedman Weidenbener believes McIntosh struggled on other levels as well to connect with voters and reporters in Indiana. "He didn't have the right personality. He had a Washington mindset going for him...," she said. "McIntosh never seemed to understand that if he criticized the governor for something, that the reporters were not just going to report that, but were going to ask him a bunch of questions to back up his claims. And when we would ask him questions, he never seemed to be able to answer them. I really think reporters ended up killing his campaign before it ever had a chance to get off the ground."[26]

McIntosh, desperate to get voters to connect with his 25 percent guarantee, declared in the closing weeks of the campaign that if he failed to cut property taxes by "an *average* of 25 percent" in the first four years of his term, he would not seek a second term.

FISHY BUSINESS

Fish, as strange as it seems, particularly those in the White River, figured prominently in both of O'Bannon's campaigns for governor. In 1996, O'Bannon ran a memorable TV ad that reviewed the troublesome record accumulated by a private foreign firm contracted by Mayor Goldsmith to operate the Indianapolis wastewater treatment facilities. The resulting fish kills in the White River were the centerpiece for the ad that featured a goldfish (read: Goldsmith) swimming in a small tank and the announcer proclaiming, "Steve Goldsmith: Bad for fish. Wrong for Indiana."[27]

In 2000, the fish were back again, but this time coming from Republican nominee David McIntosh. Trailing badly in the polls, McIntosh came out swinging in September with an ad that criticized Governor O'Bannon's handling of a massive fish kill in the White River that began in late December 1999 and stretched into the first few days of 2000. Calling it "The O'Bannon Fish Kill," McIntosh said the campaign was entering the "comparative phase" as his campaign bought time in all TV markets in Indiana for an issue that many outside of central Indiana had never heard of before. The ads said O'Bannon was attacking McIntosh to draw attention away from his administration's mismanagement. "But when an unknown polluter killed 117 tons of fish, O'Bannon said nothing—even refused to alert residents along the river. Nearly a year later, O'Bannon has spent $1.4 million and still no one has been punished. And now he wants our vote? Frank O'Bannon: Bad for fish. Wrong for Indiana."[28]

In fact, the White River fish kill was the largest eco-disaster in the state's history and required years of work by the Indiana Department of Environmental Management, the Indiana Department of Natural Resources, the Indiana State Department of Health, and the governor's office.

The governor did not wait, however, for the legal challenge for the fish kill to be completed. He ordered a clean-up of the river, and on the same day, he personally delivered to federal court the state's suit against the Guide Corporation of Anderson in late April 2000. He and First Lady Judy O'Bannon pulled on boot waders and personally helped restock the first 4,000 fish into the river from Broad Ripple Park in Indianapolis. A storm of environmental protestors on the shoreline and in rowboats in the river showed up as did many schoolchildren the O'Bannons had invited. One protestor called the governor's action a "publicity stunt staged to cover up how poorly he has protected the White River" and shouted while the governor spoke. One protest sign, held up behind the governor as he spoke accused him of "environmental crimes." Another protestor floated a "fish casket" on the river to symbolize the fish killed earlier, while still another was arrested for throwing something into the river.

The hoped-for positive nature of the event, however, was not lost in total. O'Bannon told the schoolchildren that each of them had a role to play with him in helping keep the environment safe. One child asked the governor why the protestors were present. Perhaps not realizing his voice was being captured by a nearby microphone, the governor told her, "It's their place in life to complain all the time, not to help, but that serves a purpose, too!"[29]

While the White River fish kill remained a big issue mostly in central Indiana, reporters asked about it across the state as McIntosh's ads continued to air.

"We have moved quickly, and it's in the legal process now to punish the polluter and collect the money to reimburse the state for its expenses for the cleanup," O'Bannon said during an Elkhart television interview. "It is the state's responsibility and the governor's responsibility to make sure we have safe and clean rivers, and when there is a polluter, we'll clean the river, punish the polluter, and restore the river to what it was before."[30]

O'Bannon also pointed out the difference between this environmental catastrophe and the one under Mayor Goldsmith. The City of Indianapolis's wastewater treatment plant, operated by the mayor and the city, was the polluter then. In the 1999-2000 White River fish kill, a private corporation was identified as the polluter.

O'Bannon was winning the public relations battle elsewhere, however, as the case against Guide Corporation continued to move forward in federal court. At hand now was the 2000 campaign, and in the weeks that followed, O'Bannon's campaign indeed did defend itself. Running a series of scathing ads, the governor's campaign called attention to some of the more troubling aspects of McIntosh's conservative voting record in Congress, including support of cuts for environmental protection laws, programs for seniors, and school lunch programs. The ads repeatedly noted that McIntosh had assembled that year's record for most missed votes of any member of the U.S. House. Calling McIntosh "desperate," the ads proclaimed that "he has a record we just can't trust."[31]

The *South Bend Tribune*'s Colwell asked O'Bannon, "What kind of governor do you think David McIntosh would be, given what you know about him and his record?"

O'Bannon paused briefly then replied, "I think he would be a very different governor than I am, at least based on his past record in the Congress...Generally, in Congress, he has voted against free or reduced school lunches for needy children, against drug-free schools, sponsored legislation to do away with the Department of Education, and on environmental issues, with polluters who kill fish in our rivers, he voted against environmental laws including the Clean Water Act."[32]

The White River fish kill issue was eventually settled in the state's favor on June 18, 2001, when the Guide Corporation of

Anderson pled guilty to seven separate counts related to the release of toxic chemicals and violation of the Clean Water Act and paid fines of $2 million for each count.

"When we filed the suit last year, I promised the people of Indiana that the polluter would be held accountable for harming one of Indiana's most important natural resources," O'Bannon said. "We've made good on that promise."[33]

THREE DEBATES

As he did in 1996, O'Bannon participated in three face-to-face debates with his opponents in 2000, one each in Indianapolis, Fort Wayne, and Evansville. The first debate, sponsored by the Indianapolis Press Club, was a preview of an even more aggressive performance by McIntosh at the Evansville meeting. During the Indianapolis debate, McIntosh took shots at the governor on almost every subject, including the economy, nursing home oversight, loss of Fortune 500 headquarters in the state, and a plan to address expected increases in property taxes for most homeowners following reassessment. Mismanagement was a common theme, again, with McIntosh saying, "We've seen scandal after scandal, mistake after mistake. It's been a legacy of mismanagement."[34]

O'Bannon took the high road, firmly emphasizing the progress of the previous four years, becoming irritated with McIntosh at one point, admonishing him to "Get your facts straight." He added, "We've learned a lot tonight about what's wrong with Indiana. I think you need a leader who is willing to stand up and say what's good about Indiana. The choice is really about who has the experience and who can you trust with Indiana's future."[35]

McIntosh was not done, breaking the debate rules by bringing along a prop pledge that he signed at his podium promising to cut taxes. He encouraged O'Bannon and Horning to do the same. Horning took the bait, but the governor ignored the stunt, pointing out that McIntosh's "guarantee" of a 25 percent tax cut was misleading. "Congressman, I've had a plan out since last December," O'Bannon said to McIntosh. "Let me tell you, when you sign an agreement and guarantee a 25 percent tax cut, that can't happen for everyone. You're fooling the public." He reiterated he had offered a specific plan for property tax restructuring and signed into law more than $1.5 billion in tax cuts during his first term. "I'll stand on my record," O'Bannon said.[36]

CAUGHT IN THE MIDDLE

Dr. Suellen Reed, a career educator from Rushville, Indiana, was often quoted as saying, "Children don't come to school with Rs or Ds on their heads." Her point, made in her own soft and kind way, has been to convince voters and politicians in Indiana that the state's schools are far too important for partisan politics. She was perhaps never more in the middle than during the 2000 campaign, when Republican gubernatorial nominee McIntosh continued to make claims about the state's schools that seemingly undercut Reed's own campaign for reelection.

WISH-TV political reporter Jim Shella took up Reed's unusual position in the middle between McIntosh, whom she endorsed, and O'Bannon, with whom she had worked closely during his first term. "Dr. Reed is probably closer to Governor O'Bannon on education issues than she is to Congressman McIntosh," O'Bannon campaign chair Tom New told Shella.[37]

McIntosh was airing statewide TV ads that claimed one in three Indiana high school students either dropped out or failed the ISTEP test at least five times and cited other statistics where schools needed to show improvement. O'Bannon took issue with McIntosh's claims on drop-out and ISTEP results, repeated in their Fort Wayne debate and noted that he was using statistics that Republican nominee Dr. Reed was also using. O'Bannon's campaign aired an ad with Reed calling McIntosh's assertions wrong, despite Reed saying she had been quoted out of context. She later told Shella that the state's graduation rate was a new record, consistent with what O'Bannon had said and disagreed with McIntosh's assertion in one of his ads that O'Bannon deserved an "F" on his report card for education leadership.[38]

During the Indianapolis gubernatorial debate, McIntosh continued the low-ball pitches and included claims that a third of all high school students in Indiana were failing the graduation qualifying exam. His attacks were so strident, Governor O'Bannon finally remarked, "To anyone running for office that says our schools are at the bottom, I suggest they give (Dr. Reed) a call so she can straighten them out."[39]

Reed felt the pressure but also felt prepared. "Seriously, the truth of the matter is, I never wavered from what I thought was right. I thought that as long as I did that, I would be okay. I always remembered, 'To thine own self be true, and thou cannot be false to any man.' So I stuck with my story. The thing that I hoped would happen was that both sides would see that education was above politics, and we should not make a political football out of something that was so important to our children and to our state's future. We were making some important and significant progress and to deny that was unfair to the kids as well as to everyone who had put in so much effort."[40]

Reed felt continued pressure, however, to put space between her positions and those of the Democratic governor. But not all Republicans gave her grief. "Republicans were not all of the same mind...There were many, many Republicans who agreed with me 100 percent who could see beyond petty politics and see that what we were doing was bigger than any one election, or any one office," Dr. Reed said. "There were those, though, who gave me a significant amount of criticism and told me that all these sort of things were going to happen to me...I think those were a selected few who were looking more at the short-term political goal rather than looking at the big picture when it came to education policy in Indiana."[41]

As the campaign came down to its final days, newspaper editorials went almost universally O'Bannon's way—including a surprise endorsement from the editors of the *Indianapolis Star*. The *Star*, normally a safe endorsement for any Republican running for any office, endorsed O'Bannon in an unenthusiastic editorial, noting that of the candidates running for governor, O'Bannon appeared to be the best prepared to lead. His endorsements were more favorable elsewhere including in the *Louisville Courier-Journal,* the *South Bend Tribune,* and the *Fort Wayne Journal Gazette.*

POLLING OUR WAY

Most reporters, political party observers, and even voters could see that the 2000 race was basically over long before Election Day. Labor Day, the traditional opening of fall campaigns, found the first polls confirming O'Bannon's lead. The *Indianapolis Star* reported on September 1, 2000 that O'Bannon had support from 50 percent of voters surveyed, with McIntosh trailing at 29 percent.[42]

The last polls taken before the November vote showed O'Bannon maintained a double-digit lead, and the once hopeful Republican Party, thinking it finally had returned to the "promised land," again looked like a loser. A poll by the Public Opinion Laboratory at IUPUI the weekend before the election found O'Bannon's lead was twenty-two points, matching internal O'Bannon campaign polls that showed him with a twenty-two-point edge. In fact, the closest the O'Bannon polls ever showed the race was a solid 49 to 37 lead O'Bannon held in the May 2000 sampling, prior to the gas tax suspension.[43]

McIntosh was not deterred, at least not publicly (and probably in a fruitless attempt to help Republicans to gain a majority in the Indiana House of Representatives). "We have to convince people that if they're voting for George W. Bush and Dick Lugar, then they need to vote for Murray Clark and me," McIntosh said.[44] He told the AP in the final weekend of the race as he visited every courthouse in his own congressional district, "I was never ahead in the polls in 1994. When we came here in our bus tour six years ago, we were six points down at that time and we won by ten percentage points in the poll that counted. We're going to do it again."[45]

Ironically, O'Bannon also campaigned heavily in McIntosh's district the last weekend, with campaign spokesman Thad Nation telling reporters, "The second district is an area where Governor O'Bannon has run strong in the past. It is McIntosh's district, but we're willing to battle down to the final vote."[46]

Winston (in 2000 serving as state Democratic chair) noted that the strength of O'Bannon's 2000 campaign was impressive for another reason: The presence of Senator Richard G. Lugar on the ballot seeking his fifth term.

"On their side, they had Dick Lugar...on the ballot, and we still won...I think, once again, some of the people continue to underestimate Frank O'Bannon. I mean, you had to be with that man, driving around the state and seeing how he would not get tired, would not give up, and would not stop working, and you could see how intent he was on becoming governor," Winston said.[47]

Also on the ballot in 2000 was O'Bannon confidant David Johnson, who accepted the task of challenging Senator Lugar. Johnson knew and respected Lugar from his early career stint as a staff attorney for Democratic members of the U.S. Senate prior to returning to Indiana and accepted the challenge at O'Bannon's request.

"Governor O'Bannon was concerned in the 2000 race that it was going to be difficult to get someone to take that position for all the reasons that it turned out to be," Johnson said about his first and only run for public office.[48]

There was no question that Lugar could be harmful to the Democratic statewide ticket, including Democrats seeking or defending seats in the Indiana House of Representatives. Many Democratic strategists figured a "busy Lugar" was a "good Lugar"—meaning if he had an engaged race for reelection, he would be less able and less likely to give of his time, talent, and treasure to McIntosh or other GOP candidates in 2000.

In the end, Johnson raised more than $1 million and staged a credible challenge to Lugar, but ended his campaign as the other Democrats who had come before him—conceding to the popular Lugar on Election Night.

The 2000 campaign completed, Yang said he felt grateful his firm had accepted Bill Schreiber's invitation in 1995 to talk to Frank

O'Bannon of Indiana. "Governor O'Bannon was just an incredible guy to work with and to be with," Yang said. "He was always humble and gracious, and we had a wonderful time working for him. He did important things, and I am proud to have been a part of that..."[49]

2000 POSTSCRIPT: THE MISMANAGEMENT MANTRA

The Indiana Republican Party engaged in a "mismanagement mantra" against the O'Bannon administration throughout the first term—the strategy apparently to try to kill the Democrats with a million drops of water. More than once, however, the Republicans crossed over the line with rude and insensitive attacks on the governor and members of the administration.

"We were desperate for a candidate, and David McIntosh presented himself, much to the chagrin of a lot of people who thought he was nutty to give up a safe U.S. House seat to do this," former GOP state chair Mike McDaniel said. "But David said he and his wife talked this over, and they decided that they wanted to do this. At the time, we're trying to figure out who you are going to run against an incumbent governor, and it is not too often that an incumbent governor in Indiana ever loses, and to have a sitting member of Congress step up and say that they are willing to do that, well, as state chairman, I had to say, 'Yes, he's our best shot. We have to take our best shot at this.' I didn't see anybody else out there who was going to make a big difference or give us a chance."[50]

McDaniel credits McIntosh for working hard, "but there were days that he did not exactly peg the 'warm and fuzzy' meter out there. I mean, he is a nice, friendly guy, but sometimes the policies that he put out there came off a little strident for some people."[51]

Winston said O'Bannon was particularly good at combating the Republican's drumbeat of "mismanagement." "Our candidate did a good job of laying out what we were doing. Evan Bayh did a good job of laying the groundwork over eight years that showed we knew how to manage and that we weren't a bunch of wild-eyed liberals. Frank was a continuation of that."[52]

Democrats fired back aggressively against the accusations of mismanagement, keeping a running count of the number of congressional votes McIntosh was missing back in Washington in order to campaign back home in Indiana, and sent out a daily fax to reporters known as "Today's Reason to Reject McIntosh."

THE LAST ELECTION DAY

November 7, 2000 was the last Election Day Frank O'Bannon would face as a candidate. He'd placed his name on the ballot for state senate five times from 1970 to 1986, twice for lieutenant governor in 1988 and 1992, and twice for governor in 1996 and 2000. Frank and Judy began their day early by walking down 46th Street to vote at St. Thomas Aquinas School, just a block from the governor's residence and just a short walk east of where they had begun their marriage at Fairview Presbyterian Church more than four decades before. Throughout the day, they visited polling places, phone banks, and other places where campaign volunteers and voters could be found.

While returning to the governor's residence for a late lunch, campaign spokesman Thad Nation took a call on his cell phone informing him that exit polling in Indiana showed O'Bannon way ahead. Nation said, "I got off the phone and told the governor, 'It looks like we're going to win.' And he just said, 'Okay, that's good,' and he leaned his head back and went to sleep in the car on the road back to the residence. That just sort of set the stage for that night over at the Hyatt where we watched the returns come in...It was a very muted celebration up there. We all just sort of watched it, congratulated him, and went on with the night. It was the most calm victory I have ever experienced in a campaign."[53]

By late afternoon, the O'Bannon family sat down for a simple meal of homemade vegetable soup and salad prepared by P.J. Irvine and Connie Watson, members of the governor's residence staff who gave up their state holiday on Election Day to make sure the family had something to eat.

The O'Bannon-Kernan team spent the days leading up to the 2000 vote on a bus tour that barnstormed forty Indiana cities in three days, finishing with a statehouse rally the day before the vote. The *Corydon Democrat* reported, "By then, the governor said that morning, it was out of his hands. He had done what he could; the election rested with party organizations still feverishly getting out the vote and the voters."[54]

FOUR MORE YEARS

In the end, Governor O'Bannon won reelection easily, gathering 1,232,525 votes to McIntosh's 908,285—a wider margin than his historic 1996 win. Libertarian nominee Andrew Horning, Jr., gathered 38,458 votes statewide.[55]

O'Bannon won in seventy-seven of the state's ninety-two counties and came close in many traditionally Republican counties.[56] McIntosh called O'Bannon at 7:40 p.m. on Election Night to concede. The Voter News service, a partnership of various news organizations, found in exit polling that more than 25 percent of Republican voters crossed over to support O'Bannon, while nine out of ten Democrats supported him.[57]

O'Bannon and family watched the returns and then made their way to the Indiana Convention Center but not before pausing to hear that Vice President Al Gore had won the presidency. It would later be reversed by the networks, declaring Texas Governor George W. Bush as the winner.

At the convention center, the governor told the celebratory crowd, "I want to thank all the people in the state of Indiana who said that we're moving in the right direction. We're going to continue to move in that right direction," he said. "It's been a remarkable, remarkable year, and we're glad it's come to a victory here on this night."[58]

His victory came amidst an up and down night nationally for Democrats who first believed Gore had won, only to face a stunning defeat after several more weeks of recounts and challenges focused on a terribly flawed General Election vote in Florida.

A Strong, Clear Message

O'Bannon said the voters sent a "strong, clear message" and said, "The thing I really emphasized during the last month of the campaign, as I spoke around the state, was changing the direction of public school education. We've taken the first step (with new standards). The real challenge in the next four years is to make sure those high standards are aligned with the testing, and we're giving teachers the professional development to get to that point."[59]

In a prelude to a theme that would dominate the second term, O'Bannon acknowledged to reporters that state tax revenues were running behind projections, which would cause limitations to what could be done on taxes and state spending. Those declining revenues threatened to take away any mandated power or authority O'Bannon may have normally received after such a convincing reelection.

During the campaign, O'Bannon made few expensive promises knowing that he would have to be conservative about spending if the downward trend continued.

O'Bannon's fiscal cautiousness made sense politically, Nation believes. "O'Bannon ran his administration in a manner that reflected his commitment to fiscal responsibility. There was always an abundance of caution, a real commitment to keeping the Rainy Day Fund strong and little interest in just going out and spending money willy-nilly. The foundation of Democrats winning in Indiana had been set by then, and in a conservative state like Indiana, you have to prove your fiscal responsibility first and then you can go from there. O'Bannon always took that to heart," he said.[60]

A Historic Day

O'Bannon asked his friend Randall T. Shepard, chief justice of the Indiana Supreme Court, to administer the oath of office to him for his second term as governor on January 8, 2001. As he finished the oath, the governor reached over and gently hugged Judy and could be overheard saying into her ear, "I love you."[61]

The event took place in front of the largest crowd ever assembled for a gubernatorial inauguration in Indiana. More than 27,000 people came to the RCA Dome in downtown Indianapolis to witness the event, including about 25,000 fourth-grade Indiana history students from across the state, getting their own chance to make a little Hoosier history. O'Bannon and Lt. Governor Joe Kernan entered the arena from an upper deck, wading their way through the excited and supportive students. State Trooper Larry Gershanoff followed them closely each step of the way.[62]

"The governor and the lieutenant governor went from one side of the upper deck around, walking and waving and these kids were thrilled to death that he would do this," Donna Imus recalls. "He really, really believed in public education, so what better way than to involve kids in the political process in this important way."[63]

Gospel singer Sandi Patty of Anderson sang the National Anthem and led a youth choir, the Madison County Character Counts singers, while her husband, Donald Peslis, director of the Center on Character Education, also offered remarks. The audience included two former governors, Evan Bayh and Robert D. Orr. Five members of the Indiana congressional delegation attended, including Democrats Julia Carson, Baron Hill, Timothy Roemer, Peter Visclosky, and Republican Brian Kerns.

In his speech, O'Bannon described it accurately as "an extraordinary day" and "the start of a new millennium, a new century, a new term in state government—and you." His remarks were optimistic, focused more on the future than on the previous four years as he cited fresh challenges and opportunities before every Hoosier in the new century.

Governor O'Bannon heavily emphasized education in his remarks when he said, "We must give every student the best teachers Indiana has to offer, by supporting them and giving them the tools for quality teaching...I have seen firsthand the wonderful work your teachers do for the children of Indiana."[64]

He asked the fourth-graders then to stand and thank their teachers with a round of applause. Perhaps even more customary, and in an attempt to reach out to the many youngsters present in terms they could understand, O'Bannon called on his love of bird watching to make his point. He recounted watching sparrows, gold finches, juncos, and cardinals eating alongside one another in a bird feeder near his Harrison County home, when a blue jay swoops in chasing the others away. "I guess life always has barriers and events that act as the blue jay. They disrupt and prevent people from participating. They determine conditions and actions. And if that weren't the case, then I guess we would not need a thing we call government. But like the bird feeder, we have a diversity of people and we all need to participate. Government is the institution that helps balance the needs, opportunities, and responsibilities before us all."[65]

Lt. Governor Joe Kernan was sworn in by his sister, Barbara Kernan Christin. The Kernans, a big, outgoing, and loving family, proudly gathered around Joe as he told his sister Barbara, "Don't be bashful," and Maggie Kernan drew a laugh when she added, "Yeah, don't start now." Barbara momentarily forgot one of the lines of the oath, but quickly recovered. Following his oath, Kernan turned to Shepard and said, "I think the first thing I have to do is ask the chief justice if that causes any problems." Kernan's remarks drew even more attention than normal, as even as early as this day in early 2001, Democrats and Republicans were watching his every move as evidence of his plans to run for governor himself in 2004.[66]

19
Tough Times Ahead

THE RIGHT TIME TO BE HERE

Frank O'Bannon was only the fourth governor to earn two consecutive terms in office. His second term, however, would bear little resemblance to his first. O'Bannon's two terms in office stood in stark contrast to one another, altogether opposite images in terms of how state government could and would be managed.

During the second term, political life proved painful and difficult. Gone were the days when the governor could afford to be out front on new spending programs or major initiatives or services that cost money. In fact, on the day he was inaugurated for his second term inside the RCA Dome, the governor's budget director, Betty Cockrum, was across the street in the statehouse laying out the governor's two-year, $21-billion budget for the start of the 2001 session of the General Assembly. The budget was balanced, but it relied heavily on gaming revenue to shore up sagging tax revenues elsewhere and spent down the state's surplus to just below $1 billion—below what the governor had previously said was acceptable. It provided only a 2 percent increase for public schools, meaning with inflation and other increased costs, they would basically stay even over the upcoming biennium. Cockrum told legislators it was "a starting point" and reminded them, "We continue to see signs of a slowing economy. We are faced with some hard choices."[1]

Legislators needed more convincing that day and many of them for weeks and months to follow—Republicans seemingly on a one-note theme of "cut and manage your way out of this" and some Democrats not wanting to deal with the budget realities at all, concerned that any tax increase or program cuts would be harmful. The reality remained, however, that the budget submitted by the governor bore little resemblance to the final version enacted at session's end.

Amidst the slew of bad news on the state's economy and the resulting assault on the state's operating budget, the governor worked hard to remain optimistic and confident. Some of us on the staff sometimes groused about how bad things were or worried about how much worse it could get. The biting criticism from opposition Republicans and the sagging or sometimes nonexistent support from Democrats made the situation worse. Frank O'Bannon was not having fun in the midst of a record budget crisis, but he had an edge on his younger staff: He'd been through this before. When we would meet and discuss the latest round of program cuts, delayed payments, or tax increases, the mood was heavy and difficult to absorb, but O'Bannon remained hopeful. The state's economy had rolled up and down the hill many times before, so the governor knew we had tough choices to make but still seemed confident that problems could be solved. "This is the time to be here, when you face the tough challenges," he said to staff one Friday morning during a surprise visit to our regular weekly gathering. He was determined to keep moving forward, even though in his heart of hearts, he had to know the situation was becoming worse than Indiana had ever faced before.

"I think it was horrible for him," Cockrum said. "...When you begin to run out of money and have to grapple with that...not only can you not start new initiatives or respond to opportunities that come along, you can't even effectively respond to the daily challenge of operating the core business of state government."[2]

In these times, however, O'Bannon kept his own counsel for the most part. Judy said he did not often talk about the tough times at work when he would return to the governor's residence in the evening. "In those times, he would just be quieter than he normally was," she said. "Now, if something happened that was good, he would be so excited he couldn't stand it. If he visited a factory and they were doing some new process on something, or building something new, he'd go on and on about that, especially on days he chaired meetings of the Education Roundtable. He just loved that!"[3]

Judy said during most evenings when the governor was not scheduled to be at an event, he enjoyed quiet evenings on the second floor of the Governor's Residence, eating a bowl or two of Cheerios cereal (with water, rather than milk, which his stomach wouldn't tolerate), and spent long hours reading or playing solitaire on his desktop computer.

Cockrum stayed at her post until the end of the '01 session, a session that reflected some of the worst of the remaining tension between O'Bannon and legislators. Not only had O'Bannon surprised members of both parties by handing down a veto to a proposed pay increase for legislators and judges, but he also refused to sign the 2001-03 biennial budget, taking the rare step of letting it become law without his signature.

Officially, O'Bannon was increasingly worried about revenue projections that went from bad to worse—even during the period of January to June as legislators crafted the budget. Given that the events of September 11, 2001 were still in the future—further taking a bite out of the U.S. and Indiana economies—fiscal restraint was in limited supply in the first months of 2001.

"On the budget, I have to give a tip of the hat to him," said John Gregg, who served six years as speaker of the house between 1996 and 2002. "He called us in to talk about the budget, and the doom and gloom had not really hit nationally on the economy. To his credit in that case, we would have all been better served in the house and senate if we had known at the start (of the session) what we knew at the end. He told us it was a bad, bad budget, and he understood it well from all his years on Senate Finance, and he told us that it was not going to work."[4]

The budget became law without the governor's signature, and Cockrum departed from her role, replaced by a familiar face, Marilyn

Schultz. Schultz said she learned quickly during the warm summer months of 2001 that state government was running out of options, about as quickly as tax revenues were dwindling, and that there was little appetite among legislators to seek a tax increase or any other fix to the budget they'd just passed. Democratic leadership, in fact, said a general tax increase of any kind was a "non-starter."

"We had a huge deficit and there were no alternatives left," Schultz said. "The only alternative was to try and piece together a plan to work with the budget we had as best we could, and that included asking the Medicaid program to find $250 million in savings, dollars that would not be available to people in need."[5]

Schultz believes the downturn at the start of the twenty-first century was many times worse than what she and other legislators faced in the early part of the 1980s and again in the early 1990s because the makeup and distribution of the state's biennial budget had changed. "It was worse in a number of ways," she said. "If you look at the expenditure pie, about a third went to education, about 19 percent went to property tax relief, and together, that means you have a huge portion of the budget where you really have no control or few options. You had a budget in this period that the legislature and the governor actually had less control over than they did in the 1980s."[6]

Created was "an extraordinarily deep hole, but one that we were always truthful about," Schultz said.[7]

O'Bannon, despite not having signed the budget, would bear heavy criticism for the difficult cuts in state services and expenditures that were on tap. Public and private polling showed the governor's approval rating beginning to slide. Hoosiers seemed to struggle to connect with the idea that a national recession was to blame—and with the nation entering wars in Afghanistan and Iraq in 2001-02, patriotic Hoosiers were reluctant to do anything but support President Bush and his policies.

Political columnist Ed Feigenbaum, publisher of *Indiana Legislative Insight*, noted that "Republicans, led by State GOP Chair Jim Kittle, Jr., have fed public perception that the nation's oldest governor (O'Bannon)...is a great guy who just doesn't have a firm handle on the switch of state government."[8]

O'Bannon was not alone among the nation's governors facing the wrath of voters—California Governor Gray Davis, a fellow Democrat, couldn't survive a recall effort that swept him from office a little over a year into his second term. "(O'Bannon's) counterparts from coast to coast are enduring painfully low approval ratings," Feigenbaum said. "Maybe that's why Governor Frank O'Bannon can't seem to buy a break—or credit for anything he's done, even though an objective analysis might suggest that he has accomplished as least as much under trying circumstances as many of his gubernatorial colleagues—perhaps even some of his more recent Hoosier predecessors."[9]

Legislators fell back into comfortable roles—Republicans urging the governor to make more cuts and avoid tax increases and Democrats saying the budget and the economy were going to improve soon enough, meaning no tax increase was necessary. Someone had to be the goat, and that was often O'Bannon.

Gregg believes O'Bannon deserved better treatment. "From 2001 to 2003, when everyone was going on and on about the budget, the first guy I ever heard talk about the need for fiscal restraint because of the coming challenges was Frank O'Bannon," Gregg said. "...He was trying to warn us about the coming problems."[10]

DEALING WITH THE THIRD FLOOR

The promise of the O'Bannon administration, from the start, was that this man, well known and well liked by legislators of both parties, would enjoy a positive working relationship with the third floor of the statehouse. The reality proved to be quite challenging.

O'Bannon, like Governors Bowen and Orr, came up in state government through the legislative branch. Unlike Governor Bayh, he was a known quantity to most legislators and was not directly blamed for the political sea-change Bayh's 1988 victory brought, leaving simmering resentment among desperate Republicans. But there were differences. In Bowen and Orr's era, the political nature of the General Assembly was vastly different than in O'Bannon's era. The days when a sitting governor could go into a legislative district and make a world of difference (and thereby influence a legislator's vote) were mostly gone. It wasn't that modern-day governors didn't try. And in many districts, O'Bannon did make a difference, including one in Indianapolis where he and Judy O'Bannon campaigned tirelessly for Jeb Bardon who scored an upset win for the Indiana House by defeating an incumbent Republican. O'Bannon's support for legislative candidates in Northwest Indiana and Southern Indiana also seemed to have a positive impact. But in this era in which two sessions of the house found the body evenly divided or with razor-thin majorities by either party in the lower house, the edge of one or two seats was critically important.

Former state senator Mike Gery, who became a key legislative adviser to Governor O'Bannon, said, "Most legislators don't feel they owe the governor credit for winning their seats. Whenever I used to hear the phrase in the governor's office that 'they wouldn't be here if it weren't for us,' I would laugh. I can tell you, as a legislator, when you have just gone through a campaign and raised a lot of money and worked hard, the fact that the governor came in for a day...does not mean he is the reason you won. It's not like that."[11]

In real terms, O'Bannon won some major victories in the legislature during his terms as governor but also suffered some major defeats. He often endured the expressed scorn and railing of some members, Republicans and Democrats alike. It seemed everyone was looking for someone to blame, and the modest O'Bannon made an easy target for some.

"I give him very high marks in an era where it is very difficult to get things done. There were some very major accomplishments," Gery believes. "In the long run, no matter how hard it was, or what his style was, I think his administration will get positive marks for what got accomplished...It probably would have been nice for a lot of people to see the governor just give these fiery speeches or ones that brought tears to people's eyes...but in the long run, I am not sure that gets you much."[12]

The session that was perhaps toughest was 2001—a year in which O'Bannon came into his second term riding a large margin in a relatively easy campaign for reelection, but was unable to embark on much of a 'mandate movement' because of limited or diminishing state resources. Despite that, an agenda was crafted which legislators largely ignored; instead they continued enacting spending bills often forcing O'Bannon to veto them, including the two most unpopular vetoes of his entire time in public office—a veto killing a proposed pay raise for legislators and judges and another that would have shielded legislators' e-mails from the state's open records law.

The pay raise bill passed the house and senate in the light of day and, for once, was not slipped into another bill in the waning hours of the session. Following the suggestion of editorial writers and other pundits, both parties agreed to move a pay raise bill "out in the open" and expected—and thought they had—O'Bannon's support. They didn't get it. O'Bannon, citing growing pressures on the state budget, vetoed the bill.

Former speaker Gregg said the bill was handled in a public way on purpose. He and Senate President Pro Tem Robert Garton decided that since a legislative pay raise had not occurred since 1986, the time was right to proceed.

O'Bannon's veto shocked legislators, Gregg said. "You could have knocked me over with a feather, and I'm a big boy. I had every, and I mean every, reason to think that bill was going to be signed. I had every assurance from every person possible that it was going to be signed. I was just shocked. I can tell you, that caused a serious break. When I left in 2002, that wound had not even started to heal."[13]

Representative Pat Bauer notes, "There absolutely was a difference between dealing with Frank O'Bannon and dealing with his staff, and I think Frank O'Bannon had a good heart and a mind and he wanted to do good things. But I think, sometimes, people would turn him the other way, and one of those was on the pay raise for legislators. I can tell you, he lost a lot of friends on that issue. The legislature would not have passed that bill without the tacit or explicit approval or understanding that he was going to let it become law."[14]

Thad Nation, who served as press secretary for the first six months of 2001, does not believe O'Bannon broke faith with legislators. "The governor did not believe he ever made that promise, so I don't think he believed that he ever broke his word on that," Nation said. "It was extremely unpopular with them, but basically, everything that needed to get done in 2001 did not get done, and there is no question that it had a negative fiscal impact and was something the state could not afford."[15]

Whether O'Bannon gave his word or not, he believed strongly conditions had changed. O'Bannon said, "I have said before that I believe legislators and judges are overdue for a pay raise. However, the state's current financial situation demands that even worthy initiatives be delayed until better economic times."[16]

O'Bannon also vetoed House Enrolled Act 1083 that sought to shield legislators' e-mails from public review. The governor was equally firm in his determination, despite knowing it would anger many members of the General Assembly. He recalled his first days in the legislature when committee hearings were not always open to the public, when committee votes were taken in private, and when floor amendments could be offered without being printed and distributed in advance. "I believe an open government is essential to a free society…The legislature's records should be open to the public, with a few carefully crafted exceptions. Although the legislature, as a separate branch of government, clearly has the power to exempt itself from the Public Records Act and address these issues in its rules, this is not a step that should be taken hastily or without careful deliberation and meaningful opportunity for public comment."[17]

In total, O'Bannon set his veto pen to thirteen bills in the 2001 session, almost all of them because of their fiscal impact. Another fourteen bills would die at the end of his pen following the 2002 session—again, because of fiscal concerns.

Further angering some legislators, especially budget negotiators at the end of the 2001 session, was the governor's unusual step of allowing the 2001-03 biennial budget to become law without his signature. In doing so, he said, "…I respect the energy and the effort so many have put in to crafting House Enrolled Act 1001, the budget for the next biennium…(but) I remain concerned that this budget is just plain unrealistic when it comes to paying for the spending the

General Assembly has put in place. If economic conditions grow more challenging, the state is in real danger of coming up short. I want to be sure that all expenditures—especially any spending that would draw down our important Rainy Day Fund—are fully justified. I do not want to put Indiana in a position where a general tax increase is unavoidable, or we don't have enough funds to meet an emergency."[18]

"I recognize that under the current conditions, this very well may be the best budget that the legislature can come up with. Therefore, I will allow the legislature's budget to go forward and become law, but without my signature."[19]

PRESERVING THE VETO

Veto powers for Indiana governors have never been as significant as other states, or that of the U.S. president. A simple majority is all that legislators need to override the veto of an Indiana governor. Be that as it may, the governor's veto at least had the power to remain in place until the next session of the legislature when an override could be considered. Nursing home owners, angry at an O'Bannon veto that would have cut into their stranglehold on dollars for care for the elderly and people with disabilities, sued claiming that O'Bannon had, in effect, delivered his veto back to legislators too soon. In *D&M Healthcare, Inc. vs. O'Bannon*, nursing home interests argued that he was in violation of the Indiana Constitution.[20]

In the first round, the nursing home side won—with the Indiana Court of Appeals ruling unanimously in August 2003 that the constitution required that a governor deliver a veto on the first day of the next session. More than a few jokes made their way through the halls of the statehouse noting that appellate court judges were among those denied a pay increase with O'Bannon's earlier veto—and that their ruling smelled of "payback." As unlikely as that was, regardless, the governor appealed the decision to the Indiana Supreme Court—and had plenty of motivation to do so. O'Bannon's practice of immediately returning vetoes had been the practice in place for a generation—Governors Bayh, Orr, and Bowen had used the same practice O'Bannon employed. The impact of ruling that practice unconstitutional was startling, calling up the question: Did delivering vetoes "too soon" since 1972 mean that all those bills vetoed by the last four governors were actually legal and should become law? It was a question worthy of pursuit, but one that became moot when the Indiana Supreme Court ruled in the governor's favor, saying in effect that one could not fault a governor for essentially turning in his homework early.[21]

BUDGET BOTTOM DROP

By the end of the first quarter of the new State Fiscal Year in 2001-02 with the new budget in hand, state revenues continued to plummet and were $142 million off projection, yet lawmakers were still reluctant to return for a hoped-for Special Session to address that issue and property tax restructuring. O'Bannon responded by announcing more spending cuts and reluctantly freezing state employee salaries. One of O'Bannon's budget cutting moves gained little notice due to no fault of his own— announced on September 10, 2001, news of the cuts soon faded amidst the sad news the following day when terrorist attacks rocked the nation.

In making the case for cuts, O'Bannon said, "Some will say that this is not that bad, but we cannot allow ourselves for one minute to think that we are beginning to work ourselves out of this crisis. There is absolutely no news, information, or event that indicates our economy will get better anytime soon."[22]

The strategy that fall was to have the governor out front, trying to convince voters and legislators that the problem was real. It would culminate with a rare statewide television address O'Bannon made on the evening of November 15, 2001. O'Bannon had a sober message for Hoosiers: The state must do something to address its fiscal concerns or face even more difficult cuts and reductions in services. "The fact is, our state is in a fiscal crisis...I can tell you—without fear of overstating the case—that this crisis threatens our very way of life in Indiana," O'Bannon said.[23]

He attempted to head off criticism and questions about the state's now-gone record surplus by reminding voters that Democrats and Republicans had agreed together to enact a series of tax cuts and new spending measures (including road improvements, funding teachers' pensions, and investments in university technology) to spend down the surplus during flush times.

"We all thought it prudent to reduce the surplus in ways to help Hoosiers," O'Bannon said. "And it was prudent—at that time, with the information we had."[24]

O'Bannon outlined how he had reduced spending in all state agencies by 7 percent, imposed a hiring freeze and suspended pay increases for state employees, delayed state construction projects, and reduced spending for Medicaid services.

He concluded by appropriately linking his Balanced Budget Plan with his already announced 21st Century Tax Restructuring Plan. "The situation, then, is clear: We will not grow our way out of this dilemma, and we cannot cut our way out. We've cut the fat and even the muscle; more drastic cuts threaten the very backbone of state services—our public schools, our public safety, our health... A Republican legislative leader recently told me that he and his colleagues had to hear from you before they'll address this budget crisis. Take him at his word. Ask your legislators to pass the program I've just outlined. You should expect nothing less from us. To do less would mean we have broken faith with you, the people who have elected us as leaders."[25]

Appropriate to the glum mood of the speech, thousands of loud and messy starlings descended on the upper reaches of the statehouse that night as they often did, roosting there from the cold November wind—their presence so imposing, state troopers on the governor's security detail carried umbrellas over the governor and Mrs. O'Bannon as they entered and exited the statehouse to shield them from the bird droppings.

Hoosiers, it seems, were in an equally bad mood. Whether from a twisted sense of loyalty to the president in a time of war or some other reason, the governor bore the brunt of the criticism for the situation. It was clear that voters were beginning to blame the messenger about the bad news of state surpluses reduced to possible deficits, spending cuts, and proposed tax increases. While the governor was determined to "talk straight" to voters and legislators, he ran the very real danger that he would be weakened to such a point that it would be impossible to get legislators to follow any needed corrective course of action in the upcoming session. He would need all of his strength and courage to withstand the withering weeks and months that lay ahead.

TAXES

The taxes paid by Indiana citizens have been at the center of political debate for decades, and it was never truer than in the O'Bannon-Kernan years. At times, the debate has been nasty, or even silly, with most everyone agreeing that some sort of major reform was needed to Indiana's antiquated system of taxation. Getting agreement on what direction to go, regardless of what particular tax was in discussion, was always difficult. Lawsuits brought by taxpayers challenging the state's property tax assessment system served to tip the system on its head. Judges agreed that the state's assessment system was unfair or at least unevenly applied from township to township across the state. As a result, the court ordered the state to enact a new property tax assessment system—one based on a property's market value. Fears ran high that some homeowners, especially those with older homes, would face a major jump in their property taxes—possibly forcing some of them to sell their homes to avoid the tax bill.

O'Bannon and legislators focused a considerable amount of time and energy on tax cuts, particularly during the governor's first term when they agreed to about $1.5 billion in cuts. However, because the tax cuts were spread out in many different areas, political advisers became concerned that Hoosiers didn't always realize they had received the cuts. In fact, during focus groups conducted for the 2000 campaign, pollster Fred Yang found some voters doubted O'Bannon's claim of $1.5 billion in tax cuts.

During his first term, O'Bannon formed the Citizens Commission on Taxes, which made a series of recommendations on various forms of tax reform—many of which were adopted into the governor's legislative agendas in subsequent sessions. Progress was slow, however, during years when the state enjoyed record surplus levels. Reform measures always came to this: Lower a tax here, and you have to raise a tax there to remain "revenue neutral."

While the Citizens Commission on Taxes did not make the full progress needed to reform Indiana's property tax restructuring program, the O'Bannon-Kernan administration did not give up. The court's looming order made it imperative that something be done. State government did work on establishing new assessment rules for local officials to use at the Department of Local Government Finance and even delayed implementation of them to help taxpayers avoid large increases without realizing a cut somewhere else.

On October 18, 2001, O'Bannon and Kernan summoned a standing-room-only crowd of lobbyists, legislators, and state leaders to a meeting room at the Indiana Government Center South. There they announced the most comprehensive and sweeping reform of Indiana's property tax system in a generation and, in doing so, won cautious support in many Republican corners, some dubbing it "credible" and "substantive."

"The Lieutenant Governor (Joe Kernan), with the governor's blessing, decided to think outside the box…and the result was a total revamp of the state's business taxes," Feigenbaum wrote. "We still remember the looks of shock and awe when the plan was unveiled…which more than compensated for the looks of 'aw shucks' when the governor's first attempt at bringing together disparate groups to cobble together a new tax scheme fizzled in his first term…"[26]

Speaker Gregg and other Democratic members of the house and senate stood with O'Bannon and Kernan as the plan was unveiled. However small that support may have seemed, combined, these acts represented no small feat in the dog-eat-dog environment that had become Indiana politics. The plan had many component parts

representing the squeezed balloon that the state budget was: Squeeze
it in one area, and another area popped out. That meant to lower
property taxes on average for homeowners or to eliminate the business
inventory tax or the gross receipts tax, other taxes would have to be
raised elsewhere to even out the pain for all and keep state revenues at
existing levels. The plan was not meant for budget relief but was also
not intended to leave homeowners and businesses paying more taxes
than before.

O'Bannon was animated and agitated when questions were raised
during the announcement about whether this was the "right time" to
reform the state's property tax system. "What happens if we do nothing?
If no one does anything, on average, homeowners' bills go up 33 percent
which really translates into that much of a tax increase."[27]

Kernan, who led the group of six bipartisan architects who worked
on the 21st Century Tax Restructuring Plan for more than five months
(including no legislators), said, "I remember that we had two plans, one
was very targeted, and one was broader. I went to the governor, and I
called the broader one the 'go big or stay home plan' and...I said to him,
'Governor, I think we should go big or stay home. This opportunity is
not going to present itself again. The last time anything close to this
happened was thirty years ago.' He smiled and told me, 'Go for it, I'm
with you on it.'"[28]

Perhaps no one but O'Bannon himself could have engendered the
level of trust Kernan could—with Democrats and Republicans alike.
Kernan had built a solid reputation as lieutenant governor and was
personally as popular as O'Bannon among legislators and others—
regardless of party. People gravitated to Kernan naturally.

"It was long overdue, but give them credit, they came up with a plan,
they sold it to the public, they sold it to the legislature, and that was a great
plan...For the years of budget struggles we went through there, it was
truly significant that we got something like that passed," Gregg said.[29]

Feigenbaum wrote, "While critics might suggest that O'Bannon
was late in coming to the table and left the heavy lifting to his trusted
deputy, Lt. Governor Joe Kernan, the bottom line here is that he brought

a comprehensive plan to the legislative table, maintained a dialogue, and brought lawmakers back in special session to hammer out the final details," Feigenbaum concluded.[30]

SEPTEMBER 11, 2001

On September 11, 2001, America experienced change in ways that it had not in more than a generation. For post-World War II Americans, a new sense of fear and vulnerability entered our lives for the very first time. For older Americans, such as Frank O'Bannon, who had lived through and in the shadow of the last "great war," the events of that bright September day rang eerily familiar to them, and it was reflected in how the governor approached that day.

The attacks on New York City and Washington, D.C. (and the subsequent aborted attack on Washington that ended in a Pennsylvania field) began as Governor O'Bannon departed the governor's residence for the statehouse to start his day.

Tim Joyce recalls, "Governor O'Bannon was in the car on the way to the office when this all started, and when he got there, it was probably twenty or twenty-five minutes and the second tower was hit."[31] O'Bannon met with Bob Small, executive assistant for public safety, the superintendent of the state police (Mel Carraway), the major general of the National Guard (George Buskirk), and the executive director of SEMA (Pat Ralston).

State leadership had to decide what to do next. Among the mayors, Bart Peterson of Indianapolis wanted to take a different route than the governor. He sent his employees home.[32] O'Bannon allowed those state employees who wanted to leave the opportunity to do so. He did want at least a minimal number of workers to remain so that state government could continue operating.

Throughout the morning, O'Bannon continued to take in information from all appropriate sources, including information passed on to the nation's governors that day from the FBI and the White House. But the governor's TV remained turned off.

"We didn't have a television on in his office…The decisions and the questions and the commentary coming through the telephone from all these variety of sources, now that I look back on it, were clearly being driven by the visuals…on television," Joyce said. "Yet, what Governor O'Bannon was doing, which is so typical of him, was listening."[33]

Before the morning was out, O'Bannon issued his first official statement, a written one which said, "I am saddened by the tragic events that have occurred in Washington, D.C. and New York City. As we await more information on what has transpired, it's important that our citizens remain calm and avoid panic. Let me assure you that the state of Indiana has moved into a state of alert and has implemented precautionary plans to ensure that our citizens are safe. Security at all government buildings has been enhanced. All Indiana state troopers are on standby, ready to respond if needed. We are still gathering information through our Emergency Operations Center, the state police, and the Indiana National Guard."[34]

Later, he stood before reporters and remarked, "Like all Americans, I am horrified and saddened by the tragic events that have occurred today in New York City and our nation's capital. Make no mistake: This was not just terrorism. In my mind, this was an act of war. I fully support President Bush in his deliberation to protect our people and our freedom."[35]

He assured Hoosiers that all public buildings were on their highest security alert, military sites in Indiana had been secured, and the state's Emergency Operations Center had been activated.

Recalling the attack on Pearl Harbor decades before, he added a word of compassion and hope, "After my parents told me about the attack at Pearl Harbor, I remember just trying to understand why someone would do that. Many of us—adults and children—are wondering the same thing today. The horror of these acts is beyond comprehension. I am heartsick for the many, many people who were killed or injured—and for their families and loved ones. My sympathy and my prayers go out to them.

As a people, we all must look inwardly and gather strength from and for each other to get through this tragedy. I am heartsick for our children, who had a little bit of their childhood stolen from them today. And I am heartsick for our country, which stands for life and liberty and the pursuit of happiness and idealism and compassion and caring about one another.

"No cowardly act of war like that we have witnessed today will undermine the spirit of Americans. We're seeing that spirit today among the rescuers who are trying to help the injured, and among the hundreds of people lining up to donate blood. I'm calling on Hoosiers to do what they can. I know I don't have to do much in the way of persuading; the people of Indiana *always* step up in time of need...This is a time for all of us to pull together; to remember what America is made of; to remember what we're made of."[36]

Joyce said O'Bannon only watched the horrifying images of September 11, 2001 many hours after the attacks and after he had spoken to the press. "In retrospect, one could make the argument and ask, 'Why weren't you using that technology to stay up to date?' And I think he would say, and I think this is why he did it, because he had people coming in and going out doing what they were supposed to be doing: advising him about the situations in Indiana and any potential dangers in our state related to that...He was letting his experts give him information to help keep the public safe. He was not being emotionally driven by what he saw on TV...He clearly kept out all the fuzz and listened to his staff."[37]

Later that month, O'Bannon heeded President Bush's request to activate the Indiana National Guard to be on guard at commercial airports in the state. In total, four thousand guard members were called up for the task.

FOB at Ground Zero

Governor O'Bannon took an unannounced and unscheduled side trip on October 10, 2001, just twenty-nine days after two terrorist-driven airplanes crashed into the World Trade Center Towers in

New York City, killing thousands of Americans and leveling the buildings to smoking piles of rubble. In New York for an important National Governors' Association meeting on educational standards, O'Bannon accepted the invitation of New York Governor George Pataki (b. 1945), a Republican, to visit what had become known as "ground zero" and to take in the devastation firsthand. Television reporters captured a somber governor as his late evening flight returned to Indianapolis. He told them, "It made me angry. I think you have feelings of anger and sorrow and certainly of sympathy for the people who are really suffering and you get a strong dose of the reality that it happened." Viewing what he called "a crater in the middle of civilization" reminded him of bombed-out European and Japanese cities at the end of World War II.[38]

At the site, O'Bannon shook hands with two New York City police officers, including one who grew up in Indiana. "We've all got those connections that mean a lot to us when we've suffered a great loss like this, and we say that we've got to help those who have been hurt in all the ways we can and try to make this country as safe as we can," O'Bannon said. The governor sounded themes of hope, however, saying, "It takes all of us being vigilant, working together, and we will fight terrorism and root it out and make the United States safe again. And hopefully with the coming together of the countries of the world to fight terrorism, we might have brought the people of the world closer together."[39]

Indiana Counter-Terrorism Security Council

The New York trip was an appropriate prologue for the next day, October 11, 2001, as O'Bannon and Lt. Governor Kernan launched the state's new fifteen-member Counter-Terrorism and Security Council to be headed by Kernan, with Clifford Ong serving as the day-to-day director. Although the state had had an anti-terrorism task force in place since 1997, the goal of this panel was to proactively work to prevent terrorism in Indiana, as unlikely a target as the state may seem. But, as Lt. Governor

Kernan said, it was important that Indiana prepared for the worst in order that it might prevent the worst: "While the odds are small that anything like this could happen in Indiana, we believe the risks are too great for Indiana not to be fully prepared." The plans included a comprehensive threat assessment to all aspects of the state's infrastructure, including many factors not previously considered threats (such as utilities, health, airports, water supplies) and Kernan declared, "There is no such thing as turf in this effort, we're all in this together."[40]

O'Bannon, along with all public leaders in this period, tried hard to strike a balance between appropriate cautiousness and the freedom to live one's life. "Even without witnessing the scene in New York, anyone can understand why Americans are frightened, but we must not give in to fear, because we are a courageous people."[41]

The Indiana effort was meant to mirror the national Homeland Security agency created by President George W. Bush in the wake of the terrorist attacks. At that time, Bush and Homeland Security Director Tom Ridge (b. 1945), a former Republican governor of Pennsylvania, pledged widespread support and information sharing with the states. In the first few weeks, information flowed freely, and members of Bush's cabinet conducted telephone conference calls with the nation's governors; O'Bannon participated in all of them.

The new state-federal relationship was headed for a major strain, however. To exacerbate the terror of the attacks of September 11, a series of "anthrax attacks" had also occurred via the U.S. mail in the weeks that followed, killing and injuring postal workers and others in Washington, D.C. and Florida.

ANTHRAX IN INDIANA

On October 26, 2001, postal inspectors converged upon the Critical Parts Center, a company housed in a simple one-story office building near the Indianapolis International Airport that held contracts to clean and maintain equipment from the U.S. Postal Service. Days earlier, two postal workers at the Brentwood post office in Washington, D.C. died from exposure to anthrax being sent to national leaders via the mail. Officials feared equipment from that station was sent to Indianapolis, possibly exposing workers there to anthrax. Postal officials had gathered samples from the equipment with the help of their own professional health experts and shipped them to a lab controlled by the Centers for Disease Control and Prevention. Meanwhile, company officials, seemingly seeking their own answers, called the Indiana State Department of Health asking for assistance with not only testing but with obtaining high-grade antibiotics to offer to their employees. They did not know the test results and neither did state health officials, but within a week, the test results would be known, and it would not speak well of the newly formed state and federal efforts to address terrorism.

NBC *Nightly News* reported on October 30, 2001 that tests from the Indianapolis facility were positive for exposure to anthrax. This was big news to the state and the nation, and sadly, unknown news to everyone in state government in Indiana who had been closely monitoring the situation. The O'Bannon administration scrambled through the night and into the next day to get the details, working closely with Indianapolis Mayor Bart Peterson and his public health and public safety officials. Tensions grew that the anthrax threat had spread beyond the nation's costal region to the Midwest and that important information about the scope and level of that threat had been withheld not only from the public, but from the state and local officials charged with ensuring the health and safety of all Hoosiers. The governor conferred with state and national public health officials, and he and Peterson felt strongly that it was important to tell the public everything officials knew. Finally, by mid-afternoon on October 31, the governor and lieutenant governor planned a public announcement along with Peterson and Dr. Gregory Wilson, the state health commissioner. The governor delayed going before reporters, however, until he could speak personally to Secretary Ridge and, as the governor later said, "express to him my concern that there be better communications with us whenever there is anything in Indiana that we should be concerned about or could be a threat."[42]

The governor's remarks were carried live on statewide television and reported nationally. O'Bannon was uncharacteristically annoyed and even more uncharacteristic of him, willing to express his annoyance publicly. "As you all know, yesterday, on a national news network report, it was reported anthrax had been found in Indianapolis. Last night, when the reports were issued (on the network news), we had not yet received confirmation on tests done on the equipment. Today, we know that in forty-four tests on postal equipment there, one sample was positive for a few anthrax spores. What this means is that the equipment tested had been exposed to anthrax in Washington, D.C., but that the exposure was very limited, and at this level of exposure, anthrax is not a threat to human health here in Indiana."[43]

The governor noted that the public health threat in Indiana was minimal and that the equipment in question had not handled Indiana mail, "so there is absolutely no reason for Hoosiers to be alarmed." But he added, with postal officials standing nearby, "I am concerned, however, about how the postal service handled this situation as far as notification. The possibility of anthrax exposure was never reported to any official by the postal service or by the Centers for Disease Control. To be fair, the postal service had not yet determined that anthrax was present in its Brentwood facility before the equipment was shipped here to Indiana...But they have known since early last week that the machine was possibly exposed and that it was here in Indiana. Dr. Wilson found out about the situation only after (company) officials telephoned to find out about how they could obtain antibiotics for their workers."[44]

"I urge all of us to be vigilant, but not give into fear. The people who delivered anthrax through the postal service are enemies and are trying to make us live our lives in fear. I hope you will join me in not letting these terrorists win."[45]

Remembering Those Who Died

On September 11, 2002, O'Bannon and Peterson led a large remembrance ceremony on the west steps of the Indiana Statehouse.

Ten empty chairs were assembled at the front of the crowd for the total of nine Hoosiers killed in the terrorist attacks a year earlier and the one Hoosier Marine killed to that point in time in the new war on terrorism. The ceremony also honored 318 Hoosiers who had responded and survived the crises in both New York and Washington as fire and police rescue workers, medical personnel, and others. Earlier that day, O'Bannon dedicated a new marker, made of Indiana limestone, on the south lawn of the statehouse, bearing the words of President George W. Bush (b. 1946): "Terrorist attacks can shake the foundations of our biggest buildings, but they cannot touch the foundation of America."

In his speech, O'Bannon said, "Like the rest of our great country, Indiana rose up on September 11 and remembered the greatness that comes from working together, unselfishly, to meet the need for help. It is up to us all now to continue to act this way, to be our brother's keeper in good times and in bad. In so doing, we will honor what we lost as we saw the worst of what man can do to man. And we will keep hold of what we gained as we witnessed the best that we can do for one another."[46]

O'Bannon asked all Hoosiers to "tell your children, and other young people, the stories of the heroes who stood in the midst of destruction to risk and, in too many cases, to give their lives to help others get to safety. Tell your children the stories of the officers who ran into the fire to help as others rushed out. Tell them the stories of the ordinary Americans on Flight 93 who overcame terrorists on a suicide mission so that others would not die. And tell them of the people who found other ways to help, who reached out to their neighbors to rebuild a nation that will never fall to attacks of hate and who made sure our foundation remains strong, that our hearts remain open, and that our land remains free. These are the stories of heroes."[47]

THE WAR ON TERRORISM

Governor O'Bannon was determined to be a public and full supporter of President Bush's effort to combat terrorism in response to the events of September 11, 2001. While some Democrats parted with the president on policy decisions he made related to the war and terrorism, O'Bannon remained publicly aligned with Bush's approach. In private, he was likewise supportive, encouraging staff to support the president during this difficult period. As part of that, he insisted upon attending departure ceremonies for Indiana troops being called up as the nation prepared for the pending war in Afghanistan and later in Iraq. In February 2002, O'Bannon helped send off 380 soldiers to a peace-keeping mission in Bosnia that freed up regular army troops for duty in Afghanistan. Just after Christmas in December 2002, O'Bannon greeted about 600 Hoosier troops as they departed Fort Knox, Kentucky for an undisclosed assignment in the Middle East. O'Bannon told the troops, "We talk a lot about patriotism in this country and what each of us can do to show our pride as Americans...but you show your patriotism every day by representing Indiana in the National Guard. You show the rest of the country, and the world, that Indiana is full of brave, selfless, patriotic people who realize what a privilege our freedom is, and that you choose to defend it."[48]

He would return to Fort Knox again in late January 2003 when another 650 Indiana troops were deployed for overseas duty.

The nation officially started combat operations just two months later, known as "Operation Enduring Freedom," on March 18, 2003. President Bush's announcement of the commencement of military operations was expected at some point during that evening, and Governor O'Bannon insisted on returning to the statehouse so that he could make a statement as well—but only after the president had addressed the nation. As it turned out, Governor O'Bannon's statement could not be made until just after 11 p.m., allowing television stations across the state to carry it live. In it, he said, "Tonight, we have learned that America is at war. We are at war to defend our country's very essence—freedom, tolerance, the pursuit of happiness, and self-determination. Despite the differences Americans have expressed over the last several months, we are united tonight in support of the brave men and women who are standing at the doorstep of a country led by a tyrant whose illegal weapons of mass destruction are a threat to the world. Fifteen hundred of these strong, courageous men and women are Hoosiers. Our hearts and minds are with them and their loved ones tonight, and we pray that they return home safely—and quickly. Let us stand shoulder to shoulder with them. As they face down an enemy half a world away, let us refuse to give in to terrorists who wish to frighten us here at home and undermine the American way of life. Let us keep our troops in mind, but let us continue to go about our daily lives."[49]

His closing remark was perhaps the most he was willing or able to do. The governor was aware that many of the nation's Democratic leaders were opposed to the war, or at least opposed to the argument used by President Bush leading to war. Some of that opposition was even present among members of O'Bannon's personal staff, but as in other times, it was the governor's opinion that was the publicly stated one, and differences among staff on the issue of the war were kept private. O'Bannon said, "Let me close by saying that no one is happy about this turn of events. But we *are* at war. We must and will support our troops; we must and will support our president; we must and will support our American way of life."[50]

The governor's commitment to the troops would continue. Throughout the remaining months of his life—and his term in office—he sent letters of encouragement to troops and their families that he heard from and was particularly diligent about sending letters of condolence to the families of those killed in the war.

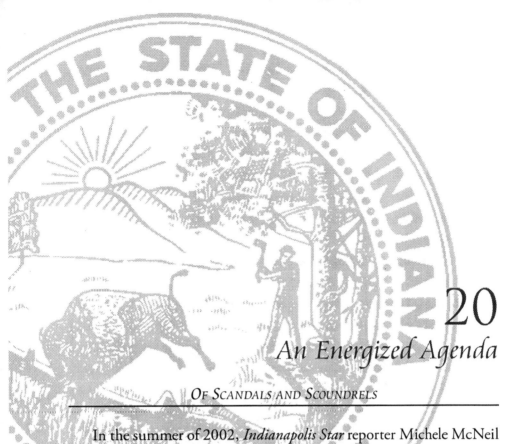

20

An Energized Agenda

OF SCANDALS AND SCOUNDRELS

In the summer of 2002, *Indianapolis Star* reporter Michele McNeil walked into the governor's press office and made a startling statement. She revealed she had been investigating an anonymous tip left on her voice mail suggesting that Walter Kevin Scott, the investment manager of the state's Public Employees Retirement Fund (PERF), was actually a convicted felon who had previously been accused of stealing the personal identity of another individual of a similar name.

As the days wore on, it was revealed that Scott had served time on a criminal charge involving identity theft—and now had immediate and high-level access to the identities of thousands of active state employees and retirees. McNeil, it seems, had stumbled onto a major story and a major embarrassment for PERF and the administration.

Scott, it was later revealed, was dumped by Cook, Inc., a Bloomington-based medical device company that seemed happier to get rid of him than to accurately reflect his sordid past. O'Bannon expressed outrage at PERF's lax hiring process and the fact that Cook gave Scott excellent references.[1]

McNeil said she could tell that the story "wore" on the O'Bannon team, particularly Diana Hamilton, the governor's trusted adviser for PERF and other quasi-governmental agencies. It was Hamilton, however, who had insisted on a criminal background check—where Scott subsequently used the Social Security number of an Ohio man with the same name in order to pass. He used his own Social Security number for payroll and other hiring purposes.

"...This really started a lot of people thinking about these quasi-governmental agencies and how they operate, and the level of checks and balances that are in place for them," McNeil said.[2]

In private, O'Bannon was completely dumbfounded by the level of deceit employed by Scott to pull off the charade. The governor frequently shook his head in disbelief as the details of the case unfolded before him. It seemed, at times, beyond his capacity to understand how a person could conduct so many massive lies. O'Bannon acted quickly, however, by ordering a complete investigation by attorney Forrest Bowman to ensure the PERF funds were secure, along with the identities of the members. He repeatedly stated publicly that all PERF funds would be secure—they were.

He also pressured the PERF board to fire its director, William Butler, who had hired Scott and replace him with a trusted O'Bannon adviser, Craig Hartzer, who left his post as head of the Department of Workforce Development to lead PERF out of the deep waters.

While O'Bannon's office was not responsible for hiring Scott, he said, "...I know that the buck stops here, and so I will do whatever it takes, and I will hold people accountable, to make sure this kind of thing never happens again."[3]

Hartzer believes the PERF events deeply troubled O'Bannon. "He had never campaigned against the bureaucracy of state government... so when there were complaints about the behavior of state employees, he seldom, if ever, immediately assumed that the state employee was wrong or that the bureaucracy was wrong." The troubles at PERF were "totally counter-intuitive to him," Hartzer said.

AT THE CENTER

Whether legitimate or not, the governor becomes the center of many stories, and his comment or opinion is sought on various situations. One "hot situation" came in the midst of the 2000 reelection campaign when the trustees of Indiana University finally reached the end of their rope and decided to dismiss legendary men's basketball coach Bob Knight. The move was front-page news across the state and the nation, given Knight's long and well-known career that included seemingly as many outbursts and tangles with others as wins. O'Bannon reluctantly commented on Knight's dismissal, saying, "This is a disappointing end to a long and distinguished career at Indiana University. Bob Knight has contributed greatly to the university, the state of Indiana, and the world of basketball...I have known Bob Knight for many years and am personally saddened by this outcome...Nonetheless, I am confident that IU's action today is in the best interest of the university, and I fully support its decision."[4]

Current events often drove public policy in the O'Bannon era, reflected in two major bills the governor signed into law, including House Enrolled Act 1253 increasing jail time for persons who burn, vandalize, or burglarize a house of worship. The act increased penalties from a range of six months to three years to a new range of six to twenty years in jail. "When someone violates a church, he also violates each and every person who worships there...We must do more to deter these repugnant crimes," O'Bannon said.[5]

The governor also signed legislation requiring Indiana motorists to slow down or pull over into an adjoining lane when a law enforcement or other emergency vehicle is stopped alongside a roadway. The 1999 law came after four Indiana State Police troopers were killed in motor vehicle crashes along roadsides in the four previous years. O'Bannon signed the law seated next to Cindy Winzenread, widow of State Trooper Andy Winzenread who was killed in a 1997 accident along Interstate 74 near Greensburg. The death moved State Representative Cleo Duncan, a Greensburg Republican, to push for passage of the bill.

O'Bannon also jumped into the fray when federal Medicaid officials ordered states to begin paying for Viagra, an impotency drug, for Medicaid-eligible clients. Indiana paid those claims for just one month in 1998 until O'Bannon himself called a stop to it, defying federal orders. In letters to President Clinton and Donna Shalala, secretary of the U.S. Department of Health and Human Services, O'Bannon said he disagreed with the federal mandate and did not plan to honor it. O'Bannon said he was concerned about black-market reselling of the drug and reports of abuse and inappropriate use of the drug, but mostly he was concerned about asking Hoosier taxpayers to pay for the cost of the impotency drug under a public health program (Medicaid funds to eligible clients in Indiana were about two-thirds federal, one-third in state matching funds). O'Bannon's defiance held, and Indiana never again paid for a Viagra claim under Medicaid.

President Clinton's 1998 impeachment by members of the U.S. House of Representatives as a result of statements he gave about an extra-marital sexual relationship with a White House intern put all political leaders on the hot seat. Reporters love hearing what other politicos have to say when one of their own is sizzling away—and Clinton's troubles did not escape the nation's governors for comment, including O'Bannon. O'Bannon kept his statement short, simple, and written only, "This is a deep personal tragedy for Bill Clinton and his family. I'm very glad that he had come forward to admit he misled the public and that he takes full responsibility for what he did. He also said it's time to move forward. I, too, hope we as a people can put this matter behind us, and the sooner, the better."[6]

Despite Clinton's personal failings, O'Bannon felt, like many Americans, that the president's leadership in so many other areas, including the unprecedented economic growth and strength of the U.S., had to be considered in the context of Clinton's whole life.

Also during O'Bannon's second term, the U.S. Mint announced a popular program to reissue U.S. quarters and to include a state-specific design on the reverse side following the order each state was admitted. Indiana's quarter was issued in the second year for the program, and the governor wanted to go "all out."

O'Bannon asked staffer Cheryl Reed to work with the U.S. Mint, and the state sponsored a quarter design contest. All kinds of designs came in, including ones honoring Chief Little Turtle and George Rogers Clark. The design the governor favored featured an Indy-style racing car and a basketball player going for two points. Of the racing car-basketball design, Mint officials were concerned it was too busy.

O'Bannon made a difficult choice for any Hoosier—the basketball player would have to go from the design.

"Governor O'Bannon knew the quarters would go worldwide and that Indiana is recognized for racing, and basketball players were more ubiquitous," Reed said. "He knew he'd take some flak for that, and he did."[7]

To roll out the new quarter, O'Bannon truly did pull out all the stops. The head of the U.S. Mint had made trips to each state for the first day of the quarter issue. In Kentucky, they had staged an event at Churchill Downs. In Ohio, they used an airplane hangar at Dayton and invited former astronaut and O'Bannon favorite John Glenn. For Indiana, nothing other than the Indianapolis Motor Speedway would do.

"The event was a record-breaker at the time for the Mint in terms of attendance and activity," Reed said.[8]

In addition, a special "first day cancellation" was offered specific to the event by the U.S. Post Office. "That was huge for the stamp collectors, too, so we had all the coin collectors, the stamp collectors, the race fans who wanted to meet the drivers, and of course, a lot of kids and adults who wanted a free quarter," Reed said.[9]

O'Bannon rode around the track in a two-seat Indy-style racing car driven by one of only four women to ever race in the Indianapolis 500, Sarah Fisher.

Energize Indiana: A Vision for Indiana's Future

The last major push of the O'Bannon administration, the governor's historic economic development proposal in 2002-03, was dubbed "Energize Indiana." In an important way, the program helped energize the administration as well. Fresh off a surprising victory for his plan to restructure property taxes in Indiana during the '02 session, O'Bannon and Kernan came forward with a sweeping ten-year program of more than $1.25 billion in new investments in key sectors of the Hoosier economy.

"Energize Indiana is our commitment to build on our past, strengthen our present, and blast forward into the future," O'Bannon said. "It is our commitment to fire up our state's economy. And it does not use one state tax dollar."[10]

The Energize Indiana program was far reaching and focused on investment targeted to creating high-skill, high-wage jobs in four industry sectors to which Indiana could stake a claim—advanced manufacturing, life sciences, information technology, and twenty-first-century logistics, or high-tech distribution. It would help businesses get started, conduct research, market new ideas, and create jobs, O'Bannon said.[11]

Energize Indiana also focused on current workers by assessing their skills and matching them with appropriate jobs; by providing educational opportunities to improve their skills; and by extending unemployment benefits for people who, because of the national recession, could not find work within the normal thirteen-week benefit period. It also provided a one-time investment of $200 million into K-12 education, college scholarships for as many as 22,000 students to pursue studies in the four targeted areas and who remained in Indiana after graduation, and provided money so universities could build new facilities.

The program relied on a series of innovative funding mechanisms, including a proposal to securitize a portion of future payments to the state from the national tobacco settlement and permitting new bonding authority for the state's port commissions and investments from the state's Public Employees' Retirement Fund and the Teachers' Retirement Fund.

Republican House Minority Leader Brian Bosma of Indianapolis said the tobacco settlement was "questionable" as a funding device and, along with others, was quick to criticize efforts to tap future payments under the tobacco settlement for money now (a concern abandoned by GOP legislators less than a decade later as they endorsed leasing the state's future revenue from the Indiana Toll Road to foreign investors).[12]

"Again, the usual suspects in the statehouse were amazed at the breadth of the plan, and the governor has gotten some good press—outside Indiana, of course—about his willingness to tackle and see to completion such a big issue at a time when other governors had to devote their total attention to budget woes," Ed Feigenbaum said.[13]

O'Bannon told *Inside Indiana Business* television host Gerry Dick, "We said we were going to take overt steps to provide businesses with the specially skilled workforce they need—and help young people get those skills. For the first time in Indiana, we're addressing the 'brain drain' by making specific overtures to students to stay in Indiana after they graduate."[14]

To sell the Energize plan, O'Bannon and Kernan went into a full-court press, meeting with legislators, business and education leaders, editorial boards across the state, and local officials from both parties as often as they could.

Initial opposition melted as quickly as the snow in the spring of 2002, as Republicans and Democrats alike realized the plan was the boldest move the state could make amidst a deep national recession and the resulting lean state budget. In embracing and passing the plan while combining it with the state's biennial budget, O'Bannon said "lawmakers acted on our most urgent priority—passing a budget—and they also addressed our vitally important need—job creation—by passing Energize Indiana. These economic-development measures will encourage innovators to test creative ideas, inspire researchers to pursue proposals, and prompt business owners to grow their companies. Energize Indiana will allow Hoosiers to follow their dreams and make them a reality in Indiana."[15]

The governor's enthusiasm over the passage of Energize Indiana was dampened, somewhat, by the state budget legislators handed him.

"We're glad, certainly, that the situation in Indiana is better than it is in some other states, where there are massive teacher layoffs and other severe cutbacks," the governor said. "Still, this budget presents some difficult challenges—and, unfortunately, the legislature has tied our hands in dealing with some of them."[16]

The new budget flat-lined the appropriation for Medicaid, the joint state-federal healthcare program for the poor, pregnant women, and children and people with disabilities, even though the number of people served by the entitlement program increased from fewer than 740,000 people in 2002 to more than 817,000 expected by 2005.

He said the new budget reduced the level of funding proposed by another $218 million and "tied our hands by restricting us in how we operate the program and making it virtually impossible to make significant reductions."[17] O'Bannon's remarks reflected his growing frustration with legislators who demanded more cuts in spending but often set about undoing those cuts when they proved unpopular by restricting the governor's role in managing the budget.

"For a guy often portrayed as asleep at the wheel, O'Bannon worked deftly and largely behind the scenes to make both tax restructuring and Energize Indiana happen," Feigenbaum said.[18]

Feigenbaum said O'Bannon's behind-the-scenes approach led to him not getting deserved credit for his efforts. "While some politicians are willing to lay claim to anything that slightly resembles an utterance they made at some point in the past, O'Bannon and Kernan aren't your typical politicians. They're much more likely to work quietly, build consensus, shun self-congratulations, and share credit."[19]

SAY IT AIN'T SO, JOE

Just five days after O'Bannon and Kernan launched Energize Indiana, Joe Kernan stunned the political world by announcing he would not be a candidate for governor in the 2004 election.

Widely expected to be the Democratic nominee, and the party's best chance to hold on to the governor's office, Kernan had raised about $2 million toward an expected '04 campaign but instead said it was time to go home to South Bend. "Upon completion of my term as Indiana's lieutenant governor, I will return to private life," Kernan said. "This was a very personal decision on the basis of what I believe is the best for Maggie and me at this time in our life."[20]

Just days before, Kernan phoned Governor O'Bannon to tell him and Judy of his plans as he and Maggie drove from South Bend to Indianapolis. The O'Bannons were stunned but accepted what he told them.

O'Bannon did not try to talk Kernan out of his decision but reminded Kernan he could take more time to think it over. In the end, he didn't need more time—the decision had been made, and Kernan moved quickly to step aside in order to allow other Democrats interested in the party's nomination for governor to step up.

Governor O'Bannon did not attend the packed news conference in Kernan's third-floor statehouse office, instead attending previously scheduled meetings in Washington, D.C. But Judy O'Bannon did. She was gracious but emotional when she spoke to reporters afterward, her voice briefly cracking. "Here's a man who sat in a prisoner of war camp for eleven months, and in those days, he really thought about what life meant to him. Each day is so precious. We've taken fifteen of his years, and he ought to have some of his own if he wants them."[21]

Republicans called it an "early Christmas present," noting that Kernan would have been the toughest Democrat in Indiana to beat. Within minutes, speculation centered on a host of other Democrats to run for governor in 2004, including former U.S. representatives Baron Hill and Tim Roemer, former house speaker John Gregg, Indianapolis Mayor Bart Peterson, former state and national Democratic Party chair Joe Andrew, State Senator Vi Simpson of Bloomington, and even U.S. Senator and former two-term governor Evan Bayh. In the end, only Andrew and Simpson would launch campaigns—and those would only last through 2003 until the political world changed dramatically again.

THE GOVERNORS COME TO INDIANA

O'Bannon was thrilled to announce that the 2003 National Governors' Association (NGA) summer meeting would take place in Indiana—the nation's governors last gathered in Indiana at French Lick in the summer of 1931. Indianapolis was chosen as the host city from a field of four other cities.

O'Bannon remained active in the NGA and all issues related to the states, employing a full-time federal liaison office in Washington, D.C. comprised of Jeff Viohl, Gerry del Rosario, Chris Priest, and Rob Kidney.

Kentucky Governor Paul Patton (b. 1937), serving as the chair of the NGA, helped land Indiana the job as host state. A fellow Democrat who became lieutenant governor of Kentucky just two years after O'Bannon's election in 1988, Patton was perhaps O'Bannon's closest friend among the nation's governors.

"Frank and Judy were very proud and pleased to host it, and they worked very hard at providing a good meeting...," Governor Patton said. "When it came time to host the NGA meeting at Indianapolis, we did that because Kentucky did not have the convention facilities that they had to host such a large event, and I knew Frank really wanted to have it in Indiana..."[22]

Patton's wife, Judi, was equally close to her first lady counterpart in Indiana. She too had high praise for the NGA preparations in Indiana. "They were so thoughtful about everything," Judi Patton said. "They had so much for the families and the first spouses, and it was just an outstanding event. I think many of them just could not believe all that Judy had planned for us, to include us."[23]

Governors O'Bannon and Patton were both dedicated members of the NGA, active in both the annual winter meeting in Washington, D.C., and again in the summer meeting. "I always viewed the NGA as very important as we attempted to address issues with the administration or the Congress," Governor Patton said. "The governors and the states often need to speak with one voice, and the governors have a lot more in common than they have in political differences, as it relates to the federal government."[24]

Federal issues of importance were virtually the same for all states—federal highway funding dollars, Medicaid funding, and welfare reform. Patton believes O'Bannon was an influential force among the governors of his time, particularly regarding issues like Medicaid.

The governors were successful in 2002 in convincing Congress and the Bush administration to release an additional $20 billion reallocation to the states for rising Medicaid expenses.[25]

"The National Governors' Association is important, particularly for smaller states like Indiana and Kentucky. It's not that our two states are all that small, but when compared to California, New York, and some others, well, they can pretty much row their own boats up there in Washington. The rest of the states don't have that kind of clout, so we get that collectively through NGA," Governor Patton said.[26]

THE LAST IDEA: ON TOP OF THAT DOME

In late August 2003, Governor and Mrs. O'Bannon attended the Indiana Democratic Editorial Association annual meeting at French Lick, Indiana—as they had for every year of their marriage. It would be the last IDEA convention the governor would ever attend, but those who were in attendance recall it as one of his best.

Brian Howey, publisher of the *Howey Political Report*, reported later that "Governor Frank O'Bannon gave his final speech at the Democratic Editorial convention. He spoke without notes. As he was at the National Governors' Association in Indianapolis last month, Governor O'Bannon was lucid and in stride, operating out of a maximum comfort zone; he was at the top of his game."[27]

Howey noted that O'Bannon recalled how then-New York Governor Franklin D. Roosevelt had attended the National Governors' Association meeting just up the street in the 1930s, and Roosevelt was able to see firsthand the largest dome of its kind in the world at that time at the historic West Baden Springs Hotel. "I wonder what he thought," O'Bannon said, before talking with pride about his own recent and historic achievements, the just-passed Energize Indiana economic development plan and the successful property tax restructuring effort in the 2002 session of the General Assembly.[28]

Finally, O'Bannon recalled Harrison Albright, the visionary architect of the West Baden Springs Hotel. Albright "stood on top of the dome as the supports were taken out," O'Bannon explained, despite the fears of many that such a large domed structure would collapse. Instead, it's stood long into another century. "I feel like I'm on that dome tonight," O'Bannon said.[29]

GREETING THE PRESIDENT

Governor O'Bannon interrupted his scheduled vacation following the IDEA confab to go to Indianapolis on September 5, 2003, as President George W. Bush visited Hendricks County to tout an economic stimulus proposal and raise campaign cash for the upcoming 2004 election. At the airport, O'Bannon was at the front of the line to greet the president as he descended the steps from Air Force One. "I just signed your letter," Bush said succinctly, informing the governor that he had approved O'Bannon's just days-old request for federal emergency disaster relief for flooded Southern Indiana counties.

"The president brought us some very good news today," O'Bannon told reporters afterward. "I am especially pleased that the people who have suffered because of these storms and floods have learned so quickly that help is on the way."[30]

It would prove troubling later when reporters would repeat unconfirmed and unattributed statements that said O'Bannon's speech appeared slurred when he spoke to the president. Todd Siesky, a member of the governor's communications staff, staffed him that day and noticed nothing unusual about his speech, other than he appeared more relaxed than normal and more talkative than he was at times when he was tired.

A Slow, Quiet Float

Governor O'Bannon and his friend and Harrison County neighbor Bob Sawtel loved to take canoe rides down the Big Blue River. It seemed like a great way for the governor to spend his last official "day off" on this mini vacation on Saturday, September 6, 2003.

"We went on a float trip down the Big Blue River that day with the Bob and Missi Sawtel outfit, and it was just wonderful, just a lot of fun," Judy said. "We came home that night and sat outside in lawn chairs and just looked up at the sky and at the stars. We got our binoculars out, like we always did, and he just loved that."[31]

The governor's official schedule would creep in on his life soon enough, but this slow, quiet Saturday was spent as Frank O'Bannon loved most—being outside and enjoying nature and the company of his family and friends.

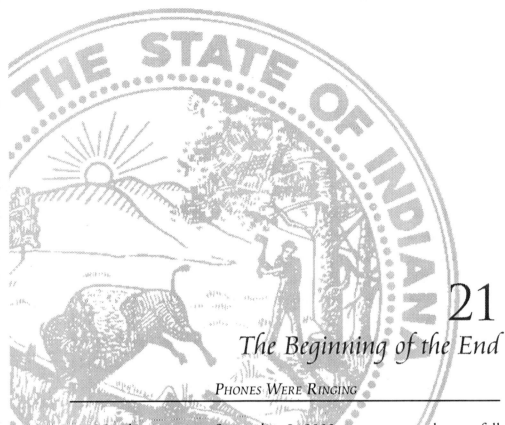

21

The Beginning of the End

Monday morning, September 8, 2003 was a sunny, pleasant fall day in Indiana. The weather would be the only good news that day for this day would signal the beginning of the end of the O'Bannon administration. For all of us in the small world of the governor's staff, our lives were too full of work and demands to ponder much that day, but as the hours wore on, it was clear—nothing would ever be the same.

At about 9 a.m., phones were ringing in three separate places. All bore the same news: The governor was stricken, unconscious, and being rushed to the hospital.

Ray Raney's phone rang first at the front of the governor's office. On the phone was Trooper Alex Willis telling him the unthinkable: He was unable to contact the governor at his room at the Palmer House Hilton Hotel in downtown Chicago—either by phone or by knocking at his door.

"He was always very prompt," Willis said. "When he said he was going to be somewhere, he was there. But that morning, when I went back up to his room, you could hear this snoring sound coming from the room. I couldn't believe that he was still asleep, and I found that to be kind of unusual, so I knocked on the door…there was no response, but the snoring sound was still there, and it's pretty loud. I knocked a little harder and still no response."[1]

Raney alerted Tim Joyce and Cindy Athey and told them, "We've got a problem."[2]

Willis and Raney hoped that the governor had taken out his hearing aids as he slept and couldn't hear the knocks. As Willis spoke to Raney on his cell phone, Joyce, the governor's chief of staff, and Athey, his executive assistant, joined on the line. They suggested Willis go back to his own room and try ringing the phone in the governor's room.

Meanwhile, Cindy Athey placed a quick call to Lt. Governor Kernan, also in Chicago for the conference. Kernan and his top aide, Tom McKenna, were preparing for the day's events downstairs when Athey called and said O'Bannon was running late and that Kernan may have to stand in for him at the public events now just moments away.

"We wanted to do this as low-key as possible," Raney said. "We didn't want anyone involved with the conference or any outside people involved; we just wanted the hotel people to give us a key to get into the room."[3]

"Tim Joyce told me, 'You don't want to do anything to embarrass the governor, like busting in the door,'" Willis said. By then, the hotel maintenance staff had delivered a room key for O'Bannon's room. "I tried the room key, and it got the door open a few inches, but he had put on the chain, or sliding lock on the door. It was so dark in the room, the sheets on the bed were all I could see," Willis said.[4]

Willis called out, "Governor! Governor!" but got no response, as the snoring sound continued. Hotel security removed the sliding lock, and Willis entered the room alone.

He turned on the lights and could see O'Bannon was lying on his back, near the foot of his bed and partially inside a small closet. Still in his pajamas, he remained unresponsive. "I went over to him, and this time, I said, 'Frank! Frank!' and I got no response. So I rubbed his sternum, and I got no response, but he *was* breathing. I opened his eyes, and I saw that his pupils were very small," Willis said.[5]

Trained as a first responder but not as an emergency medical technician or as a paramedic, Willis (like all state troopers) was prepared to address persons who have stopped breathing or are bleeding profusely. In O'Bannon's case, he was beyond the medical help Willis could provide.

As Willis tended to the governor, he yelled out to hotel security personnel in the hallway to call 911 immediately and held on to his cell phone to tell Raney, Joyce, and Athey what he was finding.

Lt. Governor Kernan said, "The more I thought about it, the more I thought what Cindy said just didn't sound right. The governor was always very punctual, and it just didn't feel right to me."[6]

Kernan decided to go to O'Bannon's room upstairs himself and found Illinois state troopers and hotel personnel waiting in the hallway and Willis inside the room with O'Bannon. Kernan's entrance was a welcome sight for Willis. He was relieved to see someone he could trust and was appropriate to have present at such a private moment in the governor's life.[7]

Kernan and Willis continued to tend O'Bannon as he lay on the floor, Willis cupping O'Bannon's head in his hands speaking quietly to him, as the lieutenant governor softly cleaned his face with a wet washcloth he retrieved from the bathroom. Within moments, paramedics arrived and followed Willis's instructions that the governor, still clad in his pajamas, be removed from the hotel via a private elevator and entrance—away from the conference participants and other hotel guests in the main lobby. Willis grabbed the governor's briefcase and his reading glasses as the group raced to the elevator and down to a waiting ambulance.

Kernan believes Willis "had done all the right things...I knew that a lot had changed but I did not know to what degree."[8]

Within moments of these events, a second call was coming in to the governor's office in Indianapolis, this time to Mary Dieter's office in the Press Office. On the phone was an officer from the Chicago

Fire Department, calling as a courtesy to let her know that their EMS ambulance was in the process of transporting O'Bannon to Northwestern Memorial Hospital. He was unconscious; that was all they knew.[9]

As this was taking place, Joyce had placed a call to First Lady Judy O'Bannon at the governor's temporary residence. He told her what he knew: The governor did not wake up, was unresponsive, and was en route to the hospital.

Moments later, Mrs. O'Bannon placed a call to Jonathan Swain. "Frank is ill; something is wrong with him." Soon, Joyce and Raney were asking Swain to meet Mrs. O'Bannon and fly by helicopter to Chicago as she rushed to be at her husband's side. As Swain hurried from downtown along I-70, he prayed for the O'Bannons.[10]

Back in Chicago, the ambulance raced north from the hotel the 1.6 miles up Michigan Avenue to nearby Northwestern Memorial Hospital with Governor O'Bannon in the back and Lt. Governor Kernan riding in the front passenger seat. Willis followed behind in a Chicago Police Department vehicle.

At the hospital, doctors told Willis O'Bannon needed immediate surgery. When Willis told them Judy was en route, they insisted they could not wait. He told them to do what they had to, their patient was the governor of Indiana.[11]

As Swain arrived at the state police post so did Mrs. O'Bannon in a car driven by Trooper Larry Gershanoff. A state police helicopter was warming up and ready for them to board. Mrs. O'Bannon had already arranged for the helicopter to make one stop more, on the parking lot at Hinkle Fieldhouse at Butler University so Jennifer O'Bannon could get on board. From there, the helicopter flew north the 180 miles from Indianapolis to Chicago, as Mrs. O'Bannon placed hurried cell phone calls to her other children in Southern Indiana. "Dad got sick; he didn't wake up today," she told both of them. That was all she knew.[12]

Back at the statehouse, Joyce, Dieter, and Athey were receiving another update from Willis and Lt. Governor Joe Kernan, who was riding in the ambulance to the hospital. And perhaps not surprisingly, word was getting out at an alarming rate. The phones kept ringing in the press office and reporters began to walk in seeking information. Dieter and I worked feverishly to gather more information by phone, and Dieter sat down, as she had many times before as a reporter, and hammered out as much of a written statement as she could with the scant details known.

Statehouse reporter Kate Shepherd from WIBC and Network Indiana was one of the first to get through on the phone. She reported to me that Chicago radio stations were reporting that O'Bannon was stricken. "Kate, I have no information to give you on that now. I'll have to call you back," I told her and hastily hung up. It was Kate's second dead end. She had also placed a call to Swain's cell phone. She reached him aboard the helicopter with Mrs. O'Bannon. "Kate, I can't talk right now. You have to call the press office." He hung up, too. Shepherd would understand and would soon have the story that would be breaking live on her station and across the state on radio and TV in moments.[13]

The truth could not be avoided: The governor had suffered a massive, debilitating stroke and was in need of emergency surgery to save his life.

At 10:26 a.m., Dieter issued a brief written statement that said: "Governor Frank O'Bannon, who was in Chicago to attend the U.S. Midwest Japan Conference this morning, has been taken to Northwestern Hospital. More information will be released as it becomes available."[14]

Moments later, Dieter would read the statement to reporters who had already set up a mini-encampment in the south atrium of the statehouse just outside the governor's office, Room 206. She was unable to elaborate much and was disciplined in avoiding speculation and encouraged the reporters to do the same.

The state police helicopter carrying Mrs. O'Bannon and Jennifer made the hour-long flight to Midway Airport in Chicago in near silence. Upon landing at Midway Airport in Chicago, Lt. Governor Kernan met them. Kernan informed Mrs. O'Bannon that she was to call the doctors at the hospital immediately, before departing.

"We were prepared for them to tell us he had died," Swain said. "Instead, they wanted her to know that they had to proceed immediately with a surgery to relieve the swelling of his brain, and to save his life."[15]

Mrs. O'Bannon, Jennifer O'Bannon, and Swain were loaded into an unmarked Indiana State Police car escorted by a marked Chicago Police car. It bothered the first lady that the police car rolled with their lights and sirens blaring up the Stevenson Expressway for the thirteen-mile trip into the downtown loop to Northwestern Memorial Hospital.

"Can't we ask them to turn off those sirens. We should turn those off!" Mrs. O'Bannon said. But the sirens were in the car in front of them and were clearing the way to the hospital. Chicago and Illinois State Police were under orders from Illinois Governor Rod Blagojevich and Chicago Mayor Richard M. Daley to do all they could to assist the O'Bannons and the ISP.[16]

Regardless, the entourage arrived at Northwestern Memorial as Kernan and his aide, McKenna, boarded the same helicopter that had borne Mrs. O'Bannon's party, for a return flight to Indianapolis. With the governor unconscious, it was imperative that the lieutenant governor return to Indianapolis—state government must have a leader.

Back in Indianapolis, Dieter, Joyce, and I met privately in the chief of staff's office discussing what we could say to the media—and when. The story, as Dieter and I insisted, was getting away from us. Indianapolis TV and radio stations were already reporting live on details from their Chicago affiliates. Those reports soon became the most current news we could get. Dieter worked the phones with Northwestern Memorial Hospital, securing that the hospital was to make no public statements about the governor without coordinating with the Indiana Governor's Office. Beyond newly enacted HIPAA requirements ensuring even a public figure like O'Bannon medical privacy, state government had not faced such a crisis in the modern age. The last governor stricken was more than a century before. I was successful at reaching a media relations person at the hospital and gathered for the first time the preliminary information they had given Chicago media, an attempt to get at least *even* with reporters who, in the first few hours of this event, seemingly knew more than we did and knew it before we did.

At 11 a.m., Joyce assembled all of the governor's office staff who were present in Room 101 of the statehouse, our normal room for staff meetings. Several staff members did not know many of the details, and still others were hoping the health issues involved were minor. As Joyce gave the staff as much news as he could, sobs rose among some of the staff members as others comforted them. Pat Rios, the deputy chief of staff, said out loud in a sad voice, "Oh no," to no one in particular. Staff members from all levels hugged and supported one another and then quietly filed back to their offices, "back to work" as Joyce had reminded them that Governor O'Bannon would want and expect them to do.

The News Is Official

At about 12:45 p.m., officials at Northwestern Memorial Hospital in Chicago, under their own pressure from Chicago and Indiana media to answer questions, agreed with Dieter that they and the governor's office in Indianapolis would release simultaneously the same information as it was known at the time. Dieter said she would read a prepared statement for reporters who had set up a pool microphone in the south atrium. Dieter delayed the statement's release until the state police confirmed Mrs. O'Bannon was inside the hospital safely and not likely to encounter reporters' questions. Dieter's voice was strong but quick as she read the very limited details we knew:

"We have information from Northwestern Memorial Hospital in Chicago that the governor is undergoing surgery—right now," she told them. "He has been in surgery since approximately 11 o'clock this morning."[17]

She added, "He was stricken in his hotel room at the Palmer House in Chicago...The emergency room physician, Patrick Connor, M.D., has issued a prepared statement that said the governor was unconscious and nonresponsive when he arrived at the emergency room of the hospital, and he was determined to be suffering from a cerebral hemorrhage."[18]

A stickler for accuracy, Dieter refused to speculate on various reports coming from Chicago reporters who seemed to be covering their end of the story every bit as aggressively as those in Indianapolis and across Indiana. In fact, many of the questions asked just could not be answered yet, including any sort of detailed answer on what sort of specific transfer of power was needed or would be approached.

"Because the governor is in surgery, his staff and the staff of the lieutenant governor have been researching what happens in this kind of a situation. And it has been determined that Article 5, Section 10 of the Indiana Constitution makes a provision for the lieutenant governor to assume the role of acting governor under certain circumstances," Dieter told reporters. It would be the first of many references to this previously unheard of term, "acting governor."[19]

Behind her, just inside the doors of the governor's office, General Counsel Jon Laramore was quietly returning from a private meeting he had with State Supreme Court Chief Justice Randall Shepard informing him of what was happening. Laramore was in close consultation with Lt. Governor Kernan and his legal counsel, Kevin Murray, and an outside attorney Kernan trusted closely, Dick Nussbaum.

Legislative leaders were similarly being notified quietly. Laramore was charged with conducting research, using the state's 1851 constitution as the guide. At the same time, Governor O'Bannon underwent an extensive surgery, attended to by some of the best neurosurgeons in the country. They worked feverishly to not only stabilize the governor but to do anything they could to reduce the swelling of his brain that was beginning to overtake him.

LT. GOVERNOR KERNAN IN THE STATEHOUSE

Upon his arrival in Indianapolis from Chicago, Lt. Governor Kernan's every step was broadcast live on television. As his helicopter landed at the Indianapolis Heliport, cameras followed Kernan and McKenna as they entered a car and greeted aide Matt Sikora.

Once at the statehouse, Kernan walked quickly without comment to his third-floor office where he met privately with McKenna and Joyce. Soon, the attorneys would join the discussion and the "acting governor" concept was fully discussed. It was agreed Kernan would issue a few brief remarks to reporters in one news conference, but they all wanted to avoid any situation that looked like he was being too aggressive in stepping up. However, the fact was Governor O'Bannon was unconscious and unable to perform the duties of his office at that hour, and the pubic needed to see who was in charge.

At 3 p.m., reporters crammed into Kernan's office, Room 333 of the statehouse, and carried his remarks live on statewide television. Kernan detailed what he could about what had occurred in Chicago and encouraged all Hoosiers to pray for the governor. He reiterated that Governor O'Bannon was the governor, a statement he would repeat many times over the next several days, and that the state's constitution provided a "common sense" clause that allowed him to serve simply as "acting governor" for the time being. Reporters' questions, however, continued to center on whether the "acting governor" status needed to be made official and whether a transition of power was occurring.

Kernan told reporters, "There is no transition taking place. Governor O'Bannon remains the governor of Indiana. The lieutenant governor serves as the acting governor in his place." He said he was not seeking to influence in any way whether the position of acting governor needed to be made official in any capacity. "The state constitution is designed specifically that the other two branches of government are engaged in this decision. Therefore, I will not interfere with it, and I will not encourage it."[20]

He refused to speculate on any large or important decisions before him, instead saying, "What remains on my mind, as well as all of the people who work in this building, is the well-being of the governor. We all continue to say a prayer and hope for the best." Kernan pushed aside questions that state government was making plans for Governor O'Bannon's condition to remain undetermined on a long-term basis. In order to "go on with the business of the state of Indiana," Kernan confirmed that he would attend Wednesday's previously scheduled Energize Indiana forum in Indianapolis, the tenth and last one he and Governor O'Bannon had scheduled.[21]

On a personal level, Kernan said, "I think all of us are still in a state of disbelief that this could happen to someone who is so vital, who has so much energy. But at the same time, you recognize that in his absence, it is our responsibility, it is exactly what he would tell us to do, and that is what we need...to step up and do."[22]

First Physician's Briefing

By 5 p.m., matters had begun to settle into the fashion they would follow for the next few days. At Northwestern Memorial Hospital in Chicago, a trio of doctors emerged from the hospital to address a large group of reporters gathered to get an update on the governor's condition. Indianapolis television stations carried the briefing live, as members of the governor's staff crowded into Dieter's office and mine to watch the two TV sets carrying the unbelievable news about our boss, and our friend.

Hiding in plain view in the crowd was Jonathan Swain, the first lady's chief of staff, trying to hear the doctor's update firsthand. Swain went undetected at that time because Indianapolis media were initially relying on their Chicago counterparts to ask the questions of the physicians and none of the Chicago reporters knew Swain.

Dr. Hunt Batjer introduced both Dr. Patrick Connor, the emergency room doctor who attended the governor as he arrived at the hospital, and Dr. Wesley Yapor, the neurosurgeon who performed the governor's emergency surgery. Dr. Yapor reported that the governor was "under sedation for management of his problem of the brain. He came into the emergency room unresponsive. We took him to surgery as soon as humanly possible. The surgery went very well." Yapor said the surgery involved removing blood from both sides of O'Bannon's brain which had accumulated due to a massive stroke. Some of the blood on his brain, however, may have come from the governor hitting his head when he collapsed, the doctor said.

"As far as whether he is going to make it, the next twenty-four to forty-eight hours are critical," Dr. Yapor said. "We certainly are doing everything possible to assure that he will regain as much normal function as possible. In the meantime, he cannot be governor, or at least function as governor, in the normal sense of his duties, because he remains in critical care and he is in very serious condition."[23]

Dr. Connor confirmed that the governor was "near death" when he arrived in the emergency room. "He was quite unresponsive when he arrived, and his blood pressure was very high as well," Dr. Connor said.[24]

Dr. Batjer attempted to put the governor's potential recovery in perspective. "The recovery is really in terms of weeks and months, and not in terms of hours and days. That puts us in a very difficult position to try and predict what the future holds. A lot of things can happen in that amount of time, both good and bad."[25]

By day's end, Raney had begun to assemble a plan to provide ongoing, twenty-four-hour security for not only Governor and Mrs. O'Bannon at the hospital, but also for Lt. Governor Kernan back in Indianapolis. Willis was assigned to return to Indianapolis, but not before Mrs. O'Bannon asked him to see the governor in the intensive care unit following his surgery.

"I was not going to go in there and see him, and then right before I went to leave, Mrs. O'Bannon said, 'Before you leave, I want you to see him.' I didn't want to, but she said, 'I want you to see him the way he is now, because I don't want your last memory of him to be him lying there on the floor in that hotel room.' So we walked in there, and she held my hand, and she said, 'Frank, Alex is here.' And she said, 'You remember all the times you guys went floating down Blue River.' And that was just killing me."[26]

Willis soon departed and drove his state police car back to Indiana alone through the dark and tearful night—unsure as everyone was about what the future held.

The next day brought little news from Chicago, other than that the governor was stable and breathing well, almost without the assistance of the ventilator. Lt. Governor Kernan, who avoided detailed comments to reporters on Monday, went over many of the things he had said the day before. Although no formal declaration of the "acting governor" status had yet been made, state government was in the solid hands of Kernan, who acted decisively, purposefully, and appropriately at every turn. During the day on Tuesday, he walked to the Indiana Government Center South Auditorium to meet with all agency department heads and key state personnel. He walked shoulder to shoulder with Tim Joyce, Governor O'Bannon's chief of staff, in a symbolic move to remind all that Governor O'Bannon was still the governor. To the appointed leaders of state government, Kernan was direct and clear: Governor O'Bannon would want and expect that everyone in state government continue to do the people's business, to answer the phones, to provide services just as we do each day. Lt. Governor Kernan asked each one to pray for the governor and to get back to work and do the best they could. It was inspiring and typical of the "can do" attitude with which Joe Kernan approached every task before him.

By this time, Mrs. O'Bannon had been joined in Chicago by Jonathan and Soni and Polly Zoeller. Her son-in-law, Tom Zoeller, remained in New Albany taking care of their children. Jon Swain, who also remained in Chicago, assisted Mrs. O'Bannon in preparing a statement to give to the multitude of reporters who had been asking for comment from her. In it, she said, "Today, we are filled with the comfort and awe of being part of a wonderful, diverse family. We thank you for uplifting us with your prayers, skills, services, and friendship…Words cannot describe the comfort we feel from the people of Indiana and beyond, and we truly feel we are on this journey together."[27]

SEPTEMBER 10, 2003

On Wednesday morning, House Speaker B. Patrick Bauer, a South Bend Democrat, and Senate President Pro Tem Robert Garton, a Columbus Republican, signaled they would proceed with the formal declaration that Governor O'Bannon was temporarily incapacitated and unable to perform the duties of his office. The constitution required that Bauer and Garton make that information known to the State Supreme Court and that the court make the final determination as to whether to elevate the lieutenant governor officially to acting governor.

"I want to tell you, that was a very, very difficult thing to do, because what we were really saying was that he was incompetent to carry out the duties of governor," Bauer said. "Bob Garton really struggled with this because he really liked Frank O'Bannon a great deal and came into the senate with him in 1971 and worked with him in the senate every day for almost twenty years...But we really had to do it, because this was going on over a two- or three-day period, and we had people calling it a crisis."[28]

Garton and Bauer had several requisites for proceeding, however. They said they wanted to get official word from O'Bannon's doctors regarding his condition, wanted assurances from the governor's staff that they agreed the governor was incapacitated, and wanted to talk to, if they could, Mrs. O'Bannon, so they could get reassurance from her about how she felt about the transition that needed to take place.

The letter from O'Bannon's doctor, Dr. Wesley Yapor, was to the point: "Gentlemen: This letter certifies that Governor Frank O'Bannon is currently unable to discharge the responsibilities and duties of his office."[29]

Mrs. O'Bannon also reached out to Bauer and Garton.

"Judy called us, we were on a speaker phone, and she really boosted our spirits," Garton said. "She said it was the appropriate thing to do, the right thing to do, and that her family was all there and they were in agreement. She was quite upbeat, as Judy always is, or at least in public she always is. She said this was appropriate and that Frank would want it that way. She told us not to have any second thoughts about it."[30]

Bauer recalls it this way: "She said, 'Bob, Pat, you have to do this. We're praying for his recovery, but even if he lives, he won't probably be able to be governor again, and it is going to take some time.' Well, that woman, she is something else, she is just incredible. I always knew she was someone special, but I really knew it that week."[31]

At mid-morning, as Bauer and Garton walked quietly from Bauer's third-floor statehouse office south a few steps down the hallway to the office of Chief Justice Shepard, about a dozen photographers and reporters followed them each step of the way. "That was quite dramatic," Garton said. "We handed the letter to the chief justice, and Pat shook his hand, and the chief justice had tears in his eyes...Then Pat choked a bit, and I grabbed the chief justice's shoulder and said, 'Don't do this to us!' I knew we had to turn around and walk back out, and I didn't want them to catch us all in tears."[32]

Shepard said, "It was just a stressing period of several days...I think that all of the people who had some role to play in those days did so in ways that really bordered on the heroic. We all felt this terrible sense of sorrow for the tragedy and wanted people to know what a special affection and respect we had for the first lady and the governor. We wanted to assure the public in general that the government would go on."[33]

"All of this happened while recognizing that we were writing what might turn out to be precedent that we had hoped would never be used. Everyone worked very hard, their level best, to get it right," Shepard said. "When the question arose of whether the governor's authority should be formally transferred, there were meetings and a series of conversations with the governor's staff, with the speaker, the president pro tem, and me, and the lieutenant governor. The Supreme Court did meet and go over what was actually known about the relevant sections of the state constitution. I don't recall if any statutes were in play or not. We regarded this not as classic litigation, but that we had this highly unusual role to play that was really more political, if you will, or administrative, than judicial."[34]

The entire matter took about forty-five minutes. Once the court had voted, Bauer and Garton then met with reporters on the floor of the

Indiana House in a news conference again carried live on Indianapolis television. "We have today presented a letter to the Indiana Supreme Court, pursuant to Article 5, Section 10, suggesting that Governor O'Bannon is unable to discharge the duties of his office," Bauer said.[35]

"Our colleague is in a drug-induced coma," Garton told reporters. "The reports that we hear from the medical doctors are that many signs are positive, and we are praying for as full a recovery as possible."[36]

Garton and Bauer stressed that they had followed the constitution. Bauer was quick to note that "upon his recovery, Governor O'Bannon may seek a ruling from the Supreme Court declaring that his inability to serve has ceased."[37]

Lt. Governor Kernan's role was simply expanded, they explained, to include the title of acting governor. He would, in effect, serve in both capacities for the time being.

Shepard believes state leadership acted appropriately. "None of us wanted to take any action, and certainly no leadership in the legislature or the judiciary wanted to take any action that seemed precipitous or in any way deemed premature or somehow uncaring," he said. "Everybody tried to come to a common understanding about what was appropriate...we did not think of it as judicative, however, in the traditional sense."[38]

The provisions enacted during these days were approved by voters in 1978.

An hour or so later, doctors in Chicago provided a brief update saying the governor's breathing had improved dramatically and that he was "breathing over" the ventilator and had shown some responses to stimuli, but it was uncertain whether the responses were voluntary or involuntary. For example, Dr. Yapor said the governor retracted his legs at the knee when asked to move his feet.[39]

Lt. Governor Kernan, now the state's acting governor, kept his word and attended the last Energize Indiana forum scheduled that day for the IUPUI Conference Center in Indianapolis. Afterward, he agreed to talk with reporters, his comments broadcast live on Indianapolis television. He told the reporters, "This is the first time in about fifty-six hours that

I felt like smiling. The news that we got about Governor O'Bannon this morning was very, very encouraging. It gives us all great hope and great confidence that he is on the road to recovery, and it feels good to know that he is doing as well as could be expected."[40]

Kernan was accompanied by attorneys Murray and Nussbaum to assist in answering constitution-related questions. Some of the first questions were about what would happen if O'Bannon were to expire. Nussbaum explained that the acting governor would be elevated to governor, and a special session of the legislature would be required in that instance, to consider his selection of a new lieutenant governor.

Kernan said the day's events "demonstrated that there is consensus among all three branches of Indiana government, the judicial, the legislative, and the executive, that this was the proper and appropriate next step to take. The Indiana Constitution works."[41]

Kernan expressed publicly what many wanted to believe, that Governor O'Bannon was going to get better. He cautioned that it was too soon to tell for certain, but there was certainly hope. "There is a period of uncertainty here, and we are all prepared to do all that is necessary to do the business of the state of Indiana until Governor O'Bannon returns."[42]

In Chicago, Mrs. O'Bannon asked Swain to read her statement to reporters about the governor's condition and the proceedings in Indianapolis.

"We all have an understanding of Frank's condition today, and we have total confidence in his medical team. We are also aware of the formal process that is occurring in Indiana, and in it, we are seeing what we have always known: Our state government is a strong institution based on a constitution. We are so appreciative that the leadership of both the legislative and judicial branches have included us in their deliberations. We understand and fully support the actions being taken today. Our family recognizes that our sense of confidence in the spiritual, emotional, and physical strength that we now find in ourselves comes from our association with Frank O'Bannon and from God."[43]

SEPTEMBER 11, 2003

The second anniversary of the September 11, 2001 terrorist attacks would come and go in Indiana rather quietly, with smaller observances conducted at various sites around the state. Two years removed from that tragedy, state government and the media were still focused on the condition of the state's forty-seventh governor. Because of that focus, the governor's office issued an advisory reminding the media that flags would be flown at half-staff on state buildings, consistent with President Bush's order, in observance of the anniversary of the September 11th terrorist attacks.

News from Chicago was limited to written statements that provided brief overviews of his condition. One Chicago report upset many of the governor's office staff when a spokeswoman for Northwestern Memorial Hospital suggested that the governor could end up "brain dead" and not be able to function at his normal level in the future. Dieter spoke to Kelly Sullivan, the public information specialist at the hospital, and asked her whether the information coming from the hospital might more appropriately offer that strokes can affect the brain in a wide range of ways, rather than jumping to the idea of being "brain dead." The doctors apparently agreed, as an updated statement from the hospital later that day said, "There can be a whole range of damage, from mild in the form of slurred speech, to severe resulting in much more debilitation." The statement quoted Dr. Yapor saying, "As with nearly every significant stroke, it is certain there has been damage to the brain, but it is still too early to tell the degree of disability or prognosis at the present time."[44]

The frankness of the statements from the hospital startled many in the governor's office, some of them becoming angry and upset when I forwarded the AP story on the subject via e-mail. The hospital's statements were less hopeful and optimistic than the prevailing positive thoughts that most were operating under. The staff struggled to get back to regular tasks, although the governor's mailboxes were overflowing with bags and bags of get-well cards. Schoolchildren from all corners of the state were especially generous, writing and drawing beautiful cards and letters. Staff members wiped tears from their eyes when they read some of the cards passed from person to person.

Flowers and other gifts filled the front lobby office of 206 Statehouse; flowers sent to the hospital were discouraged, but those that did arrive were redirected by Mrs. O'Bannon to the pediatric and geriatric units of the hospital.

At the statehouse, no one went inside the governor's formal office. No one was told to stay away; it just seemed like the right thing to do, to leave Governor O'Bannon's office as he had left it, in hopes that he would soon return there.

Acting Governor Kernan conducted his duties from his third-floor office and met as often as possible with both his own staff and the governor's staff. Everyone worked to "get back to normal."

Governor's office staff and many Hoosiers were operating at a certain level of ignorance, one buttressed by our hope against hope that Governor O'Bannon would get better. Quiet conversations took place among staff, many expressing a similar theme: the hope that Frank O'Bannon might be able to get back home to a well-deserved retirement in Corydon.

In Chicago, President Bush had missed Mrs. O'Bannon when he attempted to call her at the hospital, so he issued a handwritten statement that was given to her in which he said, "All of our very best wishes to you and your family. George W. Bush."[45]

Former president Bill Clinton had better luck and reached Mrs. O'Bannon by phone. The two spoke for nearly forty-five minutes, remembering the last time they were together as a group in May 2003 at the Indianapolis 500. At that event, Clinton and Governor O'Bannon had their normal conversation about what books each one was reading, and the governor had been pleased a few days later when a package arrived from Clinton carrying a couple of the books he thought Governor O'Bannon would enjoy. Clinton told Mrs. O'Bannon, "Here, I called to try and lift your spirits, and you ended up cheering me up!"[46]

Jennifer O'Bannon now believes, however, that her father's condition was much graver and his hope of recovery far less likely than most knew or believed. "In a case like my father's, what they call a wet stroke...In the condition they found him in, they would not try to resuscitate him or work on him," she said. "...But I think they went ahead without that based only on my father's status as governor."[47]

Swain said, "It's not that Judy was not hopeful, but we were all on this roller coaster, and there certainly was this reality that he probably would never go back and work in the governor's office again."[48]

Back in Indiana, Willis spoke to Mrs. O'Bannon by telephone. "I could look on the news, and they would say he was getting better, but I knew better. I asked her about it, and she said, 'There really is no change. We're just waiting. It may soon be time to make a decision.'"[49]

The O'Bannon family had taken rooms at the Wyndom Hotel across the street from the hospital in Chicago, and Swain had gone to a nearby Walgreen's drugstore to buy toiletries and other needed items. Hotel sinks served as washing machines for some of their clothes until a change of clothes could be brought up from Indianapolis by Cindy Athey.

The family visited the governor often in the intensive care unit. Jonathan Swain did as well. "They had brought up some CDs for him, some music, because the doctors had told the family that playing some music that he liked was good for him."[50]

By Thursday night, it was decided that Jennifer O'Bannon and Polly Zoeller would return to Indiana to attend to the needs of their young children (being cared for by thoughtful and giving family and friends back home).

SEPTEMBER 12, 2003

The news from Chicago had slowed down to a more normal grind, and reporters were moving on to more analytical stories about the week's incredible occurrences. Press calls had slowed considerably as most moved into thinking the governor's condition could remain as it was for a very long time.

Swain had returned to Indianapolis and confided to Dieter late in the day on Friday that Mrs. O'Bannon had told him the buildup of pressure on the governor's brain had increased somewhat from Thursday to Friday and that a shunt had been inserted to help drain blood from the brain. The O'Bannon family, however, was not prepared to release further details about the governor's condition on Friday.

Trying to take a cue from "Acting Governor" Kernan and our chief of staff, Tim Joyce, I decided to go ahead with a planned trip to a Medicaid conference in Denver, Colorado. A cold mountain wind brought the threat of early snow flurries to Denver that day, and as I returned to my hotel from dinner, I was struck by the heavy change in the weather and the cold wind that suddenly blew in from the west. I had no idea that just over a thousand miles away in Chicago, privately but surely, Governor O'Bannon's life was slipping away.

22
A Governor Comes Home

I would come to regret going to Denver. By late morning, Jon Swain's call to my cell phone brought the news: "Governor O'Bannon is going to die today; they expect he won't make it beyond just a few more hours," he said. There I sat, alone in a hotel room far from home and far from my other duties in the press office, scrambling to get the earliest flight I could back to Indiana.[1]

In Chicago, Mrs. O'Bannon was already starting to do what she knew had to be done and agreed that some highly confidential, internal notifications should occur that the governor's condition "had taken a turn for the worse" overnight. Swelling of the governor's brain had caused his blood pressure to rise dramatically and was affecting other vital functions as well.

As Saturday morning arrived, Joyce called Lt. Governor Kernan at home and said, "Joe, we've lost him."

"Maggie and I knew that the whole world had changed then," Kernan said.[2]

Within moments, Laramore called Dieter at home and told her he had received a message from Joyce that they needed to get to the statehouse. Joyce had also advised Swain to get to the Indiana State Police hangar at the Indianapolis International Airport and prepare to return to Chicago. As had been the case all week, cell phones were burning up as frantic calls were placed back and forth among staff.[3]

Mrs. O'Bannon was alone in Chicago with her son Jonathan. Earlier plans to have her daughters return with the older grandchildren to visit their ailing grandfather were shelved. Instead, daughters Polly and Jennifer would have to remain where they were as their father's wonderful and full life slowly slipped away.

A composed Judy O'Bannon reached Swain by phone just as he prepared to board a state police plane at the airport. "Judy called and she said, 'Things aren't going well,' and I told her I was waiting to get on a plane to come up. 'You won't need to come up; he probably won't make it through the morning. We need to start setting things in motion. Once things are wrapped up here, we'll take care of how his body will be transported, and I will be back.' I can't remember all of it, but it was pretty straightforward," Swain said.[4]

Judy was composed but very tired, Swain said. He remembered that she wanted him to do whatever he could to set up a foundation immediately so donations in the governor's name could be made to the benefit of others. Swain was able to reach a banking friend in Fort Wayne, Deborah Sturgis, and got help getting an account set up immediately so that donations could be accepted.

"She had been up most of the night because they had let her know at some point that he was failing," Swain said. "She had decided that she would move forward with the living will, and…they took him off the machines."[5]

Back at the statehouse, Joyce, Dieter, Laramore, Athey, and Swain converged and began notifying key leaders and coordinating what would happen when the governor finally succumbed. "Tim Joyce was particularly distraught," Dieter recalls. "He was the one who spent hours each day with the governor, and I hugged him."[6]

Kernan remained away from the statehouse in order to avoid tipping off reporters.

A short discussion centered on when the "official announcement" of O'Bannon's death should be made. Some wanted the word to go out almost immediately after the governor's death. Others wanted to wait until Mrs. O'Bannon was not only away from the hospital but back home in Indiana.

"Tim Joyce was very concerned that the information did not get out before Governor O'Bannon actually had passed away, and he wanted to do whatever would work best for Mrs. O'Bannon," Swain said. "...The day we left the hospital, photographers followed our car as we left...The photographers had captured Judy early one of those mornings when she was going to the hospital; others wanted to release it as soon as Judy had left the hospital. I said they needed to wait until we knew that Judy was on the plane at Midway Field—and that's only a difference of fifteen minutes."[7]

Dieter was keeping constant contact with her counterpart at the hospital, Kelly Sullivan, who called Dieter from the ICU at Northwestern Memorial Hospital. Doctors had stopped the medication that holds down pressure on the brain but had not yet removed the ventilator when the governor died naturally, precisely at 11:33 a.m. (Indianapolis time).

Todd Siesky, John Zody, and Tamara Mitchell, the press office administrative assistant, arrived to help in dealing with the coming onslaught of reporters.

At 2:25 p.m., State Police Superintendent Mel Carraway notified the governor's office that the plane carrying Mrs. O'Bannon and her son had departed from Midway Airport in Chicago. Fifteen minutes later, Dieter officially issued the news that was slowly but surely beginning to slip out. Under the headline "Governor O'Bannon Dies," the statement was direct and sad:

Governor Frank O'Bannon died at 11:33 a.m. EST today in the neurointensive care unit of Northwestern Memorial Hospital. He was 73 and in the seventh year of his tenure as governor. The governor's condition worsened early this morning as he experienced an increase in the swelling of his brain. Despite all measures administered by physicians to control his intracranial pressure, it continued to rise and subsequently caused his vital signs to go from stable to unstable. The governor experienced a drop in both blood pressure and heart rate. Based on the governor's living will, First Lady Judy O'Bannon and the family decided to use no further means of support and care and the governor died naturally. Northwestern officials have scheduled a press briefing with physicians for 7:30 p.m. CDT/EST today. The conference will be held at the hospital, 251 E. Huron St., on the third floor of the Feinberg Pavilion. Mrs. O'Bannon will be arriving at the Indiana State Police hangar sometime after 3:15 p.m. Governor O'Bannon designated that he wished to donate organs, so his body will arrive in Indianapolis later this evening."

The news set off a maelstrom of calls and inquiries from reporters near and far. "My calls to the reporters were succinct. 'I'm sorry to tell you this, but Governor O'Bannon has died. We've put out a statement by e-mail.' Several burst into tears, none of them tried to quiz me; the news was so stunning that they were literally dumbfounded," Dieter said.[8]

As Mrs. O'Bannon's flight made its way to Indianapolis, Lt. Governor Kernan (who had slipped into the statehouse virtually unnoticed) prepared to meet her at the airport. Maggie Kernan had returned to Indiana just a day or so before, cutting short a foreign trip once she learned of Governor O'Bannon's stroke.

Swain said he and Kernan made their way to the airport quietly using an elaborate back way from the statehouse to the car. "...We wanted to get him out of the building and into the car and on his way to the airport before people could talk to him. He and I went out to the airport, and Maggie (Kernan) met us out there. There was already media out there, but they weren't allowed inside the fence."[9]

Siesky had been dispatched to the airport and kept reporters at the agreed-to location—outside the airport fence where they could capture Mrs. O'Bannon's arrival on videotape and film but not ask questions.

En route to the airport, Swain and the new governor talked quietly in the back of the car. "He and I talked about how Judy was doing. He asked about how I was doing, always concerned, and wanted to know if I had talked to Judy's kids that morning and how they were doing," Swain said. "We rode the rest of the way in silence and when we got to the airport, Maggie Kernan was there. When he was lieutenant governor, a lot of us called him 'Joe,' and as the plane was coming up, and I remember saying something about 'Joe,' and then I corrected myself and said, 'I mean the governor,' Maggie turned to me and said, 'It's always just Joe. He's still Joe.' I said something to the effect that, 'Well, no, now he's governor.'"[10]

Judy and Jonathan O'Bannon emerged from the plane. Mrs. O'Bannon began immediately comforting others, something she would do thousands of times over in the days to follow. Her compassion and grace were overwhelming, as she freely offered up hugs and embraces to all who were present. Troopers Willis and Gershanoff, clearly fighting to keep from breaking into tears, held Mrs. O'Bannon closely for several moments. Lt. Governor Kernan and Maggie Kernan did likewise, with Mrs. Kernan wiping tears from her face as she spoke to Judy. Mrs. O'Bannon retired to the Harrison House at Fort Benjamin Harrison, the temporary governor's residence.

Around 4:30 p.m., Joyce, Dieter, Laramore, and Swain went to the third floor to confer with Lt. Governor Kernan and his closest aides, including McKenna, Murray, Nussbaum, and Mary Downes. They discussed at length how to handle the swearing-in ceremony, whether to conduct it privately with just one still and one video photographer present in a "pool" arrangement. Kernan preferred letting every reporter in the room who could fit.

The ceremony would be at 6 p.m. Supreme Court Justice Theodore Boehm would administer the oath, as Chief Justice Shepard was out of town. Most legislators were also out of town, although Senate President

Pro Tem Robert Garton hurriedly drove from Columbus to Indianapolis for the ceremony. Most Hoosiers would see Joe Kernan become the state's forty-eighth governor via live television, as only a small number of administration officials fit into the remaining chairs in the gallery. Among Kernan's closest advisers present were Downes, his former chief of staff, who had previously left state government, and Tina Noel, who had just recently accepted a private sector position. Her successor, Katherine Bull, ended up starting her new job in Kernan's office at a historic time.

Mrs. O'Bannon had called to say she wanted to attend Kernan's ceremony, and so Pat Rios was asked to escort her into the building. "Judy very much wanted to be there," Swain said. "She thought it was important that she be there and that she be supportive of the new governor."[12]

As she entered the statehouse, reporters left her alone, taking video and pictures of her arrival but not asking her questions. Mrs. O'Bannon went immediately to the governor's office where current and former staff had begun to pour into the outer lobby—so that they might have others with whom to share their grief and sense of loss.

Swain said, "She felt it was important to let them know how appreciative she was to all of them gathered. There were people who had worked for him for years. They may not have been on the governor's staff at that time, but they had worked for him at some point in the past. She walked into 206, and before we could close the door, everyone was applauding, probably because that was the only way they could express their support for her. She had been through total hell that week, and the people on the staff always had such tremendous respect and affection for Judy."[13]

THE FORTY-EIGHTH GOVERNOR OF INDIANA

Joseph E. Kernan, Jr., was sworn in as the state's forty-eighth governor just after 6 p.m. on Saturday, September 13, 2003 in the chambers of the Indiana Supreme Court. Justice Boehm administered the oath as Maggie Kernan solemnly held the family Bible under her husband's left hand. In the front row watching the proceedings was now former first lady Judy O'Bannon, surrounded by her son Jonathan O'Bannon, Tim Joyce, and Jonathan Swain. She was the first to rise in applause once the oath was completed.

"I would have gone to that if I had to crawl, or if I had cried the whole time," Judy said. "Joe Kernan deserved all of the support and encouragement that any of us could give. As much as he had been a supporter as well as a team member with Frank, he deserved for me to stand there with whatever credibility I had from Frank and watch him be sworn in. I had to do that on a personal and an official level, and it was not hard to do. He had been so faithful to Frank. I had to be faithful to him."[14]

Moments after taking the oath of office and accepting the thunderous applause of those present, Kernan stood alone at the front rail in the courtroom chambers. He told all Hoosiers there and the multitude watching statewide on live television, "I've lost my governor and my friend. So too has every Hoosier lost their governor and their friend...Today, without reservation, Maggie and I accept these new responsibilities that we have with humility, understanding of the challenges that lie ahead, but also with resolve, understanding that as we work together, going forward from here...that we can do well, that we can do the best for all Hoosiers."[15]

FRANK O'BANNON COMES HOME

On that cool Saturday night in September, Judy O'Bannon and her children huddled into the small office at the Indiana State Police hangar at the Indianapolis International Airport. Only the state's new governor, Joe Kernan, State Police Superintendent Melvin Carraway, Trooper Willis, Joyce, and I were inside. I had made my way home from Denver, going immediately from my return flight to the small hangar to try and offer some help during this long, taxing day for everyone.

Inside the hangar office, the group talked softly and waited patiently for the C-130 military transport plane to arrive at the hangar. Television cameras stood in waiting, still broadcasting the day's events unseen before by generations of Hoosiers. Reporters present did not have to be reminded to ask no questions—they conducted themselves at all times during these days with incredible class and courtesy—proving ubiquitous media critics wrong. In the days since the governor had been stricken, and in the days that followed, they worked long hours, filed countless stories, and quietly offered condolences and support to those they had known personally and professionally for these many years. Their stories were touching and beautiful and reflected positively on the quality of Indiana and its news media.

As the C-130 transport plane came to a rest, a hearse from Crown Hill Mortuary silently rolled forward. Moments later, the O'Bannon family stood quietly along the edge of the tarmac with Kernan and Carraway at their side. Chief of Staff Tim Joyce and I stood a few steps removed. The State Police Honor Guard carefully lifted the governor's flag-draped coffin from the stand at the back of the plane and down a small ramp. Major General George Buskirk of the Indiana National Guard preceded the casket and gently greeted Mrs. O'Bannon. Behind the casket was the head of the governor's security detail, Ray Raney. He quietly walked behind the honor guard, following his governor home from another trip. A few feet away, we could hear the quiet sounds of the family's weeping and the last of the summer's crickets chirping. Just beyond where we stood in sad silence, commercial planes, one after another, rolled in and out of the gates at the airport's main terminal. For the people on those flights, their trips were just beginning or ending. Those of us standing there knew, as did the tired and devoted O'Bannon administration soldiers watching from home late that Saturday night, the O'Bannon administration had come to an end.

Before departing, Mrs. O'Bannon again offered hugs to every member of the security detail, to Joyce and me, as well as Governor Kernan. Mrs. O'Bannon's ability to think of others in these moments made my heart quake—she told me, "Frank always appreciated so much all the work you did for him; you were such a loyal friend and such a good writer. Thank you for all you have done."[15]

The O'Bannon family then took their place in the ubiquitous green minivan that had transported Frank and Judy O'Bannon up and down the roads from Corydon to Indianapolis many, many times. The O'Bannons always favored the van over any fancy car. It had lots of room for family and was good enough for them. The governor's body was loaded carefully by the State Police Honor Guard into the back of the hearse. As it slowly departed the terminal area, a news helicopter followed the small entourage all the way to the funeral home. As Saturday gave way to Sunday, Frank O'Bannon was back home again in Indiana. He was cremated in private the next day, his remains given to his beloved wife, Judy. Some of those ashes have been placed beneath a favorite tree at the O'Bannon family barn in Harrison County—Judy's hope is that they will help the treasured wildflowers there grow even more beautifully. The rest remain in an urn in her possession, someday to be placed at their final resting place at the O'Bannon family plot at the historic Cedar Hill Cemetery in Corydon.

SEPTEMBER 14, 2003

Mrs. O'Bannon was in a familiar setting Sunday morning—in worship with her church family at the Central Avenue United Methodist Church in Indianapolis. News photographers captured her and her daughter Jenny, daughter-in-law, Soni, and her chief of staff, Jonathan Swain, as they walked to the historic church building that the O'Bannons had worked hard with members of the congregation to save.[16]

Just a mile or so away, the state's new governor, Joe Kernan, and his wife, Maggie, took their regular Sunday Mass outside at Military Park in downtown Indianapolis as part of the annual Irish Festival. The state's first Catholic governor had gone for prayer and Mass earlier in the week as well at St. John's Roman Catholic Church across from the RCA Dome. Inside the dome this particular Sunday, where Frank

O'Bannon had started his second term as governor, more than 54,000 Indianapolis Colts fans gathered for one of the season's first home games and stood and formed a rousing choir singing "Back Home Again in Indiana" as images of Governor O'Bannon's life and service were shown on the giant screens inside the dome.

Faith played an important role for Judy and the entire O'Bannon family as they struggled to deal with the loss, and Judy believes God was with her throughout.

"I had a marvelous experience the day before Frank (fell ill). I went to the dedication of the interfaith peace temple with the Dali Lama who was in Bloomington. At that ceremony, different faith-based denominations presented their offering of prayer to the group. They were wonderful, and the Methodists were there, too! There were Quakers, Buddhists, there were Hindus, Muslims, and everyone came offering prayers very humbly," she said.[17]

At the event, cellist Michael Fitzpatrick performed. "The piece he played was the result of the meeting between Roman Catholic monks at Gethsemane Monastery outside Louisville, Kentucky and Tibetan monks, Buddhist monks. 'East meets West' they called the gathering, and they wanted to compose and perform a piece of work for that," Judy said.[18]

Fitzpatrick agreed to compose and perform a piece but wanted to do so from deep inside Mammoth Cave. "It sounds sort of odd, but he explained that by saying it was in the bowels of the earth, and it came from a commonness that we had of the foundation of life that is represented in material things of the earth," Judy said.[19]

Fitzpatrick gave Judy one of his CDs at the request of her friend Jane Owen, from New Harmony, Indiana. "The music reminds me again that music can sometimes do what words, either written or spoken, cannot do. It just reaches inside of you and pulls out something spiritual. Well, I was listening to that, it turns out, just the time Frank was having his stroke...and when the piece was over, I said to myself, 'It's over,' and I got the phone call, and it was."[20]

New Eyes to See

Before Governor O'Bannon's life officially ended, a surgery was conducted at Northwestern Memorial Hospital because the governor had committed himself to be an organ donor years before. "He had the card in his wallet when he died...that he wanted to be an organ donor, and he had it on his driver's license," Judy O'Bannon told WISH-TV in the weeks following the governor's death.[21]

Frank O'Bannon got the idea of becoming an organ donor when he attended the Organ Transplant Survivors Olympics during the time he was lieutenant governor. Judy believes his donation was an extension of his commitment to public service. "I am sure we did not have great conversations about that, but it was such a natural thing for us to believe in, and he wanted to do that," Judy said.[22]

In fact, O'Bannon had signed legislation in April 1999 that reduced the waiting time for Hoosiers in need of organ transplants.

For Becky Lindsey, who lives outside of Chicago, Illinois, O'Bannon's donation of his cornea meant that her life could be more than it might have been otherwise. Slowed by growing blindness, Lindsey had stopped driving and worried about being able to carry on a normal life. "It broke my heart to think that I was gonna be blind," she told WISH-TV reporter Karen Hensel. Lindsey had never heard of Frank O'Bannon before—she's from Illinois and had not kept track of who the governor of Indiana was. When Hensel presented her with a picture of O'Bannon so she could see who her donor had been, she said, "He's a nice, kind-looking man; he's got brown eyes. Maybe God sent me an angel, huh?" Lindsey kept the picture and said she wished she could thank the governor herself but knows she never can.[23]

Another Rare Choice

Governor O'Bannon made another unusual choice in preparing in advance for the end of his life. He designated that he wished to be cremated, a choice made by only a quarter of all persons in the

U.S. and by even less in Indiana. An industry group, the Cremation Association of North America, reports that just slightly more than 14 percent of all Hoosiers were cremated in 2001, about half the national rate. In fact, only seven states reported lower cremation rates than Indiana. The cremation was consistent with the O'Bannon family wishes as well, Mrs. O'Bannon said at the time, and meant that the governor's body would not lie in state at the statehouse as others had done before.[24]

23

Farewell for a Governor, a Friend

Do Justice, Love Mercy, Walk Humbly

Shortly after Governor O'Bannon's death, Judy sat down with her children and some of the governor's staff and began planning memorial services that would be appropriate for a sitting governor.

"I wanted them to, as best we could, embody the spirit of Frank. He was very much a Hoosier, and we tried to have a Hoosier event. The one in Indianapolis, I thought, needed to celebrate a leader, celebrate our state, and what it was about," Judy said.[1]

The Indianapolis ceremony occurred on Friday, September 19, 2003 on the west steps of the Indiana Statehouse, the very place Frank O'Bannon had taken the oath of office more than seven years before. A crowd of more than 5,500 crammed onto the statehouse lawn and moved west down the street dividing the Indiana Government Center. The service reflected Judy's deliberate efforts to include ecumenical elements, including Jewish, Muslim, and Christian prayers, as well as personal touches that Frank himself would have loved: a barbershop quartet singing "Oh Danny Boy!" and the Key School Strummers, a ukulele and mouth harp band from the Indianapolis Public Schools' Key School who had performed previously at the governor's residence and the National Governors' Association meetings. They closed the memorial service with a rousing and upbeat version of one of the governor's favorite songs, "Back Home Again in Indiana." Carrie Newcomber and Sandy Patti performed as well.

Speakers included U.S. Senator Evan Bayh, U.S. Representative Julia Carson, the Reverend Richard Hamilton, Chief of Staff Tim Joyce, and Governor Kernan. Also in attendance were former governors Whitcomb, Bowen, and Orr as well as sitting governors from several states—Governors Paul Patton of Kentucky, Gary Locke of Washington, Mike Huckabee of Arkansas, Phil Bredeson of Tennessee, Dirk Kempthorne of Idaho, Bob Holden of Missouri, and Rod Blagojevich of Illinois. Iowa's lieutenant governor, Sally Pederson, attended as well as two former Alabama governors, Don Siegelman and Jim Folsom, Jr. The U.S. Deputy Secretary of Agriculture, James Moseley, officially represented President George W. Bush. The entire Indiana congressional delegation was present along with former U.S. senator Birch Bayh.

Michigan Governor Jennifer Granholm was unable to attend the Friday ceremony, but surprised Mrs. O'Bannon with a visit to Corydon, Indiana the next day for visitation at the Corydon United Methodist Church there. Vermont Governor James H. Douglas ordered the Indiana state flag flown over the Vermont Statehouse in Montpelier on the day of O'Bannon's memorial service.

In honor of the governor's role as commander in chief of the Indiana National Guard, a nineteen-gun salute was offered from cannons fired along West Street. (Twenty-one-gun salutes are reserved for presidents and other heads of state.) An Air Force flyover, featuring F-16 jets flying at 300 miles per hour, roared overhead in the traditional "missing man" formation. The service concluded with the playing of "Taps."

The Indianapolis service followed a day-long living memorial inside the statehouse featuring photos and mementos from the

O'Bannon years and the governor's official portrait on display in the statehouse rotunda. Since O'Bannon had been cremated, his casket did not lie in state as had other governors in Indiana history.

Hundreds of Hoosiers filed through the statehouse on Thursday, September 18, to see the displays and to sign dozens of memory books placed outside the governor's office. Just outside the door of the governor's formal office sat an extraordinary, large black wreath and flower arrangement—given by the men of Phi Gamma Delta, the governor's beloved fraternity.

"When we were younger, and a couple we knew lost a child, and when President Kennedy died, I remember thinking, 'How do people get through these things?' But by the time Frank died, I understood he was very much a public figure, public property. And it didn't make it any harder; it probably made it easier," Judy said.[2]

Kentucky Governor Patton and his wife, Judi, perhaps the closest friends the O'Bannons had among sitting governors, were especially moved by the sudden death of Frank O'Bannon. Patton's security detail was notified almost immediately by members of the Indiana State Police when O'Bannon died.

"It was a very personal loss for me for a lot of reasons," Governor Patton said. "I felt very close to Frank, closer to him than any other governor I served with. We were neighbors and we had a similar background and similar views."[3]

Judi Patton immediately called her friend Judy O'Bannon. "I talked to her on the phone and tried to comfort her. I can tell you that they were so loved and respected by all the governors and first ladies across the nation. Some people you just bond with, and we did that with them. His death has been a tragic loss, and we miss him terribly," Mrs. Patton said.[4]

Kay Harrod and Rex Lyons, two staff members from the Kentucky governor's office, came along with the Pattons to Indianapolis for the O'Bannon memorial service and manned the phones inside the governor's office so every member of the staff, and every state employee who wanted to, could attend the memorial service.

The Portrait

The governor's official portrait on display that week was created by Michael Chelich of Hammond, selected in 2000 from among thirty-two artists living and working in Indiana. It was the second gubernatorial portrait he painted, the first being Governor Evan Bayh. (He also painted the portrait of U.S. Senator Richard G. Lugar of Indiana that is displayed in the Senate Agriculture hearing room in the U.S. Capitol in Washington, D.C.)

Little did Chelich know when he spent those many hours with Governor O'Bannon that his work would become the centerpiece of the memorial services and remembrances for the governor. The O'Bannon family chose Chelich's oil painting of O'Bannon for display in the statehouse rotunda because it so wonderfully captured the image of the governor. The painting was also the first of the governor's portrait collection to ever leave Indianapolis, as it was also displayed at the Corydon United Methodist Church and the old Indiana statehouse in Corydon on September 20 and 21.

Chelich made the unusual choice to depict O'Bannon seated at his desk, turned as if he were greeting a visitor or guest. He said he intentionally painted O'Bannon with his jacket open. "He was a very open person, so the attempt is to have his body appear to be very open to people. There was nothing in front of him to create any sort of barrier to who he was...I also had him with the chair scooted back from the desk so it looks like he's getting up from there to greet you."[5]

Corydon Pays Tribute

Events in the governor's honor in his hometown of Corydon reflected the kindness and simple grace of this beautiful community. Throughout the day on Saturday, September 20, dozens of Harrison County and Southern Indiana residents stopped at the Corydon United Methodist Church on the town square to view the O'Bannon family photos that were on display two days before in Indianapolis, as well as the governor's official portrait. Judy Miller, organist at the church, played hymns and songs she knew the governor loved from his days in the church choir. Judy O'Bannon had planned to just visit the church a short time and then return to her home for some rest. She ended up staying most of the day, unable to pull herself away from those who shared her grief, her sense of loss, but also shared her history and memories of this fine man.

On Sunday, September 21, 2003, more than 3,000 white folding chairs were carefully set up on the lawn of the town square, just east of the original Indiana statehouse. The Hurley Conrad Memorial Bandstand, which had served as the launching point for the 1987 O'Bannon for Governor campaign, served as the stage for the memorial service. O'Bannon's former law partner, Ron Simpson, and his high school teacher and former Harrison County historian Fred Griffin offered remarks. Governor Kernan also spoke, this time remembering more of the personal attributes and good times he enjoyed through the years with O'Bannon. One of O'Bannon's most trusted and important advisers ever, Tom New, spoke of a man who had meant so very much to his life, both professionally and personally. Governor Whitcomb attended this service as well, and although fewer dignitaries attended the Corydon service than the one in Indianapolis, the town square and closed streets around it were filled to capacity.

"I knew all of these events would be highly visible, and so they were statements of who he was as a man, and what he thought was important for Indiana. We celebrated Frank and Indiana, in a happy way, and that was important to me," Judy said.[6]

WORDS SPOKEN IN GRIEF

When a sitting governor passes, the words and expressions of grief are widespread and numerous. That was certainly the case when Governor O'Bannon died. Tributes poured in from Hoosiers and from many others, including national and state leaders.

President George W. Bush issued this statement from the White House: "Frank O'Bannon was a dedicated public servant and a good and decent man. He led a distinguished career, including service in the Air Force, in the Indiana State Senate, and as Lieutenant Governor, being sworn in as Governor of Indiana in 1997. He has served the people of his state with integrity and devotion. Laura joins me in sending our thoughts and prayers to his wife Judy and their family."[7]

Former president Bill Clinton said, "I loved Frank O'Bannon and his wife, Judy, and I think of him and of her tonight."[8]

Michigan Governor Jennifer Granholm, a fellow Democrat, also praised O'Bannon. "Governor O'Bannon reflected the best of America's heartland. He was a dedicated public servant who worked hard every day to serve his citizens with integrity, honesty, and a vision for a bright future in Indiana. His loss will be felt keenly here in Michigan and across the Midwest. Both Dan and I were proud to have had the opportunity to serve with Governor and Judy O'Bannon and our hearts go out to the entire O'Bannon family."[9]

North Dakota Governor John Hoeven, a Republican, served with Governor O'Bannon on several committees in the National Governors' Association. When O'Bannon passed, he said, "I regarded him not only as a colleague, but also as a friend. I will always remember him as a kind and open man, as willing to take counsel as to give it. He was also able to set aside partisanship to get the job done, which is a true sign of leadership."[10]

Idaho Governor Dirk Kempthorne, a Republican who was installed as the new chair of the NGA during its annual meeting in Indianapolis, said, "The state of Indiana has lost a fine man, a kind man, and a man who cared deeply about his state. The nation has lost a dedicated public servant whose passion for children and for making life better for his citizens was a daily commitment. Frank O'Bannon never let partisan politics stand in the way of good public policy. I had the honor of working with Frank as members of the NGA, and I never saw him prouder than just a few short weeks ago when he and Indiana's first lady, Judy O'Bannon, hosted the nation's governors at the NGA annual meeting in Indiana. He was a wonderful host, beaming with Hoosier pride and Hoosier hospitality."[11]

The Indiana University Alumni Association, under the leadership in 2003 of Ken Beckley, said, "We express our sorrow over the death of our illustrious alumnus, our governor, Frank O'Bannon, one of the greatest alumni of this university. He was admired and respected in his every step through life. Our university and our state have been the beneficiaries of his servant life and will always be grateful."[12]

Indiana University president, Dr. Adam W. Herbert, said, "Governor Frank O'Bannon's legacy to higher education is one that leaves our institutions strong and poised for excellence in the years ahead. We are proud that he was an IU alumnus...His death is a loss for Hoosiers everywhere."[13]

Frederick F. Eichhorn, Jr., president of the IU Board of Trustees, said, "Governor Frank O'Bannon provided unwavering support for Indiana University. This is truly a sad day, and all of us at Indiana University offer condolences to the entire O'Bannon family."[14]

Washington Post political columnist David Broder (who just a few weeks before had quoted O'Bannon as saying the attempt to recall fellow Democratic Governor Gray Davis in California was "political hysteria") offered that O'Bannon's death had "cost the state one of the most decent, down-to-earth political leaders in its long history."[15]

Rachel Gorlin said, "His death upset the order of the universe for me; it seemed so profoundly cruel that a man who had given so much would be denied a chance to see his work through. Of course, intellectually, we know that life and death don't work that way, but it seemed in the case of Frank O'Bannon that they *should*."[16]

Statehouse political analyst Brian Howey wrote, "What became clear about Frank O'Bannon since he was stricken...was how the Hoosier people perceived him. Many of them had been distressed about the direction of the state and disagreed with his policies, but they loved the grandfatherly Frank O'Bannon who was, as Harrison Ullman wrote, 'As Hoosier as Hoosier can be.'"[17]

In the days following the governor's death, members of the Indiana congressional delegation and other members of Congress took to the floor of both the U.S. House of Representatives and the U.S. Senate to offer their thoughts. Senator Evan Bayh, who along with U.S. Representative Julia Carson perhaps knew O'Bannon best, said, "Frank O'Bannon died as he lived, in service to the people of Indiana. Frank O'Bannon was my friend, and he spent the best years of his life in public service."[18]

Bayh continued, "In a calling characterized all too frequently by ego and hubris, Frank O'Bannon was always humble and gentle, giving credit to others even when he deserved the lion's share. We mourn, but we can take comfort in the knowledge that our loss has been Heaven's gain. That the life and legacy of Frank O'Bannon will not end with our grieving or with my few inadequate words, but will remain everlasting in the hearts of Hoosiers everywhere..."[19]

Indiana House members who spoke in memory of O'Bannon were Carson, Peter Visclosky, Baron Hill, along with Republicans Dan Burton, Chris Chocola, John Hostettler, Mike Pence, and Mark Souder.

Governor O'Bannon's influence on the lives of those who worked for him should not be underestimated. His staff also offered moving tributes to their governor and, in many cases, valued friend.

Donna Imus said, "It's hard to talk about his impact on my life. He gave me so much as far as confidence and the ability to do what I do today...He was someone I considered a friend."[20]

Marilyn Schultz, his former legislative colleague and budget director, said although O'Bannon had been in politics throughout his adult life, "it was not his whole life. He was a man who loved to read, who loved photography, who loved to walk in the woods, who loved his family, and they had a lot of fun together. So often in politics you see the spouse being left behind, you see this separation between the political person and their personal life. That was never the case with Frank and Judy."[21]

Ray Raney, who headed the O'Bannon security detail, said, "He was a very patient man. I think from that, my patience has been improved somewhat. He took life as it came. Frank O'Bannon was the same guy in the White House that he was in Corydon, Indiana...I never saw him treat anyone bad, and when situations became political or things came up that may have been unfair to him, he took them in pretty good stride."[22]

Raney added, "I can still see him as I'm walking up to the big porch of his house, the barn at Corydon, and seeing the back of his head with him working inside on his computer. He loved that computer. He loved being around his kids and grandkids. He enjoyed golf a great deal. He was a simple guy."[23]

O'Bannon seemed to strike up a particularly close friendship with several members of the security detail, including Alex Willis, who was with him the day he collapsed.

"The fact that he was the governor made it an honor to serve that position. But the fact that he was who he was made it an even more special honor," Willis said. "He treated you like a person, a friend. He invited us to do things with him, he included us a lot, he worried if we got anything to eat at events we could go to. He was like a mentor to me. He taught me a lot of things, about a lot of subjects, not just the environment, and I felt comfortable asking him a lot of questions. I will never forget him."[24]

PERMANENT TRIBUTES

In the months and years that followed Governor O'Bannon's passing, a variety of thoughtful and important tributes were developed throughout the state to pay honor to the departed governor. Although it may seem as though Hoosiers went a little overboard, in modern times, the state had never lost a governor while in office and never had the state had a governor whose roots ran deeper in Indiana's history than Frank O'Bannon.

At the start of the 2004 session, both the house and the senate unanimously passed a Concurrent Resolution to Memorialize and Honor Governor Frank O'Bannon "for his lifetime of dedicated service to the people of Indiana." Judy O'Bannon addressed both the house and the senate, thanking them for their generosity of spirit and thoughtfulness to her and her family. Both chambers rang with loud and sustained applause for Mrs. O'Bannon as she was introduced. The resolution said, "Frank O'Bannon was the epitome of a true country gentleman in his dealings with everyone with whom he came in contact and was truly friend to all the citizens of Indiana...The lives of all members of the General Assembly have been enriched by our friend Frank O'Bannon, and we will miss him."[25]

Knowing that the Indiana State Museum at White River State Park was an important personal accomplishment for Frank and Judy, O'Bannon's friend and successor in the state senate, Senator Richard Young of Milltown, Indiana, introduced legislation in 2005 to rename the Great Hall in the museum for Governor O'Bannon.

Throughout his time in public service, O'Bannon was always a staunch advocate for improving education and educational opportunities. After his death, Hoosiers sought to honor that service. At Ivy Tech State College in Bloomington, the annual summit of the Center for Civic Engagement is now known as "The O'Bannon Institute" operating under the themes of "engage, serve, and lead." The center's goal is to graduate students from Ivy Tech who contribute to both the workforce and community service.[26] The State Student Assistance Commission also renamed its Indiana Higher Education Grant the "Frank O'Bannon Grant." Students eligible for the Frank O'Bannon Grant must graduate from high school, be an Indiana resident, and plan to enroll in an eligible Indiana post-secondary institution.

In October 2004, the Frank O'Bannon Elementary School was officially dedicated at 1317 173rd Street in Hammond, Indiana. The 115,000-square-foot school was created from two other elementary schools that were closed, the James Whitcomb Riley Elementary School and the Woodrow Wilson Elementary School.

Mrs. O'Bannon helped students and others cut a giant ribbon at the school in a ceremony led by Hammond Mayor Thomas McDermott, Jr., and the school's principal, Ezekiel Barber. The school's architect, Ronald Fanning, said, "Frank O'Bannon was the education governor in action, not just talk. During his first term, he undertook the most ambitious plan for education in the country. He was a great Hoosier who fought to put children first."[27]

The soccer fields along East 16th Street in the shadows of the thundering overpasses for Interstates 70 and 65 in downtown Indianapolis are now named "The Frank and Judy O'Bannon Soccer Park." Mrs. O'Bannon had joined Governor Evan Bayh in dedicating the park many years before, during a period when the O'Bannons lived just a few blocks away on Broadway Avenue. Today, Saturday and Sunday afternoons throughout the year, the park is ablaze with the colorful jerseys of dozens of soccer teams from across the city that play in a park named for a man and a woman who cared about that neighborhood when it was far from what it is today. A summer league baseball park near Corydon has also been named in his honor.

In December 2004, the State of Indiana made a particularly moving choice in renaming the Wyandotte Woods State Recreation the O'Bannon Woods State Park. The woods, covering 2,000 acres, includes the Wyandotte Caves, a separate area of forty to sixty acres to the north, Horseman's Hideaway, and 281 public camp sites. The Blue River, a canoeing favorite for Frank O'Bannon, runs through the woods. As a state senator, O'Bannon had worked to upgrade the area from a state recreation area to a state park. His grandfather, Lew M. O'Bannon, had planted trees in the area as part of observations for the state's centennial in 1916.

The legislature also created a Frank O'Bannon Memorial Commission to create a bust of O'Bannon for a small alcove just across from the entrance to the state senate in the Indiana statehouse. Ken Ryden of Yorktown, an artist-in-residence at Anderson University, was selected in a juried process to create the bust, paid for with $20,000 in private funds. O'Bannon's bust was unveiled in February 2006.

The town of Corydon is also exploring a statue or remembrance suitable for their favorite son, Frank O'Bannon. Leah Porter, the governor's niece, is coordinating the project expected to be completed in the coming years.

In October 2004, Governor Joe Kernan, U.S. Representative Baron Hill, and INDOT commissioner Bryan Nicol led a dedication ceremony for the new "Frank O'Bannon Highway" at Doolittle Mills, Indiana, just north of Interstate 64 in Perry County. "The late Governor Frank O'Bannon enjoyed driving the winding, hilly roads of Southern Indiana as often as possible. He'd pack binoculars, a bird guide, and whatever other supplies he needed as he enjoyed the terrain reminiscent of his Corydon home," the *Jeffersonville Evening News* reported. Judy O'Bannon spoke to the crowd assembled, saying, "Is there a more beautiful place to be in the world than in Southern Indiana in the hills?" she asked. "To have this name on a road is such a big honor for our family."[28]

The legislation creating the highway was authored and sponsored by State Representative Jerry Denbo of French Lick, who called the bill his proudest moment in more than a decade in the legislature. "I've never had such a great privilege in my fourteen years in the legislature," Representative Denbo said. "Everyone in Indiana loved Frank O'Bannon."[29]

In March 2004, a new state government office building opened on Broadway Avenue in downtown Gary. State Representatives Charlie Brown and Vernon Smith of Gary and Mayor Scott King dedicated the building as the new Frank L. O'Bannon Memorial Building. The building houses a variety of state and local offices and was built through a cooperative effort of the city of Gary and the state.

The Hoosier State Press Association gave its "Indiana Newspapers Publishers' Free Freedom Award" to Governor O'Bannon in January 2004. The highest award the association can award, the award recognized his work during thirty-three years in state government and his dedication as a newspaper publisher. The association also announced a new special award named for Frank O'Bannon, the "Frank O'Bannon Sunshine Award" to recognize citizens and government officials for their work in keeping government open.

THE KERNANS MOVE ON

Joe and Maggie Kernan went home to South Bend early in January 2005, as Kernan's sixteen months as Indiana's forty-eighth governor came to an end. It was the end of a nearly two-decade run in public office, first as mayor of South Bend, then as O'Bannon's loyal lieutenant governor and finally as governor.

"I look back on it as an extraordinary opportunity over sixteen months to be able to serve Indiana, and I tried to do so in a way that was proactive and aggressive," Kernan said upon arriving home. He told reporters among his proudest memories is when Democrats and Republicans came together for the good of the state in the troubled days during Governor O'Bannon's stroke and death. "It was because of a lot of support and help and good people in the statehouse, but also all over Indiana, that we were able to work through this. I did not get a lot of sleep for the first couple of months, but neither did a lot of other good folks who helped make it work."[30]

Maggie Kernan, who was thrust into the role of first lady and who put aside her full-time work at a South Bend bank, said coming home was like starting anew. "I'm not trying to come back to South Bend to recreate my old life. I've changed. A large part of what I'll be doing is creating a new life," she said.[31]

Joe Kernan believes all of his experiences were really blessings. "I would just say that I never even imagined I would be mayor of my city. I've had extraordinary opportunities to serve South Bend and Indiana, and I've been honored to do so. I have no regrets, and I consider myself blessed in every way."[32]

Kernan took a particular view of his sixteen months as governor: He did not intend to be a caretaker. "I believed then, and I believe today, that with the new responsibility that I had, the new job that I had, came the idea that I had to do my best. I was not going to sit there and wait for the phone to ring. I was not going to take a sixteen-month hiatus…Sixteen months in government and politics is a lifetime in terms of the kinds of things that can be accomplished, or neglected," Kernan said.[33]

Tops on Kernan's priority list was an innovative new attempt to offer full-day kindergarten in Indiana's schools—a whole new effort that included a funding plan to make it happen despite the state's still cash-strapped budget. As 2004 wore on, however, Republicans in the legislature seemed unable to put aside the prospects of possibly taking back the governor's chair in the November election. As a result, many said they supported Kernan's push but not everyone was willing to help the recently installed governor complete the O'Bannon and *now* Kernan agenda.

Kernan's selection of the state's first female lieutenant governor, Kathy Davis of Indianapolis, made history but also reflected his commitment to do the job. Davis had never sought political office before, but she won over any skeptics and quickly became an outstanding complement to the energetic and outgoing Kernan. Davis was asked to serve and agreed to without knowing whether Kernan planned to change his mind and run for governor in 2004. "I wanted to work with the best person I could find, and I think I made the right choice," he said.[34]

Kernan and Davis lost the 2004 election—ending an incredible run of sixteen years of Democrats in the governor's office. Judy O'Bannon campaigned vigorously through her grief for Kernan-Davis and was dubbed the "Conciliatory General" by reporter Kevin Rader during WTHR's coverage of the November 2004 election. She offered support to a disappointed room of Indiana Democrats, including many young campaign volunteers who had never known the "wilderness years" she and her husband knew prior to 1988. "We've had some years where we've swept the decks, and other years when it's a little sparser," she said. "One of the wonderful things about living in a representative democracy is that days that don't come out exactly how we want them are often followed by days that turned out the way we want."[35]

Judy said she was happy that, looking into the ballroom at the Westin Hotel, she didn't see a collection of only older volunteers. "I'm looking at the most capable, trained, caring, and concerned young people," she said. "Don't put your head down and feel sad. Sometimes you start the next campaign the day after the last one."[36]

Upon his departure from office in January 2005, the *Indianapolis Star* and many other Indiana newspapers paused to thank the Kernans for their service. The *Star* said Kernan "has the right to be proud of his service to the people of Indiana" and said "Kernan saw his greatest challenge as striking a delicate balance between O'Bannon's legacy and the need to put his own stamp on...that he did."[37]

FRANK'S KIDS REMEMBER THEIR DAD

On February 13, 2006, about five hundred people gathered at the statehouse to witness the unveiling of the new bust created to honor Frank O'Bannon. As part of the ceremony, each of Frank O'Bannon's children and grandchildren were introduced, and fittingly, a long, warm applause filled the room. It was as if those present were trying to offer to "the O'Bannon kids" one more hug and one more "thank you" for all of their sacrifice and grace. Just as they had always, Frank O'Bannon's children and grandchildren shared him in death as they had in life, with the people of Indiana. Their grief, hard to subdue at times, reflected the same grief thousands of Hoosiers felt about this man who was gone too soon.

"We were never angry about sharing our father," Jennifer O'Bannon said. "I do wish he had gotten a retirement, that they would have had some time where they did not have things to do, or places to go."[38]

Jennifer hopes her father got to hear the wonderful words spoken of his life as he crossed over into his rest. "I think he got the respect and remembrance that he deserved and he had earned," she said. "Here is my dad, who never wanted to look dumb and was sometimes his own worst critic...I hope he was able to see the memorial services, and maybe get to hear the wonderful accolades spoken about his life, that his good soul and spirit had allowed him to do a good job here on this earth."[39]

Jonathan O'Bannon believes his father was still in awe of the idea of being governor of Indiana, even during the seven years he served in the office—particularly at special times when he could meet the winner of the Indy 500, talk to the IU basketball team before and after their Final Four games in 2002, or even meet golfer Arnold Palmer (b. 1929) or Hoosier-born rocker John Mellencamp (b. 1951).

"Every once in a while, he'd look at you and say, 'Did you ever think we'd be doing something like this?' I mean, he really, truly knew that he would never have been governor of Indiana if he did not have a lot of good people around him," Jonathan said.[40]

Jennifer adds, "I always said, even before he passed, I was not sure what they would do once he was out of office, but I knew my mother was just getting started."[41]

Judy Lives Forward

Judy O'Bannon said she never considered life without her husband Frank—she always thought she would die first. But it wasn't to be that way. After the public ceremonies to honor her husband were finished, the 2004 campaign and the nearly year-long string of events concluded where his name was permanently remembered and honored, Judy began a new, different period of her life—living on her own for the first time in more than forty years.

"My life has changed in ways I would not have thought," Judy said. "I thought it would be more like, as an individual, I could set that apart in my mind and my heart and say, 'I miss Frank,' and that I could just understand it that way. But it's not like that. It's like half of me is just not here. I mean, I try and go on and do more than I did before but I am trying to do it with just half of me."[42]

But Judy is hopeful. "I've decided that I'm going to live to be an old woman, so I have to find the other half of myself that I know is within me!"[43]

At the time of Frank's illness and death, people asked her repeatedly, "How are you holding up?" and she replied, "This is God in me somehow. I don't mean God made me this great saint all of a sudden, but it was God's strength in there that gave me insights...that told me things are going to be okay, however they come out."[44]

Legacy

In traveling this state and sitting and talking with the people who knew Frank O'Bannon well or worked with him as a senator or a governor or just loved him as a husband, father, brother, or friend, I attempted to narrow down with all of the people I talked with, for all time, just what *is* "the O'Bannon legacy?" I can recall vividly the "legacy" word making its way more and more into conversations in the governor's office as the second term stretched into its sixth and seventh year. There was even talk at one point of a formalized process for the end of the seventh year and into the eighth, before the election for the next governor overtook the common agenda to remind Hoosiers of who their governor was and what Frank O'Bannon had meant to them. Time and fate did not allow for that work to occur, and it may have been best that way. Even after his death, the discussion continued about his "legacy" and his overall impact and import not only to the office of governor but also to the more than six million people who lived in Indiana at the time of his death.

Political columnist Ed Feigenbaum wrote a "legacy piece" about Governor O'Bannon in June 2003, three months before he died. In it, he said, "But a case can be made that Frank O'Bannon has had a pretty good run, despite the devastating effects of the national recession (and maybe, in some minor ways, because of them)."[45]

Feigenbaum noted that O'Bannon's accomplishments had all come without the benefit of controlling both houses of the legislature, something Governors Branigin, Whitcomb, Bowen, and Orr had all enjoyed. He added that O'Bannon "has done something that the late U.S. Representative Morris Udall of Arizona cautioned fellow politicians: Never use up all your chits during your first term, and never fail to cash them all in before you leave office."[46]

In the end, Feigenbaum said that "in this television-obsessed age, Frank O'Bannon is unlikely to get the credit he may deserve until the next generation of history books are written" and predicted "Corydon's Capital Candidate…still has some additional big-picture, outside-the-silos thinking up his sleeve."[47]

Sadly, he'd never get to reveal what was "next"—likely a second, last attempt at full-day kindergarten.

Judy O'Bannon said her husband was not all that comfortable with "legacy talk" when it was brought up to him prior to his death—even becoming embarrassed at times, personally, during campaign seasons when the praiseworthy rhetoric would grow too strong. "He was not comfortable with that. He did not want to think about that," Judy said. "I think there are two kinds of legacies left with people. I think one of them is the acknowledgement that decent people, good people, nice guys can be leaders and that public service is a high calling, and a gentlemanly person did okay at it."[48]

Judy believes it's best to leave it to others to roll up the list of policies, programs, or initiatives that ultimately define the "work" of the O'Bannon administration and to someday place those in the context of all the men (and perhaps one day women) who serve this state as governor. O'Bannon enacted an impressive number of public policy initiatives and efforts to draw from for the list. Noteworthy among those are property tax restructuring, focus on a new high-tech economy for Indiana, increased educational opportunities for the youngest Hoosiers and adults who seek continuing education, and new opportunities for lives of freedom and choice for people with disabilities.

But the legacy in every person I encountered on this journey was one we perhaps too quickly overlook. They had many ways of saying it. Some said, "Frank O'Bannon proved that nice guys can finish first." Or they said, "He was the kindest, most compassionate man I ever knew," or even, "He was a true Hoosier gentleman, always." So is this his legacy that he was a man who worked diligently at being fair, honest, and kind to those whom he knew and those whom he did not know and who sacrificially gave of himself and his life so that his state, his community might grow and improve?

The chief justice of the Indiana Supreme Court, Randall T. Shepard, said at his memorial service, "...Even people who have known about our first family only through news accounts or television, or by word of mouth, came to the conclusion over time that the O'Bannons have stood for something uncommonly good. People have held the conviction that Frank and Judy O'Bannon have given over their lives to achieve the very best for our families, for our neighbors, and our state."

Rabbi Sandy Eisenberg Sasso of the Indianapolis Hebrew Congregation sounded a similar theme. "It is not just death that has brought us together. We come together to celebrate a life whose generosity of spirit and sincerity of purpose have touched us all, a life that continues to live in the halls of government; in the streets, schools, and gardens of Indiana, and in each of us."[49]

Perhaps we have found the legacy when we experience the better part of ourselves, when we willingly put aside partisanship and strife, and instead work together with others toward a common good. It is in these times we follow the lead, the legacy, if you will, of the simple, kind man from Corydon who never sat and dreamed of power but accepted power as a responsibility for action.

Rabbi Eisenberg Sasso's words from the Indianapolis memorial service for the governor still echo in my heart and mind:

> An ancient Jewish sage taught of the various crowns of distinction a person may wear: the crown of leadership, the crown of service, and the crown of wisdom. Frank O'Bannon wore all of these crowns with honor, as a political leader, public servant, and discerning statesman. Yet above all these crowns is the greatest crown of all, the crown of a good name. Throughout his life, Frank O'Bannon wore with dignity and with humility the crown of a good name. He knew the deepest wisdom of all that his destiny was to serve you, oh God, by serving others. Allow us, oh God, to continue to unwrap the gifts of mind and heart which your beloved servant Frank O'Bannon has bequeathed to us. Let us carry with us from this hallowed place and this sacred time, the example of his life. May the memory of our beloved governor and friend ever be a source of inspiration and blessing. Blessed was he in his coming, blessed is he as he goes forth to life eternal, and as he lived in peace, so may he rest in peace. Amen.[50]

Appendix

THE STAFFING OF GOVERNOR FRANK O'BANNON'S OFFICE
1997-2003

Staffing the governor's office during the O'Bannon administration were many dedicated, loyal, and intelligent men and women who gave of their time and talent for the betterment of our state. In policy positions, Governor O'Bannon employed the "Executive Assistant" model first created under Governor Otis R. Bowen.[1]

The author has attempted to assemble a comprehensive list of all of the persons who served at any time during the six years, nine months, and three days that comprised the O'Bannon terms. Cindy Athey, executive assistant, and Carla McIntire, office manager, and others assisted in compiling this list.

Governor O'Bannon's Staff	Staff Position(s)
Regina Alexander	Administrative Assistant, Transportation
David Allen	Deputy Legislative Director

Laura Alt	Administrative Assistant, Scheduling
Cindy Athey	Executive Assistant, Scheduling Director
Angela Belden	Deputy Press Secretary; Deputy Communications Director
Steve Bella	Policy & Communications Adviser
Amy Small Bilyeu	Deputy Legislative Director
Fred Biesecker	General Counsel
Tasha Smith Bonds	Administrative Assistant, Transportation, Environment & Natural Resources
Phil Bremen	Press Secretary
Katy Brett	Program Assistant, First Lady's Office
Russ Brown	Special Assistant, Governor & Scheduling
Margaret Burlingame	Chief of Staff; Deputy Chief of Staff
Thelma Burns	Executive Housekeeper, Governor's Residence
Steve Campbell	Communications Director; Deputy Press Secretary
Nancy Cira	Governor's Residence Director
Beth Compton	Executive Assistant, Environment & Natural Resources
Annette Craycraft	Special Assistant, Constituent Correspondence & Service

Carol Darst	Program Manager, First Lady's Office
Jennifer Davis	Administrative Assistant, General Counsel and Public Safety
Mary Beth Davis	Administrative Assistant, Press Office
Amanda Deaton	Administrative Assistant, Fiscal and Legislative Policy
Angie DeMauro	Administrative Assistant, Governor & Scheduling Office
Steve DeMougin	Executive Assistant, Community Affairs
Mary Dieter	Press Secretary & Communications Director
Jennifer Dunlap	Administrative Assistant, Press Office
Angie Dye	Program Assistant, First Lady's Office
Mike Edmondson	Staff Assistant, Boards & Commissions
Jean Farison	Coordinator, Boards & Commissions
Amy Levander Flack	Deputy Legislative Director
Alpha Garrett	Scheduling/Press Assistant, First Lady's Office
Mike Gery	Deputy Legislative Director
Sue Gilstrap	Constituent Correspondence & Service
Deborah Glenn	Switchboard Receptionist
David Goldwater	Administrative Assistant, Health & Human Services

Cheryl Gonzalez	Special Assistant, Legislative Team
Larry Grau	Executive Assistant, Education
John Grew	Executive Assistant, Budget & Fiscal Policy
Christina Hale	Staff Assistant, Boards & Commissions
Craig Hartzer	Policy Director
April Hayes	Switchboard Receptionist
Bart Herriman	Executive Assistant, State Tax Board, Revenue, TRF/PERF, and State Board of Accounts; Legislative Team
Rose Hicks	Housekeeper, Governor's Residence
Demika Holland	Switchboard Receptionist
Wyatt Hornsby	Constituent Correspondence & Service
P.J. Irvine	Executive Housekeeper, Governor's Residence
Brenda Jacobs	Administrative Assistant, Public Safety, Education & General Counsel Policy; Switchboard Receptionist
Tim Joyce	Chief of Staff; Deputy Chief of Staff
Priscilla Keith	Deputy General Counsel; Executive Assistant, Public Utilities
Sharon Kendall	Special Assistant, Constituent Correspondence & Service
Kasey Kendrick	Special Assistant, Governor & Scheduling

Doug Kinser	Deputy Legislative Director; Executive Assistant, Insurance & Financial Institutions
Bob Kovach	Legislative Director
Lee Lamb	Special Assistant, Constituent Correspondence & Service
Jon Laramore	General Counsel
Lisa Love	Administrative Assistant, Scheduling
Jessica MacIntosh	Special Assistant, Constituent Services
Heather Macek	Executive Assistant, Education Policy; Secretary, General Counsel & Public Safety
Jim Maguire	Chief of Staff
Jeannette Marquez	Administrative Assistant, Legislative Team
Joyce Martin	General Counsel; Executive Assistant, Environment, Natural Resources & Public Utilities
Aja May	Scheduling Assistant, First Lady's Office
Nancy McGann	Special Assistant, Constituent Correspondence & Service
Carla McIntire	Office Manager
Tamara Mitchell	Administrative Assistant, Press Office
Terry Mumford	Legislative Director
Deirdre Murphy	Staff Assistant, Boards & Commissions

Thad Nation	Press Secretary; Policy & Communications Adviser
Tom New	Chief of Staff
N. Bryan Nicol	Deputy Chief of Staff
Catherine O'Connor	Executive Assistant, Public Safety, Corrections & National Guard
Marty Peters	Executive Assistant, Community Affairs; Program Director, First Lady's Office
Dexter Powell	Butler, Governor's Residence
Ron Powell	Policy & Communications Adviser
Kendra Price	Secretary; Switchboard Receptionist
Cheryl Reed	Deputy Press Secretary; Deputy Communications Director
Kimberly Reed	Secretary, General Counsel & Public Safety
Pat Rios	Deputy Chief of Staff; Deputy Legislative Director; Executive Assistant, Public Health
Terri Roney	Special Assistant, Constituent Correspondence & Service
Marya Rose	Deputy Legislative Director
Anne Runden	Program Assistant, First Lady's Office
Jonathan Siebeking	Staff Assistant, Boards & Commissions
Todd Siesky	Deputy Communications Director

Addison Simpson	Executive Assistant, Transportation, Bureau of Motor Vehicles & Hoosier Lottery
Bob Small	Executive Assistant, Public Safety, Corrections & National Guard
Joe Smith, Jr.	Deputy Team; Executive Assistant, Transportation, Bureau of Motor Vehicles & Hoosier Lottery
Kathy Smith	Executive Assistant, Education
Jason Spindler	Special Assistant, Constituent Correspondence & Service
Angela Spittal	Communications Director
Anne Sterling	Coordinator, Constituent Services; Scheduling Assistant, First Lady's Office
Amy Stewart	Deputy Chief of Staff
Lois Stewart	Secretary, Chief of Staff & Deputy Chief of Staff
Carrie Stiers	Administrative Assistant
Jayne Stites	Program Director, First Lady's Office
Andrew Stoner	Deputy Press Secretary; Executive Assistant, Human Services
Jonathan Swain	Chief of Staff & Press Secretary, First Lady's Office
Jennifer Swenson	Program Director, First Lady's Office
Jennifer Swickard	Scheduling Assistant, First Lady's Office

Pat Terrell	Policy & Communications Adviser
Robin Tew	Director, Constituent Services; Executive Assistant, Indiana Arts Commission; Tobacco Prevention Agency; Professional Licensing Agency; and Governor's Fellow Program
Linda Ventura	Receptionist & Secretary
Kelly Voorhees	Special Assistant, Governor & Scheduling
Carl Waiters	Staff Assistant, Governor's Residence
Connie Watson	Housekeeper, Governor's Residence
Deborah White	Secretary & Switchboard Receptionist
Robin Walker	Administrative Assistant, Scheduling; Switchboard Receptionist
Molly Wilkinson	Administrative Assistant, Environmental & Health/Human Services and Community Affairs
Carlis Williams	Executive Assistant, Public Health & Human Services
Jayelynn Willman	Administrative Assistant, Public Safety & Transportation
Carter Wolf	Executive Assistant, Community Affairs
Floyd Worley	Executive Assistant, Transportation, Bureau of Motor Vehicles and Hoosier Lottery
John Zody	Deputy Communications Director

End Notes

Chapter 1

1. Videotape of C-SPAN Broadcast of Sept. 19, 2003, "Governor Frank O'Bannon Memorial Service," Indiana Statehouse, Indianapolis, IN
2. Ibid.
3. Ibid.
4. Ibid.
5. *Indianapolis News*, Aug. 28, 1979.
6. Ibid.

Chapter 2

1. Biographical Directory of the United States Congress: 1774-Present. The Library of Congress. Cleaves, Freeman. *Old Tippecanoe: William Henry Harrison.* New York, N.Y.: Scribner's Sons, 1939. Goebel, Dorothy. *William Henry Harrison: A Political Biography.* Philadelphia: Porcupine Press, 1974. Gray, Ralph D. *Gentlemen From Indiana: National Party Candidates 1836-1940.* Indianapolis: Indiana Historical Society. Pp vii. 1, 1977.
2. Ewbank, Louis B., and Dorothy L. Riker, eds. *The Laws of Indiana Territory, 1809-1816.* Indianapolis: 1934. Indiana Historical Collections, XX, pp. 335-338. Esarey, Logan. *A History of Indiana.* (2 volumes). Fort Wayne, IN: 1924, I, pp. 239-242.

3. Ibid.

4. *Corydon Democrat*, Feb. 17, 1943.

5. *Corydon Democrat*, Jan. 9, 1909.

6. *Corydon Democrat*, Jan. 9, 1907.

7. Indiana Yearbook. (1918). Pp. 983-1,005.

8. Oral interview of Senator Robert P. O'Bannon conducted by Jerry Handfield, 1978. *Indiana Historical Bureau and Centennial History of the Indiana General Assembly.* Indianapolis: Indiana State Library Manuscripts.

9. Rosamond Sample interview with the author, Corydon, IN, Nov. 20, 2004.

10. Jane Parker interview with the author, Plainfield, IN, Dec. 20, 2004.

11. Minutes of the Indiana Historical Commission, April 24, 1915. Indiana Commission on Public Records, Indianapolis, IN.

12. Robert P. O'Bannon oral history interview with Jerry Handfield, 1978. Robert P. O'Bannon file, Indiana Division, Indiana State Library.

13. *Corydon Democrat*, Oct. 8, 1924.

14. *Indianapolis Star*, Nov. 4, 1924.

15. Ibid.

16. *Indianapolis Star*, Nov. 5, 1924.

17. *Corydon Democrat*, Nov. 5, 1924.

18. Robert P. O'Bannon oral history interview with Jerry Handfield, 1978. Robert P. O'Bannon file, Indiana Division, Indiana State Library.

19. Ibid.

20. Ibid.

21. *Corydon Democrat*, May 19, 1920.

22. *Corydon Democrat*, Feb. 17, 1943.

23. Robert P. O'Bannon oral history interview with Jerry Handfield, 1978. Robert P. O'Bannon file, Indiana Division, Indiana State Library.

Chapter 3

1. Paul C. Bulleit column, *Louisville Courier-Journal*, 1976. Reprinted in *A Place To Begin: Images of Corydon, Indiana, 1850-1975.* Goshen, KY: Town of Corydon, Harmony House Publishers, 2000.

2. Diane Miller interview with the author, Corydon, IN, July 16, 2005.

3. Jane Parker interview with the author, Plainfield, IN, Dec. 20, 2004.

4. Rosamond Sample interview with the author, Corydon, IN, Nov. 20, 2004.

5. Jane Parker interview with the author, Plainfield, IN, Dec. 20, 2004.

6. Judy O'Bannon interview with the author, Indianapolis, IN, Feb. 9, 2005.

7. Judy O'Bannon interview with the author, Indianapolis, IN, Feb. 23, 2005.

8. Jane Parker interview with the author, Plainfield, IN, Dec. 20, 2004.

9. Ibid.

10. David Allen e-mail to the author, May 17, 2006.

11. Judy O'Bannon interview with the author, Indianapolis, IN, Feb. 9, 2005.

12. *Indianapolis Star*, Nov. 19, 1996.

13. *Indianapolis News*, undated, 1970.

14. *Indianapolis Star*, Nov. 19, 1996.

Chapter 4

1. Fred Griffin interview with the author, Corydon, IN, Nov. 19, 2004.

2. *Corydon High School Pantherette,* October 1947.

3. Ibid.

4. *Louisville Courier-Journal*, Feb. 1, 1948.

5. *Corydon Democrat*, March 3, 1948.

6. O'Bannon, Frank, Foreword to Beck, Bill. *Play On: Celebrating 100 Years of High School Sports in Indiana.* Louisville, KY: Four Color Imports Ltd., 2003.

7. Ibid.

8. *Corydon Democrat*, May 26, 1948.

9. Fred Griffin interview with the author, Corydon, IN, Nov. 20, 2004.

10. Jane Parker interview with the author, Plainfield, IN, Dec. 20, 2004.

11. Ibid.

12. Governor Frank O'Bannon news release, December 2002.

13. Fred Griffin interview with the author, Corydon, IN, Nov. 20, 2004.

14. Wells, Herman B "Being Lucky: Reminiscences and Reflections" (1980) Bloomington, IN: Indiana University Press. Pp. 217-218.

15. *Louisville Courier-Journal*, Sept. 19, 2003.

16. John M. Kyle letter to the author, 2005.

17. Budd Weed letter to the author, 2005.

18. Donald E. "Monk" Lambert letter to the author, 2005.

19. William C. Reed, Jr. letter to the author, 2005.

20. Rod Howard letter to the author, 2005.

21. Thomas Hoadley letter to the author, 2005.

22. Robert Williams, M.D. letter to the author, 2005.

23. William Boaz letter to the author, 2005.

24. Arbutus yearbook (1950). Bloomington, IN: Indiana University.

25. *Louisville Courier-Journal*, Sept. 19, 2003.

26. Arbutus yearbook (1952). Bloomington, IN: Indiana University.

27. George Fleetwood interview with author, Indianapolis, IN, Feb. 7, 2005.

28. Judy O'Bannon interview with the author, Indianapolis, IN, March 8, 2005.

29. Donald E. "Monk" Lambert letter to the author, 2005.

30. Phil Gutman interview with the author, Fort Wayne, IN, May 5, 2005.

31. Donald E. "Monk" Lambert letter to the author, 2005.

32. Judy O'Bannon interview with the author, Indianapolis, IN, Feb. 9, 2005.

Chapter 5

1. Judy O'Bannon interview with the author, Indianapolis, IN, Feb. 9, 2005.

2. Ibid.

3. Ibid.

4. Ibid.

5. Ibid.

6. Ibid.

7. Ibid.

8. Ibid.

9. Ibid.

10. "Uncharted territory: Being the first," Mosaic newsletter, Louisville Theological Seminary, Spring 2003.

11. Judy O'Bannon interview with the author, Indianapolis, IN, Feb. 9, 2005.

12. Ibid.

13. Ibid.

14. Charles Asmus quotes from Boys and Girls Club Horatio Alger Award videotape, undated.

15. Judy O'Bannon interview with the author, Indianapolis, IN, Feb. 9, 2005.

16. Remarks by Governor Frank O'Bannon, Athenaeum celebration, Indianapolis, IN, May 2002, event attended by the author.

17. Judy O'Bannon interview with the author, Indianapolis, IN, Feb. 9, 2005.

18. Ibid.

19. Ibid.

20. "Uncharted territory: Being the first," Mosaic newsletter, Louisville Theological Seminary, Spring 2003.

21. Judy O'Bannon interview with the author, Indianapolis, IN, Feb. 9, 2005.

22. Ibid.

23. *Louisville Courier-Journal*, Sept. 18, 1957.

Chapter 6

1. *Corydon Democrat*, Jan. 14, 1959.

2. Ron Simpson interview with the author, Corydon, IN, July 16, 2005.

3. Ibid.

4. Ibid.

5. Ibid.

6. Ibid.

7. Ibid.

8. Ibid.

9. Ibid.

10. Gordon Pendleton interview with the author, Corydon, IN, July 16, 2005.

11. Judy O'Bannon interview with the author, Indianapolis, IN, Feb. 9, 2005.

12. Gordon Pendleton interview with the author, Corydon, IN, July 16, 2005.

13. *Corydon Democrat*, Nov. 23, 1963.

14. Gordon Pendleton interview with the author, Corydon, IN, July 16, 2005.

15. Judy O'Bannon interview with the author, Indianapolis, IN, Feb. 9, 2005.

16. Callie Zimmerman interview with the author, Corydon, IN, July 16, 2005.

17. Judy O'Bannon interview with the author, Indianapolis, IN, Feb. 9, 2005.

18. Ibid.

19. Judy O'Bannon interview with the author, Indianapolis, IN, Nov. 17, 2005.

20. Jennifer O'Bannon interview with author, Indianapolis, IN, Oct. 24, 2005.

21. Jonathan O'Bannon interview with the author, New Albany, IN, July 18, 2005.

22. Ibid.

23. Jennifer O'Bannon interview with the author, Indianapolis, IN, Oct. 24, 2005.

24. Jonathan O'Bannon interview with the author, New Albany, IN, July 18, 2005.

25. Polly O'Bannon Zoeller interview with the author, New Albany, IN, July 18, 2005.

26. Jennifer O'Bannon interview with the author, Indianapolis, IN, Oct. 24, 2005.

27. Ibid.

28. Polly O'Bannon Zoeller interview with the author, New Albany, IN, July 18, 2005.

29. Judy O'Bannon interview with the author, Indianapolis, IN, Feb. 23, 2005.

30. *Indianapolis Star*, Nov. 19, 1996.

31. Ibid.

32. Videotape of HGTV broadcast, *Barns Reborn*, Nov. 14, 2001.

33. Associated Press report, Jan. 7, 2001.

34. Jonathan O'Bannon interview with the author, New Albany, IN, July 18, 2005.

35. Polly O'Bannon Zoeller interview with the author, New Albany, IN, July 18, 2005.

36. Videotape of HGTV broadcast, *Barns Reborn*, Nov. 14, 2001.

37. Ibid.

38. Alex Willis interview with the author, March 4, 2005.

39. Larry Gershanoff interview with the author, Greencastle, IN, March 15, 2005.

40. Videotape of HGTV broadcast, *Barns Reborn*, Nov. 14, 2001.

41. Ibid.

42. Tom Zoeller e-mail to the author, Oct. 1, 2005.

43. Ibid.

44. Beau Zoeller e-mail to the author, Oct. 1, 2005.

45. Ibid.

46. Chelsea Zoeller e-mail to the author, Sept. 27, 2005.

47. Demi Zoeller e-mail to the author, Sept. 27, 2005.

48. Ibid.

49. Asher O'Bannon Reed e-mail to the author, Nov. 15, 2005.

50. Ibid.

Chapter 7

1. *Louisville Courier-Journal*, Sept. 19, 2003.

2. O'Bannon for Senate flyer (1970). Uncatalogued collection, Indiana State Archives, Indianapolis, IN.

3. *Corydon Democrat*, Nov. 5, 1970.

4. *Corydon Democrat*, Oct. 23, 1970.

5. *Cordon Democrat*, Oct. 28, 1970.

6. Election returns, Harrison County only. *Corydon Democrat*, Nov. 4, 1970.

7. *Corydon Democrat*, Oct. 20, 1974.

8. Ibid.

9. Ibid.

10. *Corydon Democrat*, Oct. 30, 1974.

11. Letter to the author from Marian McGrath Pearcy, Attorney for Zelpha Mitsch, Aug. 11, 2005.

12. *Corydon Democrat*, Oct. 30, 1974.

13. *Louisville Courier-Journal*, Sept. 19, 2003.

14. Don Park interview with author, Muncie, IN, March 23, 2005.

15. Ibid.

16. Wayne Townsend interview with the author, Hartford City, IN, March 19, 2005.

17. Robert Garton interview with author, Indianapolis, IN, Sept. 19, 2005.

18. *Indianapolis News*, Sept. 8, 1987.

19. *Indianapolis News*, March 5, 1971.

20. Mike Gery interview with the author, Indianapolis, IN, Jan. 24, 2005.

21. Ibid.

22. Don Park interview with the author, Muncie, IN, March 23, 2005.

23. Robert Kovach interview with author, Elkhart, IN, May 6, 2005.

24. Phil Gutman interview with author, Fort Wayne, IN, May 5, 2005.

25. *Lafayette Journal & Courier*, May 30, 1988.

26. C-SPAN videotape, *States of the Nation*. September 1985. O'Bannon family video collection.

27. Ibid.

28. *Indianapolis Star*, Nov. 6, 1988.

29. Ibid.

30. Robert Garton interview with the author, Indianapolis, IN, Sept. 19, 2005.

Chapter 8

1. Mike Gery interview with the author, Indianapolis, IN, Jan. 24, 2005.

2. Wayne Townsend interview with the author, Hartford City, IN, March 19, 2005.

3. Mike Gery interview with the author, Indianapolis, IN, Jan. 24, 2005.

4. Graham Richard interview with the author, Fort Wayne, IN, March 23, 2005.

5. Julia Carson interview with the author, Indianapolis, IN, April 9, 2005.

6. Graham Richard interview with the author, Fort Wayne, IN, March 23, 2005.

7. Randall Shepard interview with the author, Indianapolis, IN, Sept. 26, 2005.

8. Graham Richard interview with the author, Fort Wayne, IN, March 23, 2005.

9. Wayne Townsend interview with the author, Hartford City, IN, March 19, 2005.

10. Ibid.

11. *Indianapolis News*, undated 1979 column. O'Bannon family clipping collection.

12. Ibid.

13. Ibid.

14. Ibid.

15. *Louisville Courier-Journal*, undated 1978 column. O'Bannon family clipping collection.

16. Louis Mahern interview with the author, Indianapolis, IN, Feb. 16, 2006.

17. Ibid.

18. John Whikehart e-mail to the author, July 22, 2005.

19. Tom New remarks, O'Bannon bust dedication, Indiana Statehouse, Feb. 13, 2006.

20. *Indianapolis Star*, Nov. 6, 1988.

21. George Fleetwood interview with the author, Indianapolis, IN, Feb. 7, 2005.

22. Robert Garton interview with the author, Indianapolis, IN, Sept. 19, 2005.

23. George Fleetwood interview with the author, Indianapolis, IN, Feb. 7, 2005.

24. Walsh, Justin E. *Centennial History of the Indiana General Assembly, 1816-1978*. The Select Committee on the Centennial History of the Indiana General Assembly and the Indiana Historical Bureau, Indianapolis, IN, 1987, p.607.

25. *Indianapolis Star*, Jan. 19, 1977.

26. Ibid.

27. Ibid.

28. Ibid.

29. Ibid.

30. Ibid.

31. Ibid.

32. Ibid.

33. Robert Kovach interview with author, Elkhart, IN, May 6, 2005.

34. *Indianapolis Star*, Jan. 19, 1977.

35. *Indianapolis Star*, April 25, 1973.

36. Governor Frank O'Bannon news release, May 12, 1997.

37. Marilyn Schultz interview with the author, Indianapolis, IN, Oct. 5, 2005.

38. Walsh, Justin E. *Centennial History of the Indiana General Assembly, 1816-1978*. The Select Committee on the Centennial History of the Indiana General Assembly and the Indiana Historical Bureau, Indianapolis, IN, 1987, p.631.

39. Ibid., p. 628.

40. Ibid., p. 629.

41. Mike Gery interview with the author, Indianapolis, IN, Jan. 24, 2005.

42. Don Park interview with the author, Muncie, IN, March 23, 2005.

43. Ibid.

44. Judy O'Bannon interview with the author, Indianapolis, IN, March 8, 2005.

45. Ibid.

Chapter 9

1. Otis Bowen interview with the author, Bremen, IN, May 6, 2005.

2. Watt, William J. *Bowen: The Years as Governor*. Indianapolis: Bierce Associates, Inc., 1981.

3. *Indianapolis Star*, Jan. 11, 1984.

4. Walter Helmke interview with the author, Fort Wayne, IN, May 5, 2005.

5. Lawrence Borst interview with the author, Indianapolis, IN, Feb. 21, 2005.

6. Louis Mahern interview with the author, Indianapolis, IN, Feb. 16, 2006.

7. *Louisville Courier-Journal*, March 8, 1996.

8. Tom New remarks, O'Bannon bust dedication ceremony, Indiana Statehouse, Feb. 13, 2006.

9. *Corydon Democrat*, Aug. 6, 1997.

10. Ben Schreiber interview with author, Indianapolis, IN, Aug. 19, 2005.

11. Ibid.

Chapter 10

1. *Indianapolis Star*, Nov. 15, 1987.

2. *Indianapolis Star*, Nov. 13, 1987.

3. *Indianapolis Star*, Nov. 8, 1987.

4. *Indianapolis Star*, Nov. 13, 1987.

5. Steve Daily interview with the author, Kokomo, IN, July 12, 2005.

6. Ibid.

7. Lee Hamilton interview with the author, Bloomington, IN, April 5, 2005.

8. Ibid.

9. Ibid.

10. *Indianapolis News*, Sept. 8, 1987.

11. Ibid.

12. David Johnson interview with the author, Indianapolis, IN, Sept. 15, 2005.

13. *Corydon Democrat*, Jan. 14, 1987.

14. *Corydon Democrat*, O'Bannon Campaign Souvenir Edition, May 17, 1987.

15. Ibid.

16. Ibid.

17. Frank O'Bannon Gubernatorial Campaign Kick-Off Speech, Corydon, IN, May 17, 1987.

18. Ibid.

19. Ibid.

20. *Louisville Courier-Journal*, May 18, 1987.

21. Larry Conrad remarks, O'Bannon for Governor Kick-Off Rally, Corydon, IN, May 17, 1987.

22. Chuck Coffey e-mail to the author, Feb. 1, 2005.

23. *Louisville Courier-Journal*, Sept. 19, 2003.

24. Donna Imus interview with the author, Indianapolis, IN, Sept. 14, 2005.

25. Robert Pastrick interview with the author, French Lick, IN, Aug. 27, 2005.

26. *Indianapolis News*, Sept. 8, 1987.

27. John Goss interview with the author, Indianapolis, IN, April 9, 2005.

28. Ibid.

29. Ibid.

30. David Johnson interview with the author, Indianapolis, IN, Sept. 15, 2005.

31. John Goss interview with the author, Indianapolis, IN, April 9, 2005.

32. *Indianapolis News*, Sept. 8, 1987.

33. *Corydon Democrat*, Jan. 27, 1988.

34. Handwritten notes by Frank O'Bannon, Indiana State Archives, January 1987. Uncatalogued collection, Indiana State Archives, Indianapolis, IN.

35. Jane Parker interview with the author, Plainfield, IN, Dec. 20, 2004.

36. Evan Bayh interview with the author, via telephone, Sept. 13, 2005.

37. *Indianapolis Star*, Jan. 10, 1988.

38. Ibid.

39. Undated, O'Bannon 1988 campaign file, notes from "BEB Meeting." Uncatalogued collection, Indiana State Archives, Indianapolis, IN.

40. Ibid.

41. Joe Hogsett interview with the author, Indianapolis, IN, Oct. 26, 2005.

42. Judy O'Bannon interview with the author, Indianapolis, IN, March 8, 2005.

43. David Johnson interview with the author, Indianapolis, IN, Sept. 15, 2005.

44. Louis Mahern interview with the author, Indianapolis, IN, Feb. 16, 2006.

45. Project 88-206 Report, O'Bannon 1988 campaign files. Uncatalogued collection, Indiana State Archives, Indianapolis, IN

46. *Indianapolis News*, Aug. 28, 1995.

47. Evan Bayh interview with the author, via telephone, Sept. 13, 2005.

48. Joe Hogsett interview with the author, Indianapolis, IN, Oct. 26, 2005.

49. John Goss interview with the author, Indianapolis, IN, April 9, 2005.

50. *Indianapolis Star*, Jan. 21, 1988.

51. Joe Hogsett interview with the author, Indianapolis, IN, Oct. 26, 2005.

52. Judy O'Bannon interview with the author, Indianapolis, IN, March 8, 2005.

53. John Goss interview with the author, Indianapolis, IN, April 9, 2005.

54. George Fleetwood interview with the author, Indianapolis, IN, Feb. 7, 2005.

55. Louis Mahern interview with the author, Indianapolis, IN, Feb. 16, 2006.

56. David Johnson interview with the author, Indianapolis, IN, Sept. 15, 2005.

57. *New Castle Courier-Times*, Feb. 6, 1995.

58. *Indianapolis Star*, Jan. 22, 1988.

59. Steve Daily interview with the author, Kokomo, IN, July 12, 2005.

60. Mike McDaniel interview with the author, Indianapolis, IN, June 16, 2005.

61. Ibid.

62. Ibid.

63. Ibid.

64. *Indianapolis Star*, Jan. 19, 1988.

65. *Indianapolis Star*, Sept. 17, 1987.

66. Mike McDaniel interview with the author, Indianapolis, IN, June 16, 2005.

67. Ibid.

68. Joe Hogsett interview with the author, Indianapolis, IN, Oct. 26, 2005.

69. Ibid.

70. Jim Shella interview with the author, Indianapolis, IN, June 25, 2005.

71. John Goss interview with the author, Indianapolis, IN, April 9, 2005.

72. *Corydon Democrat*, Jan. 27, 1988.

73. 1988 Primary Election Report, Indiana Secretary of State Evan Bayh, Indianapolis, IN.

Chapter 11

1. Mike McDaniel interview with the author, Indianapolis, IN, June 16, 2005.

2. Jim Shella interview with the author, Indianapolis, IN, June 25, 2005.

3. Steve Goldsmith interview with the author, via telephone, Aug. 12, 2005.

4. Mike McDaniel interview with the author, Indianapolis, IN, June 16, 2005.

5. Ibid.

6. John Goss interview with the author, Indianapolis, IN, April 9, 2005.

7. Marilyn Schultz interview with the author, Indianapolis, IN, Oct. 5, 2005.

8. Ibid.

9. John Goss interview with the author, Indianapolis, IN, April 9, 2005.

10. *Indianapolis Star*, Nov. 6, 1988.

11. Ibid.

12. Ibid.

13. Ibid.

14. "Bylines with Bob McIntosh," radio interview of Frank O'Bannon at New Albany, IN, Nov. 5, 1988.

15. 1988 General Election Report, Indiana Secretary of State Joseph H. Hogsett, Indianapolis, IN.

16. *Corydon Democrat*, Jan. 11, 1989.

17. Videotape of WTHR-TV live coverage of Jan. 9, 1989 Inaugural Ceremonies, Indiana Statehouse, Indianapolis, IN.

18. Inaugural Address of Lt. Governor Frank O'Bannon, Jan. 9, 1989. Indiana Statehouse, Indianapolis, IN.

19. *Indianapolis Star*, Dec. 18, 1987.

20. Craig Hartzer interview with the author, Indianapolis, IN, Sept. 2005.

21. Darryl Voelker interview with the author, Corydon, IN, July 16, 2005.

22. Ibid.

23. Marjorie O'Laughlin interview with the author, Indianapolis, IN, May 9, 2005.

24. Ibid.

25. "Bylines with Bob McIntosh," radio interview of Frank O'Bannon, undated tape.

26. Tom New remarks, Frank O'Bannon bust dedication, Feb. 13, 2006. Indiana Statehouse, Indianapolis, IN.

27. "Bylines with Bob McIntosh," radio interview of Frank O'Bannon, undated tape.

28. Judy O'Bannon interview with the author, Indianapolis, IN, April 5, 2005.

29. Frank O'Bannon remarks to Citizens Concerned for the Constitution convention, reported in Brian Howey column, Indianapolis News, Oct. 9, 1995.

30. Susan Williams interview with the author, Indianapolis, IN, Sept. 29, 2005.

31. Ibid.

32. Judy O'Bannon interview with the author, Indianapolis, IN, April 5, 2005.

33. Videotape of WSBT-TV unedited news video. Interview of Frank O'Bannon and Joe Kernan, Red Square, Moscow, Russia, July 9, 1990.

34. Ibid.

35. John Goss interview with the author, Indianapolis, IN, April 9, 2005.

36. Evan Bayh interview with the author, via telephone, Sept. 13, 2005.

37. Judy O'Bannon interview with the author, Indianapolis, IN, April 5, 2005.

38. Evan Bayh interview with the author, via telephone, Sept. 13, 2005.

39. James Maguire interview with the author, Indianapolis, IN, Oct. 18, 2005.

40. Louis Mahern interview with the author, Indianapolis, IN, Feb. 16, 2005.

41. Associated Press report, June 19, 1993.

42. Videotape of WISH-TV news report, June 18, 1993.

43. Robert Garton interview with the author, Indianapolis, IN, Feb. 16, 2005.

44. John Ketzenberger interview with author, Indianapolis, IN, July 1, 2005.

45. Kevin Corcoran interview with the author, Indianapolis, IN, Aug. 23, 2005.

46. Robert Garton interview with the author, Indianapolis, IN, Feb. 16, 2005.

47. Ibid.

48. Ibid.

49. Mike Smith interview with author, Indianapolis, IN, June 16, 2005.

50. Videotape of WISH-TV news report, June 19, 1993.

51. *Louisville Courier-Journal*, June, 20, 1993.

52. Ibid.

Chapter 12

1. Frank O'Bannon gubernatorial campaign announcement speech, Harrison County Courthouse, Corydon, IN, Jan. 30, 1996.
2. Joe Hogsett interview with the author, Indianapolis, IN, Oct. 26, 2005.
3. *Indianapolis Star*, Jan. 31, 1996.
4. Judy O'Bannon interview with the author, Indianapolis, IN, April 5, 2005.
5. Baron Hill interview with the author, Seymour, IN, May 2, 2005.
6. Ibid.
7. David Johnson interview with the author, Indianapolis, IN, Sept. 15, 2005.
8. Ibid.
9. *Louisville Courier-Journal*, Sept. 19, 2003.
10. Geoff Garin interview with the author, via telephone, Dec. 1, 2005.
11. *Cook Political Report* as reported in Brian Howey's column, *Indianapolis News*, Aug. 28, 1995.
12. Fred Yang interview with the author, via telephone, Feb. 23, 2006.
13. Geoff Garin interview with the author, via telephone, Dec. 1, 2005.
14. *Corydon Democrat*, Sept. 27, 1995.
15. Frank Greer interview with the author, via telephone, July 7, 2005.
16. Ibid.
17. David Johnson interview with the author, Indianapolis, IN, Sept. 15, 2005.
18. Ibid.
19. Ibid.
20. Fred Yang interview with the author, via telephone, Feb. 23, 2006.
21. Videotape of O'Bannon for Governor, 1996 campaign ad.
22. Videotape of O'Bannon for Governor, 1996 campaign ad.
23. Ibid.
24. Ibid.
25. Fred Yang interview with the author, via telephone, Feb. 23, 2006.
26. Videotape of O'Bannon for Governor, 1996 campaign ad.
27. Fred Yang interview with the author, via telephone, Feb. 23, 2006.
28. Jennifer O'Bannon interview with the author, Indianapolis, IN, Oct. 24, 2005.
29. Jonathan O'Bannon interview with the author, New Albany, IN, July 18, 2005.
30. Videotape of O'Bannon for Governor, 1996 campaign ad.

31. Text of Goldsmith for Governor 1996, campaign ad.

32. *Howey Political Report*, 10th Anniversary Review, January 2004.

33. Ibid.

34. Mary Dieter interview with the author, Zionsville, IN, July 14, 2005.

35. John Ketzenberger interview with the author, Indianapolis, IN, July 1, 2005.

36. Steve Goldsmith interview with the author, via telephone, Aug. 12, 2005.

37. Videotape of Goldsmith for Governor 1996, campaign ad.

38. Jim Shella interview with the author, Indianapolis, IN, June 25, 2005.

39. Videotape of WTHR-TV news report, October 1996.

40. Videotape of WTHR-TV interview with Frank O'Bannon by John Stehr, Jan. 8, 1997.

41. Fred Yang interview with the author, via telephone, Feb. 23, 2006.

42. Frank Greer interview with the author, via telephone, July 7, 2005.

43. Geoff Garin interview with the author, via telephone, Dec. 1, 2005.

44. Ibid.

45. Rachel Gorlin e-mail to the author, March 25, 2005.

46. Geoff Garin interview with the author, via telephone, Dec. 1, 2005.

47. David Johnson interview with the author, Indianapolis, IN, Sept. 15, 2005.

48. Mike Edmondson interview with the author, Indianapolis, IN, April 27, 2005.

49. Ibid.

50. Ibid.

51. Robin Winston interview with the author, Indianapolis, IN, April 19, 2005.

52. Ibid.

53. Ibid.

54. Governor Frank O'Bannon news release, Nov. 24, 1998.

Chapter 13

1. Robert Garton interview with the author, Indianapolis, IN, Sept. 19, 2005.

2. John Ketzenberger interview with the author, Indianapolis, IN, July 1, 2005.

3. Mike Smith interview with the author, Indianapolis, IN, June 16, 2005.

4. Jim Shella interview with the author, Indianapolis, IN, June 25, 2005.

5. Joe Kernan interview with the author, South Bend, IN, May 20, 2005.

6. Ibid.

7. Ibid.

8. Judy O'Bannon interview with the author, Indianapolis, IN, April 5, 2005.

9. Ibid.

10. Ibid.

11. *Corydon Democrat*, June 5, 1996.

12. *Corydon Democrat*, June 12, 1996.

13. Ibid.

14. Videotape of WISH-TV live interview with Frank O'Bannon by Jim Shella & Debby Knox, United Center, Chicago, IL, Aug. 29, 1996.

15. Ibid.

16. Ibid.

17. *Indianapolis Star*, Aug. 30, 1996.

18. *Indianapolis Star*, Aug. 31, 1996.

19. John Ketzenberger interview with the author, Indianapolis, IN, July 1, 2005.

20. Jim Shella interview with the author, Indianapolis, IN, June 25, 2005.

21. Kevin Corcoran interview with the author, Indianapolis, IN, Aug. 23, 2005.

22. *Louisville Courier-Journal*, Nov. 7, 1996.

23. Louis Mahern interview with the author, Indianapolis, IN, Feb. 16, 2006.

24. Videotape of Frank O'Bannon remarks, WFYI-TV coverage of September 1996 debate, DePauw University, Greencastle, Ind.

25. Judy O'Bannon interview with the author, Indianapolis, IN, April 5, 2005.

26. Kevin Corcoran interview with the author, Indianapolis, IN, Aug. 23, 2005.

27. Steve Goldsmith interview with the author, via telephone, Aug. 12, 2005.

28. Associated Press report, Oct. 26, 1996.

29. *Indianapolis Star*, Jan. 16, 1997.

30. Fred Yang interview with the author, via telephone, Feb. 23, 2006.

31. *Louisville Courier-Journal*, Nov. 5, 1996.

32. Geoff Garin interview with the author, via telephone, Dec. 1, 2005.

33. Jim Shella interview with the author, Indianapolis, IN, June 25, 2005.

34. Steve Goldsmith interview with the author, via telephone, Aug. 12, 2005.

35. Julia Carson interview with the author, Indianapolis, IN, April 9, 2005.

36. Ibid.

37. Judy O'Bannon interview with the author, Indianapolis, IN, April 5, 2005.

38. Kevin Corcoran interview with the author, Indianapolis, IN, Aug. 23, 2005.

39. *Indianapolis Star*, Nov. 6, 1996.

40. *Jeffersonville Evening News*, Nov. 6, 1996.

41. *Corydon Democrat*, Nov. 13, 1996.

42. Jane Parker interview with the author, Plainfield, IN, Dec. 20, 2004.

43. Rosamond Sample interview with the author, Corydon, IN, Nov. 19, 2004.

44. Judy O'Bannon interview with the author, Indianapolis, IN, April 5, 2005.

45. 1996 Election Report of the State of Indiana, Indiana Secretary of State Sue Ann Gilroy, Indianapolis, IN.

46. *Louisville Courier-Journal*, Nov. 6, 1996.

47. Steve Campbell interview with the author, Indianapolis, IN, June 29, 2005.

48. Steve Goldsmith interview with the author, via telephone, Aug. 12, 2005.

49. Associated Press report, Nov. 6, 1996.

50. Mike Smith interview with the author, Indianapolis, IN, June 16, 2005.

51. Howey Political Report, 10th Anniversary Special Edition, January 2004.

52. Kevin Corcoran interview with the author, Indianapolis, IN, Aug. 23, 2005.

53. DeLaney, Ann. *Politics for Dummies*. Foster City, CA: IDG Books Worldwide, Inc., 1995.

54. Judy O'Bannon interview with the author, Indianapolis, IN, April 5, 2005.

55. *Corydon Democrat*, Nov. 7, 1996.

56. *Louisville Courier-Journal*, Nov. 10, 1996.

57. Ibid.

58. Ibid.

59. *Louisville Courier-Journal*, Nov. 12, 1996.

60. *Corydon Democrat*, Nov. 13, 1996.

Chapter 14

1. *Indianapolis Star*, Nov. 10, 1996.

2. *Indianapolis Star*, Nov. 7, 1996.

3. *Louisville Courier-Journal*, Nov. 7, 1996.

4. *Indianapolis Star*, Nov. 10, 1996.

5. Ibid.

6. *Louisville Courier-Journal*, Nov. 6, 1996.

7. John Gregg interview with the author, Indianapolis, IN, Feb. 1, 2006.

8. *Louisville Courier-Journal*, Jan. 12, 1997.

9. *Jeffersonville Evening News*, Nov. 6, 1996.

10. John Gregg interview with the author, Indianapolis, IN, Feb. 1, 2006.

11. B. Patrick Bauer interview with the author, Indianapolis, IN, June 3, 2005.

12. *Louisville Courier-Journal*, Jan. 14, 1997.

13. *Louisville Courier-Journal*, Jan. 14, 1997.

14. Donna Imus interview with the author, Indianapolis, IN, Sept. 14, 2005.

15. Ibid.

16. *Louisville Courier-Journal*, Jan. 14, 1997.

17. Videotape of WISH-TV live coverage of Gubernatorial Inaugural Ceremonies, Indiana Statehouse, Indianapolis, IN, Jan. 13, 1997.

18. Governor Frank O'Bannon Inaugural Address, Jan. 13, 1997.

19. Ibid.

20. Videotape of WISH-TV live coverage of Gubernatorial Inaugural Ceremonies, Indiana Statehouse, Indianapolis, IN, Jan. 13, 1997.

21. Nancy Milakovic McGann e-mail to the author, Feb. 22, 2006.

22. Watt, William J. *Bowen: The Years as Governor.* Indianapolis: Bierce Associates, Inc., 1981.

23. Governor's Office Memo, "Communication Between Agencies and the Governor" dated August 1999.

24. Robin Winston interview with the author, Indianapolis, IN, Sept. 19, 2005.

25. Tim Joyce interview with the author, Indianapolis, IN, July 27, 2005.

26. Lesley Stedman Weidenbener interview with the author, Indianapolis, IN, June 24, 2005.

27. *Brian Howey Political Report* via www.IndianapolisEye.com, undated.

28. Mary Dieter interview with the author, Zionsville, IN, July 14, 2005.

29. Phil Bremen interview with the author, Indianapolis, IN, Aug. 1, 2005.

30. Mary Dieter interview with the author, Zionsville, IN, July 14, 2005.

31. *Louisville Courier-Journal*, Jan. 31, 2004.

32. Ibid.

33. Associated Press, March 17, 2000.

34. Ibid.

35. John Ketzenberger interview with the author, Indianapolis, IN, July 1, 2005.

36. Ibid.

Chapter 15

1. Governor Frank O'Bannon to the author, July 2002.

2. Alex Willis interview with the author, Anderson, IN, March 4, 2005.

3. Joe Smith, Jr., interview with the author, Indianapolis, IN, Jan. 13, 2006.

4. John Zody correspondence to the author, Sept. 1, 2005.

5. Ibid.

6. Ray Raney interview with the author, Indianapolis, IN, Sept.14, 2005.

7. Judy O'Bannon interview with the author, Indianapolis, IN, April 5, 2005.

8. Ibid.

9. Alex Willis interview with the author, Anderson, IN, March 4, 2005.

10. Donna Imus interview with the author, Indianapolis, IN, Sept. 14, 2005.

11. Ibid.

12. Cheryl Reed correspondence to the author, Oct. 10, 2005.

13. Ibid.

14. Ibid.

15. Governor Frank O'Bannon State of the State address, Jan. 28, 1997.

16. Ibid.

17. Governor Frank O'Bannon State of the State address, Jan. 13, 1998.

18. Ibid.

19. Governor Frank O'Bannon State of the State address, Jan. 12, 1999.

20. Governor Frank O'Bannon State of the State address, Jan. 15, 2002.

22. Ibid.

23. Governor Frank O'Bannon news release, April 13, 2000.

Chapter 16

1. Governor Frank O'Bannon news release, Feb. 6, 1997.

2. Governor Frank O'Bannon news release, Sept. 9, 1997.

3. Governor Frank O'Bannon news release, Oct. 21, 1997.

4. Governor Frank O'Bannon news release, Jan. 5, 1999.

5. Suellen Reed interview with the author, Indianapolis, IN, Dec. 16, 2005.

6. Governor Frank O'Bannon news release, Jan. 8, 1999.

7. National Education Goals Panel (NEGP) news release, Feb. 23, 2000.

8. Governor Frank O'Bannon news release, Jan. 8, 1999.

9. Suellen Reed interview with the author, Indianapolis, IN, Dec. 16, 2005.

10. Ibid.

11. Ibid.

12. Ibid.

13. Michelle McNeil interview with the author, Indianapolis, IN, July 29, 2005.

14. Governor Frank O'Bannon news release, Jan. 14, 1999.

15. Governor Frank O'Bannon State of the State address, Jan. 12, 1999.

16. Governor Frank O'Bannon news release, Jan. 27, 1999.

17. Ibid.

18. Ibid.

19. Suellen Reed interview with the author, Indianapolis, IN, Dec. 16, 2005.

20. John Ketzenberger interview with the author, Indianapolis, IN, July 1, 2005.

21. Borst, Lawrence M. *Gentlemen, It's Been My Pleasure: Four Decades in the Indiana Legislature*. Indianapolis: Guild Press Emmis Books 2003.

22. David Johnson interview with the author, Indianapolis, IN, Sept. 15, 2005.

23. Steve Campbell interview with the author, Indianapolis, IN, June 29, 2005.

24. Phil Bremen interview with the author, Indianapolis, IN, Aug. 1, 2005.

25. Edited pool videotape, Full-Day Kindergarten Statehouse rally, Indianapolis, IN, April 12, 1999.

26. Ibid.

27. Ibid.

28. Ibid.

29. Mike Smith interview with the author, Indianapolis, IN, June 16, 2005.

30. Jim Shella interview with the author, Indianapolis, IN, June 25, 2005.

31. John Gregg interview with the author, Indianapolis, IN, Feb. 1, 2006.

32. David Johnson interview with the author, Indianapolis, IN, Sept. 15, 2005.

33. Governor Frank O'Bannon remarks to joint meeting of Indiana School Boards Association & Indiana Association of Public Schools Superintendents, Indiana Convention Center, Indianapolis, IN, Sept. 29, 1999, as reported by *Howey Political Report*.

34. Governor Frank O'Bannon news release, April 30, 1999.

35. Suellen Reed interview with the author, Indianapolis, IN, Dec. 16, 2005.

36. Michelle McNeil interview with the author, Indianapolis, IN, July 29, 2005.

37. Phil Bremen interview with the author, Indianapolis, IN, Aug. 1, 2005.

38. Tom New remarks, Governor Frank O'Bannon bust dedication ceremony, Indiana Statehouse, Indianapolis, IN, Feb. 13, 2006.

39. Ibid.

40. Governor Frank O'Bannon news release, May 23, 2000.

41. Governor Frank O'Bannon news release, June 19, 2000.

42. Governor Frank O'Bannon news release, Oct. 17, 2000.

43. Governor Frank O'Bannon news releases, July 25, 2000 and Aug. 15, 2000.

44. Governor Frank O'Bannon news release, Aug. 15, 2000.

45. Governor Frank O'Bannon news release, Sept. 13, 2001.

46. John Gregg interview with the author, Indianapolis, IN, Feb. 1, 2006.

47. Bill Moreau guest column, *Howey Political Report*, Sept. 20, 2003.

Chapter 17

1. Judy O'Bannon interview with the author, Indianapolis, IN, Aug. 31, 2005.
2. Ibid.
3. Susan Williams interview with the author, Indianapolis, IN, Sept. 29, 2005.
4. Ibid.
5. John Goss interview with the author, Indianapolis, IN, April 9, 2005.
6. Governor Frank O'Bannon news release, June 24, 1998.
7. Paul Patton interview with the author, via telephone, Sept. 21, 2005.
8. Videotape of WRTV-TV, NewsChannel 64 live coverage of Governor Frank O'Bannon news conference, Evansville, IN, Jan. 9, 2003.
9. Ibid.
10. Governor Frank O'Bannon Statement on the Petition of Clemency of Kevin L. Hough, April 30, 2003.
11. Ibid.
12. Ibid.
13. Ibid.
14. Judy O'Bannon interview with the author, Indianapolis, IN, Aug. 31, 2005.
15. Ibid.
16. *Indianapolis Star*, Nov. 18, 1997.
17. "Indiana Executions Since 1900, The Death Penalty in Indiana." Clark County Prosecutor's Website.
18. Rosamond Sample interview with the author, Corydon, IN, Nov. 20, 2004.
19. Governor Frank O'Bannon Statement on the Petition of Clemency of Kevin L. Hough, April 30, 2003.
20. Videotape of 1997 Beacon of Hope Awards remarks by Judy O'Bannon, Indianapolis Athletic Club, Indianapolis, IN.
21. Videotape of *"Consider This"* television interview with Judy O'Bannon, IUPUI Department of Political Science, Sept. 15, 2000.
22. Videotape of *The Heartland Garden* television interview of Judy O'Bannon, WFYI-TV, Indianapolis, IN, Summer 2000.
23. Videotape of *Interview on the Arts* television interview of Judy O'Bannon, American Cablevision, Indianapolis, IN, Sept. 8, 1997.
24. Judy O'Bannon interview with the author, Indianapolis, IN, Aug. 31, 2005.
25. Ibid.

Chapter 18

1. Videotape of O'Bannon for Governor, 2000 campaign ad.

2. *Indianapolis Star*, Jan. 19, 2005.

3. *Corydon Democrat*, March 29, 2000.

4. Fred Yang interview with the author, via telephone, Feb. 23, 2006.

5. Robin Winston interview with the author, Indianapolis, IN, Aug. 19, 2005.

6. Ibid.

7. Ibid.

8. *Indianapolis Star*, May 12, 2000.

9. *Louisville Courier-Journal*, June 12, 2000.

10. O'Bannon-Kernan 2000 campaign news release, Oct. 20, 2000.

11. Videotape of *Politically Speaking with Jack Colwell*, David McIntosh interview, WNIT-TV, Elkhart, IN, undated.

12. Frank Greer interview with the author, via telephone, July 7, 2005.

13. Fred Yang interview with the author, via telephone, Feb. 23, 2006.

14. Thad Nation interview with the author, via telephone, Dec. 29, 2005.

15. Indianapolis Star Library Online Factfile, www.indystar.com.

16. *Corydon Democrat*, June 21, 2000.

17. Robin Winston interview with the author, Indianapolis, IN, Aug. 19, 2005.

18. Fred Yang interview with the author, via telephone, Feb. 23, 2006.

19. Thad Nation interview with the author, via telephone, Dec. 29, 2005.

20. Lawrence Borst interview with the author, Indianapolis, IN, Dec. 21, 2005.

21. Jim Shella interview with author, Indianapolis, IN, June 25, 2005.

22. Mike Smith interview with the author, Indianapolis, IN, July 16, 2005.

23. *Louisville Courier-Journal*, Nov. 8, 2000.

24. Videotape of *Politically Speaking with Jack Colwell*, David McIntosh interview, WNIT-TV, Elkhart, IN, undated.

25. Robin Winston interview with the author, Indianapolis, IN, Aug. 19, 2005.

26. Stedman Weidenbener interview with the author, Indianapolis, IN, June 24, 2005.

27. Videotape of O'Bannon for Governor, 2000 campaign ad.

28. Videotape of David McIntosh for Governor, 2000 campaign ad.

29. Videotape of WRTV-TV news report, April 28, 2000.

30. Videotape of *Politically Speaking with Jack Colwell*, David McIntosh interview, WNIT-TV, Elkhart, IN, undated.

31. Videotape of O'Bannon for Governor, 2000 campaign ad.

32. Videotape of *Politically Speaking with Jack Colwell,* Frank O'Bannon interview, WNIT-TV, Elkhart, IN, undated. 32

33. Videotape of WISH-TV news report, June 18, 2001.

34. Videotape of 2000 O'Bannon-McIntosh debate, Indianapolis, IN, Sept. 22, 2000.

35. *Louisville Courier-Journal,* Sept. 23, 2000.

36. Ibid.

37. Videotape of WISH-TV news report, Oct. 12, 2000.

38. Ibid.

39. *Louisville Courier-Journal,* Sept. 23, 2000.

40. Suellen Reed interview with the author, Indianapolis, IN, Dec. 16, 2005.

41. Ibid.

42. *Indianapolis Star,* Sept. 1, 2000.

43. Fred Yang interview with the author, via telephone, Feb. 23, 2006.

44. *Louisville Courier-Journal,* Nov. 5, 2000.

45. Associated Press report, Nov. 7, 2000.

46. Ibid.

47. Robin Winston interview with the author, Indianapolis, IN, Aug. 19, 2005.

48. David Johnson interview with the author, Indianapolis, IN, Sept. 2005.

49. Fred Yang interview with the author, via telephone, Feb. 23, 2006.

50. Mike McDaniel interview with the author, Indianapolis, IN, June 16, 2005.

51. Ibid.

52. Robin Winston interview with the author, Indianapolis, IN, Aug. 19, 2005.

53. Thad Nation interview with the author, via telephone, Dec. 29, 2005.

54. *Corydon Democrat,* Nov. 15, 2000.

55. 2000 General Election Report of the State of Indiana, Secretary of State Sue Ann Gilroy, Indianapolis, IN.

56. Ibid.

57. *Louisville Courier-Journal,* Nov. 8, 2000.

58. Ibid.

59. *Louisville Courier-Journal,* Nov. 12, 2000.

60. Thad Nation interview with the author, via telephone, Dec. 29, 2005.

61. Videotape of 2001 Gubernatorial Inaugural Ceremony, RCA Dome, Indianapolis, IN, Jan. 8, 2001.

62. Ibid.

63. Donna Imus interview with the author, Indianapolis, IN, Sept. 14, 2005.

64. Governor Frank O'Bannon Inaugural Address, RCA Dome, Indianapolis, IN, Jan. 8, 2001.

65. Ibid.

66. Videotape of 2001 Gubernatorial Inaugural Ceremony, RCA Dome, Indianapolis, IN, Jan. 8, 2001.

Chapter 19

1. Associated Press report, Jan. 9, 2001.

2. Betty Cockrum interview with the author, Indianapolis, IN, Oct. 14, 2005.

3. Judy O'Bannon interview with the author, Indianapolis, IN, Aug. 31, 2005.

4. John Gregg interview with the author, Indianapolis, IN, Feb. 1, 2006.

5. Marilyn Schultz interview with the author, Indianapolis, IN, Oct. 5, 2005.

6. Ibid.

7. Ibid.

8. *Indiana Legislative Insight*, June 2, 2003.

9. Ibid.

10. John Gregg interview with the author, Indianapolis, IN, Oct. 5, 2005.

11. Mike Gery interview with the author, Indianapolis, IN, Jan. 24, 2005.

12. Ibid.

13. Ibid.

14. B. Patrick Bauer interview with the author, Indianapolis, IN, June 3, 2005.

15. Thad Nation interview with the author, via telephone, Dec. 29, 2005.

16. Governor Frank O'Bannon veto statement, May 3, 2001.

17. Governor Frank O'Bannon veto statement, May 10, 2001.

18. Governor Frank O'Bannon budget statement, May 11, 2001.

19. Ibid.

20. Jon Laramore correspondence with the author, June 1, 2005.

21. Ibid.

22. Governor Frank O'Bannon statement to reporters, Oct. 3, 2001.

23. Governor Frank O'Bannon Statewide Address, Nov. 15, 2001.

24. Ibid.

25. Ibid.

26. *Indiana Legislative Insight*, June 2, 2003.

27. Videotape of WISH-TV news report on Governor Frank O'Bannon news conference, Oct. 18, 2001.

28. Joe Kernan interview with the author, South Bend, IN, April 7, 2006.

29. John Gregg interview with the author, Indianapolis, IN, Feb. 1, 2006.

30. *Indiana Legislative Insight*, June 2, 2003.

31. Tim Joyce interview with the author, Indianapolis, IN, July 27, 2005.

32. Bart Peterson interview with the author, Indianapolis, IN, Nov. 21, 2005.

33. Tim Joyce interview with the author, Indianapolis, IN, July 27, 2005.

34. Governor Frank O'Bannon Statement I, Sept. 11, 2001.

35. Governor Frank O'Bannon Statement II, Sept. 11, 2001.

36. Ibid.

37. Tim Joyce interview with the author, Indianapolis, IN, July 27, 2005.

38. Videotape of WRTV-TV and WTHR-TV news reports on O'Bannon return from New York City, Oct. 11, 2001.

39. Ibid.

40. Governor Frank O'Bannon news release, Oct. 11, 2001.

41. Ibid.

42. Videotape of WISH-TV and WTHR-TV live reports, O'Bannon-Kernan-Peterson-Wilson news conference, Oct. 31, 2001.

43. Ibid.

44. Ibid.

45. Ibid.

46. Governor O'Bannon speech, Sept. 11 Commemorative Ceremony, Indiana Statehouse, Indianapolis, IN, Sept. 11, 2002.

47. Ibid.

48. Governor Frank O'Bannon statement to Indiana troops, Fort Knox, Ky., Dec. 27, 2002.

49. Governor Frank O'Bannon statement on the war, March 18, 2003.

50. Ibid.

Chapter 20

1. Governor Frank O'Bannon news release, Sept. 23, 2002.

2. Michelle McNeil interview with the author, Indianapolis, IN, July 29, 2005.

3. Governor Frank O'Bannon news release, Sept. 23, 2002.

4. Governor Frank O'Bannon news release, Sept. 10, 2000.

5. Governor Frank O'Bannon news release, May 11, 1999.

6. Governor Frank O'Bannon statement on impeachment of President Clinton, Aug. 18, 1998.

7. Cheryl Reed correspondence to the author, Oct. 10, 2005.

8. Ibid.

9. Ibid.

10. Governor Frank O'Bannon news release, Dec. 4, 2002.

11. Ibid.

12. Videotape of WRTV-TV news report, Dec. 4, 2002.

13. *Indiana Legislative Insight*, June 2, 2003.

14. Videotape of Governor Frank O'Bannon remarks on *Inside Indiana Business with Gerry Dick*, WFYI-TV, April 11, 2003.

15. Governor Frank O'Bannon news release, April 27, 2003.

16. Ibid.

17. Ibid.

18. *Indiana Legislative Insight*, June 2, 2003.

19. Ibid.

20. Videotape of WRTV-TV news report, Dec. 9, 2002.

21. Ibid.

22. Paul Patton interview with the author, via telephone, Sept. 21, 2005.

23. Judi Patton interview with the author, via telephone, Sept. 21, 2005.

24. Paul Patton interview with the author, via telephone, Sept. 21, 2005.

25. Ibid.

26. Ibid.

27. Posting in Brian Howey column, www.IndianapolisEye.com, March 15, 2004.

28. Ibid.

29. Ibid.

30. *Indianapolis Star*, Sept. 6, 2003.

31. Judy O'Bannon interview with the author, Indianapolis, IN, Aug. 31, 2005.

Chapter 21

1. Alex Willis interview with the author, Anderson, IN, March 4, 2005.

2. Ray Raney interview with the author, Indianapolis, IN, Sept. 14, 2005.

3. Ibid.

4. Alex Willis interview with the author, Anderson, IN, March 4, 2004.

5. Ibid.

6. Joe Kernan interview with the author, South Bend, IN, April 7, 2006.

7. Ibid.

8. Joe Kernan interview with the author, South Bend, IN, April 7, 2006.

9. Mary Dieter interview with the author, Zionsville, IN, July 14, 2005.

10. Jon Swain interview with the author, Indianapolis, IN, Jan. 25, 2005.

11. Alex Willis interview with the author, Anderson, IN, March 4, 2005.

12. Jon Swain interview with the author, Indianapolis, IN, Jan. 25, 2005.

13. Reporter Kate Shepherd to the author, via telephone, Sept. 8, 2003.

14. Governor Frank O'Bannon news release I, Sept. 8, 2003.

15. Jon Swain interview with the author, Indianapolis, IN, Jan. 25, 2005.

16. Jennifer O'Bannon interview with the author, Indianapolis, IN, Oct. 26, 2005 and Jon Swain interview with the author, Indianapolis, IN, Jan. 25, 2005.

17. Videotape of Mary Dieter Statehouse statement, WISH-TV live special report, Sept. 8, 2003.

18. Ibid.

19. Ibid.

20. Videotape of Lt. Governor Joe Kernan Statehouse news conference, WISH-TV live coverage, Sept. 8, 2003.

21. Ibid.

22. Ibid.

23. Videotape of physicians' news conference at Northwestern Memorial Hospital, Chicago, IL, WRTV-TV, Sept. 8, 2003.

24. Ibid.

25. Ibid.

26. Alex Willis interview with the author, Anderson, IN, March 4, 2005.

27. Judy O'Bannon written statement, Sept. 9, 2003.

28. B. Patrick Bauer interview with the author, Indianapolis, IN, June 3, 2005.

29. Letter from Dr. Wesley Yapor to Senator Robert Garton and Representative B. Patrick Bauer, Sept. 10, 2003.

30. Robert Garton interview with the author, Indianapolis, IN, Sept. 19, 2005.

31. B. Patrick Bauer interview with the author, Indianapolis, IN, June 3, 2005.

32. Robert Garton interview with the author, Indianapolis, IN, Sept. 19, 2005.

33. Randall Shepard interview with the author, Indianapolis, IN, Sept. 2005.

34. Ibid.

35. Videotape of B. Patrick Bauer Statehouse statement to reporters, WTHR-TV live coverage, Sept. 10, 2003.

36. Videotape of Robert Garton Statehouse statement to reporters, WTHR-TV live coverage, Sept. 10, 2003.

37. Videotape of B. Patrick Bauer Statehouse statement to reporters, WTHR-TV live coverage, Sept. 10, 2003.

38. Randall Shepard interview with the author, Indianapolis, IN, Sept. 2005.

39. News release from Northwestern Memorial Hospital, Chicago, IL, Sept. 10, 2003.

40. Videotape of Lt. Governor Joe Kernan statement to reporters from IUPUI, WISH-TV live coverage, Sept. 10, 2003.

41. Ibid.

42. Ibid.

43. Judy O'Bannon written statement, Sept. 10, 2003.

44. News release from Northwestern Memorial Hospital, Chicago, IL, Sept. 11, 2003.

45. Faxed White House handwritten note from President George W. Bush to First Lady Judy O'Bannon, Sept. 11, 2003.

46. Jonathan O'Bannon interview with the author, New Albany, IN, July 18, 2005.

47. Jennifer O'Bannon interview with the author, Indianapolis, IN, Oct. 26, 2005.

48. Jon Swain interview with the author, Indianapolis, IN, Jan. 25, 2005.

49. Alex Willis interview with the author, Anderson, IN, March 4, 2005.

50. Jon Swain interview with the author, Indianapolis, IN, Jan. 25, 2005.

Chapter 22

1. Jon Swain telephone call to the author, Sept. 13, 2003.

2. Joe Kernan interview with the author, South Bend, IN, April 7, 2006.

3. Mary Dieter interview with the author, Zionsville, IN, July 14, 2005.

4. Jon Swain interview with the author, Indianapolis, IN, Jan. 25, 2005.

6. Ibid.

7. Mary Dieter interview with the author, Zionsville, IN, July 14, 2005.

8. Jon Swain interview with the author, Indianapolis, IN, Jan. 25, 2005.

9. Mary Dieter interview with the author, Zionsville, IN, July 14, 2005.

10. Jon Swain interview with the author, Indianapolis, IN, Jan. 25, 2005.

11. Ibid.

12. Mary Dieter interview with the author, Zionsville, IN, July 14, 2005.

13. Jon Swain interview with the author, Indianapolis, IN, Jan. 25, 2005.

14. Ibid.

15. Judy O'Bannon interview with the author, Indianapolis, IN, Nov. 17, 2005.

16. Judy O'Bannon interview with the author, Indianapolis, IN, April 5, 2005.

17. Judy O'Bannon to the author, Sept. 13, 2003.

18. Ibid.

19. Ibid.

20. Ibid.

21. Videotape of Judy O'Bannon interview, WISH-TV news report, Oct. 13, 2003.

22. Judy O'Bannon interview with the author, Indianapolis, IN, Nov. 17, 2005.

23. Videotape of WISH-TV news report, Oct. 13, 2003.

24. *Fort Wayne Journal Gazette*, Sept. 18, 2003.

Chapter 23

1. Judy O'Bannon interview with the author, Indianapolis, IN, Nov. 17, 2005.

2. Ibid.

3. Paul Patton interview with the author, via telephone, Sept. 21, 2005.

4. Judi Patton interview with the author, via telephone, Sept. 21, 2005.

5. Michael Chelich interview with the author, Hammond, IN, May 20, 2005.

6. Judy O'Bannon interview with the author, Nov. 17, 2005.

7. President George W. Bush statement, Washington, D.C., Sept. 13, 2003.

8. Remarks from former President Bill Clinton, Congregation Beth el Zedek, Indianapolis, IN, June 8, 2005.

9. Governor Jennifer Granholm statement, Lansing, MI, Sept. 13, 2003.

10. Governor John Hoeven statement, Bismarck, ND, Sept. 13, 2003.

11. Governor Dirk Kempthorne statement, Boise, ID, Sept. 13, 2003.

12. Indiana University Alumni Association statement, Bloomington, IN, Sept. 12, 2003.

13. President Adam Herbert statement, Bloomington, IN, Sept. 13, 2003.

14. Indiana University Board of Trustees statement, Bloomington, IN, Sept. 13, 2003.

15. *Washington Post*, Sept. 17, 2003.

16. *Indianapolis Star*, Sept. 18, 2003.

17. www.IndianapolisEye.com posting, March 15, 2004.

18. Videotape of Evan Bayh statement, floor of the U.S. Senate, Washington, D.C., Sept. 15, 2003.

19. Ibid.

20. Donna Imus interview with the author, Indianapolis, IN, Sept. 14, 2005.

21. Marilyn Schultz interview with the author, Indianapolis, IN, Oct. 5, 2005.

22. Ray Raney interview with the author, Indianapolis, IN, Sept. 14, 2005.

23. Ibid.

24. Alex Willis interview with the author, Anderson, IN, March 4, 2005.

25. House and Senate Concurrent Resolution, January 2004.

26. Ivy Tech Bloomington campus news release, undated.

27. *Times of Northwest Indiana*, Oct. 9, 2004.

28. *Jeffersonville Evening News*, Oct. 24, 2004.

29. Ibid.

30. *Indianapolis Star*, April 11, 2005.

31. *South Bend Tribune*, Feb. 6, 2005.

32. *South Bend Tribune*, Dec. 19, 2004.

33. Joe Kernan interview with the author, South Bend, IN, April 7, 2006.

34. Ibid.

35. *Indiana Daily Student*, Nov. 3, 2004.

36. Ibid.

37. *Indianapolis Star*, Jan. 7, 2005.

38. Jennifer O'Bannon interview with the author, Indianapolis, IN, Oct. 26, 2005.

39. Ibid.

40. Jonathan O'Bannon interview with the author, New Albany, IN, July 18, 2005.

41. Jennifer O'Bannon interview with the author, Indianapolis, IN, Oct. 26, 2005.

42. Judy O'Bannon interview with the author, Indianapolis, IN, Nov. 17, 2005.

43. Ibid.

44. United Methodist Profiles, www.UMC.org posting.

45. *Indiana Legislative Insight*, June 3, 2003.

46. Ibid.

47. Ibid.

48. Judy O'Bannon interview with the author, Indianapolis, IN, Nov. 17, 2005.

49. Rabbi Sandy Eisenberg Sasso, O'Bannon Memorial Service, Indianapolis, IN, Sept. 19, 2003.

50. Ibid.

Appendix

1. Watt, William J. *Bowen: The Years as Governor*. Indianapolis: Bierce Associates, Inc., 1981, pp. 30-31.

Index

Printed in the United States
59745LVS00003B/67-510

9 781600 080128